OVERDRIVE

L.A. CONSTRUCTS THE FUTURE, 1940–1990

EDITED BY WIM DE WIT AND CHRISTOPHER JAMES ALEXANDER

THE GETTY RESEARCH INSTITUTE

CONTENTS

FOREWORD

STUDYING LOS ANGELES'S URBANISM

Thomas W. Gaehtgens

IN THE PAST FEW DECADES, MAJOR STUDIES OF LOS ANGELES have deepened our understanding of how this metropolis evolved. Just as postwar art was illuminated by the Getty's Pacific Standard Time initiative in 2011–12, the architecture of Los Angeles, its modernism in particular, is now presented in an exhibition that surveys new interpretations of the city's history and establishes Los Angeles as a developed urban center deserving of recognition as a model for the future. The Getty Research Institute holds extensive collections of archives, drawings, and models that have been donated or purchased in recent decades. Thanks to these extraordinary resources, augmented by loans from other institutions, it has been possible to conceive of bringing the local history of this metropolis into public view.

To visitors, Los Angeles can seem incomprehensible, confusing, and off-putting. The sun, sea, and mountains, which play such an integral role in the city, barely persuade people of its appeal. The feeling of disorientation is so powerful, it can seem difficult to surmount. Tourists have little time to get to know a city. They quickly develop prejudices, which can only be revised through patient learning, and, in the case of Los Angeles, through driving.

Los Angeles seems to challenge all European customs of experiencing a city. Where is the center? Where are the cathedral and town hall that mark the heart of a community? Los Angeles also has these structures, yet they have shaped neither the geographic nor the urban center of the city. From a European perspective, the absence of this core is one obvious reason why many visitors feel lost.[1]

In Los Angeles, almost every dinner party conversation begins with comments about the traffic, much as people in London talk about the weather. Everybody quickly agrees that the situation is serious— as though cities such as Beijing, Mumbai, São Paulo, and Shanghai do not have their share of traffic jams. Yet, in Los Angeles, it seems to diminish the quality of life more drastically than elsewhere, perhaps because of the city's immense size. Los Angeles is a behemoth, ever expanding eastward, seemingly without systematic planning. Simply put, many people think of Los Angeles as urban and environmental chaos.

FIGURE 1.
View north of Wilshire Boulevard between La Brea Avenue and Highland Avenue, Los Angeles, ca. 1935.
Los Angeles, Getty Research Institute.

FIGURE 2.
View north of Wilshire Boulevard between La Brea Avenue and Highland Avenue, Los Angeles, 1955.
Los Angeles, Getty Research Institute.

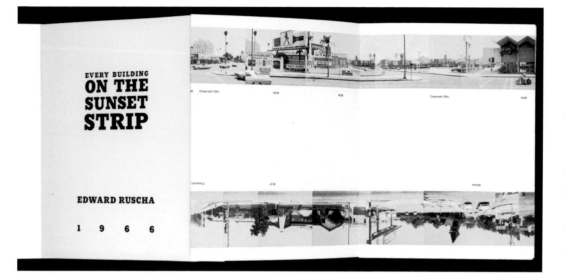

FIGURE 3A.
Ed Ruscha (American, b. 1937).
Sunset Boulevard at Crescent Heights Boulevard,
Los Angeles.
From Ed Ruscha, *Every Building on the
Sunset Strip* (1966), n.p.
Los Angeles, Getty Research Institute.

Although he spent his exile living in a comfortable home in Santa Monica, Bertolt Brecht best described this sense of being a rootless European: "I / Who live in Los Angeles and not in London / Find, on thinking about Hell, / that it must be / Still more like Los Angeles."[2] Such literary commentaries about the city are legion, and films often evoke this hellish image of Los Angeles. Fascination and revulsion alike determine the perception of the city. Whereas the cityscapes of London, Paris, Rome, and New York are easily grasped, Los Angeles is experienced as an incomprehensible urban entity.

This perception, however, contradicts the orderly development of Los Angeles. Although the growth occurred at an unusual speed, it was by no means unplanned (fig. 1). The first author to intensively study the landscape and urban planning of Los Angeles came to this same conclusion. Anton Wagner, a German geographer and geologist, published a comprehensive study of Los Angeles in 1935. In this work, Wagner analyzed the shocking speed with which the metropolis had reached a population of two million immigrants in just a few years.[3] The author's extensive explorations of Los Angeles were undertaken by foot—an inconceivable feat today. At the time, this was the most convenient way to study the proportions of diffuse settlements.

By the 1960s, Los Angeles had tripled in size (fig. 2).[4] Given these numbers, Wagner's method of analysis seems historically remote. To recognize the city's uniqueness, new methodologies of observation became necessary. European cities could no longer be used as a point of comparison; a value system that distinguished between culturally significant buildings at the center and insignificant suburbs at the margins was not applicable to this metropolis. To understand the city's expansive development, it had to be examined from the perspective of technological and economic growth. The focus shifted from the role of urban squares and theaters to the supply of water and electricity and the function of freeways, gas stations, shopping centers, and parking garages. The city could not be analyzed as the product of visionary planning; rather, it had to be regarded as the result of sharply increasing needs.

The product of this technological and social upheaval was generally considered ugly. The suburbs did not evolve as "green lungs," as they had around 1900, during the metropolitan construction boom in Europe and the "city beautiful" movement in the United States; instead, areas were built quickly and cheaply and were characterized by their uniformity and banality. Yet, by the 1960s, this conventional condemnation of the endless and unmanageable urban sprawl had been overcome.

The cultural distinctiveness of these urban areas was analyzed and completely reassessed through the writings of authors such as Tom Wolfe and Joan Didion and, most prominently, in *Learning from Las Vegas* (1972), the groundbreaking book on the theory of architecture by Robert Venturi, Denise Scott Brown,

FIGURE 3B.
Ed Ruscha (American, b. 1937).
Sunset Boulevard at Hayvenhurst Drive, Los Angeles.
From Ed Ruscha, *Every Building on the
Sunset Strip* (1966), n.p.
Los Angeles, Getty Research Institute.

and Steven Izenour. They recognized the suburbs as the actual living spaces of the modern age, a result of a
new attitude toward life—one in which buildings are not subject to a style. The city is no longer planned from
above; rather, it is built and developed by the people living in it. The city is determined not by an aesthetic
norm but by its diversity of cultures and interests. The authors chose Las Vegas as an example of the modern
American city because it represented, in its size and density, a tangible model for analysis. However, Los
Angeles was the true center of this modern American city culture; the city's image was shaped not by buildings but by billboards: "The graphic sign in space has become the architecture of this landscape."[5]

The view through the windshield determines the impression of the city's image; it is characterized not by church steeples but by neon advertising signs. The symbols signifying urbanity are not planned
spaces in which the community is reified but a luminescent world of images encroaching upon us. Los
Angeles is to be viewed while moving. Its vitality can only be grasped through constantly changing commercial images, the sole purpose of which is to attract and hold our attention. Photography and movies
have familiarized us with this perception of Los Angeles. For instance, Ed Ruscha's *Every Building on the
Sunset Strip,* published in 1966 as an accordion fold, conveys a street scene from the perspective of the
mobilized spectator (figs. 3a, 3b).[6] Fierce debates raged over whether cities like Los Angeles were entirely
at the mercy of commercialization, thereby precluding the possibility of architecture as design. Within this
discourse, certain voices became more demanding of a reversal of traditional aesthetic priorities. In the era
when pop art was celebrating its triumph, the hierarchy of the academic system that placed high art above
popular culture collapsed. The semiotic turn, which measured the world of neon signs and moving images
in terms of their aesthetic quality, initiated an entirely new understanding of so-called suburbanization and
urban sprawl. According to this insight, the modernity of a city is characterized precisely by the inability to
limit it to a fixed space because its borders and boundaries are constantly changing. Vitality and mobility
are determined not by concepts of urban planning but by the needs of residents, who design their own
living spaces.

Simultaneous to Scott Brown, Venturi, and Izenour researching Las Vegas, Reyner Banham was writing about Los Angeles. His 1971 book, *Los Angeles: The Architecture of Four Ecologies,* was published at just the right moment. Banham also questioned the traditional criteria of urban planning for analyzing cities. The Eurocentric perspective centering on the gaze seemed, to him, inadequate for understanding the development of Los Angeles. Banham was quite aware that he had to overcome a "relatively conventional implicit definition of 'architecture'" in order to do justice to the modernity of this city and its role as a model for the future.[7] Instead of undertaking a formal consideration of outstanding individual architectural works as his point of departure, he accomplished a convincing comprehensive view of the city, which he interpreted as the result of a new urban reality and a new way of life. According to him, a key element for understanding the history of Los Angeles up to the present day is mobility. "The language of design, architecture, and urbanism in Los Angeles is the language of movement."[8] He follows with a central thesis: "Mobility outweighs monumentality." Banham communicates his own experience to the reader: "I learned to drive in order to read Los Angeles in the original."

The originality of Banham's analysis also lies in his ability to place the urban development of Los Angeles within a historical context. The network of freeways that forms the arteries of the community had not been recklessly inscribed into the city. It relied instead on the long-existing roads, with which the first residents had traversed this vast plain. Banham's description of Los Angeles as "a city built on transport" referred back to the city's earliest history.[9] Freeways, parking lots, drive-ins, and gas stations did not destroy its urban development; rather, they are an integral part of a naturally growing urban space. Banham went a step further, however, describing the aesthetic qualities of the freeways' lines as grand sweeping arcs elegantly permeating the grid system of municipal districts. Banham enthusiastically remarked that the intersection of the Santa Monica (10) and San Diego (405) Freeways was "one of the greater works of Man" (fig. 4).[10]

Like Scott Brown, Venturi, and Izenour in their study of Las Vegas, Banham points out that the ubiquitous billboard images in Los Angeles should not be described as "visual pollution by commercial advertising." On the contrary, the "proliferation of advertising signs is an essential part of the character of Los Angeles; to deprive the city of them would be like depriving San Gimignano of its towers or the City of London of its Wren steeples," thus reversing the hierarchy of the traditional architectural canon.[11]

The debates around high and low, academic and vernacular art that took place during the era of pop art find their counterpart in the reevaluation of the urban image. Seen from this perspective, Los Angeles gains a new status: it eludes the accusation of not complying with norms and instead presents itself as a model of urban modernity. Moreover, Banham calls on contemporary architects to study Los Angeles as the epitome of urban planning: "If Los Angeles is one of the world's leading cities in architecture, then it is because it is a sympathetic ecology for architectural design, and it behooves the world's architects to find out why."[12]

The Getty Research Institute's *Overdrive: L.A. Constructs the Future, 1940–1990* is the first exhibition to present an extended investigation of this alternative urban history. By displaying a wide range of rich and varied original materials, the exhibition traces the gradual transformation of Los Angeles, in just a few generations, from a small number of settlements into a metropolis. The exhibition assesses the transportation system and the technological requirements for supplying individual urban areas with water and electricity, which

FIGURE 4.
Santa Monica (10) and San Diego (405) Freeway interchange, looking northwest, Los Angeles, 8 August 1964.
Sacramento, California Department of Transportation, Library and History Center.

manifested in an architectural diversity of buildings. Shopping centers, industrial buildings, sports arenas, and cultural event spaces are presented both in their architectural form and in their function in urban planning. But this exhibition is also devoted to residential areas, with their denial of a stylistically unified architectural idiom. By studying the works of a range of architects, from Rudolph Schindler to Frank Gehry, *Overdrive* reveals the dynamic process by which a modern architectural language asserts itself.

This exhibition follows on the heels of Pacific Standard Time: Art in L.A., 1945–1980, a rare collaboration among a wide range of cultural institutions that provided comprehensive insight into Los Angeles's postwar art scene. Encompassing more than sixty exhibitions across Southern California, it confronted visitors with an unexpected wealth of artistic ideas. Pacific Standard Time represented a journey of discovery to a largely uncharted territory that had been dominated by renowned names such as John Baldessari, Sam Francis, David Hockney, and Ed Ruscha.

The architecture of California is more firmly ensconced in the general public's mind. The well-known photographs of Julius Shulman have played a large role in establishing the importance of modernity in the history of architecture as represented by Charles and Ray Eames, Frank Gehry, John Lautner, Richard Neutra, Rudolph Schindler, and numerous other architects.[13] But this was not always the case, and for many years modern architecture in California faced a great deal of criticism. When the first modern structures in California were built, predominantly reflecting the Bauhaus style, many judged them to be overly uniform and dismissive of an individual's freedom and taste. Modern architecture also got caught in the turbulent waters of politics and was accused of being socialist—even downright communist. Much has been written about modernity's long road to recognition, and California modernist architecture has long since been regarded as a classic chapter in the history of world architecture. Los Angeles has become a museum of twentieth-century architectural history, the study of which provides the basis for future urban planning in other parts of the world.

This book and the accompanying exhibition would not have been possible without the enthusiastic support of colleagues throughout the Getty, especially James Cuno, president and CEO of the J. Paul Getty Trust; Deborah Marrow, director of the Getty Foundation; Timothy Potts, director of the J. Paul Getty Museum; and Tim Whalen, director of the Getty Conservation Institute. In addition, the curators of the exhibition, Wim de Wit and Christopher James Alexander, have taken on the Herculean task of elucidating forty years of the history of the built environment in Southern California with consummate skill and intelligence.

NOTES

This text was translated from German by Zaia Alexander.

1   André Corboz, *Looking for a City in America: Down These Main Streets a Man Must Go . . . : An Essay* (Santa Monica: Getty Center for the History of Art and the Humanities, 1992).

2   Bertolt Brecht, "On Thinking about Hell" ["Nachdenkend über die Hölle," 1941], in Bertolt Brecht et al., eds., *Poems, 1913–1956* (New York: Methuen, 1976), 367.

3   Anton Wagner, *Los Angeles: Werden, Leben und Gestalt der Zweimillionenstadt in Südkalifornien* (Leipzig, 1935).

4   Compare census data for Los Angeles County from 1930 (2,209,492) and 1960 (6,742,696). See *Fifteenth Census of the United States: 1930,* vol. 3 (Washington, D.C.: Government Printing Office, 1932), pt. 1, 252; and *The Eighteenth Decennial Census of the United States: Censuses of Population and Housing 1960,* vol. 5 (Washington, D.C.: Bureau of the Census, 1961), pt. 5, 25.

5   Robert Venturi, Denise Scott Brown, and Steven Izenour, *Learning from Las Vegas* (Cambridge, Mass.: MIT Press, 1972), 9; see also the excellent study by Martino Stierli, *Las Vegas in the Rearview Mirror: The City in Theory, Photography, and Film,* trans. Elizabeth Tucker (Los Angeles: Getty Research Institute, 2013).

6   Charles G. Salas and Michael Roth, eds., *Looking for Los Angeles* (Los Angeles: Getty Research Institute, 2001).

7   Reyner Banham, *Los Angeles: The Architecture of Four Ecologies* [1971] (Berkeley: University of California Press, 2009), 4, with Antony Vidler's evocative introduction. The book initiated a variety of commentaries. See Peter Plagens, "Los Angeles: The Ecology of Evil," *Artforum* 11, no. 4 (1972): 67–76; and Thomas S. Hines, *"Los Angeles: The Architecture of Four Ecologies* by Reyner Banham," *Journal of the Society of Architectural Historians* 31, no. 1 (1972): 75–77.

8   Banham, *Los Angeles,* 4–5.

9   Banham, *Los Angeles,* 57.

10   Banham, *Los Angeles,* 70–71.

11   Banham, *Los Angeles,* 121.

12   Banham, *Los Angeles,* 226.

13   For the best and most impressive overview, see the recently published monumental work by Thomas S. Hines, *Architecture of the Sun: Los Angeles Modernism, 1900–1970* (New York: Rizzoli, 2010)

INTRODUCTION

PROVOKING NEW PERCEPTIONS OF LOS ANGELES

Wim de Wit and
Christopher James Alexander

DURING THE TWENTIETH CENTURY, LOS ANGELES rapidly evolved into one of the most populous and influential industrial, economic, and creative capitals in the world (figs. 1, 2). Architectural innovations of this era transformed the "first modern and widely decentralized industrial city in America" into a vibrant laboratory for cutting-edge design.[1] *Overdrive: L.A. Constructs the Future, 1940–1990* provides an examination of these built experiments and their impact on progressive design. The architectural drawings, models, images, and written analyses highlighted in the *Overdrive* exhibition and catalog reveal the complex and often underappreciated facets of Los Angeles and illustrate how the metropolis became an internationally recognized destination with a unique design vocabulary, canonized landmarks, and a coveted lifestyle.

THE GETTY'S LAYERED ENGAGEMENT WITH L.A. ARCHITECTURE

The programs of the J. Paul Getty Trust have been dedicated to the research, documentation, preservation, and promotion of Los Angeles's built environment for several decades. J. Paul Getty himself collected an impressive series of black-and-white photographs documenting Los Angeles's transformation from a fledgling pueblo in the mid-1800s to a vibrant urban center in the 1940s (fig. 3).[2] The Getty Research Institute (GRI) has continued to build on his regional interest and is committed, alongside other leading institutions, including the University of California, Santa Barbara; the University of California, Los Angeles; the University of California, Berkeley; California State Polytechnic University, Pomona; the University of Southern California; the Los Angeles Public Library; the Huntington Library; and the Library of Congress, to conserving significant architectural archives.

   After an intense period of strategic acquisitions, the GRI's Los Angeles–related architecture and design special collections now consist of more than 50,000 original drawings, 250,000 photographic prints and negatives, nearly 100 models, and a vast array of papers, including letters, notebooks, records, posters, and other ephemera. Archives include the seminal works of Reyner Banham, Welton Becket, Franklin Israel, Ray Kappe, Pierre Koenig, William Krisel, John Lautner, Leonard Nadel, Julius Shulman, Camilo José Vergara,

FIGURE 1.
View of Westwood, north from Pico Boulevard at Westwood Boulevard, Los Angeles, ca. 1935.
Los Angeles, Getty Research Institute.

FIGURE 2.
View of Westwood, northwest from Pico Boulevard, Los Angeles, 1955.
Los Angeles, Getty Research Institute.

FIGURE 3.
Early photo of Los Angeles collected by
J. Paul Getty, 1886.
Los Angeles, Getty Research Institute.

and the Frank Brothers Furniture Company, as well as the architectural drawings for Los Angeles's Union Station. Similarly, the Getty Foundation has long been engaged in the study and preservation of architecture in Southern California through conservation initiatives such as PreserveLA and various research projects. Years of meticulous archival cataloging efforts, ambitious digitization projects, popular exhibitions, and diverse international publications have made these fascinating materials accessible to broad audiences at the Getty Center and around the globe.

As a result of increasingly enlightened civic practices and the grassroots efforts of the Los Angeles Conservancy, more than nine hundred buildings have been designated as Historic-Cultural Monuments since 1962.[3] In an effort to bolster these numbers, the Getty Conservation Institute (GCI) and the City of Los Angeles embarked in 2000 on a multimillion-dollar initiative to develop the first comprehensive inventory of Los Angeles's built heritage. The collaboration resulted in the establishment of the city's Office of Historic Resources and the successful implementation of SurveyLA, which will document every significant structure within the city's borders through a custom-designed field-survey database system. In March 2012, the GCI launched the Conserving Modern Architecture Initiative, which will "advance the practice of conserving twentieth-century heritage, with a focus on modern architecture, through research and investigation, the development of practical conservation solutions, and the creation and distribution of information through training programs and publications."[4] The GCI's inaugural field project for this innovative, international venture is the Eames Residence (Case Study House #8), built in 1949 by Charles and Ray Eames in the Pacific Palisades neighborhood of Los Angeles and the Bernheimer residence, also known as Yamashiro, in the Hollywood Hills.

NEW DIMENSIONS OF DISPLAY AND INTERPRETATION

The J. Paul Getty Trust is now embarking on an ambitious new investigation of L.A. architecture that builds upon its other ongoing architectural initiatives. During the past three decades, there have been an impressive series of successful exhibitions in the region that highlighted specific dimensions of L.A. architecture and featured monographic presentations of its prolific architects. Unfortunately, since the retrospective *Architecture in California, 1868–1968,* curated by David Gebhard and Harriette Von Breton at the University of California, Santa Barbara, Art Gallery in 1968, there has not been a major exhibition dedicated to a comprehensive survey of all forms of this area's diverse architecture and infrastructure.

Pacific Standard Time Presents: Modern Architecture in L.A. is a collaborative Getty venture that seeks to catalyze the next decade of research about this terrain. As with Pacific Standard Time: Art in L.A. 1940–1985, staged across Southern California from 2011 to 2012, the primary motivation for this project was to research and disseminate ideas embedded in existing architectural collections and reveal resources from previously unknown or underutilized archives. In 2011, the Getty Foundation began funding the development and implementation of a series of exhibitions and programs dedicated to the analysis of Los Angeles's vibrant architectural landscape. Initial institutional partners include the A+D Architecture and Design Museum of Los Angeles; the Armand Hammer Museum of Art and Culture Center; Cal Poly Pomona; the Los Angeles Conservancy; the Los Angeles County Museum of Art; the MAK Center for Art and Architecture; the Museum

FIGURE 4.

**View of downtown Los Angeles showing the
Four-Level Interchange, 1950s.**

Los Angeles, Getty Research Institute.

of Contemporary Art, Los Angeles; the Southern California Institute of Architecture; and the University of California, Santa Barbara.

The centerpiece of this initiative is the Getty Research Institute's exhibition at the Getty Museum titled *Overdrive: Los Angeles Constructs the Future, 1940–1990.* This presentation endeavors to reframe the public's perception of Los Angeles's dynamic built environment and amplify the exploration of its vibrant architectural legacy. Instead of a chronological or architect-based organization, the exhibition (and the plate section of this catalog) is structured into five broad categories that reveal the complex dimensions of the region's built landscape.

The first section of the exhibition, titled "Urban Networks," highlights Los Angeles's robust water and power infrastructures and vast transportation network, which allowed the region to grow at an unprecedented pace (fig. 4). Los Angeles's global identity is inextricably linked with the attitude and aesthetic of the automobile. In "Car Culture," exhibited renderings of imaginative automobile designs reveal the industrial forms and materials that inspired and enabled architects to create whimsical new buildings geared toward motorized living. A captivating display of eye-popping coffee shops, gas stations, movie theaters, and strip malls also highlights some of the curbside landmarks that punctuated Los Angeles's horizon line (pl. 18).

The region's unprecedented influx of capital, materials, and skilled labor provided L.A. architects with both visionary patrons and infinite avenues for creativity. The "Engines of Innovation" section of the exhibition features an array of building types and design strategies commissioned by global leaders in international commerce, aerospace, media and entertainment, higher education, and the oil industry (pl. 22). "Community Magnets" explores how designers met the compelling architectural challenge of creating spaces that attract and unite people throughout the four-thousand-square-mile metropolis. This portion of the exhibition examines structures dedicated to sports, culture, consumption, and faith that have become destinations for both Los Angeles residents and tourists worldwide (pl. 36).

Many of Los Angeles's most famous architectural landmarks are nestled in quiet neighborhood side streets, hidden from public view. The exhibition's "Residential Fabric" narrative provides a unique insight into the region's influential residences, from sleek modernist homes to massive housing developments (pl. 52). While aesthetically diverse, all of the exhibition's highlighted structures—including corporate office towers, movie theaters, places of worship, and shopping malls—reveal insights into architects' pioneering incorporation of bold forms, advanced materials, and new technologies.

THE NEXT PHASE OF SCHOLARLY ANALYSIS

This new architectural investigation builds upon the groundbreaking work of a legion of historians, theorists, curators, critics, and activists who have researched and expounded upon the development of Los Angeles. Thanks to the efforts and contributions of leading experts—including Reyner Banham, Mike Davis, John Entenza, David Gebhard, Thomas S. Hines, Esther McCoy, Kevin Starr, D. J. Waldie, and many others—we have a keen understanding of Los Angeles's built legacy, potential opportunities, and pending obligations.

For this venture, we have been very fortunate to engage skilled authors whose thought-provoking essays shed more light on the complex narratives presented in the exhibition. While not structured in exactly the same thematic manner as the exhibition, the book has four categories that reflect a similar methodological approach toward analyzing the city and its architectural design. The catalog begins with a series of assessments of Los Angeles's physical landscape and is followed by sections about Los Angeles and modernism, its residential architecture, and its buildings for commerce and transportation.

The first section of the book is dedicated to issues of planning and how the Southern California terrain was shaped into the megalopolis that we know now. The book starts with an audacious look at the region's landscape, literally going back thousands of years. Philip J. Ethington traces all the elements that had an impact on the natural environment of the Los Angeles Basin, from the prehistoric settlers to the commercial enterprises of recent times, thus indicating what made the basin into a center of political and cultural power.

After this expansive history, William Deverell zooms in on Los Angeles's open space and focuses especially on the unexecuted plans for a comprehensive park system. Enumerating the various twentieth-century proposals for an overarching approach to Los Angeles's parks, beaches, and other accommodations for recreation, he points out that Angelenos instead preferred to spend their time in their private green space—the backyard—bringing into question the roles of public versus private interests in city planning.

Eric Avila looks at another major intervention in the landscape: the freeway system. Avila argues that while the freeways connect various parts of the city, they also divide neighborhoods, especially when the construction of these traffic arteries was used to clear out neighborhoods controversially designated as slums in need of redevelopment. At the same time, Avila contends, the freeways had such an impact on the minds of the people who used them that they also became cultural icons, playing roles in literary and painterly works and even providing a canvas for murals and graffiti.

The last essay in this section, by Sandy Isenstadt, deals with Los Angeles's built landscape. Isenstadt is, however, interested in looking at the buildings not during the daytime, when they are lit by the California sun, but rather after dusk, when they become beacons of light. In Isenstadt's opinion, the modern city comes to life at night when neon and searchlights call attention to the inhabitants of the buildings, and the glowing interiors of the steel-and-glass structures illuminate the urban surroundings.

The book's second section explores the concept of modernism in Southern California: how it was taught and promoted, how it relates to modern movements in other parts of the world, and what the preservation issues are for modern architecture. Wim de Wit presents modern architecture as a trend that, after its early developments before World War II, was promulgated in Southern California by a number of publications. It was first accepted for public and commercial buildings and later for residential architecture. The taste for modern buildings, however, was always in flux.

Ken Breisch examines the history of the four major architecture schools active in the Southern California region during and after World War II. He shows how these schools responded to the demands of modern society and aimed in different ways to prepare their students to work in that environment. He demonstrates convincingly that curricula are not inalterable documents. Instead, he argues, they are produced by educators influenced by the thinking of their time and are therefore constantly subject to change.

The vicissitudes in architectural theory and professional practice were impacted by forces from many different sources, both inside and outside the United States. The ongoing contributions from central Europe to

Los Angeles's architectural scene have been discussed widely.[5] The connections between Los Angeles and Latin America or Asia, however, have just begun to be assessed. Jeff Cody, Hugo Segawa, and Fernando Atique have examined these relationships and produced studies that, the authors feel, are still works in progress. In his examination of the relationship between Los Angeles and Asia, Cody focuses on postwar interactions, which he challenges us to think of not as influences from one part of the world on the other but as confluences, flows of ideas back and forth that impacted both worlds. Segawa and Atique investigate the relationship between Los Angeles and the countries south of the border. They call attention to the astute role the magazine *Arts & Architecture* played in bringing the work of Latin American architects to the attention of a North American audience.

The preservation of the numerous experimental buildings produced in the period between 1940 and 1990 requires an in-depth study of how to conserve materials that were either new in the period when the building was constructed or do not exist anymore, as well as a thorough education of a public that does not always want to understand why a recent building should be saved. Susan Macdonald addresses these and other issues; the questions she raises are not all answered yet, but she and her team at the Getty Conservation Institute are searching for solutions.

The three essays in the residential section explore what Los Angeles is best known for: its huge tracts of land covered with homes. Becky Nicolaides looks at the suburban landscapes of Los Angeles in the post–World War II era and points out that they are not all the same. She focuses on two types: the "sitcom suburbs" of the 1950s and '60s and the "corporate suburbs" of the 1970s and '80s. It is especially the latter type—with its huge, standardized, and sometimes-anonymous developments centered on office towers and shopping malls—that generated the label of "sprawl." The word's negative connotation affected Los Angeles's identity for many years, making the city's name synonymous with such notions as monotony, facelessness, and car dependence. Dana Cuff does not think in terms of the American dream. Instead, she shows that the introduction of tract houses was driven by merchant builders, not by architects or buyers. Most architects, according to Cuff, did not profit from the new developments, as their experiments were not acceptable to the standardized designs that homebuilders preferred. Los Angeles architects did, however, experiment with new materials, especially those that had first been developed by the local aviation and aerospace industries. Dana Hutt writes about the use of materials such as steel, aluminum, fiberglass, and plastics, and about the clients who, often working in those industries themselves, were not afraid of unusual materials, demonstrating that architectural experiments will always remain visions on paper unless there is a client who is willing to pay for the realization.

If aviation provided new ideas to architects for the use of materials, what happened to the design of the buildings for aviation itself? This question and other issues about industry and commerce are examined in the last section of the book. Vanessa R. Schwartz's study of Los Angeles International Airport (LAX) takes us away from the design of the individual terminals and urges us to look at the facility's in-between spaces to examine the calibrated flow of passengers on the ground. She points out that, with the rapid growth of air travel in the post–World War II era, airports were bound to require expansion and modernization. The team of William Pereira and Charles Luckman was able to create an airport that could be adapted easily to modern needs, and as a result, Schwartz argues, LAX became the quintessential jet-age airport.

Stephen Phillips sheds new light on the so-called L.A. Ten group of architects by framing their work of the 1970s and '80s as inspired by the gritty industrial environment in which they lived and worked, rather than by the context of deconstructivism, which many others have claimed as a major influence on the group. This new reading enables us to better understand the work of the L.A. Ten and their desire to integrate the functions of domesticity and industry into modern society.

In the final essay, Chris Nichols looks at the popular expressions of architecture—Googie coffee shops, bowling alleys, drive-in theaters, and motels—in the San Gabriel Valley, where, after an economic downturn in the 1970s, many modern buildings were preserved through neglect. In doing so, Nichols draws our attention to some of the fortuities of urban life, where an area long considered unfashionable becomes a treasure trove of midcentury modern architecture.

EVOLVING PERCEPTIONS OF THE PERPETUAL CITY OF THE FUTURE

Although Los Angeles is consistently accused of developing without intention or order, this exhibition and catalog outline how the region's rapid ascent was deliberately willed into existence by a shifting array of vested interests, powerful alliances, enlightened patrons, and innovative designers. In 1958, *Los Angeles Times* reporter Norris Leap wrote, "This is the day of supersonic flight, of the one-man helicopter and the moon rocket, of the miracles of chemistry and physics and engineering. It also is the day when dreamers include the architect and the builder and the hard-headed banker. And this day's dreamers say it's well past the dawn's twilight of a new Los Angeles era."[6]

The modern landscape successfully conceived and constructed by these ambitious visionaries served as the "blueprint of the modern American city" and enticed millions of souls eager to capitalize on the legendary L.A. promise of personal rejuvenation and professional reward.[7] The title of this exhibition and catalog refers to the extraordinary pace and global impact of the region's unprecedented growth. The term *overdrive,* however, has a dual meaning; it alludes to the fact that an engine burning at an incredible speed often overheats and shuts down. This metropolis's expansionist aspirations and aggressive growth did not come without a price. The environmental degradation, disturbing economic disparities, and daunting civic encumbrances that resulted from the region's meteoric rise can often make Los Angeles boosterism seem like a cruel hoax. Through it had a seductive lure, Los Angeles also effectively disillusioned and repelled generations of urban critics and skeptics. A 1988 *Los Angeles Times Magazine* feature titled "L.A. 2013" mused about the future of the city: "Most of the accounts assume that Los Angeles is going to be a smoggy, overcrowded, expensive place to be caught in freeway gridlock on the way to a home besieged by crime. Certainly, these problems will exist. But, questions remain: How much worse will these urban ills become during the next 25 years?"[8]

While aspects of that dystopian vision materialized, Los Angeles's twenty-first-century incarnation also included more positive unforeseen transformations. In March 2012, the United States Census Bureau determined that the region synonymous with interminable sprawl had become "the nation's most densely populated urbanized area…with nearly 7,000 people per square mile."[9] Strategic infill projects, which amplify existing neighborhood resources instead of creating entirely new developments

FIGURE 5.
Charles H. Owens (American, 1881–1958).
A Pictorial Map of the Los Angeles Metropolitan District, 1926.
Sheet: 55.9 × 83.8 cm (22 × 33 in.);
lithograph: 48 × 69 cm (18⅞ × 27⅛ in.).
San Marino, California, Huntington Library.

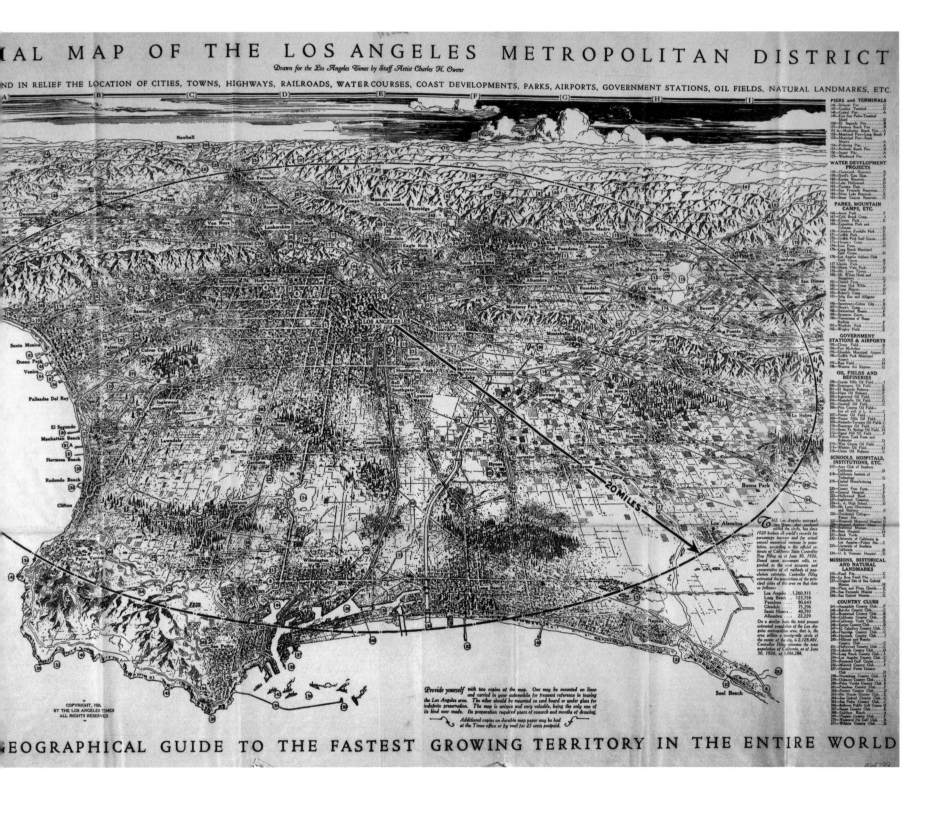

IAL MAP OF THE LOS ANGELES METROPOLITAN DISTRICT

Drawn for the Los Angeles Times by Staff Artist Charles H. Owens

ND IN RELIEF THE LOCATION OF CITIES, TOWNS, HIGHWAYS, RAILROADS, WATER COURSES, COAST DEVELOPMENTS, PARKS, AIRPORTS, GOVERNMENT STATIONS, OIL FIELDS, NATURAL LANDMARKS, ETC.

EOGRAPHICAL GUIDE TO THE FASTEST GROWING TERRITORY IN THE ENTIRE WORLD

on virgin landscapes, will continue to sustain growing population demands in the decades ahead. Concurrent with this efficient planning trend, Los Angeles was at the vanguard of the urban ecological movement, preserving thousands of acres of open space in the Santa Monica Mountains. Public transit rail corridors that were dismantled in the mid-twentieth century to make way for millions of cars were resurrected and began reconnecting the expansive corners of the region. Miles of new bike lane networks were systematically integrated into streets once entirely dominated by motorized traffic.

Los Angeles's ability to facilitate change, recalibrate, experiment, and forge ahead is one of its greatest strengths. Its rich history reveals the fact that future generations of nimble minds will continue to harness the region's enviable resources to create progressive layers of architectural innovation. As Los Angeles launches into the next phase of its urban trajectory, it is crucial that our analysis of this city keep pace with its evolution (fig. 5). This project is an exciting new dimension of an ongoing investigation, which we hope will galvanize broader public interest, spark intriguing provocations, and yield pioneering insights about this captivating metropolis on the move.

NOTES

1   Greg Hise, *Magnetic Los Angeles: Planning the Twentieth-Century Metropolis* (Baltimore: Johns Hopkins University Press, 1997), 10.

2   J. Paul Getty, compiler, "Collected Photographs and Postcards of Los Angeles, California, and Vicinity, ca. 1857–1940," 1986.IA.29, Getty Research Institute, Los Angeles.

3   "Historic-Cultural Monuments and the Cultural Heritage Commission," Office of Historic Resources, http://preservation.lacity.org /commission.

4   "Conserving Modern Architecture Initiative," Getty Conservation Institute, http://www.getty.edu/conservation/our_projects/field _projects/cmai/cmai_overview.html.

5   See, for example, Esther McCoy, *Vienna to Los Angeles: Two Journeys* (Santa Monica, Calif.: Arts + Architecture, 1975); Elizabeth A. T. Smith and Michael Darling, *The Architecture of R. M. Schindler* (Los Angeles, Calif.: Museum of Contemporary Art, 2001); Elizabeth Armstrong, *Birth of the Cool: California Art, Design, and Culture at Mid-Century* (Newport Beach, Calif.: Orange County Museum of Art, 2007); and Thomas S. Hines, *Architecture of the Sun: Los Angeles Modernism, 1900–1970* (New York: Rizzoli, 2010).

6   Norris Leap, "Suburbia 19??: It'll Stretch in All Directions," *Los Angeles Times,* 2 January 1958.

7   Joel Kotkin, "L.A.'s Economy Is Not Dead Yet," *Forbes.com,* 15 June 2010, http://www.forbes.com/2010/06/15/ los-angeles-cities-economy-opinions-columnists-joel-kotkin.html.

8   Nicole Yorkin, "L.A. 2013: Techno-Comforts and Urban Stresses—Fast-Forward to One Day in the Life of a Future Family," *Los Angeles Times Magazine,* 3 April 1988, 7.

9   "Growth in Urban Population Outpaces Rest of Nation, Census Bureau Reports," United States Census Bureau, 26 March 2012, http://2010.census.gov/news/releases/operations/cb12–50.html#.T7_nG_nVRlU.google.

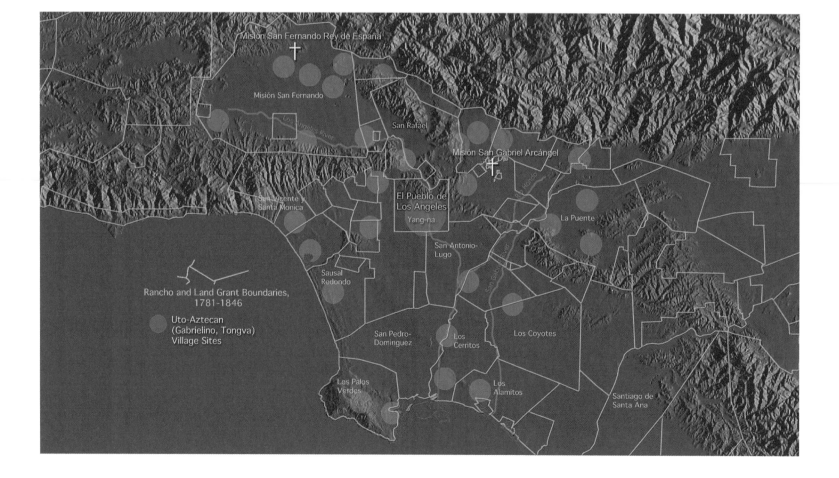

Misión San Fernando Rey de España

Misión San Fernando

Los Angeles River

San Rafael

Misión San Gabriel Arcángel

San Vicente y
Santa Mónica

El Pueblo de
Los Angeles

Yang-na

La Puente

San Antonio-
Lugo

Sausal
Redondo

Rancho and Land Grant Boundaries,
1781-1846

Uto-Aztecan
(Gabrielino, Tongva)
Village Sites

San Pedro-
Dominguez

Los
Cerritos

Los Coyotes

Los Palos
Verdes

Los
Alamitos

Santiago de
Santa Ana

TRANSFORMATIVE LANDSCAPES

THE DEEP HISTORICAL MORPHOLOGY
OF THE LOS ANGELES METROPOLIS

Philip J. Ethington

Hic, ubi nunc Roma est, orbis caput, arbor et herbae et paucae pecudes et casa rara fuit.
[Here, where now stands Rome, capital of the world, there were trees, and grass, a few sheep,
and occasional cottages.]
　　　—Ovid, *Fasti* 5.93–94[1]

TWENTY-FIRST-CENTURY LOS ANGELES is the product of more than one hundred centuries of human effort that transformed the deep ecology of the Los Angeles Basin into one of the world's greatest nodes of global power and cultural interaction. Networks of roads, freeways, rails, ports, and airports draw on the labor of about eighteen million persons and integrate a mighty concentration of power and capital that has been developed over the past few centuries around the site of an ancient settlement called Yangna.[2]

Los Angeles is the expression of successive regimes of power established by Uto-Aztecans, Spanish, Mexicans, and Americans from the United States who exploited a resource-rich basin and the people within it; the resulting riches have attracted and sustained migrants from every continent. This essay maps the geohistorical inscription of urban forms and unequal practices by successive regimes on the living environment of Los Angeles.

Bounded by the San Gabriel Mountains to the north and the Santa Ana Mountains to the southeast and interrupted by the Santa Monica and Puente ranges, the Los Angeles Basin proper is centered on the Los Angeles River, which lies in the middle of a larger drainage that connects the San Fernando, San Gabriel, and San Bernardino Valleys. These valleys are ancient alluvial plains, the sedimentary deposits from millions of years of mountain erosion carried by the Los Angeles, San Gabriel, Rio Hondo, and Santa Ana Rivers. Throughout an immense antiquity, huge and fearsome creatures inhabited these plains, canyons, and mountains: mammoths, mastodons, saber-toothed cats, giant lions, glyptodons, giant ground sloths, and short-faced bears. Megafauna, or "giant animals," thrive only in resource-rich ecoregions, so it is unsurprising

FIGURE 1.
Los Angeles Basin showing Uto-Aztecan village sites, ca. 0–1769, and Spanish-Mexican land grants, 1769–1842.

that the nomadic, spear-crafting Clovis hunters found their way into the basin about 13,200 years ago to slaughter these animals to extinction, clearing the ground for a very different culture complex known as the Archaic or Millingstone people. For ten thousand years, the Millingstone people developed a sedentary, acorn-based lifestyle; dwelt along the springs and the sheltered canyons of the foothills; practiced a low-impact hut architecture; and established the best village sites and the best routes between them—essentially inscribing the region's future urban plan.[3]

This Arcadia was shattered at about the time of Augustus Caesar, when the warlike Uto-Aztecans (today called Tongva or Gabrielino) marched westward and expelled the Millingstone people, while the Uto-Aztecans' cousins marched southward to establish the Aztec Empire (fig. 1). Numbering about five thousand in 1770, these conquerors established approximately fifty permanent villages ranging in size from fifty to two hundred persons. Each village was dominated by a single ruler, called a *tomyaar,* drawn from an aristocratic stratum. The work of hunting, fishing, and gathering was left to the commoners and to their slaves, who were taken in war. The Uto-Aztecans established a vast transportation network on land and sea, trading foodstuffs, luxury goods, and shell-string money. Built atop the Millingstone settlements, these fifty or so village sites became the model for municipalities. Their stratified societies—with a permanent ruling class, a broad middle class, and a permanent slave class—were then seized and subjugated by a few hundred Spanish invaders in the late eighteenth century.[4]

The Spanish under Carlos I continued the Roman practice that had shaped Spain itself, converting vanquished territories into *latifundia* (great farms), with the conquered peoples supplying the labor. Called *haciendas* in Mexico beginning in the 1520s, this settlement type remained an effective method of frontier agrarian production when the Spanish under Carlos III claimed California during the late eighteenth century.

From 1769 to 1781, the Spanish established a theocracy in the Los Angeles Basin. All real power was held by the Franciscan fathers in charge of the "missions"—giant haciendas worked by captive Uto-Aztecans.

Designed in a Moorish style by Father Antonio Cruzado, Misión San Gabriel Arcángel—the first of the Los Angeles Basin missions—was constructed by indigenous labor beginning in 1771 at a site central to the Rio Hondo drainage and surrounded by ancient Uto-Aztecan villages. The village of Shevaanga stood on the San Gabriel River to the west; Weniinga stood at the feet of the San Jose Hills to the east; Ashuukshanga to the northeast; Aluupkenga to the north; and Shehiikwanonga to the northwest.[5] In the foreground of Ferdinand Deppe's 1828 painting is the remains of Shevaanga, known at the time as a *rancheria,* one of many villages still active outside the mission-hacienda system established by the Spanish (fig. 2). *Rancherias* were inhabited by free Uto-Aztecans who did occasional for-hire

FIGURE 2.
Ferdinand Deppe (German, 1794–1861).
Mission San Gabriel, 1832.
Oil on canvas, 68.6 × 94 cm (27 × 37 in.).
Santa Barbara, Santa Barbara Mission Archive Library.

work for the mission priests. The long, low quarters pictured in the left of the painting housed hundreds of "neophytes," the baptized "Gabrielino" Uto-Aztecans who were subject to the absolute power of the fathers and suffered very high mortality and morbidity rates in their prisonlike quarters. The large structure in the middle held the mission offices, residences for the padres, and workrooms for the neophytes. The church itself stands at the eastern edge of the complex, under the snow-capped Mount San Antonio.

The second great hacienda church was the Misión San Fernando Rey de España (1797). With large gangs of enforced labor, the Franciscans irrigated and cultivated the arid alluvial plain, supporting a military class that hunted runaways. According to church records, by 1819, Misión San Fernando grazed 12,800 head of cattle across the San Fernando Valley, and the Misión San Gabriel herded almost 20,000 cattle, 2,938 horses, and 6,548 sheep. The Gabrielinos cultivated 163,578 grape vines and 2,333 fruit trees and applied their hands to looms and other craft industries.[6]

A "rancho system" quickly spread this hacienda economy across the Los Angeles Basin, centered on the Uto-Aztecan villages. Following Roman custom, the Spanish governor of Alta California parceled out hacienda-scale ranchos to military officers in reward for their service. These lands were held and subdivided by heirs for generations.

The Spanish and Mexican ruling stratum assumed the role of the *tomyaars* and governed about the same number of settlements.[7] The surnames of these Californios (rancheros)—Carillo, Dominguez, Lugo, Nieto, Ontiveros, Peralta, Pico, Sepulveda, Verdugo, Ybarra, and Yorba—live on in Los Angeles today in countless place and street names, as well as through their descendants. Though small in number, the Californios inscribed their institutional forms onto the landscape with the land grants they received from 1784 to 1842. Their adobe *casas grandes*—with simple geometries, public spaces, and open courtyards—inspired, not overtly but deeply, Irving Gill and the modernist architects of the twentieth century.[8] Long before the United States conquest of 1848, Spanish and Mexican families were joined by Yankee immigrant-businessmen such as Don Abel Stearns (1798–1871), also known as "Cara de Caballo" (horseface)—a Massachusetts native who in the 1820s adopted the Spanish language, converted to Catholicism, became a Mexican citizen, and married fourteen-year-old Arcadia Bandini, daughter of the great San Diego–area ranchero Juan Bandini.[9] The new Anglo ruling class learned the ways of power and its geography from its predecessor.

Founding dynasties of their own by the 1880s and 1890s, a new class of rulers with the names Harry Chandler, Edward Doheny, George Getty, William Randolph Hearst, Henry Huntington, and Harrison Grey Otis moved into the region, operating huge landed estates, employing thousands of laborers on both sides of the US-Mexican border, and collaborating openly with the Mexican dictator Porfirio Diaz. These new rulers aggressively recast the region as an emerging industrial powerhouse, invented Anglocentric cultural traditions, and defeated labor-based challenges to their rule. They created a powerful centralizing infrastructure that counterbalanced the many dispersed settlement nodes inscribed by the ranchos. They built a mighty artificial harbor at San Pedro and Wilmington; created a vast "industrial zone" centered on Alameda Boulevard between downtown and the harbor; secured millions in bond funding to create the titanic Owens Valley Aqueduct (still the longest aqueduct in all of human history); and supplied cheap electricity through a municipally owned city department.[10] Contrary to the myth of a "fragmented city," all roads, freeways, and

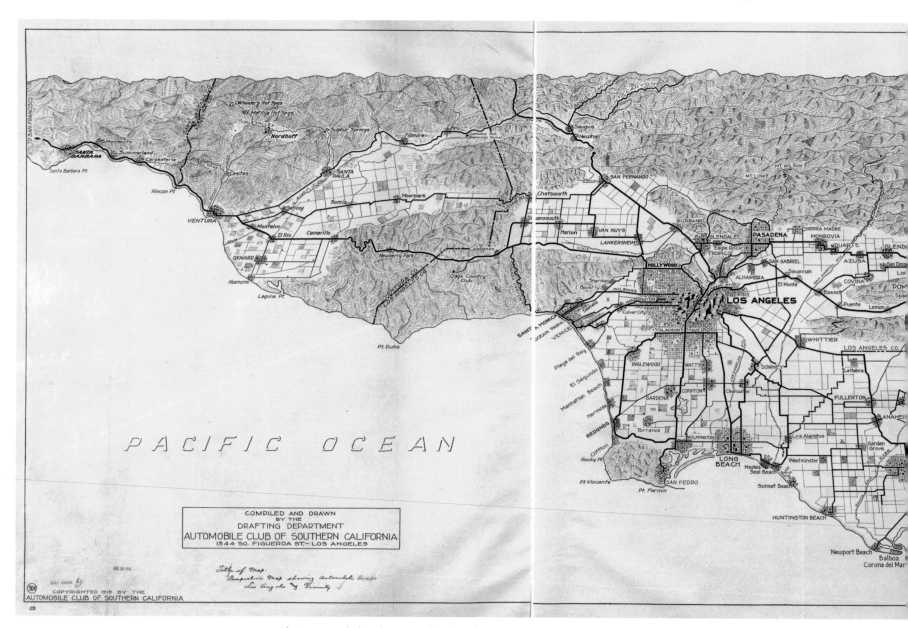

FIGURE 3.
Automobile Club of Southern California's map of Los Angeles and the San Gabriel Mountains, 1915.
Offset print, 62 × 174 cm (24⅜ × 68½ in.).
Washington, D.C., Library of Congress,
Geography and Map Division.

paths to power led to downtown Los Angeles. As a 1915 Automobile Club of Southern California map clearly shows, downtown Los Angeles served as the central hub for numerous towns and villages, from Pomona in the east to Ventura in the west, and Santa Ana to the southeast (fig. 3).

In 1915, the Los Angeles oligarchs aggressively annexed more than 400 square miles of surrounding territory, including the giant 170-square-mile San Fernando Valley. Leveraging this bountiful infrastructure in the late 1910s and 1920s, investors poured billions of dollars into the region, and, in turn, hundreds of thousands of workers migrated to Los Angeles. Developers mobilized a staggering volume of materials and

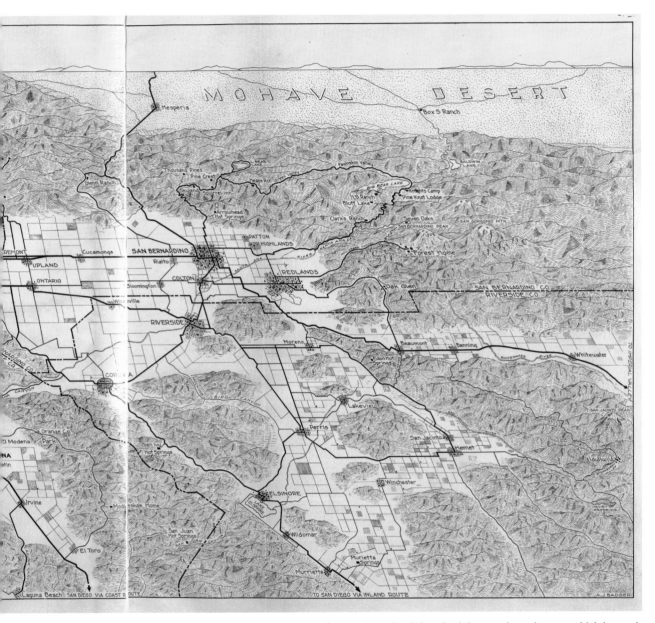

human labor to achieve the building boom of approximately six hundred thousand new homes, which housed 1.2 million new residents. Port activity at the twin harbors of Long Beach and San Pedro increased from 2.4 million tons in 1917 to 27 million tons just five years later. A wider circle of junior oligarchs—Babbit-style "booster" real estate developers—converted ranchos that they had purchased from debt-ridden Californios into incorporated growth-machine cities: Montebello (founded in 1920), Lynwood (1921), Torrance (1921), Hawthorne (1922), South Gate (1923), West Covina (1923), Signal Hill (1924), Maywood (1924), Bell (1927), and Gardena (1930).[11]

Industry was powered by the huge oil fields beneath the Los Angeles Basin, developed by Edward Doheny and other "oilmen" who not only established new dynasties but also reinforced the reactionary political culture of the Anglo oligarchy. The founders of Union Oil Company of California (later UNOCAL) also started the Christian fundamentalist movement.[12] The Gettys, George and his son J. Paul, brought their Oklahoma oil fortune to Los Angeles in 1906 and began buying up leases throughout Huntington Beach and Long Beach after Union Oil brought in a gusher at Santa Fe Springs in 1921. Oil also attracted the major auto and rubber manufacturers. Goodyear opened its plant in 1919, followed by Firestone, Goodrich, and US Rubber. The Ford Motor Company built its first branch plant in 1917 and a much larger plant in Long Beach in 1927 (it later moved to Pico-Rivera); Willys-Overland built a plant in Maywood in 1929; Chrysler began production in the City of Commerce in 1931; followed by Studebaker in Vernon and General Motors in South Gate, both in 1936. By the end of the 1920s, Los Angeles boasted the highest per capita rates of automobile ownership in the world, with one auto for every three people.[13]

With infrastructure and oil in full supply, the Los Angeles Anglo oligarchs recruited the business of two cutting-edge technologies: movies and aircraft. Southern California, supplying an average of three

FIGURE 4.

Los Angeles Basin showing municipal boundaries with dates of incorporation, aerospace production sites, boundaries of the Watts Riot of 1965, and Uto-Aztecan village sites, ca. 0–1769.

Aerospace Production Sites

1850-1939 LA City
1880-1949 Cities
1950-1979 Cities
1980-1991 Cities
Rancho and Land Grant Boundaries, 1781-1846
Uto-Aztecan Village Sites

hundred cloudless days each year, made Los Angeles an attractive film production location. The actor and studio mogul Thomas Ince headquartered his pioneering production company in Los Angeles in 1913 and developed the "central producer system" in the suburb of Culver City.[14] Soon, Universal, Triangle, Lasky, Vitagraph, Metro, Fox, and others built sprawling movie factories. Massachusetts Institute of Technology graduate Donald Douglas set up an airframe shop in Santa Monica and won his first military order in 1921 to build torpedo bombers for the US Navy. By 1928, Douglas Aircraft was worth $25 million; it expanded to El Segundo in 1932 and Long Beach in 1941.[15] Allan and Malcolm Loughead established Lockheed Aircraft in Hollywood in 1926, moving in 1927 to Burbank, where the brothers could maintain an airfield adjacent to their expandable factory space. By the end of World War II, Lockheed was the largest aircraft producer in the world, with a workforce of sixty thousand (fig. 4).[16]

Such massive economic development required a massive working class. And despite the repressive political culture imposed by the Otis-Chandler regime through their antiunion newspaper, the *Los Angeles Times,* workers organized and inspired progressive leaders to push modernist visions of social justice. The district of Edendale—once a Uto-Aztecan settlement called Maawnga[17] and, later, the home of Walt Disney's first studio (1926–39)—was one of the earliest "movie colonies," attracting artists and intellectuals. Active among these bohemians were the Austrian émigrés Richard Neutra and Rudolph Schindler, who, beginning in the 1920s, adapted the ideals of their mentors—including Frank Lloyd Wright—to create Southern California modernism for the masses through the use of advanced industrial materials and glass-enabled design principles that merged interior life with the natural landscape. Their populist and democratic ideals were absorbed by the vast post–World War II building industry, which provided the design theme that framed the space age of the military-industrial Cold War. This theme was epitomized by Case Study House #22 (1959), by Pierre Koenig, who defied gravity by using industrial materials to float a windowed refuge above the mighty metropolis (see Isenstadt, this volume, fig. 10).

By the mid-twentieth century, Los Angeles stood at the very center of the new culture and economy of postwar America—a consumer paradise for the masses made possible through new aerospace technologies, oil-burning automobiles, and an architectural aesthetic inspired by the materials and technologies of this new age. The Anglo dynasts—Getty, Huntington, and others—had amassed major collections of the world's artistic heritage, while the creative classes produced mass culture from the riches of a diverse cultural landscape. But the structure and ruling ideologies of Los Angeles also retained the prior shapes of the undemocratic and exploitative practices on which that growth had been built. These shapes of unjust power placed mestizo Mexican Indian working classes, African Americans, Asians, and many other nonwhites in segregated spaces nearest to industrial hazards and farthest from opportunities. The Los Angeles Police Department, developers, and real estate brokers enforced rigid maps of racial segregation that confined people of color to the working-class core as the affluent white middle class filled new suburban municipalities founded in the 1950s: Lakewood in 1954; Baldwin Park, Cerritos, Downey, and La Puente in 1956; Bellflower, Bradbury, Duarte, Industry, Irwindale, Norwalk, Paramount, Rolling Hills, Rolling Hills Estates, and Santa Fe Springs in 1957; Pico Rivera and South El Monte in 1958; Artesia, Lawndale, Rosemead, and Walnut in 1959; and Bell, Commerce, Cudahy, La Mirada, Paramount, San Dimas, and Temple City in 1960.

The Watts rebellion of 1965 (which left thirty-four people dead), the South Central–area ghettoes, crime, proliferating armed street gangs, police brutality, and the Los Angeles riots in 1992 (which left another fifty-five dead) represent the price paid by the region as a whole for the progress that was built on ideologies of inequality.[18]

In the late twentieth century, Los Angeles had to work out this mighty contradiction at its heart. Built on principles of segregation and centralized power, it has also been the destination of dreams for millions of global immigrants across the centuries. Adding four million individuals over four decades to its 1960 population of six million, Los Angeles County went from 81 percent white in 1960 to 68 percent in 1970, 53 percent in 1980, 41 percent in 1990, and only 32 percent in 2000.[19] The boundaries of residential segregation were not broken until the late 1970s, and, painfully but steadily, the immense waves of multiethnic masses have created vastly varied communities on the sites of their Millingstone forebears. Despite the shadows haunting these many places and the persistent entrenched inequalities, millions still follow the original Clovis hunters, pursuing the good life in a basin of abundance.

NOTES

Portions of this essay appear as excerpts from my essay "Ab Urbis Condita: Regional Regimes since 13,000 Before Present," in William Deverell and Greg Hise, eds., *A Companion to Los Angeles* (Malden, Mass.: Wiley-Blackwell, 2010), and as excerpts from my manuscript for *Ghost Metropolis: Los Angeles since 13,000 BP.*

1   Ovid, *Fasti,* trans. James George Frazer, 2nd ed., Loeb Classical Library (Cambridge, Mass.: Harvard University Press, 1977–88), 5:266 (Latin), 5:267 (English), lines 93–94. Translation altered by the author.

2   On 1 July 2009, the population estimate for the metropolitan area of "Los Angeles–Long Beach–Riverside, CA," was 17,820,893. US Census Bureau, "Annual Estimates of the Population of Combined Statistical Areas: April 1, 2000 to July 1, 2009," http://www.census.gov, CBSA-EST2009-02, table 2.

3   William McCauley, *The First Angelinos: The Gabrielino Indians of Los Angeles* (Banning, Calif.: Malki Museum, 1996).

4   These paragraphs on the Uto-Aztecans are drawn primarily from McCauley, *The First Angelinos.* I also draw on Lowell John Bean and Charles R. Smith, "Gabrielino," in William R. Sturtevant, ed., *Handbook of North American Indians* (Washington, D.C.: Smithsonian Institution, 1978), 8:538–49.

5   McCauley, *The First Angelinos,* 42.

6   Steven W. Hackel, *Children of Coyote, Missionaries of Saint Francis: Indian-Spanish Relations in Colonial California, 1769–1850* (Chapel Hill: University of North Carolina Press, 2005), 65–123; and Douglas Monroy, *Thrown among Strangers: The Making of Mexican Culture in Frontier California* (Berkeley: University of California Press, 1990), 66–67.

7   W. W. Robinson, *Ranchos Become Cities* (Pasadena, Calif.: San Pasqual, 1939), 9–13.

8   Thomas S. Hines, *Irving Gill and the Architecture of Reform* (New York: Monacelli, 2000), 77–79.

9   Antonio Ríos-Bustamante, *Los Ángeles: Pueblo y Region, 1781–1850* (Mexico City: Instituto Nacional de Antropología e Historia, 1991), 184–91.

10 William Deverell, *Railroad Crossing: Californians and the Railroad, 1850–1910* (Berkeley: University of California Press, 1996), 93–122; and Steven Erie, *Globalizing L.A.: Trade, Infrastructure, and Regional Development* (Stanford, Calif.: Stanford University Press, 2004), 43–112.

11 Philip J. Ethington, "The Spatial and Demographic Growth of Los Angeles," in Hynda Rudd, ed., *The Development of Los Angeles City Government: An Institutional History, 1850–2000* (Los Angeles: City of Los Angeles Historical Society, 2007), 663.

12 Philip J. Ethington, "Ab Urbis Condita: Regional Regimes since 13,000 Before Present," in William Deverell and Greg Hise, eds., *A Companion to Los Angeles* (Malden, Mass.: Wiley-Blackwell, 2010), 196.

13 The details in this paragraph are all drawn from Leonard Pitt and Dale Pitt, *Los Angeles A to Z: An Encyclopedia of the City and County* (Berkeley: University of California Press, 2000), 29–31.

14 Steven J. Ross, "How Hollywood Became Hollywood: Money, Politics, and the Movies," in Tom Sitton and William Deverell, *Metropolis in the Making: Los Angeles in the 1920s* (Berkeley: University of California Press, 2001), 258.

15 Greg Hise, *Magnetic Los Angeles: Planning the Twentieth-Century Metropolis* (Baltimore: Johns Hopkins University Press, 1997), 127–28.

16 Roger W. Lotchin, *Fortress California, 1910–1961: From Warfare to Welfare* (New York: Oxford University Press, 1992), 108–10.

17 McCauley, *The First Angelinos,* 56.

18 Pitt and Pitt, *Los Angeles A to Z,* 435, 537–38. The ideas in this paragraph are explored further in the manuscript for *Ghost Metropolis.*

19 These figures are all calculated by the author, based on US Census Bureau data from the years referenced.

PLATE 46. General plan for a complete system of parkways and large parks for the Los Angeles Region. (Base map by courtesy of Automobile Club of Southern California.)

DREAMS DEFERRED
PARKS AND OPEN SPACE

William Deverell

INTRODUCTION: WHAT MIGHT HAVE BEEN

OPEN SPACE IN LOS ANGELES: what is it other than a story of declension and disappointment? From the summit of possibility in the late 1920s to the valley of regret since, open-space planning in greater Los Angeles is an archetypal "if only" tale of loss. Any reckoning of the topic focusing on the second half of the twentieth century has to ponder the road not taken in the first.

That obligation takes us directly to the Los Angeles imagined by Frederick Law Olmsted Jr. More specifically, we must address the plan that his firm, Olmsted Brothers, and its collaborator, Harland Bartholomew & Associates, produced for their client, the Los Angeles Chamber of Commerce, in the late 1920s. Several years of on-the-ground survey, analysis, and design culminated in a brilliant proposal for an articulated system of neighborhood playgrounds and small parks linked to regional "reservations" along the coast and interspersed across surrounding foothills, mountains, and desert. Theirs was a daring vision encompassing a vast area of more than fifteen hundred square miles stretching from the Antelope Valley in the north to the harbor in Long Beach, from the beaches in Malibu east a hundred miles to Riverside County. Had it been brought to fruition, the Olmsted Plan would have drawn seventy thousand acres of parkland into an interconnected system of regional green space. Since then, aside from easel reveries of charrette workshops and the merely wishful sketches of an impossible landscape future, there has been nothing like the Olmsted Plan in the history of Southern California. Eighty years hence, the plan is at once a lofty commemoration of inspiration and a wistful funerary keepsake, a *memento mori* of landscape regret.[1]

Though complex in its intricacy and detail, the landscape narrative of the work can be quickly conveyed. As greater Los Angeles grew through the first decades of the twentieth century, expanding outward in bold metropolitan ambition, civic awareness of a lack of environmental planning from both public and private sectors grew as well. Urban and suburban expansion in the Los Angeles Basin occurred swiftly, well ahead of any widespread awareness of planning deficits; but a few voices were raised about the need to think more

FIGURE 1.
General Plan for a Complete System of Parkways and Large Parks for the Los Angeles Region.
From Olmsted Brothers and Bartholomew & Associates, *Parks, Playgrounds and Beaches for the Los Angeles Region* (Los Angeles: Los Angeles Chamber of Commerce, 1930), pl. 46.
San Marino, California, Huntington Library.

broadly about how Los Angeles would grow. By the mid-1920s, disparate opinions had coalesced into a mini-movement. Backed by private subscriptions from wealthy patrons, a committee spun from the Chamber of Commerce made a pitch to the Olmsted Brothers planning firm to come west from New England to design a new landscape future for the City of Angels.

Having haughtily rebuffed earlier entreaties, which began with late-nineteenth-century appeals to Frederick Law Olmsted Sr. himself, the firm accepted the job in the late 1920s. Several years of on-site planning ensued, with Olmsted Jr. presiding over a talented collection of landscape, engineering, and planning professionals. By then the most experienced design team in the nation, the firm matched visionary design with the hardheaded financial and political acumen needed to make things happen beyond the drafting table.[2]

Crammed into fewer than two hundred pages, *Parks, Playgrounds and Beaches for the Los Angeles Region* presented three essential routes toward a profoundly different Los Angeles future. First, the plan linked open-space sites and greenbelts in a design that could be described as laying a gigantic emerald necklace across much of Southern California. Second, Olmsted Jr. and his partners laid out the fiscal trails that would bring great sums of public, private, and bonded funds together. Third, the planners reminded their client that big plans necessitated big governance. The report sketched out a superjurisdictional political entity that could effectively manage a comprehensive landscape vision brought to life (fig. 1).

From the vantage of nearly a century later, it all looks so straightforward, even dry, in clarity and precision. Yet visionary planning is meant only for a shelf, or at best a wall, if it cannot be implemented and, once executed, cared for. It was precisely that expectation of "caring for" in the plan that tripped it up—fatally. The downfall was swift and dramatic. The Olmsted Plan was supposed to be printed in copies enough so its distribution could be far and wide and to many audiences. But the plan was printed in but a few hundred copies at most, and handbook became rare book.

Why? Having done so much so well, the planners made a crucial error, though one that probably caught them unawares. Olmsted Jr. misread the eventual reaction of his client—though not as to the plan, its scale, or what it would cost. As it turned out, the Chamber of Commerce, and especially its executive committee, resented the idea that a new institutional body would be created to run the greenscape system brought to fruition by the plan. Though Olmsted was shrewd in proposing that a superjurisdictional committee oversee a superjurisdictional plan, the Chamber of Commerce proved adamant in its unwillingness to cede authority to an upstart group created of whole cloth. That prospect was, to quote one Chamber member, nothing less than "terrifying."[3]

Had Chamber leaders objected to public expenditures on a big scale or to what might be considered centralized planning (though with significant private sector inputs of expertise and capital), we might characterize the opposition as politically motivated. But the antagonism was more peevish than principled. Lacking any animating reception whatsoever, the report languished and then disappeared.

The irony is almost as palpable as the misfortune. At the dawn of the Great Depression, which would usher in a period in which federal dollars and federal authority would forever alter the political and economic landscape of Southern California, the Chamber of Commerce held on to an antiquated past and an outmoded constellation of power. That stubbornness profoundly jeopardized the future.

Despite its dismissal, the mere existence of the Olmsted Plan can help us dispel tired and dead-wrong assumptions about Los Angeles and planning, environmental or otherwise. While we can wish for that plan to have been applied, the twentieth century is rife with others, though none even approach *Parks, Playgrounds and Beaches* in comprehensiveness or vision.

The Progressive Era precursors to Olmsted suggested a different park future for the region, one that was foundational and charmingly optimistic. Historian Lawrence Culver points out that during this more hopeful period, Los Angeles created the nation's first municipal Playground Department, "made outdoor recreation and nature appreciation part of the city's school curriculum, and purchased beaches and mountain camps to ensure public access."[4] Public and private entities offered and backed a variety of occasionally far-reaching plans through the first half of the century that reoriented regional space and transit through it, with undeniable consequences for the landscape and parks.[5] It is imperative to note that many of the influential among these—Olmsted included—made the same naive assumptions about melding recreation, green space, and the automobile in a seamless triad supporting leisure. Wrapping their ideas and the regional future around the contemporary meaning of *parkway,* public and private planners left unquestioned their certainty that the automobile and green space could coexist beyond tension or even consequence.

Yet, beyond quaint nods to nostalgia, we no longer refer to arterial automobile throughways as "parkways." The word raises associations oblique to our reality: freeways are many things to Southern Californians; "parklike" is not one of them. We can hardly imagine how our predecessors could have seen the world this way. But they did: the Automobile Club of Southern California put its considerable weight behind a late-1930s parkway plan that sketched the bones of the basin's freeway system; the idea was that driving around and through the basin could be impeccably woven into the pleasurable expectations of time spent in a park. The stresses of urban life would, if not fall away, at least recede as nature performed its soothing charms. But what actually receded was the attractiveness of the expectation, overwhelmed as it soon was by reality (fig. 2).[6]

In what might be understood as a regional rebound from the Olmsted fiasco, private and public planners huddled anew in and around the war years amidst the chaos of fundamental metropolitan and industrial change. Coming as a kind of social scientific coda to Olmsted, the 1941 volume *Los Angeles: Preface to a Master Plan* was, despite its tentative title, a far-reaching exploration of the necessity for Los Angeles planning at the broadest environmental and multijurisdictional levels (i.e., across the basin and across the county).[7] And while the book

FIGURE 2.
Arroyo Seco (110) Parkway, 1944.
Photo by "Dick" Whittington Studio.
San Marino, California, Huntington Library.

melded transportation, housing, and economic rationality together, it did not neglect green-space awareness and comment; the trouble was that *Preface* occupies a different genre entirely than *Parks, Playgrounds and Beaches.* Where the latter offered careful prescriptive steps to first reimagine and then recreate place, the former inaugurated a march of reports that hewed toward observation over practice, analysis over application. That is understandable; the war and postwar years, by way of accelerated growth, filled in much of the open space Olmsted had linked only a few short decades earlier. The moment had passed.

Cities Are for People (1942), a sweeping post-*Preface* follow-up aimed mostly at young people (though without the detail and intricacy of *Preface*), exhibits another problem of green-space planning of the midcentury, albeit one a long time coming. Placing the automobile into the park garden was one critical issue of the era, and given that this maneuver resulted in actual transit planning, it is a significant one. But there is also, as indicated in *Cities Are for People* and its ilk, a related or parallel problem. This would be the "merely extoll" camp of environmental or green-space planning: Los Angeles is the recipient of nature's munificence, and a reminder of that largesse is nearly enough to make it all work. This view (as well as an oft-utilized and entirely unhelpful metaphor comparing the regional ecosystem to the circulatory and respiratory systems of humans) is enthusiastic, but it cannot do the work or carry the weight of actual planning. But the hoary regional pride over nature's bounty is an empty vessel if it carries booster rhetoric alone. This early-1940s document was not the first, and certainly not the last, to take this view: "In our dreams the Los Angeles metropolitan community of the future has safe, well-planned streets on which traffic flows smoothly, convenient self-contained neighborhoods, numerous regional parks, connected by beautiful parkways, miles of publicly-owned beaches, and prosperous industries that make full use of the rich resources of our region."[8] That future looks pretty, but how do you get there?

To be fair, the region's wartime and immediate postwar planning ethos had environmental preoccupations beyond landscape and park planning. The environmental degradation created in the wake of Southern California's pivotal activity in sustaining the "arsenal of democracy" was profound.[9] Oil seeps and spills, blankets of smog in the airspace, infrastructural challenges borne of demographic explosion: if there was a zero-sum game of political will to wrestle with environmental challenges, this is where the attention and money went, not to parks.

Though couched in the similar booster language of the *Cities Are for People* primer, a 1944 report issued by the philanthropic and policy-minded John Randolph Haynes and Dora Haynes Foundation called for concerted preservation and conservation efforts on the coastline, including maintenance of public recreational facilities on sand and shore.[10] Picking up the beaches imperative from Olmsted was an important step. A companion report went inland, sketching out environmental and recreational visions for freshwater streams and rivers.[11] And a 1945 report resurrected and echoed the Olmsted Plan in spirit and title.[12] Well intentioned and deeply researched, this latter document seems, at least in comparison with its precursor, tinged with regret and marked by a relatively modest ambition: to highlight instead of remedy deficits.[13] That tendency, as well as a retreat to piecemeal efforts, describes much that has happened since. In fact, if we can characterize most of the first half of the twentieth century as an era of lost green-space opportunities, we have justification in characterizing the decades since as an era of no opportunities.

Private institutions did, if briefly, rise up post-Olmsted to support environmental planning as a public good, but a collective Angeleno retreat to literal privacy cut at cross-purposes with those efforts. The Haynes Foundation, in its wartime and postwar support of *Preface to a Master Plan* and its multiple spin-offs, is the case in point of such institutional vision. At odds with much of this was the collective consequence of millions of individual decisions by legions of cold-war Angelenos challenging that sense and sensibility. Angelenos retreated into their postwar backyards—because they wanted to and because they could. Refuge, status symbol, midbrow modernist environmental space—what have you—the backyard became for the postwar set what the garage had been for their prewar parents: the symbol of suburban times. Lawned, gardened, and pooled, backyards (at least for those whose class or racial status allowed) looked like green-space shards from the shattered Olmsted dream. Faith in parks, if not wider faith in the public good, existed in undeniable tension with the green-space, or "cement-space," landscapes of privacy. As Lawrence Culver notes, any postwar park growth in greater Los Angeles (and it did occur) was never enough to address long-standing deficits.[14]

However, we would do well to note historian Greg Hise's reminder that Los Angeles's history is not either "boom or gloom" but both and in between both.[15] Successes of groundswell activism and public policy have occurred in this arena. The 1978 establishment, and subsequent expansion, of the Santa Monica Mountains National Recreation Area is the pinnacle in this regard; that park and open green space draws in over 150,000 acres that are protected from development while crossing several jurisdictions. Established by legislation at the federal, state, and county levels, the recreational area was, in its most idealized imagining, envisioned as addressing myriad deficits. The to-be-protected landscape possessed "significant scenic, wilderness, recreational, public health, educational, scientific, natural, and archeological value," and the "maintenance of recreational open space" was simply "necessary to the urban environment" of greater Los Angeles.[16]

After the passage of the federal legislation that created the Santa Monica Mountains National Recreation Area, several decades of gradual, and often controversial, actions brought additional land into protected status. It should not be surprising that the National Park Service and its parent, the U.S. Department of the Interior, often ran into trouble trying to draw the land of both willing and unwilling sellers into the recreation area patchwork. The former raised objections to the timing (too slow) and the price (too low) offered for their lands. The latter often made arguments that too much land had already been removed from the marketplace in greater Los Angeles. Accurate or not, this sentiment echoed the anti-Olmsted line of sixty years earlier that Los Angeles has plenty of park space.[17]

In light of the earlier critiques leveled at Olmsted's (admittedly larger) governance plan for *Parks, Playgrounds and Beaches,* it would be instructive to make a concerted study of the Santa Monica Mountains Conservancy, the public agency started upon the creation of the recreation area as a superintendent of green space (fig. 3). As in the wishful Olmsted Plan decades earlier, the recreation area is a green-space chain; the various links in that chain are both different ecological habitats and a patchwork of local, state, and federal initiatives that stitch together an impressive recreational site.[18]

Thus, going to the mountains reveals redemptive atonement, or a suggestion of it, for the lost Olmsted moment. There is hope found as well in the flatlands of the Los Angeles Basin. From its headwaters in the selfsame Santa Monica Mountains, the Los Angeles River flows fifty-odd miles to the ocean; its

mouth at the Pacific is under a freeway in Long Beach. An important, integrative feature in Olmsted's vision, the Los Angeles River has recently suffered a complex and difficult environmental history. Big nineteenth- and early-twentieth-century floods scared Angelenos and had the maddening consequence of filling up great reaches of the basin with water and silt for weeks at a time. When it flooded, the tempestuous little river was dangerous, and when it carved away its banks, it carried increasingly valuable real estate worth-lessly out to sea.

By the 1910s, yielding to widespread insistence that the river had to be tamed, city and county officials, in partnership with the United States Army Corps of Engineers, embarked on a nearly century-long effort to cloak the river in a concrete jacket. That project cemented both the river and an especially rigid approach to regional flood control. And despite early-twentieth-century claims that the cool, gray regularity of concrete could be beautiful by way of early modernist aesthetics, a channeled, neglected river is a tough sell as a park or recreational space.

Yet, at the same time that preservation sensibilities began to succeed in the Santa Monica Mountains, a tiny grassroots reenvisioning of the Los Angeles River began. In 1986, poet and essayist Lewis MacAdams founded Friends of the Los Angeles River (FoLAR). The gesture—part lark, part crusade—has proven impor-tant and prophetic, as the intervening several decades have witnessed a significant rise in public awareness and appreciation of the riparian feature from which Los Angeles continues to draw its name, and its water.

Early arguments about the preservation of the river often focused on the untenable. Ripping out all the concrete along the river's bed and banks, in the absence of mitigating action elsewhere, cannot work, given the critical flood-control work that the channeled river performs. But, as the years since the mid-1990s demonstrate, ecological revitalization of the river can be undertaken even in the presence of concrete; sec-tions of the river can be restored piecemeal; recreational use of the river can be popularized; and the river can be a unifying recreational ribbon at the very heart of the city.[19] The tea leaves are as yet murky. *Parks, Play-grounds and Beaches* saw new, if circumscribed, life in facsimile reproduction in 2000, and the elderly vision served briefly as a touchstone prompting a public conversation about the uneven and inequitable distribution of outdoor recreation areas in the city and county.[20]

As context and background, recall that California voters approved Proposition 12 in early 2000. The bond measure allotted more than $2 billion to statewide park improvements and maintenance of the coastline and its beaches.[21] Not surprisingly, politicians and would-be elected officials perked up, environmentally and otherwise. Candidates in the Los Angeles mayoral race of 2000 touted the need for additional parks, play-grounds, and open space, often with explicit reference to the now-obscure Olmsted Plan from 1930. On more than one occasion, leading candidates James Hahn and Antonio Villaraigosa held the document aloft while delivering forceful commitments to restore the river; to create a new city-center park at the Cornfield site near downtown; and to cap toxic waste that endangers the health of children playing on Los Angeles Unified School District (LAUSD) playgrounds and sports fields. These and other objectives (many of which have been successfully accomplished) are not trivial. They are not Olmstedian, insofar as they lack articulated, systemic character. But they are important, and we might suggest that the Olmsted Plan (or the mere and renewed awareness of it) helped them come into being (figs. 4, 5).[22]

FIGURE 3.
View from Castro Crest in the Santa Monica Mountains National Recreation Area, 1981.
Photo by David Ochsner.
Malibu, California, Santa Monica Mountains National Recreation Area Research Library.

FIGURES 4A, 4B.
Views during and after the installation of a rainwater cistern beneath a formerly paved playground at a Los Angeles Unified School District campus, 2003–4.

FIGURE 5.
The Glendale Narrows of the Los Angeles River, 2012.
Photo by William Preston Bowling.

FIGURE 6.
**Los Angeles State Historic Park,
also known as the Cornfield, 2006.**
Photo by Gary Leonard.

Ten years after the mayoral-race flirtation with the Olmsted Plan, others have discovered and consulted the report for various reasons. The Los Angeles Department of City Planning (DCP) is considering the
creation of a ten-mile loop that would link parks with public transportation—an idea indebted (but not slav-
ishly) to *Parks, Playgrounds and Beaches.* Whereas the Olmsted and Bartholomew proposal used roads and
trails, the DCP's Urban Design Studio plan creates a reliance on a rail network to connect parks included in
the 1930 report (Echo and Elysian Parks, for example) with parks developed during the intervening eighty
years (Vista Hermosa) and those currently in development (Los Angeles State Historic Park, also known as the
Cornfield) (fig. 6).

Using facets of the Olmsted Plan as inspiration or objective is probably all we can ask of those who
have come after it. Selective implementation is, after all, the usual end result of all but the least ambitious
plans. The original study provides a framework for future interventions and a benchmark for comprehensive
investigation into the planning and development of greater Los Angeles.

The demise and partial resurrection of the Olmsted Plan is a fine case study of the fate of plans,
especially big plans: they are difficult to implement, they inevitably get broken up, and they face sliding time-
and-breadth scales of execution. Finding the right metric to express a green space to population or built environment ratio that constitutes "just enough" or "the right amount" remains challenging.[23] Greater Los Angeles
comes up short in almost all reckonings of such an equation. Thus, the salient point is that this region is still
trying to catch up to the visionary breadth of a park future proposed and damned nearly a century ago.

NOTES

1   *Parks, Playgrounds and Beaches for the Los Angeles Region: A Report Submitted to the Citizens' Committee on Parks, Playgrounds and Beaches* (Los Angeles: Olmsted Brothers & Bartholomew, 1930). For latter-day attempts to bring back Olmsted's ghost—laudable if improbable—see, for example, "Public-Interest Law Firm Organizes to Provide Parkland for L.A. Neighborhoods," *Los Angeles Daily Journal,* 28 January 2005; and "The Dry Garden: 'New Park Design in Los Angeles' Exhibit Dreams of a City Turning Back the Clock," *Los Angeles Times,* 8 June 2011. The *Daily Journal* article discusses the work of the nonprofit legal and policy organization the City Project (www.cityprojectca.org), which draws inspiration from the Olmsted Plan as the high-water mark in Los Angeles landscape and park-planning history.

2   For a brief history of urban and suburban planning in Los Angeles, including additional information on the origins and demise of the Olmsted Plan, please see Greg Hise and William Deverell, *Eden by Design: The 1930 Olmsted-Bartholomew Plan for the Los Angeles Region* (Berkeley: University of California Press, 2000). See also our collaborative piece "The Afterlife of a Master Plan," from which parts of this discussion are drawn, in David C. Sloane, ed., *Planning Los Angeles* (Chicago: American Planning Association, 2012), 204–11.

3   See Board of Directors, Los Angeles Chamber of Commerce, Stenographic Report, 7 February 1929, Los Angeles Chamber of Commerce Collection, Regional History Collections, University of Southern California Libraries; as cited in Hise and Deverell, *Eden by Design,* 39.

4   Lawrence Culver, "America's Playground: Recreation and Race," in William Deverell and Greg Hise, eds., *A Companion to Los Angeles* (Chichester, UK: Wiley-Blackwell, 2010), 421–60, quoted at 421. Note, too, that Victoria Padilla, in her classic treatment of the largely private garden landscapes of Southern California, marks the period from 1900 to 1930 as "the golden age," after which declension, inattention, and industrial/suburban sprawl ruled the day. Victoria Padilla, *Southern California Gardens: An Illustrated History* (Berkeley: University of California Press, 1961). See also Lawrence Culver, *The Frontier of Leisure: Southern California and the Shaping of Modern America* (New York: Oxford University Press, 2010).

5   As but one example of the regional planning ethos, the Metropolitan Transportation Authority (MTA) has been developing the bibliography "Los Angeles Transit and Transportation Studies, 1911–1957." At present, the chronological list includes sixty-eight documents and counting. There are ten plans from 1949 alone, including the Pacific Electric Railway Company study of passenger-loading standards; the California State Assembly examination of rapid transit for metropolitan areas; and the City of Los Angeles's assessment of street-traffic management. A similar accounting for land use, zoning, infrastructure, and urban design would generate comparable lists. The MTA bibliography is found at http://www.metro.net/about/library/archives/visions-studies/los-angeles-transit-and-transportation-studies/. See also Greg Hise and Todd Gish, "City Planning," in Tom Sitton, ed., *The Development of Los Angeles City Government: An Institutional History, 1850–2000* (Los Angeles: Los Angeles Historical Society, 2007).

6   A recent, thoughtful tour of the region's awakening to automobility is Jeremiah B. C. Axelrod, *Inventing Autopia: Dreams and Visions of the Modern Metropolis in Jazz Age Los Angeles* (Berkeley: University of California Press, 2009). It is important to note that, as late as 1971, Reyner Banham could celebrate Los Angeles with exuberance precisely because the automobile and the freeway system both bespoke and allowed freedom of movement through the basin. It is likely that Banham's buoyant view has become a classic, in part at least, because of this iconoclastic—even anachronistic—perspective. Reyner Banham, *Los Angeles: The Architecture of Four Ecologies* (New York: Harper & Row, 1971).

7   George W. Robbins and Leon Deming Tilton, *Los Angeles: Preface to a Master Plan* (Los Angeles: Pacific Southwest Academy, 1941); hereafter referred to as *Preface.* As befit the era, the plan is less an environmentally based vision of planning and the future than a collection of themes presented through social science analyses ("A Review of the Geographic Base" and "The Land Use Patterns," for example).

8   Mel Scott, *Cities Are for People: The Los Angeles Region Plans for Living* (Los Angeles: Pacific Southwest Academy, 1942), 98. The "sequel" to this report, aimed at an older audience, would be Charles W. Eliot, *Citizen Support for Los Angeles Development* (Los Angeles: Haynes Foundation, 1945). Eliot's uncle, also named Charles Eliot, had been a partner in the original Olmsted firm. See also Greg Hise, "Situating Stories: What Has Been Said about Landscape and the Built Environment," in William Deverell and Greg Hise, eds., *A Companion to Los Angeles* (Chichester, UK: Wiley-Blackwell, 2010), 393–420. Hise writes (at p. 395) of the "nature's bounty" paradigm from Fray Juan Crespi's famed diary entry of 1769, in which he describes the basin as "a most beautiful garden."

9   "Arsenal of democracy" became a popular slogan after President Franklin D. Roosevelt used it in a radio broadcast on 29 Decem-ber 1940.

10 Donald F. Griffin, *Plans and Actions for the Development of the Los Angeles Metropolitan Coastline* (Los Angeles: Haynes Foundation, 1944).

11 Charles W. Eliot, *Waterlines—Key to Development of Metropolitan Los Angeles* (Los Angeles: Haynes Foundation, 1946).

12 County Citizens Committee, *Parks, Beaches, and Recreation Facilities for Los Angeles County* (Los Angeles: Haynes Foundation, 1945).

13 A thorough exploration of the foundation's role in midcentury planning—by way of lent expertise and funding—is Tom Sitton, "Private Sector Planning for the Environment," in William Deverell and Greg Hise, eds., *Land of Sunshine: An Environmental History of Metropolitan Los Angeles* (Pittsburgh: University of Pittsburgh Press, 2005), 152–66.

14   Lawrence Culver, *The Frontier of Leisure* (New York: Oxford University Press, 2010).

15   Greg Hise, "Situating Stories," 414.

16   From the bill as proposed by Congressman Anthony Beilenson, May 1977; a copy can be found in the Edmund D. Edelman papers, box 762, Huntington Library, San Marino, Calif.

17   See, for example, Arthur F. Cole to Senator Robert Byrd, 14 September 1991, in which Cole writes: "I hope that ANY funds remaining in PARK or other land acquisition budgets will be immediately transferred to a BUDGET REDUCTION FUND." Conversely, Angeleno Nonya Finkelstein in a letter to County Supervisor Edmund D. Edelman, a key voice for the preservation of the recreational area, wrote, "These mountains have made me VERY happy [and] should remain available to all who come to Southern California." Finkelstein to Edelman, 12 July 1988. Both letters are in the Edmund D. Edelman papers, box 761, Huntington Library, San Marino, Calif. The Edelman papers are a significant source of information about the history of the recreational area and its expansion through the end of the twentieth century.

18   For an introduction to the political maneuvering inherent to the recreational area's growth, including the often controversial actions of the head of the Santa Monica Mountains Conservancy during key years of parkland expansion, see Jack Cheevers, "Striking Deals for Parkland," *Los Angeles Times,* 15 October 1991, 1.

19   FoLAR is but one of many groups and organizations at work on raising awareness of the river and its recreational potential. Bicycling organizations play an important role in the ways in which the river is seen and its banks used, as does the extremely interesting and entirely grassroots Los Angeles Urban Rangers, an organization dedicated to widespread understanding and recreational use of Southern California open and park space, from beaches to deserts. On bicycling organizations, see, for instance, the Los Angeles County Bicycle Coalition at la-bike.org; on the Urban Rangers, see www.laurbanrangers.org.

20   For example, Hise and Deverell, *Eden by Design,* in which the facsimile reproduction is at pages 65–282; see also Robert Garcia, "Mapping Green Access," *The City Project,* http://www.cityprojectca.org/ourwork/mappinggreenaccess/index.html; and Jennifer Wolch et al., "Parks and Park Funding in Los Angeles: An Equity Mapping Analysis" (Los Angeles: Sustainable Cities Program, University of Southern California, May 2002).

21   Proposition 12 is the Safe Neighborhood Parks, Clean Water, Clean Air, and Coastal Protection Bond Act of 2000. See http://primary2000.sos.ca.gov/VoterGuide/Propositions/12text.htm.

22   For a broad and important contribution to this renewed sense of possibility—which, it should be noted, may have reached a high-water mark around 2007—is Robert Gottlieb, *Reinventing Los Angeles: Nature and Community in the Global City* (Cambridge, Mass.: MIT Press, 2007).

23   Both racial and class disparities in access to green space and toxic racism realities render greater Los Angeles an especially apt and galling case study of such inequities. See, for example, Christopher Boone, "Zoning and Environmental Inequity on the Industrial East Side," in William Deverell and Greg Hise, eds., *Land of Sunshine: An Environmental History of Metropolitan Los Angeles* (Pittsburgh: University of Pittsburgh Press, 2005), 167–78. See also a recent public television documentary produced by KCET in Los Angeles, "Park Poor," which aired on 7 October 2011 and discusses park disparities between different Los Angeles communities (or zip codes); the story can be found at http://www.kcet.org/shows/socal_connected/content/health/community-health/park-poor.html.

ALL FREEWAYS LEAD TO EAST LOS ANGELES
RETHINKING THE L.A. FREEWAY AND ITS MEANINGS

Eric Avila

THE CLOSING OF THE 405 FREEWAY on a summer weekend in 2011 invited another round of clichés about Los Angeles and its freeways (fig. 1). National media outlets hyped the "Countdown to Carmageddon" and dramatized the chaos that would ensue when this vital traffic artery closed for construction. Like the Y2K bug, "Carmageddon" was another overblown spectacle invented to inflate Nielsen ratings. Nothing happened, of course, except two stunning days of empty freeways, but the media circus that ensued over this event under- scores the pervasive notion that freeways define Los Angeles, a city long stereotyped for its romance with automobiles, freeways, and oil.

This essay traces the origins of that stereotype to the early decades of the twentieth century, when Los Angeles pioneered a political and cultural environment conducive to driving a car. In a city that once boasted the nation's most extensive streetcar system, the mass adoption of the automobile necessitated the creation of a new kind of urban space, one given entirely to the automobile and its unfettered mobility. The parkway debuted in Los Angeles in the 1930s, but the interstate era of the 1950s and '60s introduced a regional network of high-speed arterials with elaborate interchanges that modeled feats of urban engineering. The engineers who designed these structures dispensed with the niceties that underlie the parkway concept, building spare concrete thoroughfares with a ruthless efficiency that eschewed sensitivity to the contextual particularities of the city's diverse neighborhoods and communities. The postwar generation of interstate freeways modeled a 1950s ideal of social and technical progress, and their new stature in the city's geography brought that ideal to bear upon the very identity of the city.[1]

Since the 1950s, the freeway has insinuated its way into popular understandings of Los Angeles and its culture, though the city's relationship to its freeways is not all that different from that of its urban counter- parts throughout the nation, especially in the Sunbelt, where automobiles and freeways dictate a sprawling, decentralized pattern of urban development. Nonetheless, freeways continue to play a central role in cultural representations of Los Angeles, which express perspectives and experiences of freeways and their role in

FIGURE 1.
Aerial view of a helicopter flying over the Four-Level Interchange, 1959.
Los Angeles, University of Southern California, California Historical Society Collection.

shaping the identity of the city. This essay explores the basis of these expressions, illuminating how the city's diverse social groups have innovated new cultural forms to assert their own unique understandings of the L.A. freeway and its place in the urban landscape. Part literature review, part historical account, and part cultural analysis, this essay examines the contested meanings of the L.A. freeway and its significance to urban identity in Southern California.

———

The historiography of Los Angeles entails a vexed relationship between the city and the automobile. Explaining the sheer scale of the city is an ongoing challenge for L.A. historians: What factors enabled Los Angeles to reign as the second-largest city in the nation? And how did its greater urban region support the twelfth-largest concentration of people in the world? Experts often point to the technologies of transportation that determined the scope and rate of urban growth in Southern California.

First, the railroad: it linked Los Angeles and its markets to the globalizing capitalist economy toward the end of the nineteenth century and sparked a series of demographic explosions in the region between 1870 and 1930.[2] Second, the streetcar: while the railroad dictated the early growth of modern Los Angeles, the streetcar takes credit for shaping the distinctive form of the city in its early-twentieth-century incarnation. This brings us to perhaps one of the greatest misunderstandings about the history of Los Angeles: the streetcar and the tracks it rolled upon, not the automobile and the freeway, initiated the decentralized, sprawling pattern of urban growth that amateur historians mistakenly associate with the automobile.

The key figure in this development was the scion of California's railroad empire, Henry Huntington, who quickly figured out that although building a streetcar network in Los Angeles was not necessarily a profitable enterprise, fortune awaited those who could tie this venture to land development and real estate promotion. Thus, Huntington built streetcar lines to vast parcels of empty land beyond the fringes of settlement, with nothing but a bandstand, a barbecue lunch, and big signs that read "Burbank," "Van Nuys," and "Monrovia" to greet future residents of the San Fernando and San Gabriel Valleys. In piecemeal increments, and with lots of fanfare, urban sprawl was born.[3]

Enter the automobile. Journalist Carey McWilliams described the boom of the 1920s as "the first great migration of [the] automobile age," emphasizing Southern California's hospitable climate for driving.[4] Indeed, registration rates soared in Southern California upon the car's introduction, making Los Angeles the national leader in private car ownership.[5] While Americans throughout the nation pursued their infatuation with driving, the private automobile had a special resonance in the cultural climate of Southern California, as it conformed to a regional ideology that favored a vision of decentralized urban growth predicated upon suburban homeownership in a Mediterranean climate. While the streetcar initiated this pattern of settlement, the automobile accelerated the outward thrust of suburbanization, spurring local ambitions to make Los Angeles the "Better City," as the progressive minister Dana Bartlett put it in his famous booster tract that upheld Los Angeles as a moral alternative to the squalor and congestion of cities like New York and Chicago.[6] The automobile suited the progressive idealization of suburban homeownership as a mitigating force against the unwieldy and destructive energies of industrial urbanization, making Los Angeles the first city of the automobile age.[7]

Less developed than older American cities, Los Angeles was well equipped to handle the onslaught of the automobile, but certain parts of the city struggled to accommodate the sudden invasion of these bulky machines. Space was tight on the early streets of downtown Los Angeles, granting little room to drivers who had to compete with cumbersome streetcars. Local boosters tied to the industries that produced automobiles recognized that downtown had to make room for the automobile, lest drivers find other places to take their business. Thus, the *Los Angeles Times,* the voice of downtown Los Angeles since 1881, campaigned to make downtown more car friendly. In 1920, a section of the newspaper was devoted exclusively to automobile news; it became a platform for promoting wider streets, more parking garages, and an end to public subsidies for streetcars, which the *Times* slandered as a socialist plot.[8]

Yet, even as downtown advocates pushed to make the city's historic core more car friendly, the mass adoption of the automobile was dictating a new urban geography that undermined the centrality of downtown. Land developers such as A. W. Ross led this effort, betting that the automobile would entice a motorized generation of shoppers to relinquish their ties to the downtown core. Ross convinced a few established retailers and businesses to relocate along the fresh pavement of Wilshire Boulevard, some five miles west of downtown, establishing the Miracle Mile. The miracle was not so much that shoppers would abandon downtown but that this scheme secured a line into wealthier suburban communities such as Beverly Hills, Hancock Park, and West Adams, thus opening the city's Westside for affluent settlements. Lavish new department stores such as Bullock's Wilshire anchored the Miracle Mile, modeling a new architecture for a dawning age of consumer affluence and automobility.[9]

The Miracle Mile spurred the development of the linear city, a distinctly twentieth-century urban form that took shape around a popular preference for the automobile and the spatial autonomy it afforded. The opening of the Arroyo Seco (110) Parkway in 1939 furthered this development. Although the urban parkway was not invented in Los Angeles, the opening of the Arroyo Seco Parkway between downtown and Pasadena modeled the early possibilities for high-speed, unfettered car travel within the city itself. The Spanish name given to the parkway upheld the region's "Spanish fantasy past," a marketable theme used for the development of Southern California at the turn of the century that drew upon the region's Spanish and Mexican history, as did the regional motifs of white stucco, palm trees, and red tile.[10] This mythology also supplied the Pasadena boosters and businessmen who lobbied for the construction of the Arroyo Seco with a familiar regional aesthetic by which to promote the parkway as part of Southern California's unique cultural mise-en-scène. As a "parkway," the Arroyo Seco was more than a route; it was also a place to appreciate sublime nature from the seat of a car moving through the city at forty-five miles per hour. A masterful orchestration of trees, shrubs, grass, arched bridges, and winding pavement, the parkway was the architectural linchpin between the garden suburbs and cemeteries of the nineteenth century and the modern highway of the interstate era.[11]

By the outset of the post–World War II period, however, the Arroyo Seco Parkway seemed quaint in comparison to a bold new highway infrastructure taking shape. While the early outlines had been on the drawing boards of city planning offices since the mid-1920s, the outlay to build this infrastructure came from Sacramento and Washington, D.C. In 1947, for example, the California legislature passed the Collier-Burns

Highway Act, which aimed to amass new revenues for extensive highway construction in California by establishing a special highway tax fund from an increase in the state gas tax and various other highway-related taxes. The act especially favored the construction of metropolitan freeways, and Los Angeles profited handsomely from this measure, garnering a larger share of revenues for highway construction than other regions of the state.[12]

The Collier-Burns Highway Act prompted a massive surge in freeway construction in Los Angeles and, undergirded by the heft of the Federal-Aid Highway Act of 1956, inaugurated a flurry of highway construction that lasted throughout the early 1970s—what we might call Los Angeles's age of the freeway. The basic geometry of the L.A. freeway system comprises Interstates 5, 10, 405, 605, and 710; the older highways, State Route 60 and US Route 101; and other recent additions. But this is only a fraction of the highway system envisioned in the "California Freeway and Expressway System," a master plan created by the California Division of Highways in 1959.[13] It outlines a vast grid of freeways that leaves no developed area of the greater urbanized region more than four miles from a freeway on-ramp. Though this plan fell about two-thirds short of its proposed ambition, today's freeway system in Los Angeles, like the basic infrastructure of the American West in general, largely reflects the reach of a federal government determined in the 1950s to secure its authority over a continent believed to be vulnerable to internal subversion and external attack. L.A. drivers, like drivers in most cities, thus owe the Cold War for bringing modern freeways into existence, though the current freeway system in Los Angeles is really a piecemeal hodgepodge of state routes and federal freeways built at different times, with different technologies, according to different criteria, and for different populations settling in disparate pockets of an ever-expanding urban region (fig. 2).

The idea of a unified freeway system in Los Angeles is thus something of a myth. That myth took shape around the construction of massive highway interchanges, which introduced a fluid architecture of movement and monumentality built on the scale of cathedrals and skyscrapers—but for cars, not for people. The Four-Level Interchange at the confluence of the Hollywood (101) and Harbor (110) Freeways (known in the vernacular as "The Stack") had its fifteen minutes of fame in the mid-1950s, when it was celebrated as an icon of progress and modernity (fig. 3). Built with funding from Collier-Burns, the Stack debuted on postcards, symbolizing how the city's new freeway system had become a familiar way of knowing the city in the popular imagination.[14]

During the early 1950s, on the eve of the interstate highway program, California's Division of Highways was working to implement the federal mandate to build more freeways in Los Angeles. That undertaking, which marked the largest public works program in the history of the city, lacked a master road builder like Baron Georges-Eugène Haussmann of nineteenth-century Paris or Robert Moses of twentieth-century New York. There simply was no überplanner to venerate as a champion of progress or despise as a villain of destruction. Instead, a byzantine hierarchy of "highly trained professional planners, engineers, traffic and right of way experts…whose only objective [was] the greatest public benefit" worked in a piecemeal fashion to coordinate the monumental task of building a regional network of freeways.[15]

The construction of a freeway system in the Los Angeles area impacted countless communities and destroyed tens of thousands of homes. The Division of Highways justified its work by invoking a familiar

FIGURE 2.
**California Freeway and Expressway System map,
California Division of Highways, September 1965.**
Sacramento, California Department of Transportation,
Library and History Center.

FIGURE 3.
**The Four-Level Interchange ("The Stack"),
Los Angeles, 1954.**
Photo by Ralph Morris.
Los Angeles, Los Angeles Public Library.

mantra of progress. After clearing some fifteen hundred homes south of Exposition Boulevard for the Harbor Freeway, for example, the Division of Highways paused to salute "the older folks [who] have resigned themselves to the fact that they should not stand in the way of progress and gladly cooperate. This is the rule rather than the exception."[16]

Yet, the Division of Highways failed to notice contemporary eruptions of protest in another part of the city. We might call East Los Angeles an unruly stepchild of Los Angeles. Situated on an unincorporated island of county land, East Los Angeles's diverse neighborhoods maintain a vibrant tradition of multiracial, working-class activism. The Chicano civil rights movement, the Communist Party, the Community Service Organization (CSO), and the Industrial Workers of the World (the Wobblies) all gained traction upon the political terrain of East Los Angeles, with the active participation of diverse ethnic groups. Like the neighborhoods of South Central Los Angeles, the communities of East Los Angeles, for much of the past century, belonged to an older mode of urbanism in which people moved on foot or by streetcar. The age of the freeway diminished this way of life, but not without a fight.

What provoked early protests against highway construction in East Los Angeles during the late 1950s and early 1960s was the fact that highway-building authorities—federal, state, and local—coordinated highway construction with slum clearance. The historian Raymond Mohl has documented the extent to which the sponsors of the interstate highway program targeted "slums" and "blighted areas" as ideal locales for building urban freeways.[17] In Los Angeles, this had dire consequences for the neighborhoods of East Los Angeles, which were hemmed in by a maze of new freeways that materialized during the late 1950s and throughout the following decade. The area had long been considered "blighted" in the local discourse of city planning. Since the 1930s, the neighborhoods of Belvedere, Boyle Heights, El Monte, Lincoln Heights, and Maravilla had been redlined by federal agencies such as the Home Owners' Loan Corporation and the Federal Housing Administration not only for the presence of blacks in the area—who were singled out on city survey files as detrimental to sound property values—but also for the "hopelessly heterogeneous" and working-class character of these communities.[18] The older housing stock of the area didn't help matters, either. The combination of these social and environmental factors exempted much of the area from public and private investment during the postwar period, fueling a pattern of disinvestment and decline. With Republicans such as Mayor Norris Poulson successfully red-baiting public housing programs in the mid-1950s, rendering them null and void, highway construction could knock out older, working-class neighborhoods without provisions for new housing. In this tangled web of policy and ideology, the modern barrio was born.[19]

But not without struggle. The citizens of Boyle Heights and surrounding communities registered their protest against the invasion of interstate freeways as early as the mid-1950s. They did so by packing public hearings before the Division of Highways, by editorializing in community newspapers such as the *Eastside Sun* and the *Belvedere Citizen,* and by picketing the work of bulldozers and earthmovers. This was a multiracial, multiethnic fight, but the freeways' encroachment upon East Los Angeles spurred the demographic transformation of the area. In the midst of rampant destruction, Jews and other white ethnics, African Americans, and Asian Americans vacated their former neighborhoods, leaving these spaces to a new influx of Mexican immigrants and Mexican Americans. By 1960, the population of East Los Angeles

had reached one million people, making it the nation's largest barrio.[20] Between the channelization of the
Los Angeles River in the 1930s and the construction of six freeways and their interchanges in the 1960s,
East Los Angeles had become a Chicano city within a city—an asphalt-and-concrete labyrinth marked with
murals, graffiti, chain-link fence, and cactus.

Not all communities endured such upheaval in the age of the freeway. Compare the fate of East Los
Angeles with that of Beverly Hills. Today, the stretch of Santa Monica Boulevard in Beverly Hills, though often
a parking lot, is nonetheless a splendid showcase of civic architecture, monumental sculpture, and lush green-
ery. In the 1950s, this boulevard was slated to become a freeway, State Route 2, which, on the drawing boards
of California's Division of Highways, ran southwest from the foothill communities of La Crescenta-Montrose
and La Cañada Flintridge all the way to the Santa Monica Pier. Accessing substantial resources and connections, the citizens of Beverly Hills muscled their way into the proposed path of this freeway, forcing its terminus some seven miles to the east, in the emerging barrio of Echo Park.[21]

Thus, East Los Angeles got seven freeways and Beverly Hills got none. This is a stark but useful
comparison in illustrating the discrepancies in the impact of highway construction upon the diverse communities of the city, even among those that staged protests against highway construction. The socioeconomic gulf
between Boyle Heights and Beverly Hills has widened considerably since the age of the freeway. This discrep-
ancy is more apparent in the landscape of the city than in the literature about that landscape, but it provides
key lessons in the history of how Los Angeles became the freeway metropolis par excellence.

———

So here we have a historical outline of the freeway and its place in the built environment of Los Angeles.
There are the facts of this history, too many to include in this brief overview, but what do these facts mean?
And where do we find those meanings? If Los Angeles's built environment registers a regional history of
socioeconomic disparity, so does its cultural landscape, which sustains diverse and competing interpretations
of the L.A. freeway and its place in the city's history. At the outset of the interstate era (a "gee-whiz" age
in which Americans marveled at the prospects of passenger jet travel and space exploration), L.A. freeways
entered the circuits of American popular culture as a wondrous feat of engineering and as a sturdy icon
of modernity, progress, and glamour, just as Parisian boulevards and the Brooklyn Bridge did in their day.
In the print culture of 1950s America—whether in government journals such as the Division of Highways
chronicle *California Highways and Public Works* or in glossy magazines such as *Time, Look,* and *National
Geographic*—images of L.A. freeways earned prominent visibility as the landmarks of a new civilization on the
cutting edge of transportation technology.

The L.A. freeway also inspired new modes of popular amusement and fun. Disneyland, for example—
that mid-1950s spectacle of corporate capital organized in the service of patriotism, family values, crowd
control, and mass entertainment—included a space in which to enshrine Southern California's new freeways.
In the Tomorrowland section of the theme park, which was dedicated to an imagined future of technological
and scientific progress, the Autopia ride simulated Los Angeles's new freeway system in miniature, replete
with gasoline-powered cars and multilevel interchanges. The Autopia ride not only cast the L.A. freeway as a
symbol of technological progress but also inculcated a younger generation with a fetish for commodities like

the automobile and planted the seeds of a mass addiction to fossil fuels. Moreover, the prescient designers of Disneyland situated their theme park alongside the planned route of Interstate 5, mapping a blueprint for a new and expansive phase of suburban sprawl.[22]

Disneyland taught Americans to love their freeways, and even by the late 1960s, as the freeway revolt erupted in cities throughout the nation, the L.A. freeway inspired glowing assessments of new urban possibilities. Reyner Banham, for one, delivered his paean to the L.A. freeway in *Los Angeles: The Architecture of Four Ecologies* in 1971, daring to compare the relationship between Los Angeles and its freeways to New York and its skyscrapers or Paris and its boulevards. For Banham, it was all about context: freeways make sense in a decentralized urban region whose horizontal growth reflected the mass adoption of the automobile. This sense, however widely shared among Angelenos, ran counter to establishment notions of the polis and all things urban. Piazzas, sidewalks, subways, and skyscrapers were the hallmarks of a great city, not billboards, gas stations, car washes, and freeways. Banham upended this old-world notion of what defined true urbanity, arguing for Los Angeles's inclusion within the canon of great cities by virtue of its democratic brand of urbanism, which rejected orthodox urban hierarchies in favor of a sprawling vernacular landscape that upheld the values of an affluent consumer society: convenience, mobility, and choice. Ever the iconoclast, Banham insisted upon the literal meaning of the L.A. freeway as a concrete expression of technology's liberating potential and the fitting centerpiece of twentieth-century urbanism.[23]

After World War II, but prior to the publication of *Los Angeles: The Architecture of Four Ecologies, sprawl* entered the discourse of urbanism, signaling anxiety about the fate of the American city, not unlike its lexical predecessor, *blight.* The rise of environmentalism in the late 1960s and early 1970s stoked antipathy toward freeways in the city, and Los Angeles earned further disdain from a new generation of ecoactivists. A slew of polemical tracts—Peter Blake's *God's Own Junkyard* (1964), Raymond Dasmand's *The Destruction of California* (1965), Richard Lillard's *Eden in Jeopardy* (1966), and William Bronson's *How to Kill a Golden State* (1968)—savaged Los Angeles as an environmental disaster. Though these writers targeted the automobile and its depletion of California's natural resources, they also diagnosed freeways, gas stations, parking lots, billboards, and car washes as the cancerous cells of visual blight, corporate hegemony, and environmental catastrophe.

Other social movements of the time asserted new perspectives on the L.A. freeway and its place in the city's culture. No one has labeled Joan Didion a feminist, but her writing about Los Angeles nonetheless suggests how freeways and the automobile afforded women a respite from the stultifying confines of suburban domesticity. In the oft-cited passage from Didion's 1970 novel, *Play It as It Lays,* the heroine, Maria Wyeth, exerts mastery over time and space by speeding down the L.A. freeway, as if she were the very muse that inspired Jim Morrison and The Doors to write their 1971 hit "L.A. Woman." This literary portrait of a woman behind the wheel begs comparison to a 1970 portrait of Didion herself, smoking a cigarette alongside her Corvette Stingray, daring the viewer to question her mastery of the automobile machine (fig. 4).

Didion's portrait of the L.A. freeway illustrates how the freeway metropolis signaled a new degree of autonomy to women, at least those who drove a car. But contrast Didion's Maria Wyeth racing down the freeway with the portrait of suburban isolation in Alison Lurie's 1965 novel *The Nowhere City.* Here, the freeway

FIGURE 4.
Joan Didion with her Corvette Stingray, Hollywood, 1970.
Photo by Julian Wasser.
Santa Monica, Craig Krull Gallery.

separates husband and wife. The protagonist, Paul Cattleman, takes his wife, Katherine, from their comfortable academic life in Cambridge, Massachusetts, to work for a research and development firm in West Los Angeles. Paul and Katherine rent a stucco bungalow in Mar Vista that, unbeknownst to them, happens to lie in the ensuing path of the 405 Freeway, which is gouging its way across the Westside. Paul takes a liking to Los Angeles, but his wife feels repulsion toward the city—literally, as she suffers severe allergies to her new environment. Leaving his wife at home, Paul speeds along Los Angeles's new freeways to pursue an extramarital affair, while his unknowing wife cowers behind venetian blinds, counting the growing number of vacancies on her block. For Paul, the freeway is a conduit for illicit pleasure; for Katherine, it brings destruction to her environment and her marriage.

Lurie, her publishers, and her readers might agree that freeways are for men, not women. Didion might dispute this premise, but it's the verdict of other Los Angeles artists who convey the gendered discrepancies built into Los Angeles's freeway metropolis. For example, Venice-based muralist Judith F. Baca, a longtime feminist and Chicana activist, has engaged the L.A. freeway in bold ways, stressing its complicit role in the oppression of women and families. Her best-known work is *The Great Wall of Los Angeles,* a mural about the city's history painted on a half-mile stretch of the concrete channel that was once the Los Angeles

River. A scene from the mural titled "Division of the Barrios" depicts a Chicano family divided into two halves—mother and son on one side, father and daughter on the other, the freeway writhing between them. Baca's image plays on the word itself, taking the *free* out of *freeway.* The mural conveys the freeway as an oppressive force, dividing and constricting instead of unifying and mobilizing. The *muralista* personifies the freeway as a serpent preying upon Chicano families and bringing the old barrios to ruin. Baca painted this image in the late 1970s, shortly before her commission by the city's Olympic Arts Council to paint a downtown section of the Harbor (110) Freeway in preparation for the 1984 Olympics.

Baca again engaged the concrete surfaces of the city's infrastructure to heighten the visibility of marginal social groups and their struggle for equality. In this instance, she went to the freeway itself, to the eastern wall of the Fourth Street off-ramp of the Harbor Freeway, the spine of the city's sprawling freeway system that marks the western edge of the downtown core. There, Baca painted *Hitting the Wall: Women in the Marathon,* a tribute to the elite female athletes who entered the marathon after the International Olympic Committee's 1981 decision to open the marathon to women runners (fig. 5). Baca painted the image of a female athlete "hitting the wall," reaching that point of extreme exhaustion, while breaking the tape of the finish line: the runner lunges toward the viewer, her arms stretched out in triumph as sunlight floods from behind. Baca's treatment of the freeway's surface wall enhances the visual impact of the mural. From both sides of the mural, the viewer sees not the smooth concrete surface of the modern freeway but rather the image of crude stone blocks forming an ancient wall that bears a vague likeness to Mesoamerican architecture. As the runner crosses the finish line, she breaks through a wall, which crumbles at her feet.

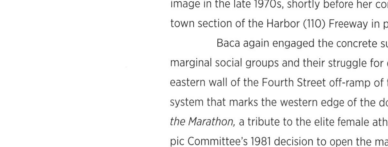

FIGURE 5.
Judith F. Baca (Mexican American, b. 1946).
Hitting the Wall: Women in the Marathon, 1984.
Acrylic on cast concrete, 6.09 × 30.48 m (20 × 100 ft.).
Los Angeles, Fourth Street off-ramp of
the Harbor (110) Freeway.
Sponsored by the Olympic Organizing Committee
for the 1984 Olympics.

Hitting the Wall disputes the sturdiness of the freeway but gives force to an ideal of feminine strength. Using paint, skill, and imagination to transform a modern freeway overpass into rubble, Baca renders the freeway as the precarious product of a man-made society. In this respect, Baca's mural reflects a public effort to feminize the freeway—to transform its rigid geometry into a blunt expression of feminine victory.

As a mural painted on the walls of a freeway off-ramp, *Hitting the Wall* illustrates what people do to the L.A. freeway, often to counter what freeways do to people, especially their homes and neighborhoods. If freeways remove drivers from the social fabric of the city, if they promote ignorance of the city's diversity—as critics such as Thomas Pynchon and Carey McWilliams have charged—then Baca forces an awareness of that diversity by using the public surfaces of freeway architecture to represent invisible or marginal social groups.[24] This strategy thrives within the sprawling and unruly body of indigenous cultural work in Los Angeles that is recognized as "Chicano art," much of which assigns a particular prominence to the L.A. freeway. Not surprisingly, given the history outlined above, the representation of the freeway in Chicana/o arts and letters tends toward critique, toward a repudiation of what happened to East Los Angeles in the age of the interstate and how its neighborhoods were disemboweled and dismembered. Today, the residents of the nation's largest Spanish-speaking barrio live beneath, above, or alongside six freeways and two massive interchanges built less than one mile apart. These structures poison their surroundings, literally, as recent studies confirm that people living in the immediate vicinity of freeways run higher risks of lung disease and respiratory illness.[25]

FIGURE 6.
Lalo Alcaraz (American, b. 1964).
Traditional Superhighway and Information Superhighway,
1994, cartoon.
First published in *L.A. Weekly.*

The "freeway revolt," as it is known to urban historians, tells a triumphant story of white middle-class city people, the ones who refused the lure of the suburbs, rising up against official plans to ram freeways through the gentrifying neighborhoods of New Orleans, New York, San Francisco, and other US cities. With access to resources, connections, and national media outlets, they implemented organized and visible forms of political protest at community and civic levels.[26] What are missing from this account, however, are the disorganized and obscured signs of revolt that persist in the landscapes of cities such as Los Angeles, especially in areas racked by poverty, homelessness, unemployment, and police brutality. These homemade expressions of dissent are invisible from the ivory tower—indeed, also from the standpoint of many policy experts—yet clear to people on the street as vernacular signs of protest. To take one cultural practice that continues to elicit a visceral fury among Los Angeles's propertied classes, graffiti on freeway signage is a ubiquitous example of a strategy to resist not only the clichéd anonymity of city life but also the invisibility of ghettos and barrios in the civic imaginary—to make the presence of the Other known by challenging the visual authority of the state and the green-and-white signs it planted on its freeways.[27]

Among other things, graffiti belongs to the broader oeuvre of Chicana/o art, and it is in this context that expressions of protest further unsettle the meaning of the L.A. freeway and its place in the city. Chicana/o artists and writers issue their own interpretation of the L.A. freeway, using wit, irony, satire, sarcasm, and other "weapons of the weak" to posit alternative understandings of the freeway and its utility.[28] In the cartoons of Lalo Alcaraz; the literature and poetry of Helena Maria Viramontes; the murals of Judith Baca; the canvas paintings of Carlos Almaraz, David Botello, and Frank Romero; and other creative works by Chicana/o artists and writers, radicalized expressions of the freeway revolt force tough questions about infrastructure and inequality and about who benefits from the planners' invocation of "public good" and who does not (fig. 6).[29]

———

This brief survey of the historical and cultural significance of the L.A. freeway rightly ends in East Los Angeles, the point of intersection of the region's major freeway arteries and where the skeins of race, poverty, and infrastructure converge. Among the diverse communities that surrendered to the imposition of the freeway, East Los Angeles bore the brunt of the postwar push to build a regional highway infrastructure; but here the revolt continues, fostering a regenerative culture of opposition that changes popular understandings of the freeway and its place in the identity of the city. A walk along the streets of East Los Angeles disqualifies Reyner Banham's Panglossian verdict that the L.A. freeway is "a coherent state of mind, a complete way of life…the fourth ecology of the Angeleno," for the concrete maze of highway overpasses and underpasses that bind East Los Angeles produces a fractured ecology that induces disorientation and isolation and disables a local sense of coherence and cohesion.

If the structure of the L.A. freeway creates dissonance and disorientation in East Los Angeles, then Chicana/o culture brings order and cohesion. This enclave of the city's contemporary cultural scene also breaches the limits of more critical analyses of the freeways. If these imposing structures fortify the boundaries of class exclusion in Los Angeles, as some trenchant critics have charged, the assertions of working-class and racial identities through both inventive and traditional forms of cultural expression—and the freeway is implicated in those efforts—subvert the hegemony of "Fortress L.A."[30] They expose cracks in the concrete, fissures that unleash dissident perspectives and alternative points of view. Satirizing the L.A. freeways in literature, poetry, and cartoons; tagging the freeways' walls and signs; painting pictures of pink freeways, freeway crashes, and freeway shootings; painting murals of freeway destruction and divided communities: these expressions of spatial struggle in contemporary Los Angeles are the residue of conflict born some sixty years ago. But this creative work is more than the rote expression of class struggle; it is also the vital means by which creative people strive to right the wrongs of malicious or misguided policy decisions, or by which they simply make themselves at home in L.A.'s expressway world.

NOTES

1 David Brodsly, *L.A. Freeway: An Appreciative Essay* (Berkeley: University of California Press, 1981); Scott L. Bottles, *Los Angeles and the Automobile* (Berkeley: University of California Press, 1987); Martin Wachs, "The Evolution of Transportation Policy in Los Angeles: Images of Past Policies and Future Prospects," in Edward W. Soja and Allen John Scott, eds., *The City: Los Angeles and Urban Theory at the End of the Twentieth Century* (Berkeley: University of California Press, 1996); and Eric Avila, *Popular Culture in the Age of White Flight* (Berkeley: University of California Press, 2004), n.p.

2 Edward W. Soja and Allen J. Scott, "Introduction to Los Angeles: City and Region," in Edward W. Soja and Allen J. Scott, eds., *The City: Los Angeles and Urban Theory at the End of the Twentieth Century* (Berkeley: University of California Press, 1996), 4–7.

3 Brodsly, *L.A. Freeway,* 68–71.

4 Carey McWilliams, *Southern California: An Island on the Land* (Salt Lake City: Peregrine Smith, 1994), 135.

5 McWilliams, *Southern California,* 236.

6 Dana Bartlett, *The Better City: A Sociological Study of a Modern City* (Los Angeles: Neuner, 1907).

7 Avila, *Popular Culture,* 190.

8 Avila, *Popular Culture,* 192.

9 Richard Longstreth, *City Center to Regional Mall: Architecture, the Automobile, and Retailing in Los Angeles, 1920–1950* (Cambridge, Mass.: MIT Press, 1998), 112–41.

10 On the Spanish fantasy past as a regional aesthetic and racialized fantasy, see Phoebe Kropp, *California Vieja: Culture and Memory in a Modern American Place* (Berkeley: University of California Press, 2006).

11 Brodsly, *L.A. Freeway,* 101; Anastasia Loukaitou-Sideris and Robert Gottlieb, "A Road as a Route and Place: Evolution and Transformation of the Arroyo Seco Parkway," *California History* 83, no. 1 (2005): 28–40.

12 Brodsly, *L.A. Freeway,* 115.

13 "Report from District VII: Freeway System Taking Shape in Greater Los Angeles Area," *California Highways and Public Works* 41 (1962): 42–57.

14 Avila, *Popular Culture,* 195.

15 *California's Freeway Planning Team* (Sacramento: California State Printing Office, n.d.), Fletcher Bowron Papers, box 48, folder 1, Huntington Library, San Marino, Calif.

16 "Rapid Progress on the Harbor Freeway," *California Highways and Public Works* 33, nos. 5–6 (1954): 5–6.

17 Raymond Mohl, "Race and Space in the Modern City: Interstate 95 and the Black Community in Miami," in Arnold R. Hirsch and Raymond A. Mohl, eds., *Urban Policy in Twentieth-Century America* (New Brunswick, N.J.: Rutgers University Press, 1993), 100–158.

18 Home Owners' Loan Corporation, 1939, Los Angeles City Survey Files, Record Group 195, National Archives, Washington, D.C.

19 Avila, *Popular Culture,* 207–10.

20 Rudolfo Acuña, *Occupied America: A History of Chicanos,* 3rd ed. (New York: Harper & Row, 1988), 246. Avila, *Popular Culture,* 217.

21 Jason Schultz, "Freeway 90210: Opposition and Politics of the Pavement in Los Angeles" (BA thesis, University of California, Irvine, 2004).

22 Avila, *Popular Culture,* 203.

23 Reyner Banham, *Los Angeles: The Architecture of Four Ecologies* (London: Penguin, 1971).

24 Carey McWilliams, "Watts: The Forgotten Slum," *The Nation* 30 (1965): 89–90.

25 Ellin Kavanagh, "Study Links Close Proximity to Freeways with Autism," *Los Angeles Downtown News,* 14 January 2011, 4.

26 Richard O. Baumbach and William E. Borah, *The Second Battle of New Orleans: A History of the Vieux Carre Expressway Controversy* (Tuscaloosa: University of Alabama Press, 1980).

27 Eric Avila, "The Folklore of the Freeway: Space, Identity, and Culture in Postwar Los Angeles," *Aztlán: The Journal of Chicano Studies* 23, no. 1 (1998): 15–31.

28 This phrase is taken from the title of a 1987 study by the Yale University anthropologist James Scott about how subaltern groups exert forms of invisible and noncoordinated resistance that mitigate against marginalization and disempowerment. See James Scott, *Weapons of the Weak: Everyday Forms of Peasant Resistance* (New Haven, Conn.: Yale University Press, 1987). For a masterful adoption of this dynamic in a US context, see Robin D. G. Kelley, *Race Rebels: Culture, Politics, and the Black Working Class* (New York: Free Press, 1994).

29 Eric Avila, *The Folklore of the Freeway: Highway Construction and the Making of Race in the Modernist City* (Minneapolis: University of Minnesota Press, forthcoming).

30 Mike Davis, *City of Quartz: Excavating the Future in Los Angeles* (New York: Verso, 1991).

LOS ANGELES AFTER DARK
THE INCANDESCENT CITY

Sandy Isenstadt

Nighttime Los Angeles had become a wonderland of light.
— Kevin Starr[1]

THE GALACTIC METROPOLIS

AT NIGHT, AN INCANDESCENT CITY BLOSSOMS, one that is only provisionally connected with its layout by day. As searchlights stretch skyward, mere two-story theaters along Hollywood Boulevard tower in the darkness, broadcasting an otherwise-modest street frontage across the region. From a vantage point in the Santa Monica or San Gabriel Mountains, episodic premieres would be the biggest place, in visual terms, in the city. The everyday street grid would still be legible at night, but its commercial vectors would be thick, almost massive with light, some of them in flickering palettes of neon, while often overlooked places like the oil fields of Torrance would pulse with burning jets (fig. 1). Beholding just this scene while descending into Los Angeles in 1988, the philosopher Jean Baudrillard saw in the radiant urbanism another transformation, just then approaching: the city, shaped by an epic struggle between masses of artificial light and "the vio- lence" of the desert sun, "condenses by night the entire future geometry of the networks of human relations, gleaming in their abstraction, luminous in their extension, astral in their reproduction to infinity."[2] The "galactic metropolis," as Baudrillard called it, twinkled best from Mulholland Drive.

Around 1940, Los Angeles was uniquely prepared to dazzle, for two main reasons. First, it had a long history of electric boosterism, with local businesses, aided by the *Los Angeles Times,* clamoring for lights to advertise their civic ambitions. Almost immediately after the first light masts went up in downtown, in 1881, the newspaper declared Los Angeles the best-lit city west of the Rockies, suggesting it would soon be the "Chicago of California."[3] Given its small population relative to East Coast cities, Los Angeles could even be said to possess the greatest "Great White Way," a reference to the brightly lit strip in New York snaking up Broadway from Fourteenth Street.[4] With Los Angeles's polycentric structure, brilliant street lighting not

FIGURE 1.
Los Angeles lights at night, ca. 1938–56.
Photo by "Dick" Whittington Studio.
Los Angeles, University of Southern California.

FIGURE 2.
**Boulder Dam (now Hoover Dam),
between Arizona and Nevada, May 1940.**
Washington, D.C., Library of Congress,
Prints & Photographs Division.

only extended the hours for shopping but diverted customers from one location to another. Commercial districts thus competed with one another to have brighter and more decorative lights. Lighting grew only more intense in the holiday season as merchants pooled resources to put on spectacular displays— an "electrified Garden of Eden," according to one account—often explicitly aimed at charming Easterners otherwise disenchanted by the warm weather and lack of snow.[5] Soon, movie premieres blasted open the night sky with wildly waving searchlights that "whizzed up like rockets," while cinema forecourts in Hollywood were blanched by floodlights and stippled with flocks of photographers' flashes as luminaries alighted from their limousines.[6]

The second factor intensifying the nighttime transformation of Los Angeles was the construction of Boulder Dam (now Hoover Dam), which was completed in 1936 (fig. 2). It was the world's greatest single source of electricity at the time, and it was the direct result of the Southern California legation in Washington, D.C., which had been advocating its construction for more than a decade. Great turbines at the dam transmuted falling water into crackling electricity; the highest-voltage transmission lines ever built then carried the current nearly three hundred miles to Los Angeles, where local electrical customers repaid almost the entirety of construction costs. When the dam opened, the entire region celebrated—with light: "On every horizon…endless shafts of light broke the skyline like slender fingers sheathed in diamond rings," all canted toward "the mother beam," a gigantic arc light downtown that was said to generate a billion candlepower.[7] The basin-wide symphony of lights appeared from the air as "a pinwheel thirty miles in diameter, first scattering its fire outward by centrifugal force, then suddenly changing and hurling the full glory of its radiance toward its blazing core." By 1940, the dam provided more than ninety percent of the city's electrical power.[8]

SOMETHING OUT OF NOTHING

By 1939, a new light, neon, had so saturated certain urban districts throughout the United States that it deserved mention in period guidebooks as a distinctive feature and sign of progress (figs. 3, 4).[9] Los Angeles, in particular, had a special relationship to neon; the first neon sign in America was installed atop a downtown Packard dealership, and, soon after, a facility was founded to make and distribute neon signs nationally. Neon was expected to dominate nocturnal Los Angeles because its light was bright but not glaring, and it was able to cut through fog, which was ideal for automobile headlights. Consequently, companies such as

FIGURE 3.
Herman Schultheis (German-born American, d. 1955).
Photo collage of neon signs, ca. 1940s.
Los Angeles, Los Angeles Public Library.

FIGURE 4.
Sunset Strip at night, West Hollywood, 1965.
Los Angeles, Los Angeles Public Library,
Herald Examiner Collection.

Standard Oil and Richfield Oil planned neon piping for service stations to punctuate the night in chains running from Mexico to Canada.

Chief among neon's virtues was its palette of color. At first, neon light was orange-red, a result of the gas's natural glow when subjected to an electrical current. By 1940, however, the spectrum had broadened considerably with phosphors coating interior surfaces of the glass tube and with the use of other gases, such as argon and krypton. More than twenty colors were commercially available then. Darkness diminishes color, but neon brought it back at night in Los Angeles. In a setting where, as the writer James M. Cain put it, the relentless sun overhead "sucks the color out of everything that it touches," Los Angeles would be at its most colorful at night. Moreover, neon shared a stunning trait with electric light: its transformation of the night was instantaneous. In *Ask the Dust,* John Fante describes the effect of a visually arid streetscape suddenly animated by light: "Beyond my window spread the great city, the street lamps, the red and blue and green neon tubes bursting to life like bright night flowers."[10] During the 1940s and '50s, blinking signs appeared not only along numerous streets but also in novels and films, giving the city and its representations a flashing multihued complexion.

By that time, however, neon's allure had already begun to dim due to its association with cheap and usually suspect amusements. Winking signs generated an excitement all their own, anticipating thrills that often were not fulfilled. "A riot of neon and jazz" appeared conspicuously in Frank Capra's *It's a Wonderful Life* (1946), as George Bailey stumbled in disbelief along the lurid streets of Pottersville, the noir doppelgänger of the genuine Bedford Falls Bailey had helped build.[11] In fact, in many noir and gangster films of the time, the falsehood of neon light stands in for the corruption of the city at large. In this way, neon was unique among the lights of Los Angeles. Where noir films rendered the city as illegible and treacherous, the shining streetlamps or beaming searchlights of movie premieres presumed the contrary—a city of energy and promise. The film *A Star is Born* (1954), for instance, refutes its darker contemporaries with an opening scene that pans the city at night to land finally at a bright and buzzing premiere. But, as urban theorist Mike Davis has observed, noir itself was "like a transformational grammar turning each charming ingredient of the boosters' arcadia into a sinister equivalent."[12] Noir, in this sense, turned a light that would have brightened the night into being itself a kind of darkness.

Bans on neon were issued across a number of communities in the late 1940s and early 1950s. Palm Springs struck a compromise between merchants and residents that allowed neon signs, but only in tasteful pastels rather than primary or acid colors. Bel Air banned them altogether to avoid any hint of the "crass commercialism of a neon sign."[13] In downtown Los Angeles, Fifth Street, west of Central Avenue, was proclaimed "a gaudy, overbright neon nightmare…a jumbled hodgepodge, glittering with cut-rate sin."[14] Thrill seekers were warned away by police, who on occasion came upon patches of blood "gleaming dully in the neon reflection."[15] Much of Orson Welles's film *A Touch of Evil* (1958) is set against a backdrop of pulsing neon signs. By then, neon was so ubiquitous that, as writer Aldous Huxley observed, it ultimately had "no effect upon us, except perhaps to make us pine nostalgically for primeval night."[16] Stephen Monk, the protagonist in Christopher Isherwood's *The World in the Evening,* was less wistful: "God curse this antiseptic, heartless, hateful neon mirage of a city!…May all its lights go out forever."[17] Neon simply promised too much. Its unwavering midnight optimism turned out to be just another fixed-grin sales pitch for cheap merchandise in a society whose very fabric seemed increasingly woven of nylon and olefin, synthetics more or less coeval with neon. Worse, as noted in a 1954 article, neon signs were advertisements that had escaped the confines of their original media; they were the commercials in the movie of Los Angeles.[18]

More than anyone else, Raymond Chandler captured neon's distinct profile in Los Angeles, making it a cipher both for wakefulness and alienation. Often in Chandler's writing, a sign blinks on and off through a long night as a character sits in contemplation of some wrongdoing; vibrant red light scuttles in and out and in and out of a miserable hotel room; reflections on a lowering sky look like the light of brushfires smoldering in the hills. Chandler captured the ambiguity of neon, from its exotic beauty to its tawdry ubiquity, its simultaneous allure and taint, with characteristic sarcasm. In his *The Little Sister,* the primary protagonist, Philip Marlowe, considers Los Angeles old and stale: "But the colored lights fooled you. The lights were wonderful. There ought to be a monument to the man who invented neon lights. Fifteen stories high, solid marble. There's a boy who really made something out of nothing."[19] The greatest transformation of all—something out of nothing—was a routine affair in Los Angeles.

As Chandler suggests, the evident artifice of such a transformation was a crucial source of its aesthetic appeal. Certainly, the magic of neon and other sorts of electric lights was as much their split-second makeover of the visible world as it was the fantastic luminous forms they brought to life. But, while all were amused by neon, entranced, perhaps, no one was fooled. It was an open secret that without its network of dams and aqueducts, Los Angeles would quickly return to the desert. Perched above the city in the Hollywood Hills in 1948, Simone de Beauvoir appreciated the nighttime view for exactly this combination of enchantment and knowing pretense, which she reckoned a substantial and legitimate new reality. She discerned a kind of dignity attending a deception that is deliberately destined to deceive no one:

Los Angeles is beneath us, a huge, silent fairyland. The lights glitter as far as the eye can see. Beyond the red, green, and white clusters, big glowworms slither noiselessly. Now I am not taken in by the mirage: I know these are merely street lamps along the avenues, neon signs, and headlights. But mirage or no mirage, the lights keep glittering; they, too, are a truth. And perhaps they are even more moving when they express nothing but the naked presence of men. Men live here, and so the earth revolves in the quiet of the night with this shining wound in its side.[20]

FLOWERING OF THE NIGHT SKY

By midcentury, Los Angeles was drenched in light. A public ceremony was held in 1955 to dedicate the one hundred thousandth streetlight, with congratulatory self-regard at the sheer number of lamps needed to illuminate the sprawling city.[21] Architecture itself became as much the source of light as the dedicated streetlamps (fig. 5). With the spread of modern architecture, buildings increasingly comprised large panels of glass. Emphasizing efficiency and function, and expressly accommodating new technologies, modernism was already a norm for manufacturing and commercial architecture. Modernism's material palette leaned toward the shiny; light was reflected by aluminum framing, enameled metal panels, extensive planes of white plaster,

FIGURE 5.
Pereira & Luckman, Architects, Engineers and Planners (1950–58).
CBS Television City (completed 1952), Los Angeles, 1953.
Photo by J. Winston Pennock.
Los Angeles, CBS Television City Archives.

and, most notably, acres of polished plate glass. Moreover, modern design efforts such as John Entenza's Case Study House Program, launched in 1945, were informing the architecture of residences. A primary aspect across every Case Study House—and a lifestyle central to core myths about the city—was outdoor living, which in every single case entailed walls of glass to bring light and outdoor beauty deep into the home's interior. Rarely mentioned is the reversibility of this outward gaze. At night, light from inside shines out.[22] Some were pleased with the effect. One resident of the newly built Bunker Hill Towers, about eight hundred feet from the Civic Center, recalled the light that streamed in at night: "It was wonderful.... We didn't even have to turn our lights on."[23] Most, however, tried to fend off the light infiltrating their homes, especially from overbright businesses nearby. Consequently, designers began to propose various visual remedies, such as ceiling-to-floor curtains, patterned glass, or even hinged opaque panels as a means of controlling ambient light.[24]

As modern aesthetic preferences turned solid building enclosures into transparent and, at night, glowing planes, lighting also began to occupy a plane high above the city streets (fig. 6). Downtown towers had since the 1920s used their height as a platform for light. Beacons were mounted on City Hall as soon as it was completed, and the Atlantic Richfield building extended its prominence into the night with its name spelled out in neon light. Building height restrictions, which had limited tall buildings to thirteen stories, were lifted in 1957. (A variance was granted for City Hall.) Over the next decade or so, at least a dozen skyscrapers were built, scattered in as many as ten distinct districts throughout the city.[25] They "spired up from the darkening land like translucent plastic harmonicas."[26] A multitude were capped with lighted signs at their tops. Such signs, many of them neon, registered postwar urban growth in a polychromatic "flowering of the night

FIGURE 6.
View of skyscrapers in downtown Los Angeles at night, with the Harbor (110) Freeway in the foreground, 1978.
Photo by Rob Brown.
Los Angeles, Los Angeles Public Library,
Herald Examiner Collection.

sky." Moreover, by night, the towers transformed the city's perceptual arrangement, providing "landmarks by which to map out the city's pattern in the dark."[27] Aloft and bright, the building signs created a geography of attention, a new urban layout hovering hundreds of feet above the ground.

At the same time, however, such signs threatened to transform architecture into something other than itself, a mere scaffolding for commercial messages. Even as structuralism inspired a search for architecture's linguistic foundation, lighted words at the top of buildings were scorned. For instance, Albert C. Martin Jr., principal of A. C. Martin & Associates, implored the owners of the twin towers he built on the site of the old Atlantic Richfield building not to allow gigantic signs. The buildings are "strong enough as architecture to make roof-level identification signs both superfluous and demeaning," he said, going on to suggest that Bank of America, the lessor, was just insecure: "No one that important really needs labeling." But modern slab towers fairly invited the signs, a point Martin made in regard to the distinctive corrugated profile of Bank of America's 1969 tower in San Francisco, which had neither need nor suitable place for a sign.[28] For writer and architect Peter Blake, the practice was the result not of insecurity but rather a territorial and ultimately infantile impulse to label objects as a way to safeguard their possession.[29]

In some ways, though, rooftop signs on tall buildings were indeed characteristic of Los Angeles. They were a "local tradition" stretching back to the first years of the twentieth century. As one writer put it, "Los Angeles stands alone in its penchant for turning buildings into signboards"; the towers for Union Bank (1968) and Crocker-Citizens National Bank (1969) are perfect examples. The proliferation of such signs can be attributed to the city's vast compass, since companies were aiming "to flag the attention of a far-off driver with a rooftop sign."[30] In some discussions, sky-high signs were marks of shame, making the metropolis appear "provincial" rather than global. In others, they were propitious. They not only gave nocturnal distinction to otherwise banal bulky boxes but also gave the entire city a new meaning. From the great postwar public space, the freeway, Angelenos "could read such words as UNION…LINCOLN…EQUITABLE," which suggested, in turn, a set of shared values appropriate to a democracy: "on the darkest night look out over the plain and see those brave words burning—HEALTH…JUSTICE…LIGHT."[31] In this rendering, Los Angeles was imagined as a civic realm that cohered around virtues broadcast to its wheeled citizenry from the tower tops. Indeed, with the "Hollywood" advertisement arguably the best-known sign in the world, the entire city is sometimes pictured in global media as an elevated and illuminated sign. Los Angeles had long been associated with strongly iconic architecture, from the fantasy homes of Beverly Hills to figurative commercial buildings such as the Brown Derby, all acting as instantly legible signs of themselves. In this context, lighted rooftop signs of the 1960s and 1970s only continued the transformation of urban form into symbolic communication. In such a process, matter and mass are themselves effectively transformed into a class of language, which, at night, is only further disarticulated from its material context.

Art Seidenbaum, a well-known columnist and editor for the *Los Angeles Times,* described his own "electric evenings" after an office building was completed on Ventura Boulevard near his home. "We have a new glare in our old view," he wrote, which one visitor (likely on break from the University of California, Berkeley, he guessed) declared "a cube of hallucinogenic sugar."[32] Illuminated signs and architectural lighting had their place, but they were increasingly overdone, Seidenbaum argued. They were "a form of visual noise at night" and often disturbed the respite of night's "black calm." In the intervals between the city's several centers, new construction was often infill between existing and inhabited buildings. Newly installed lights, as much as noise or other noxious emissions, degraded the surroundings. Thus, one building's lights could blight the neighbors' properties in the same way that an "emblazoned building is aggression in the sky, an invasion of air rights." Seidenbaum recommended creating a new regulatory agency to function as a visual corollary to the Federal Communications Commission (FCC).

The single building universally admired in this period was the municipal Los Angeles Department of Water and Power (LADWP) Building, completed in 1964 (fig. 7). Designed by A. C. Martin with a distinct profile, it needed no sign. Nonetheless, it was very much intended to advertise the agency's "products."[33] With enclosing glass walls set back from slab edges to create a stack of floating planes and a floodlit mechanical equipment screen at the roof, the building at night is a "17-story cube of blazing light."[34] At its base, eight fountains push columns of water skyward. At night, these too are illuminated.[35] Sited at the intersection of four freeways, it is splendidly situated for being viewed. Indeed, architectural historians David Gebhard and Robert Winter suggest the building is "best seen at night from the Harbor Freeway to the north. The solidity

FIGURE 7.
A. C. Martin and Associates (1945–ca. 1970).
Los Angeles Department of Water and Power Building
(1964), as seen from the Harbor (110) Freeway, 1965.
Los Angeles, Los Angeles Public Library.

of the building melts," and the driver is left only with the thin, backlit lines of the floating floor slabs.[36] It was
one of Reyner Banham's favorite buildings in Los Angeles, and he too admired it most while driving by at
night.[37] Even from the air, the building is unique—"the first big visible beacon" in the continually sprawling
city. Its "constant glow…has become a kind of comfort and traveling companion" for pilots.[38] By day, the
road ahead channels the driver's gaze as the Harbor (110) Freeway spills onto the Santa Ana (101) Freeway,
just as the pilot relies by day on the geographic landmarks of mountain range and coastline. By night, all can
orient themselves to the "cube of blazing light."

RADIANT RENEWAL AND REVERSAL

Neon's eclipse lasted about two decades. It returned in a coincidence of renewals in the 1960s and '70s. Pop
art's gimlet gaze on popular media encompassed neon (fig. 8), as evidenced by a 1975 exhibition dedicated to
it at the Los Angeles Municipal Art Gallery.[39] Preservationists became concerned that the latest trend in signs,
backlit translucent boxes, would replace now-historic signs "just as puffy cellophane-wrapped white bread
has driven the genuine staff of life almost off the market."[40] Examples from the heyday of neon were singled
out, especially the sunburst and zigzag forms woven into art deco landmarks such as the Pantages Theater

FIGURE 8.
Bruce Nauman (American, b. 1941).
La Brea/Art Tips/Rat Spit/Tar Pits, 1972.
Neon tubing and glass tubing, approximately
61.9 × 58.4 × 5.1 cm (24⅜ × 23 × 2 in.).
London, Tate.

on Hollywood Boulevard or the Franconia Apartments at Sixth and Coronado Streets. Hardly a preservationist, Banham himself was uncommonly sensitive to the vernacular merits of Los Angeles, among which he counted its neon signs, its illuminated advertising, and even its honky-tonk strips among the best the city had to offer. During a salty drive down the Sunset Strip in 1972, accompanied by Jim Morrison singing "L.A. Woman," Banham said the signs were integral to Los Angeles: "They're like an outdoor art gallery…billboards by day and by night are some of the greatest sights the city can show."[41]

Architects, too, reconsidered historic and popularly legible forms. Robert Venturi and Denise Scott Brown found a neon Mecca in Las Vegas that by the 1960s had usurped the neon crown from Los Angeles, and Charles Moore made neon a prominent feature of his Piazza d'Italia, in New Orleans, about two years after his arrival in Los Angeles. As the old studio system was restructured, even the film industry looked back to the neon heyday of the 1930s and '40s. Four of Raymond Chandler's best-known and neon-rich novels were filmed for the first time during this period, more than during his own lifetime. Neon, in short, had itself been transformed from a seedy sign to the festal "frosting of our modernity," as one writer put it.[42] Through the perspective of time, Hollywood Boulevard acquired a postmodern patina, recalling "jeweled 10th century reliquaries, grungy, weird carnival motleys with…rich rusticity and sparkling inertia." Not least, neon promised to be the low-wattage answer to a sudden dilemma brought on by the geopolitical energy crisis that took hold in 1973. Lights were dimmed citywide, even at the LADWP, which bought its energy wholesale. The crisis sparked self-reflection in a city where "lavish use of electric light seemed to be an unwritten public policy."[43]

As postmodernism went from provocateur enclave to mainstream practice, neon became part of the packaging. "You're certainly seeing a lot more of it than you did 10 to 15 years ago," said architect and theorist Steven Izenour in 1984.[44] Melrose Avenue, between Fairfax and La Brea Avenues, became a hotbed of stylishly edgy neon. Otherwise modest boutiques were seen "displaying a sizzling line of pink, red or blue light like a badge of membership in an exclusive club."[45]

Aspiring glass benders could sign up at more than a dozen schools established in the early 1980s, when the city's Museum of Neon Art was founded. As Ronald Reagan swept the nation with his appeal to renew Americans' faith in their country, neon recalled a time of unalloyed confidence, a moment when a global tide of fascism was pushed back by American military power, a good portion of it issuing from Los Angeles aircraft plants. At a moment beset by anxieties of American decline, neon signaled "a continuous festive twinkly blinking glowing whoopee" that numbed critical faculties and sparked aesthetic surrender.[46] In any case, it was an authentic urban vernacular, as much a part of the American cultural landscape as candlelight and cathedrals were to the Middle Ages. Neon fit the postmodern mood precisely for its plasticity, its knowing artifice of transformation, and its acidly satisfying "chemi-color glow."

A PSYCHOTIC GÖTTERDÄMMERUNG

The visual delight of such deliberate transformations—from the "slender fingers" of searchlights to modernist cubes of light to the "bright night flowers" of neon—was turned upside down, literally, when Los Angeles Police Department (LAPD) helicopters carried powerful lamps aloft to shine down upon an earthbound citizenry (fig. 9). The model of vision presumed by searchlights—upturned faces scattered across a wide area yet focused on and following several swinging slices of light—is reversed when they are mounted on police helicopters. Rather than advertising a singular event citywide with swoopy columns of light, skyborne searchlights carve a tunnel of visibility through the darkness to disclose those hidden, intentionally or not, under cover of night. The development was unsettling for many because it made plain that the viewer can easily become the thing viewed. Correspondingly, the blithe amusement accompanying an oblique view of a searchlight is readily transformed into considerable anxiety when finding oneself pointed at by "a finger of blinding, tell-tale light" emanating from above.[47]

First used decades earlier for military purposes, searchlights were best known in Los Angeles for their leading role at movie premieres in the 1920s and '30s. They flared up from the blanched forecourts of cinemas to project the cult of celebrity citywide, trumpeting that film stars, by the gravity of their fame, would draw into their orbit all of the evening's glamour and energy. They were, as writer Aldous Huxley noted decades earlier, an expression of the sheer joy of mobility in this, the most mobile and most joyous city in the nation.[48] LAPD helicopters began carrying searchlights in the 1960s, following the lead of several other cities. Operated by "sky cops," these "sun spots" were used at first to find missing persons or to direct rescue efforts in remote locations. Soon, they were used to track suspected criminals and locate illegal immigrants. They

FIGURE 9.
Illegal immigrants, 1983.
Photo by James Ruebsamen.
Los Angeles, Los Angeles Public Library,
Herald Examiner Collection.

were "powerful enough to turn night into day from 1,000 feet" in the air and could widen from a fifty-foot circle of light to an area the size of a city block.[49] An experiment at first, the LAPD's Air Support Division has grown into the world's largest airborne municipal law enforcement operation.

Controlling such power could be intoxicating. For example, one congressman riding along on an evening patrol had "a child's excitement operating the searchlight until the prey—docile, confused, formless" turned out to be ordinary citizens frightened and confused by the light.[50] Operated from the ground, search-lights traced patterns on an empty canvas of black. From the air, however, they raked the earth for trespasses otherwise invisible in the dark. The joy of unhindered mobility with a searchlight stands in the starkest contrast to the paralyzing effect intense light can have for anyone caught in its grip.

Just as the helicopter contravenes the city's familiar layout, so does the sun spot violate the night's economy of visibility. As the city's luminous landscape takes shape at twilight to displace the desert sun sinking into the Pacific, the sun spot rises as a kind of artificial and dedicated sun. In this sense, it confounds the city's mythology of transformations or, perhaps, deepens it. Along with the elemental desert at its edges, the Southern California sun is a major representational coordinate for the city. Described variously as intensely bright, invasive, sapping color and strength, indifferent, empty, relentless, fractured by haze, and shadowless and senseless, the sun is always "shining idiotically," in Jay McInerney's formulation in *Brightness Falls*.[51] When, finally, the sun relents at day's end, electric lighting soars in a self-radiant polymorphic urbanism native to the night, a palimpsest of garlands and beams, flashes and floods, and strokes and words of light. Numerous writers have suggested this exact transformation. Nathanael West, for example, described the "violet piping, like a Neon tube," of a Los Angeles sunset.[52] Chandler, too, succinctly captured the conversion of agricultural land, already evolved from desert, into metropolitan sprawl: "A yellow window hung here and there, all by itself, like the last orange."[53] Jack Smith, a columnist for the *Los Angeles Times,* said that at dusk and dawn the city was sublime—"both glorious and appalling, the way hell must be glorious and appalling"—as two antipodal kingdoms of light melted one into the other for a few troubling minutes. A visitor from another time would "surely believe he was witnessing the final passion of this troubled sphere," with all of humankind "annihilating itself in this magnificent, psychotic Gotterdammerung."[54]

———

The panoply of transformations underpinning Los Angeles is captured in perhaps the single most famous photograph of American architecture: Julius Shulman's portrait of the Stahl Residence (Case Study House #22), a Pierre Koenig design dating from 1959 to 1960 (fig. 10, pls. 46, 47). The photograph was taken at night. The house enjoys one of the city's most favored views, looking south from the Santa Monica Mountains. The daytime doings of city residents racing within the gridiron of streets and urban infrastructure is transformed by the night into a net of sparkling gems, appearing here as a lattice of light as dazzling and as immaterial as a sparkle. In the photograph, the southwest corner of the house's cantilevered living room projects prowlike over the grid below. Indeed, the house points to the grid, which occupies about half of the frame. Although the eye is drawn first to the staccato contrasts of light and shadow that make up the house, the grid grounds it, literally, lending it both context and meaning. All glimmer and reflection, the house, "hovering almost weightless above the bright lights of Los Angeles," as Norman Foster described it, is in some sense the

FIGURE 10.
Pierre Koenig (American, 1925–2004).
Case Study House #22, Stahl Residence (1960),
Los Angeles, 1960.
Photo by Julius Shulman.
Los Angeles, Getty Research Institute.

three-dimensional fruit of the electrified trellis supporting it and thus can represent an enduring trope of Los Angeles after dark: the transformation of utilitarian infrastructure into habitable, luminous form.[55]

The photograph registers the sun in the form of a hanging globe; it is the only visible source of light in the house and hence an analog of the point sources that align to form the grid below. But the globe appears not as a solitary, transcendent, eye-scorching orb. Rather, it is diminished, almost comic—a balloon of light playfully doubled, tripled, even quadrupled by reflections on glass. Its presumed light (actually the photographer's lights, out of frame) transforms yet again to underscore roof ribs, to coat glass walls in a merry sheen, to melt in the folds of women's dresses, even to make the concrete floor appear to float, forgetful of its debt to gravity. Shulman transforms modern minimalism—rational, even austere in its use of concrete, steel, and glass—into glimmer, glint, and glow. In this sense, Shulman pictured a third-order transformation: just as a sunbaked desert was transformed into a city, so has the city, limned by a well-lit web, been transmuted into a hillside soiree. Here, the airborne optimism of prosperous, postwar America buoys above the latticed infrastructure that serves it.

By day, sunlight presses on Los Angeles, falling equally on all things. By night, light blossoms in varied forms, adding new shapes and points of visual interest, new configurations and tensions. Strong beams of light exaggerate objects, casting long shadows from them that then join up with surrounding patches of darkness to create new and distinctive voids. By night, motion is calibrated against an episodic, even flickering visual field rather than the uniform rendering of form that comes with an even wash of daylight. By night, Los Angeles is a radiant and reflective construct, no longer beholden to the geometric structure and material resolution of the day. In Los Angeles, this transfiguration occurs daily; the twilight reshapes the city into a novel, luminous form, and then at dawn, "one by one the night-inspired illusions disappear, until finally, in the fullness of the morning light, the familiar lines of the city once more emerge."[56]

NOTES

1   Kevin Starr, *Material Dreams: Southern California through the 1920s* (New York: Oxford University Press, 1990), 157.

2   Jean Baudrillard, *America,* trans. Chris Turner (London: Verso, 1988), 51–52.

3   "A Chapter of Progress," *Los Angeles Times,* 6 May 1895, 8.

4   "Our 'White Way,'" *Los Angeles Times,* 24 November 1910, II4.

5   Mayme Ober Peak, "Few Christmas Visitors at Hollywood See 'Other Side' of Famous Movie City," *Boston Daily Globe,* 24 December 1927, 2. The tradition continued: "It may not be a white Christmas.... But it is a light Christmas—neon, fluorescent and incandescent." In "Southland Aglitter," *Los Angeles Times,* 25 December 1966, A1.

6   Aldous Huxley, quoted in David Ulin, ed., *Writing Los Angeles: A Literary Anthology* (New York: Library of America, 2002), 59–60.

7   Paul Whitney, "Lighting Spectacular as Viewed from Air," *Los Angeles Times,* 10 October 1936, 3.

8   Robert Fogelson, *The Fragmented Metropolis: Los Angeles, 1850–1930* (Cambridge, Mass.: Harvard University Press, 1967), 102; and Mel Scott, *Cities Are for People: The LA Region Plans for Living* (Los Angeles: Pacific Southwest Academy, 1942), 89.

9   Throughout, for example, Federal Writers' Project, *California: A Guide to the Golden State* (New York: Hastings House, 1939).

10   John Fante, *Ask the Dust* [1939] (New York: HarperCollins, 1980), 31.

11   Frank Krutnick, "Something More than Night: Tales of the 'Noir' City," in David Clarke, ed., *The Cinematic City* (London: Routledge, 1997), 89. This is also a general source for the description of Pottersville and noir cities.

12   Mike Davis, *City of Quartz: Excavating the Future in Los Angeles* (New York: Verso, 2006), 38.

13   "Bel-Air Area to Remain Free of Neon Lights," *Los Angeles Times,* 3 September 1949, 1.

14   "Skid Row Flares as Gaudy Nightmare in Neon Lights," *Los Angeles Times,* 18 April 1948, A1.

15   "Skid Row Flares," A1.

16 Aldous Huxley, *"The Doors of Perception" and "Heaven and Hell"* [1954, 1956] (New York: HarperCollins, 1990), 116.

17 Christopher Isherwood, *The World in the Evening* (New York: Random House, 1952), 9. The fictional story takes place in 1941.

18 Cecil Smith, "The Neon Bird in the Window," *Los Angeles Times,* 28 January 1954, A5.

19 Raymond Chandler, *The Lady in the Lake, The Little Sister, The Long Goodbye, Playback* [1949] (New York: Alfred A. Knopf, 2002). For more on Chandler and neon, see William Brevda, "The Double Nihilation of the Neon: Raymond Chandler's Los Angeles," *Texas Studies in Literature and Language* 41, no. 1 (1999): 70–102.

20 Simone de Beauvoir, *America Day by Day* [1948], trans. Carol Cosman (Berkeley: University of California Press, 2000), 122.

21 "100,000th Street Light Dedicated at Ceremony," *Los Angeles Times,* 7 April 1955, A1.

22 Case Study Houses in particular commonly contained more built-in lighting fixtures and up to twice as many electrical outlets as other homes built at the same time. Nancy C. Langley, "Modern Architecture Explained," *Los Angeles Times,* 5 May 1946, E4.

23 Jack Smith, "Looking L.A. Up and Down," *Los Angeles Times,* 3 December 1972, E1.

24 For example, Barbara Lenox, "Light Control," *Los Angeles Times,* 6 May 1956, N29.

25 John Pastier, "Tall Buildings Help to Revive Pattern of Separate Towns," *Los Angeles Times,* 5 April 1970, H1.

26 Jack Smith, "Twilight with Urban Overtones," *Los Angeles Times,* 13 November 1968, G1.

27 Jack Smith, "Neons Light of His Life," *Los Angeles Times,* 9 January 1972, E1.

28 Mitchell Schwarzer, *Architecture of the San Francisco Bay Area: History and Guide* (San Francisco: William Stout, 2007), 67.

29 Peter Blake, *God's Own Junkyard: The Planned Deterioration of America's Landscape* (New York: Holt, Rinehart, & Winston, 1964), 127.

30 John Pastier, "'This Modern Skyline Is Being Brought to You by…'" *Los Angeles Times,* 20 July 1972, C7; and Art Seidenbaum, "Rare Restraint: Letting Building Speak for Itself," *Los Angeles Times,* 9 February 1976, OC C8.

31 Jack Smith, "Neons," E1.

32 Art Seidenbaum, "Electric Evenings," *Los Angeles Times,* 4 December 1970, SF1.

33 Karl Klokke, "Building Designed to Stand for a Century," *Los Angeles Times,* 24 June 1965, E8.

34 John Pastier, "The Light Show Dims at DWP Building," *Los Angeles Times,* 23 July 1973, OC B1.

35 Albert Martin, "New Techniques Integrate Lighting, Air Conditioning," *Architectural Record* 129 (1961): 142–44.

36 David Gebhard and Robert Winter, *A Guide to Architecture in Los Angeles and Southern California* (Santa Barbara, Calif.: Peregrine Smith, 1977), 221. (This view is now partially obstructed by the later L.A. Construction Services Center on Figueroa Street.)

37 Reyner Banham, *Los Angeles: The Architecture of Four Ecologies* [1971] (London: Penguin, 1990), 134–35.

38 Seidenbaum, "Electric Evenings," SF1.

39 William Wilson, "Neon Artist's Exhibit Lighting Up a Future," *Los Angeles Times,* 20 July 1975, T66.

40 Pastier, "Neon—When Will We See the Light?" P1.

41 "Reyner Banham Loves Los Angeles (1972) BBC," YouTube video, from a 1972 broadcast by the British Broadcasting Company, posted by "modcinema," 27 February 2011, http://www.youtube.com/watch?v=hwSw9sYBSh4.

42 William Wilson, "Where Has All the Neon Gone?," *Los Angeles Times,* 19 April 1970, O8.

43 Pastier, "The Light Show Dims at DWP Building," OC B1.

44 "The Art of Bending Glass," *Los Angeles Times,* 30 April 1984, E2.

45 Elaine Woo, "The Glass Menagerie," *Los Angeles Times,* 24 February 1985, WS1.

46 William Wilson, "A Paean to Neon," *Los Angeles Times,* 19 January 1986, AC12.

47 John Cornell, "Light Beams Probe Night and Sentries Pace Strand," *Los Angeles Times,* 17 January 1942, 16.

48 Huxley cited in Ulin, *Writing Los Angeles,* 59–60. See also David Karnes, "The Glamorous Crowd: Hollywood Movie Premieres between the Wars," *American Quarterly* 38, no. 4 (1986): 553–72.

49 "Searchlight-Equipped Copters Go on Patrol," *Los Angeles Times,* 2 February 1969, OC12.

50 Robert Scheer, "Waste, Hope," *Los Angeles Times,* 11 November 1979, 1.

51 See, for example, Ivan Noe (possibly screenwriter Yvan Noé), "As a Parisian Views Hollywood," *New York Times,* 3 May 1931, X6; James M. Cain, "Paradise" [1933], cited in Ulin, *Writing Los Angeles,* 110; and Edmund Wilson, *The Boys in the Back Room* (San Francisco: Colt, 1941), Alison Lurie, *Nowhere City* (New York: Coward-McCann, 1965), and Jay McInerney, *Brightness Falls* (New York: Knopf, 1992), cited in William McClung, *Landscapes of Desire: Anglo-Mythologies of Los Angeles* (Berkeley: University of California Press, 2002), 52–53, 66.

52 Nathaneal West, *The Day of the Locust* [1939] (New York: Penguin, 1983), 23.

53 Raymond Chandler, *Farewell, My Lovely* (New York: Vintage, 1988), 36–39.

54 *Götterdämmerung,* the title of the fourth and final opera in Richard Wagner's Ring cycle, and translated as "twilight of the gods," denotes the end of an era or the collapse of a world. Jack Smith, "Twilight with Urban Overtones," *Los Angeles Times,* 13 November 1968, G1.

55 In James Steele, *Pierre Koenig* (New York: Phaidon, 1998), 5. Contemporary filmed images of the nighttime grid are discussed in Norman Klein, *The History of Forgetting: Los Angeles and the Erasure of Memory* (London: Verso, 1997), 109–10.

56 John Beckler, "Night's Magic Bejewels Freeways with Sparkling Tiaras of Lights," *Los Angeles Times,* 11 December 1955, A.

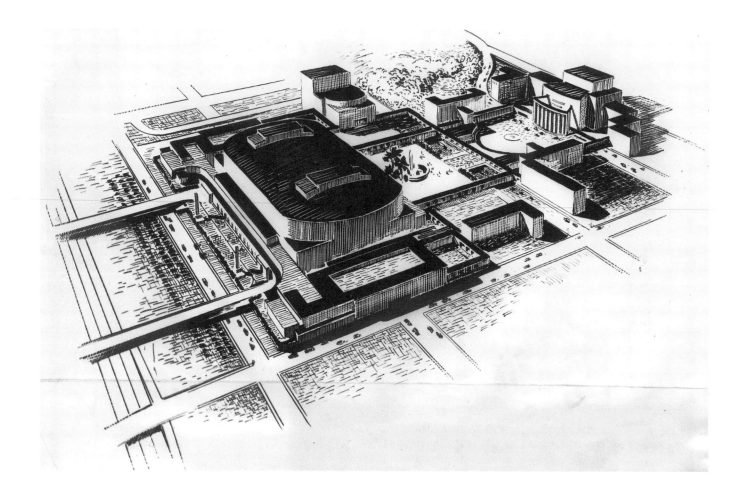

ENGAGING MODERNISM

"THE STYLE OF THE FUTURE"?
THE VICISSITUDES OF MODERNISM IN LOS ANGELES

Wim de Wit

IN JANUARY 1940, THE UNIVERSITY OF SOUTHERN CALIFORNIA (USC) organized a three-day conference to celebrate the opening of Harris Hall, the new home of its School of Architecture. The keynote speaker at this event was Frank Lloyd Wright, the septuagenarian architect who had always expressed his mind but who on this occasion was in top form. According to a reporter for the *Los Angeles Times,* Frank Lloyd Wright, "the Messiah of modern architecture," made the deliberately incendiary comment that the built environment of Los Angeles amounted to no more than "a dish of tripe."[1] Speaking before an audience of educators at what was then Los Angeles's only school of architecture, Wright chose to overlook the fact that Los Angeles had been an incubator of modernism for decades and, worse, called the city an ordinary, "common place." It should therefore come as no surprise that Wright's assessment set off a firestorm of commentary in the local press.

Within a few days of Wright's keynote lecture at USC, *Los Angeles Times* columnist Chapin Hall wrote that he actually liked the commonplace aspect of his city, which Wright had condemned. "Los Angeles and Southern California with its unlimited variety of architecture, both residential and business, is always a welcome home-coming relief after…a trip. Scarcely two houses or buildings alike, their genus is as mixed as that of an alley cat or a yellow dog, each distinctive in its own right, soothing, daring, shocking perhaps, yet offering no excuse for even an inebriated night lifer to inadvertently find the wrong key hole."[2] Hall's commentary critiques modernism's supposed monotony, according to which all the houses on a street built by a modern architect reputedly look alike, making it difficult to find one's own front door. Hall was not alone in this view. Architectural commentators stated repeatedly that the widespread preference for a range of historical styles (craftsman, colonial, or Monterrey, for example) expressed not only individual taste but also the freedom of choice that was appropriate to the American context. To them, modern architecture, with its lack of stylistic differentiation and its European roots, seemed un-American and vaguely undemocratic, possibly socialist—or, even worse, communist.[3]

FIGURE 1.
Early drawing for the Music Center (ca. 1945), 1945.
Los Angeles, Los Angeles Public Library,
Herald Examiner Collection.

Discussions such as these in the local press might suggest that there was little or no appreciation for modern architecture in Los Angeles, that no architect would be able to find a client wishing to build a modern house. This is, of course, not entirely true. While the *Los Angeles Times* reported on Wright's remarks and the various counterattacks, the same newspaper was also publishing positive reviews of exhibitions showing the work of Richard Neutra and Raphael Soriano.[4] Indeed, Neutra, Rudolph Schindler, and other modernists had already been building important modern structures in Los Angeles for a few decades.

Before World War II, a recognizably modernist formal vocabulary had become acceptable for the design of stores, offices, and small commercial structures. In the field of residential architecture, however, modernism was still widely frowned upon. Only members of an educated cultural elite were willing to hire modern architects to design their houses.[5] Those who had grown up in houses dressed up with ornamental references to grand periods of the past typically found it hard to imagine how they could live in a house that seemed to be nothing more than an off-putting structure of steel and wood with infills of glass and board. At the same time, professional and economic regulations of the period made it difficult for modernist architects to convince potential clients that this was not the case.

Architects faced a significant obstacle in the ethical rules promulgated by the American Institute of Architects (AIA), which explicitly prohibited them from pursuing advertising or publicity designed to promote their work. Prior to the rule changes in the mid-1960s, it was considered unethical for an architect, who is supposed to deliver a product that best serves the needs of a client, to promote his or her own work or become too closely associated with any kind of business, no matter if it was producing steel doors or prefabricated kitchens. Beyond such professional self-regulation, banks posed an even bigger problem. Fearing they might be saddled with unsalable property in case of foreclosure, many banks refused to provide a mortgage for a house in a modern style. Architecture critic Esther McCoy commented on this problem in 1951[6] and provoked a response from a real estate loan appraiser, who defended himself and his colleagues against the perception that they were "really old-fashioned stick-in-the-muds, ruthlessly holding back true progress in home development" (his words, not McCoy's).[7] He added: "It is extremely hard to dispose of a Modern shed-roof house, because they usually are considered ugly by the average buyer." Given the scarcity of financial support from the banks, commissioning an architect to design a modern dwelling was unaffordable for a large part of Los Angeles's population. And because architects needed to show built work in order to persuade clients to hire them, a meeting of the two seemed almost impossible.

This essay examines how, in spite of these problematic circumstances, modernism came to be accepted in Southern California, and it outlines the forces that shaped a slow but increasingly discernible change in architectural taste. Drawing on the public discourse as it was reflected in the pages of the *Los Angeles Times,* I suggest that the gradual appreciation of modernism in Los Angeles is visible not simply in the creation of modern architecture but also in its reception. In addition, I consider the roles played by the publishers and architectural critics, the developers and corporations, and, of course, the architects themselves, who eventually changed their formal vocabulary to make their work more acceptable to the public. Modernist architects tended to speak about the products of their design work as ineluctable results of such determinants as function and economy, but as is the case with all other commodities, taste is a very important factor in the salability of buildings. In the end, this essay is a study of the taste for modernism and the factors that influenced that taste.

————

It would be inaccurate to suggest that opposition to modern architecture was monolithic or entirely rigid. After all, modernism had made important inroads in the first half of the century. But the resistance that emerged in the 1930s and '40s, when modernism started to gain ground, was difficult to overcome. In 1951, a curmudgeonly commentator noted in the *Times* that the highly visible Civic Center buildings in downtown Los Angeles were going to be modern: "They say this is the style of the future. What that means I cannot imagine, for the future isn't here yet" (fig. 1).[8] When this editorial was published, the Music Center—a contemporary of New York's Lincoln Center also consisting of a music pavilion and two theaters—would not be completed for about fifteen years. But other prominent signs of change were emerging in Los Angeles's sprawling urban environment. In 1940, the famous May Department Stores Company hired the well-established firm of A. C. Martin and Associates to build a spare white box with an eye-catching curved corner of black granite and gold mosaic tile at the intersection of Wilshire Boulevard and Fairfax Avenue (fig. 2). The

FIGURE 2.
Albert C. Martin Jr. (American, 1909–45).
May Company Building (1938–40), Los Angeles, 1949.
Photo by Julius Shulman.
Los Angeles, Getty Research Institute.

CBS broadcasting corporation hired William Pereira and Charles Luckman to build its Television City (completed 1952), also in the Fairfax area (fig. 3). And the music company Capitol Records commissioned Welton Becket and Associates to design a modern building (completed in 1956) that is still one of Hollywood's most popular midcentury icons (fig. 4). In addition, while some merchant builders in the housing market remained skeptical about whether residential architecture designed in a modern style could be profitable, during the 1950s, several developers hired architects to build large tracts of modern homes, which turned out to sell surprisingly well.

In spite of these gradual transformations, architects who wanted to make themselves known to the public at large effectively had only one means to do so. Getting one's designed and built work published in both professional and popular newspapers and magazines was essential to an architect's success. Because most architectural journals were based on the East Coast, Southern California architects would have been in a disadvantageous position, were it not for the fact that they had a well-designed magazine, *Arts & Architecture,* right in their own backyard (fig. 5). Founded in 1929 as *California Arts & Architecture,* the journal was bought in 1938 by John Entenza, a well-to-do champion of the arts, who deleted "California" from the magazine's title five years later. This was a smart move, as it signified to the world of readers, writers, and advertisers not only that the content would extend well beyond works of art or architecture produced in California but also that the work of Californians deserved to be seen in an international context, alongside that of architects in Australia, Japan, and Latin America, not to mention New York City and Chicago.[9]

Entenza's next step was even more important to the success of his magazine and that of the architects published in it. In the January 1945 issue, he announced the Case Study House Program, an invitation to modern architects to build houses that could serve as prototypes for larger developments. Much has been written about this program, yet it is nevertheless appropriate to point out that the main goal of the proposal was twofold: on the one hand, Entenza wanted to help people imagine how they might live in an innovative, modernist house; on the other, Entenza's program promoted the idea of prefabrication and mass production, which he considered crucial to alleviating the unprecedented shortage of housing that was sure to emerge at the end of the war.

Prefabrication was a difficult concept to sell to a public suspicious of any trend in design that did not pretend to deliver something custom-made. Neutra, in a conversation about his Avion Village housing project near Dallas, Texas, told a *Los Angeles Times* reporter in 1941 that advertising for prefabricated housing was almost impossible. He pointed to an interesting contradiction between the promotion of cars—perhaps the most characteristic product of prefabrication and mass production—and that for housing:

> When you buy a car, you have pride in owning that make. It's been advertised and given prestige until you are proud to own that car. Prefabricated houses have been promoted in just the opposite way. It has been given no prestige by advertising. The builder tries to make the homes look deceptively as though they were individually planned. The thing has gone so far that when the company corresponds with the purchaser by mail it often uses blank envelopes so no prying neighbor can detect what his friend is up to.[10]

FIGURE 3.
Pereira & Luckman, Architects, Engineers and Planners (1950–58).
CBS Television City (completed 1952), Los Angeles, 1958. Los Angeles, CBS Television City Archives.

FIGURE 4.
Welton Becket and Associates (1949–88).
Capitol Records Tower (completed 1956), Hollywood, 1956. Los Angeles, Getty Research Institute.

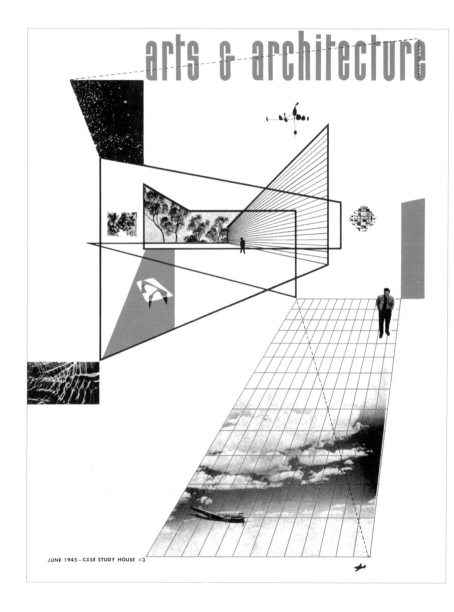

FIGURE 5.
Cover of *Arts & Architecture* 62, no. 6 (June 1945),
showing Case Study House #3, by William Wurster
and Theodore Bernardi.

FIGURE 6.
Cover of *Home* (*Los Angeles Times* magazine),
12 August 1951, showing "Space Retreat,"
by Leslie C. Guthrie Jr. and Richard O. Spencer.
Photo by Julius Shulman.
Los Angeles, Getty Research Institute.

It was in response to this problem that Entenza came up with a plan that would foreground the idea of prefabrication. The Case Study Houses encouraged people to discover firsthand that modern architecture, especially the kind with factory-produced parts, would not necessarily be experienced as impersonal or cold. To that end, he stipulated in his contracts with the architects and owners of the houses that, upon completion of each Case Study House, the owners would open it to the public. Such an open house was also a way of providing free advertisement to the industries that had delivered components of the house (the steel structure or the doors or windows) at a discount. Measured by the long lines of visitors, those open-house days were very successful.[11]

The magazine, in the meantime, played another role in changing the sentiment about modern architecture. In its pages, the design drawings for the Case Study Houses were presented to the broader world of postwar design aficionados inside and outside California. And once the construction of a house was complete, superb photographs of the structure taken by Julius Shulman circulated the work of the Case Study House architects better than any written text could have done. In addition, Shulman, a savvy businessman himself, worked hard to get his photos published not only in professional journals but also in newspapers and shelter magazines, which brought still more attention to the architects. The promotional role played by such photographers as Jack Laxer, Marvin Rand, Shulman, and, at a later date, Grant Mudford and Tim Street-Porter was as important as that of the magazine editors. Shulman in particular was a powerful figure in the architectural world, where he was able to establish a career.

Arts & Architecture was not the only venue in which architects could publish their work. *Sunset,* a magazine published in Northern California (Palo Alto), promoted the California-ranch style of living and devoted a great deal of attention to architects in Southern California, especially Cliff May. But it was *Home* magazine of the *Los Angeles Times* that provided the most opportunities for architects to have their work publicized (fig. 6). Over the years, the *Times* employed very dedicated architecture writers, including Ethel McCall Head (1940s and first half of the '50s); Esther McCoy (1950–68); Dan MacMasters (1969–78); John Pastier, who was the *Los Angeles Times*'s first architecture critic (1969–75); John Dreyfuss (1976–83); and Sam Hall Kaplan (1983–90). Each of these writers had a strong impact on people's perception of modern architecture. There was, however, a difference between the first three members of the group and the other three.

The writing of Head, McCoy, and MacMasters was generally descriptive and aimed at informing the newspaper's readers about why modern architecture deserved their attention. Many of Head's articles, for example, started with sentences like "Modern interiors make good living!" or "Young people without collections of old furniture and with modest budgets take to modern architecture."[12] Those kinds of statements were then followed by detailed descriptions of each room of a house, its color scheme, and sometimes even the furniture.

Pastier, Dreyfuss, and Kaplan were hired as architecture and design critics and were therefore not able to promote a specific architect's work. A positive review of a building by one of these critics, however, was undoubtedly helpful for an architect's career, as was recently affirmed by Thom Mayne and Eric Owen Moss, who both credited Dreyfuss with being the first writer to declare that their work carried weight and thus deserved the public's notice.[13]

In an environment marked by such strong and influential personalities, architects realized that they needed someone to mediate between the worlds of architectural design and publishing. It is therefore no surprise that, in the post–World War II period and especially after the AIA lifted its ban on advertising, large architectural firms hired public relations managers.[14] Even the small firm of Palmer and Krisel hired a public relations specialist who successfully "sold" their work to local and national publishers.[15] William Krisel was aware that a well-written article accompanied by high-quality photographs could make a house—even a modern one—very desirable and lead to new commissions.

In addition to those writing about architecture, developers and builders of tracts of land also had a powerful impact on taste, especially when the design of a house was coupled with affordable financing—for example, through postwar Federal Housing Administration (FHA) programs for GIs. By the early 1950s, developers such as Joseph Eichler and George Alexander were working with modern architects only. Eichler hired the firm of Anshen + Allen in Northern California, while the firm of Jones and Emmons served as Eichler's architects in the Los Angeles area. Meanwhile, it was Palmer and Krisel who designed the thousands of tract houses that the Alexander Construction Company built in the postwar period. As soon as competitors realized that such large-scale modernist projects were successful, many others followed.

These developers did not face the same problem as the modernist architects, such as Neutra and the Case Study House designers, when it came to marketing mass-produced houses. Eichler, Alexander, and their architects proved to be very canny about what their potential clients would accept, and they made sure that the modern look of their houses was neither monotonous nor harshly abstract. The architects introduced variations in rooflines (this is when the butterfly roof became very popular) and in floor plans, which differed slightly from one to the next but seemed more individualized than they actually were because of the different orientations they were given within the master plan of the development (fig. 7). Proud of what they had achieved, Eichler, Alexander, and others were not ashamed to advertise their houses to the "masses."[16] And young couples, who in the postwar period came in droves to Southern California to find work and start a family, adapted their taste to market conditions and eagerly purchased the affordable, modern-looking houses.[17]

In the world of office and civic building design, however, the situation was very different. The use of a modernist vocabulary had been acceptable in this area for some time. While the pre–World War II depression prevented most businesses from commissioning major office buildings, there were many stores and small office structures that had already been designed in a modern style. Modern materials, such as steel and glass, were considered to be entirely appropriate due to the connotations of efficiency, the absence of waste, and thus the good business sense that they suggested. In the postwar period, virtually every high-rise office building in Los Angeles was designed in some version of modernism. Even J. Paul Getty—who rejected the use of steel, stone, and large expanses of glass in his own house or in the Getty Villa—commissioned a high-rise office building in a stripped-down modernist vocabulary on Wilshire Boulevard for his Getty Oil Company. Claud Beelman's design, with its slim, stone-covered exterior columns separated by relatively narrow bays, gave the building as a whole the appearance of a fluted classical column, thereby softening its otherwise unornamented abstract shape (fig. 8).[18]

FIGURE 7.
Palmer and Krisel, Architects (1949–66).
Elevation drawings of tract house models A-2, A-1, and A-3 for Murray Strauss, Palm Gardens (unrealized), 1954. Pencil on vellum, sheet: 60.8 × 60.8 cm (24 × 24 in.); drawing: 57.7 × 51 cm (22¾ × 20⅛ in.). Los Angeles, Getty Research Institute.

FIGURE 8.
Claud Beelman (American, 1884–1963).
Perspective view of Getty Oil Company headquarters
(completed 1963), Los Angeles, 1961–62.
Pencil on vellum, 56.1 × 45.9 cm (22⅛ × 18 in.).
Los Angeles, Brandow and Johnston, Inc.

The public at large had also become bored with this kind of modernist architecture, which was criticized as monotonous and lacking any distinction. Throughout the 1950s, the *Los Angeles Times* published articles that display a growing sense of concern about the city's ugliness. This unease reached a climax around 1963 and 1964, when what are now considered to be Los Angeles's major midcentury monuments were nearing completion: the Dorothy Chandler Pavilion (fig. 9) and the first office buildings in Century City (fig. 10), all by Welton Becket and Associates. The public was clearly unhappy with what it saw. In October 1963, the Pasadena architect Robert Ainsworth told a *Times* reporter that "pure functionalism"—allowing the function of the building to determine its shape—was responsible for the city's unsightliness; about a year later, the literary critic Russell Kirk wrote, "The buildings of our age are vastly dull, and will starve the imagination of future generations." To drive his point home, Kirk added, "Our most pretentious new buildings are wretchedly designed."[19]

The irony in this controversy is that by the beginning of the 1960s, the modernist vocabulary had already changed significantly. Aware of the negative response to the designs coming out of their offices, many architects adjusted their styles to convey a softer and more decorative impression to the viewer. L.A. architects were not alone in this regard. They were, of course, aware of the debates taking place all over the country about how to incorporate emotion and subjectivity into modern architecture. During the second half of the 1940s and into the early 1950s, for example, *Architectural Record* (a magazine read by every self-respecting architect) published lectures and essays by prominent architectural figures, all of whom spoke in one form or another about the function of aesthetics and expression in architectural design and how to infuse modern architecture with these qualities.[20]

Several architects in Los Angeles participated in this debate, not only in writing but also through their work. The Dorothy Chandler Pavilion is a good case in point. In a long article promoting the new Music Center, Welton Becket explains the thinking behind the design: "We felt that many contemporary exterior and interior designs were too stark and unimaginative for this type of building, so we studied the classical concepts of architecture as a point of departure."[21] We may assume that Mrs. Chandler, the main client, had very specific opinions about the style in which the Music Pavilion was supposed to be "dressed" and that she was therefore part of the "we" to whom Becket refers in this quote. However, when Becket states that the materials were selected "for their inherent richness and beauty" and for the "feeling of elegance," he makes it clear that he had moved away from the abstract version of modernism to a style that evoked a sense of comfort and prosperity.

FIGURE 9.
Welton Becket and Associates (1949–88).
Rendering of the Dorothy Chandler Pavilion
(completed 1964), Los Angeles, ca. 1960.
Watercolor, pencil, and gouache on paper, mounted on
board, excluding mount, 58.1 × 94 cm (22⅞ × 37 in.).
Los Angeles, Getty Research Institute.

FIGURE 10.
Welton Becket and Associates (1949–88).
Gateway Towers (1963–64), Century City, 1966.
Photo by Julius Shulman.
Los Angeles, Getty Research Institute.

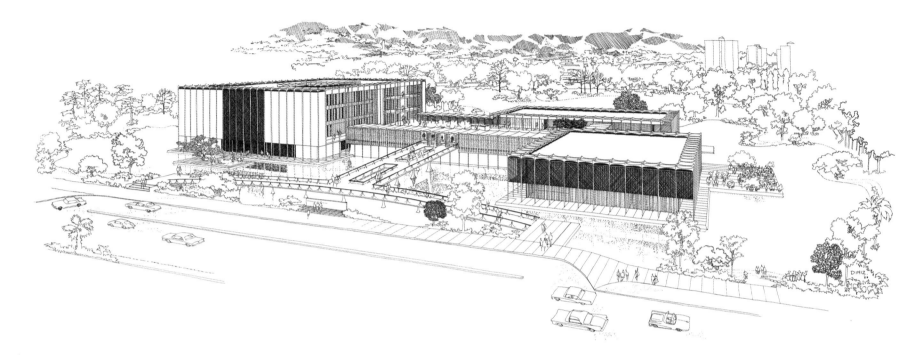

FIGURE 11.
Carlos Diniz (American, 1928–2001).
Aerial view of the Los Angeles County Museum of Art
(1961–65), by William L. Pereira and Associates,
Planning and Architecture, 1960.
Offset print on paper of pen-and-ink drawing,
11.7 × 33 cm (4⅗ × 13 in.).
Los Angeles, Edward Cella Gallery.

Becket's firm was not the only one that modified its modernist language, especially when designing civic structures. William Pereira also sought to develop a softer, more decorative kind of modernism. Having separated from his partner, Charles Luckman, reportedly because the latter was too businesslike and uninterested in the aesthetics of architecture,[22] Pereira went on to design the Los Angeles County Museum of Art (fig. 11) and buildings at the University of California, Irvine (fig. 12); the University of California, San Diego; and USC. In many of these, he used precast structural components, including columns and cornices, as decorative elements that broke down the rigidity of the boxlike structures, most likely in an effort to give the buildings a more sculptural appearance.

Edward Durell Stone should also be mentioned in this context. While Stone's career was centered in New York City, he did have an office in Los Angeles during the years that he designed a large number of university and bank buildings in the city. Having started out as a high-modernist architect involved in the design of the Museum of Modern Art in New York in 1939, Stone changed course during the early 1950s and began adding ornament (diaphanous, screen-like walls, decorative bricks, and large overhanging eaves) to his structures. Nationally, his best-known building was the Huntington Hartford Gallery of Modern Art in New York (1958); in Los Angeles, he designed striking but not always well-received buildings such as the Perpetual Savings and Loan Building in Beverly Hills (1961) (fig. 13), the Von KleinSmid Center at USC (1964), and the Ahmanson Building on Wilshire Boulevard (1967).

While Becket, Pereira, Stone, and many others were successful in getting commissions, there was a negative reaction to ornamentation, this time not from the general public but from within the architectural community. Indeed, most architects were searching for a more human style that would be appreciated by the

general public, but the more critically minded among them (including such nationally known designers as Philip Johnson and Serge Chermayeff) felt that the application of decorative elements was too simple a solution, one that lacked any theoretical grounding. As far as they were concerned, it was selling out to popular taste.[23] The criticism of Stone, Pereira, and other architects who had reintroduced ornament proved that even in the 1960s, when modernism was generally accepted as a style, architects did not form one unified movement. Instead, the concepts influencing this architectural language were complex and constantly in flux.

In retrospect, Stone's work was probably a predecessor of what came to be known as postmodernism. This style, best known for its historicizing ornamental references, began to emerge in the 1970s as an alternative to the tedium of modernist design. Interestingly, postmodernism did not gain as much influence in Los Angeles as in other cities in the United States. Not until 1984 did the *Los Angeles Times* announce the appearance of the first postmodern building on Los Angeles's skyline, the office tower at 1000 Wilshire Boulevard designed by Kohn Pederson Fox Associates.[24] Clad with a black-and-gray stone skin wrapped tightly around the interior spaces, the office building's most striking feature is its commanding placement next to the Harbor (110) Freeway, which gives the building more visibility than it probably deserves. There are, of course, some other postmodern buildings in the city, thanks to the work of Michael Graves, Charles Moore, and others.[25] The architectural debate among Los Angeles's younger architects, however, had been moving in a totally different direction.

A new generation of architects—including Frank Gehry, Thom Mayne, Eric Owen Moss, and Michael Rotondi—came to the fore in the 1970s. They too were eager to change the course of modernism but were

FIGURE 12.
William L. Pereira and Associates, Planning and Architecture (1958–85).
Langson Library (1965–68), University of California, Irvine, 1968.
Photo by Julius Shulman.
Los Angeles, Getty Research Institute.

FIGURE 13.
Edward Durell Stone and Associates (1936–76).
Perpetual Savings and Loan (1961–62), Beverly Hills, 1961.
Pencil and ink on tracing paper,
60.9 × 92 cm (24 × 36¼ in.).
Fayetteville, University of Arkansas.

not interested in returning to a classicizing vocabulary characteristic of the premodern period. Instead, as can be seen in Gehry's own house (fig. 14; see also Phillips, fig. 1), they sought a totally new language by breaking open the modernist box and allowing disparate shapes to collide with one another. Seemingly destructive, this aggressive new architecture drew universal critical attention, making Los Angeles a widely acclaimed center of architectural innovation.[26] For the general public, however, it was not easy to appreciate such a huge breach in what stylistically had become acceptable in modern architecture. As was the case forty or fifty years earlier, it was again a small group of enlightened clients (often related to the entertainment industry) who were brave enough to commission these architects to design houses or commercial buildings. And again it would have been difficult for the architects to make themselves visible to more powerful clients were it not for a globalized publishing industry that was eager to print new work in its glossy architectural magazines.

The big change came for this group of architects around 1988 when Frank Gehry won the competition for the Walt Disney Concert Hall. The decision to build a new hall for the Los Angeles Philharmonic had already given a huge boost to the pride of the city. However, the fact that the commission for this extremely important building was given to a local architect, who had never designed anything on this monumental scale, signified to the public that Gehry and his colleagues were architects worth paying attention to. Gradually, the public learned to appreciate their work, and, as a result, more significant commissions began coming in.

As often happens with large civic structures, it took fifteen years to build Walt Disney Concert Hall. In the meantime, Gehry built the Guggenheim Museum Bilbao (1997), which made him the most celebrated

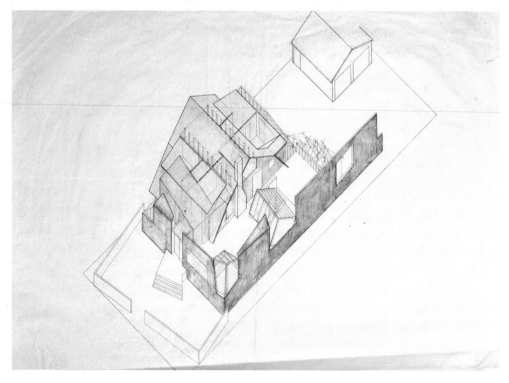

FIGURE 14.
Frank O. Gehry and Associates (1962–2001).
Axonometric view of the Gehry Residence (1977–78),
Santa Monica, n.d.
Pencil and color pencil on vellum,
91.3 × 121.7 cm (36 × 48 in.).
Santa Monica, Gehry Partners, LLP.

architect in the world. When Disney Hall was finally completed in 2003, Los Angeles had become a mecca for archi-tourism, and the city's architects were getting commissions all over the world. The latest form of modernism had been accepted.

NOTES
I would not have been able to write this essay without the research assistance of Lyra Kilston. I thank her as well as Christopher James Alexander and Nancy Troy, both of whom provided very helpful advice.

1   "Architect Wright Doesn't Like This City and Bluntly Says So," *Los Angeles Times,* 20 January 1940, A1; and "Trends in Art Traced at SC," *Los Angeles Times,* 20 January 1940, A3.

2   Chapin Hall, "What Goes On?," *Los Angeles Times,* 24 January 1940, A.

3   For example, when the Czech architect Jan Reiner came to Los Angeles to give a talk at USC, the *Los Angeles Times* reported that he liked the houses of Los Angeles and that in them he could "see the individualism and democracy of America expressing itself." "Czech Architect Praises Los Angeles Home Building," *Los Angeles Times,* 2 March 1940, 16.

4   "Exhibits," *Los Angeles Times,* 17 March 1940, C9.

5   See, for example, Thomas S. Hines, *Architecture of the Sun: Los Angeles Modernism, 1900–1970* (New York: Rizzoli, 2010).

6   Esther McCoy, "If You Don't Want to Get a Loan," *Los Angeles Times,* 15 April 1951, F13.

7   "Monday Morning Mail," *Los Angeles Times,* 20 May 1951, F25.

8   Timothy G. Turner, "Los Angelans Now Beef More Than They Boost," *Los Angeles Times,* 14 April 1950, A5.

9   For more on *(California) Arts & Architecture,* see Segawa and Atique, this volume.

10 Tom Treanor, "The Home Front," *Los Angeles Times,* 2 April 1941, 4. For further discussion of Neutra's quote about prefabrication, see also Thomas S. Hines, *Richard Neutra and the Search for Modernism* (New York: Rizzoli, 2005), 194.

11 See Esther McCoy, *Case Study Houses, 1945–1962* (Los Angeles: Hennessy & Ingalls, 1977), 9–10.

12 Ethel McCall Head, "Modern Makes Sense," *Los Angeles Times,* 23 October 1949, F7; and Ethel McCall Head, "Privacy on a City Lot," *Los Angeles Times,* 1 June 1947, F5.

13 Thom Mayne and Eric Owen Moss, in interviews conducted as part of the L.A. oral history project of California Polytechnic State University, San Luis Obispo, and the Getty Research Institute, 23 February and 17 May 2011. I thank Stephen Phillips for providing me with this information.

14 Quite a few architects' wives became the public relations managers for their husbands' firms, the most famous of whom is probably Eero Saarinen's wife, Aline.

15 William Krisel, interview by Wim de Wit, 3 November 2011.

16 In a sense, these real estate developers and merchant builders, together with their architects, worked from the opposite end of where the Case Study House architects started when planning for mass production. Like the latter, the developers also worked with some form of prefabrication: they precut most of the house parts in a factory and delivered them to the construction site, where the workers could quickly put them together. The difference is that the Case Study House designers produced a prototype and then hoped that a large builder would mass-produce them, while Krisel and others started out with a builder who had the financing to build large tracts of land. See also Cuff, this volume.

17 According to Krisel, this taste for modern houses lasted until the late 1960s, when people again began asking for traditional houses. Krisel, interview, 2011.

18 Beelman designed many office buildings in downtown Los Angeles and along Wilshire Boulevard. Robert Langdon and Ernest Wilson, the architects for the Getty Villa, joined firms with Beelman from 1953 to 1961.

19 Bob Boich, "Architect Hits Stress on Pure Functionalism," *Los Angeles Times,* 20 October 1963, O1; and Russell Kirk, "The Demise of Architecture," *Los Angeles Times,* 31 December 1964, B6.

20 See *Architectural Record,* vol. 109, no. 2; vol. 110, nos. 1, 2, 5; vol. 111, nos. 4, 5; vol. 113, nos. 3, 5; and vol. 114, no. 1.

21 Welton Becket, "A Contemporary Expression of Classic Architecture," *Los Angeles Times,* 6 December 1964, N20.

22 Hines, *Architecture of the Sun,* 693.

23 Hicks Stone, *Edward Durell Stone: A Son's Untold Story of a Legendary Architect* (New York: Rizzoli, 2011), 188–89.

24 Evelyn De Wolfe, "Post-Modern Office Tower Planned," *Los Angeles Times,* 21 October 1984, I1.

25 Some critics consider the Getty Villa, a replica of the partially excavated Villa dei Papiri in Herculaneum, to be an early example of postmodernism in Los Angeles. See, for example, Charles Jencks, "Don't Panic!," *Architectural Review* 163, no. 972 (1978): 83–85.

26 See Phillips, this volume.

PROFESSIONAL AND EDUCATIONAL DISCOURSE
TRAINING THE NEXT GENERATION OF ARCHITECTS IN LOS ANGELES

Ken Breisch

THE DECADE FOLLOWING THE END OF WORLD WAR II witnessed a tremendous demand for new construction in Southern California, especially in the realm of housing. Not only did the population surge during and after the war to feed a vast new defense and aerospace industry but tens of thousands of GIs who had passed through Los Angeles during and after the conflicts in the Pacific and Korea returned to settle in the city. The Servicemen's Readjustment Act (GI Bill of Rights) of 1944, with its low-interest housing loans for veterans, fueled this demand and the building boom it would engender. The college tuition incentives written into this same legislation encouraged millions of veterans to enroll in the nation's colleges and universities; some of those students envisioned a future in architectural design. Before the end of the 1960s, the University of Southern California (USC) offered the only professional degree in architecture in the area and thus attracted many veterans to its program. By 1970, to help meet a continuing demand for architects and planners, schools of architecture had been established at the University of California, Los Angeles (UCLA), and California State Polytechnic University, Pomona (Cal Poly Pomona). Two years later, the Southern California Institute of Architecture (SCI-Arc) was founded in Santa Monica, and an architecture major was created in 1984 at Woodbury University in Burbank.[1]

Despite a significant diversity in the stated missions, pedagogies, and curricula of these architecture programs, the design studio—a method of education that evolved during the nineteenth century at the École des Beaux-Arts in Paris—was the core of architectural education at all of these schools. Within this culture, as Dana Cuff notes, the "primary form of interaction between studio teachers and students" is the "crit," in which peers, faculty, and invited visitors critique student work produced in studio (fig. 1). These assessments culminate in the final review, "a formal ritual" to which outside jurors are invited to evaluate the students' projects.[2] It is through this "crucial attitude-forming" process, argued the British architectural historian and critic Reyner Banham, that "architects are socialized into the profession (as the great Jane Abercrombie used to phrase it) and they acquire attitudes, work-habits and values that will stay with them for life."[3] This system, more than

FIGURE 1.
"Crit" at the Southern California Institute of Architecture, ca. 1974.
Photo by Morton Neikrug.

anything else, sets architectural education apart from other disciplines and professions and underlies the formation of the practitioner.

UNIVERSITY OF SOUTHERN CALIFORNIA

In 1919, under the leadership of Arthur Clason Weatherhead, the architecture program at USC was established as an independent Department of Art and Architecture in the College of Liberal Arts; and six years later, the newly renamed School of Architecture began offering a five-year curriculum leading to a bachelor of architecture degree. As Deborah Howell-Ardila has demonstrated, by the mid-1930s, Weatherhead had begun to shift the curriculum away from the traditional and largely classical Beaux-Arts pedagogy toward a more pragmatic approach to design.[4] To further prepare students for the realities of office practice during the Depression, new studios were formed around "practical" topics, especially those associated with housing and urban planning. This new curriculum also placed a stronger emphasis on a "three-dimensional product rather than the pictorial qualities of the sketch," which, along with elaborately finished drawings, was a mainstay of the Beaux-Arts method.[5] Three-dimensional models have remained a central component of design culture at all of the region's architecture schools.

In reaction to the mounting prospect of war, and in line with his educational philosophy, Weatherhead reported in September 1941 that "population evacuation, emergency housing, the designing of arsenals, airports and the building of emergency communities for workers are lessons to be learned by the S.C. embryo architects who at the same time are given instruction in architectural principles of graphics, engineering, material studies, estimating and construction costs and research."[6] At this time, for example, Weatherhead introduced the studio course Fundamentals of Camouflage and Protective Concealment of Industrial Plants; the class was created a year in advance of Edward Huntsman-Trout's legendary camouflage assembly at the Douglas Aircraft plant in Santa Monica.[7]

Following Weatherhead's retirement, Arthur Gallion was selected in 1945 to lead what was now the School of Architecture and Fine Arts (again renamed the School of Architecture in 1949). It quickly filled with returning veterans who were able to take advantage of the GI Bill to cover their tuition, men such as Richard Dorman (BArch, 1951), William Krisel (BArch, 1949), and Conrad Buff III, Donald C. Hensman, and Pierre Koenig (all BArch, 1952).[8] Gallion's appointment coincided with the *Arts & Architecture* magazine launch in January 1945 of John Entenza's Case Study Program, a project with which many USC faculty and graduates would be involved during the following two decades. This same year, Gallion engineered the transfer of the Department of Fine Arts to the College of Letters, Arts, and Sciences; and four years later, he created the School of Architecture, a program that remains in place today.

During his fifteen-year tenure, Gallion was able to build on Weatherhead's protomodernist foundation while also integrating industrial and landscape design into the architectural curriculum; he hired Raymond F. Loewy and Garrett Eckbo to lead these new initiatives, along with Calvin C. Straub for the architecture program. Straub, who had graduated from the school in 1943, became a much-beloved third-year studio instructor; he was also an advocate for the direction Weatherhead had set for the program while Straub was a student, particularly in the area of the single-family home (figs. 2, 3). Here, Straub worked

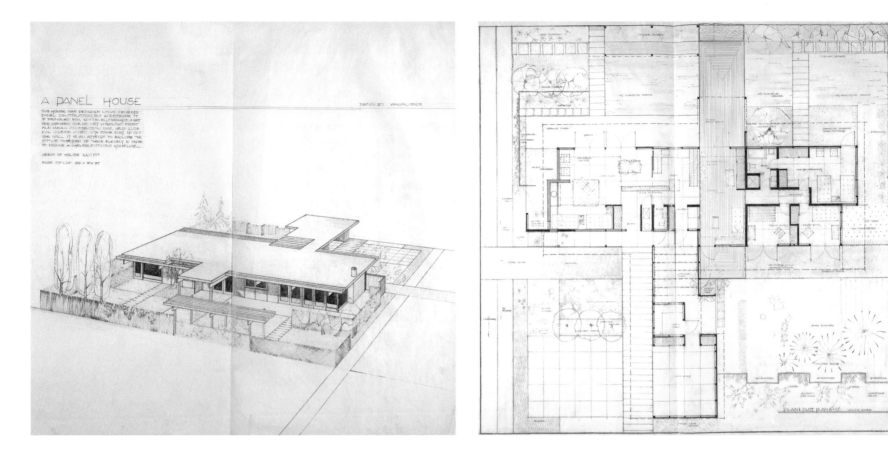

closely with Eckbo to promote a wooden post-and-beam structural system that allowed free-flowing interior spaces to open generously onto the surrounding landscape, a distinctive approach to architectural design that Esther McCoy would later dub the "Pasadena" or "USC style."[9] Other students, such as Pierre Koenig, were drawn to the more industrial aesthetic being promoted by the Case Study Program and embraced by local architects such as Craig Ellwood, for whom Koenig worked while still a student. Also as a student, Koenig built his first "steel" house (for himself) in Glendale in 1950 (fig. 4), and he went on to design two of the best-known Case Study Houses, the Bailey Residence (CSH#21, 1958) and the Stahl Residence (CSH#22, 1960).[10]

Eckbo, Loewy, and Straub were joined during Gallion's early years by an extraordinary faculty of professors, lecturers, and visiting critics, including Gregory Ain, Gordon Drake, Simon Eisner, Harwell Hamilton Harris, A. Quincy Jones, William Pereira, Whitney Rowland Smith, and landscape architect Emmet Wemple, as well as Conrad Buff III and Donald C. Hensman, both of whom were students of Straub's and began teaching shortly after their graduation in 1952 (Frank Gehry and his future partner Gregory Walsh both matriculated just two years later).

In 1955, Gallion and Eisner, along with Henry Reining Jr., dean of the School of Public Administration, established a graduate degree at USC in city and regional planning, a program that was jointly administered by the Schools of Architecture and Public Administration. Five years earlier, Gallion, who had been trained

FIGURE 2.
Gregory Walsh (American, b. 1930).
A Panel House, project for Calvin Straub's third-year studio at the University of Southern California, 1951–52.
Pencil and colored pencil on vellum,
65 × 70 cm (25½ × 27½ in.).

FIGURE 3.
Gregory Walsh (American, b. 1930).
Plan and plot plan for *A Panel House* (unrealized), 1951–52.
Pencil and colored pencil on vellum,
65 × 70 cm (25½ × 27½ in.).

as an architect, and Eisner, a city planner, had published their widely influential book, *The Urban Pattern,* and had expanded the fourth- and fifth-year architecture curriculum to include lectures and studios specifically focused on urban design. The content of these classes included "the history and planning of the city, legal background studies of zoning, subdivision problems created by the laws, the impact they have on the architect as a city builder, standards, development and application of these standards to the physical design."[11] Somewhat ironically, perhaps, the students also learned "what happens when you redesign a city and displace a great number of people."[12] A year earlier, William Pereira, who taught at USC from 1949 to 1957, and his partner, Charles Luckman, had begun work on the Bunker Hill Redevelopment Project, an urban renewal effort that would eventually displace some ten thousand inner-city residents.[13]

Following Gallion's retirement and a short interim administration, Samuel Hurst was appointed as dean of the school in 1962. Hurst reunited architecture and fine arts, and he hired Crombie Taylor—who had earlier worked for László Moholy-Nagy at the Bauhaus-inspired Institute of Design in Chicago and alongside Ludwig Mies van der Rohe at the Illinois Institute of Technology (IIT)—to lead the architecture program as associate dean. Over the next ten years, Hurst and Taylor expanded the curriculum into the building sciences, beginning with the hiring of Ralph Knowles, who would pioneer research on solar planning. Alfred Caldwell and Konrad Wachsmann, both of whom Taylor had known at IIT, were also brought to the school, as was former USC graduate Pierre Koenig. Wachsmann, who had worked with Walter Gropius on prefabricated modular housing, was recruited to reconstitute the Building Research Institute he had established at the Institute of Design in 1949 (at USC it was renamed the Institute of Building Research) (fig. 5).[14] Hurst eventually reconfigured the architecture program into a four-year undergraduate and two-year graduate degree. Following the Bauhaus model, he developed an interdisciplinary undergraduate curriculum that included architectural and landscape design, urban planning, industrial design, and building engineering. "Specialized graduate study" would then lead to more-focused professional goals, but with greater recognition of the "increasingly necessary integration" of all of these other services.[15] Acknowledging USC's long-standing emphasis on professional practice, Hurst believed that the architect had to "become again a builder in the sense that he controls the construction operation. The lingering separation between conception and execution, ie [*sic*], design and construction, is neither efficient for owner and architect nor necessary to ethical practice."[16]

FIGURE 5.
Konrad Wachsmann (German-born American, 1901–80).
Location Orientation Manipulator and other projects at the
University of Southern California, ca. 1971.
Berlin, Akademie der Künste, Baukunstarchiv.

FIGURE 6.
Heliodon at the University of Southern California, ca. 1968.
Photo by Glenn M. Christiansen, *Sunset* magazine.

Thom Mayne, who entered USC as an undergraduate student in 1963 and graduated five years later, remembers Hurst's early years as a period of radical change, during which a "series of persuasive, articulate technocrats" were brought into the school to replace many of the earlier Gallion faculty members: "The California school—Neutra, Schindler, Soriano, Ain, and Ellwood—was cleaned out except for in the fifth year. We were off doing abstract investigations: how architecture responded to dynamic forces—sun, wind, etc. Our studio was an empty space, no desks, a heliadon [*sic*] filling the whole room. For a year, we examined the properties of clay and the dynamic organization of architecture in response to the sun. The curriculum was outrageous; calculus, physics, and chemistry" (fig. 6).[17] In 1975, A. Quincy Jones, who, as a member of the "old guard" had taught fifth-year studio from 1952 to 1967, was appointed dean; his tenure was cut short due to his failing health three years later.[18] Under pressure from alumni and the architecture community in Los Angeles, he reinstated the earlier five-year bachelor of architecture degree curriculum but also retained the master of architecture degree.

Three years later, Robert Harris was selected to follow Jones. During his term as dean from 1980 to 1991, he continued to foster the school's earlier focus on planning and housing, but he developed an even stronger "urban emphasis with a focus on the design of humane and supportive urban places."[19] During the late 1980s, Harris served as cochair of the Downtown Los Angeles Strategic Plan Advisory Committee and also participated in numerous other civic and urban advisory groups. In 1985, Harris oversaw the creation of master's degree programs in both landscape architecture and building science. The following year, he used Harriet Freeman's bequest of Frank Lloyd Wright's Freeman Residence to the school—it would join the Gamble Residence, which had been gifted to the university two decades earlier—as a catalyst for new classes in historic preservation, the first of their kind in California.

UNIVERSITY OF CALIFORNIA, LOS ANGELES

Although the University of California began considering the establishment of a school of architecture and urban planning at its Los Angeles campus in the mid-1950s, it was not created until 1964, when George A. Dudley was hired to serve as dean. In the interim, the population of Los Angeles County increased by more than 1.5 million residents. To accommodate this growth, the region had embarked upon the kind of modernist reinvention of its landscape that Gallion and Eisner had envisioned in their 1950 book.[20] This effort was led by Pereira and Luckman's mid-1950s proposal to demolish the Bunker Hill neighborhood in downtown Los Angeles, a project that began in earnest in 1963, and Pereira's master plan for USC (1960–66), a scheme that, had it been fully realized, would have eradicated the West Adams neighborhood northward to the Santa Monica (10) Freeway.

Pereira further transformed himself from architect into regional planner with his 1963 proposal to turn a vast tract of the Irvine Ranch in Orange County into a new campus for the University of California. It would be adjacent to a planned residential and commercial complex, which, predicted Pereira, would by 1980 have "about 300,000 people living and working" in it.[21] Architects Welton Becket and Victor Gruen, among others, were developing Corbusian-scaled plans for Century City, Marina del Rey, Laguna Niguel, and the Century Boulevard commercial corridor adjacent to the Los Angeles Airport.[22] To facilitate access to these developments and the expanding suburbs, some 250 miles of freeway were constructed between 1955 and 1965. All of this contributed to what was widely acknowledged as an escalating air-quality crisis. As Richard Lillard noted in 1966, for many people, "Eden [had] become the world's biggest concrete and asphalt desert."[23] In 1965, in the midst of this "heroic" planning activity, the South Los Angeles neighborhood of Watts went up in flames, as an angry and disenfranchised African American population took out its frustration on its own neglected portion of the "City of Angels."

It was in reaction to this radically shifting landscape that Dudley began to formulate the curriculum for UCLA's School of Architecture and Urban Planning (SAUP); its first classes in planning and urban design were offered in 1966. A year later, he resigned, and Harvey S. Perloff was appointed to replace him as dean, a position he would hold until his death in 1983. Perloff was a specialist in economic policy planning. He had taught at the University of Chicago from 1947 until 1955, when he left for Washington, D.C., to direct Resources for the Future, Inc., a foundation and think tank concerned with the environment and urban policy.[24] Perloff, who was trained in urban policy (in contrast to the architecturally educated Gallion and Pereira), believed strongly in the application of social and behavioral sciences to the planning process. For him, that meant that the Bunker Hill urban renewal project had to be viewed as more than a "self-contained" utopian design of the type espoused by Le Corbusier and other modernists; it had to fit within the wider "context of its impact on downtown and the city."[25]

The curriculum at UCLA was developed to prepare students "to perform professional services in urban design," a discipline that was intended to bridge "the normal concerns of the architect and urban planner" and was "based on the conviction" that urban design was "closely linked to a number of interrelated disciplines." Sociology, economics, political science, engineering, law, and business were all included in the curriculum in order to permit the "dynamic interaction of [their] contrasting approaches" to the study of the urban environment.[26] This interdisciplinary pedagogy and its focus on professional practice closely paralleled a series of recommendations that Robert Geddes and Bernard Spring had published in the 1967 report *A Study of Education for Environmental Design.*[27]

To implement his vision, Perloff gathered together a diverse and progressive faculty that included urban planning experts John Friedman, Peter Marcuse, William J. Mitchell, and Edward Soja and psychologists Marvin Adelson and George Rand. They were joined by members of Archigram, a futurist avant-garde architectural group that had formed at the Architectural Association in London during the early 1960s.[28] Archigram's interest in high-tech modular structures, clip-on pods, space capsules, and mass-consumer (pop) imagery had naturally drawn them to Los Angeles, then a center of the aerospace and popular culture industries and a place the group believed to be the "city of the future as a dynamic machine."[29]

Not surprisingly, the urban design curriculum at UCLA during its early years reflected Archigram's fascination with technology and the "instant" or "plug-in" city. According to John Mutlow, who was a member of the second class (1969) in the architecture and urban design program and would go on to teach at USC, graduate studies at UCLA concentrated on "scenarios of the future" and included a close relationship with the aerospace industry and Southern California think tanks such as Rand Corporation and Systems Development Corporation, a spin-off of Rand that created early computer technology for the United States military.[30] The futuristic bent of the work produced during this period is evident in the 1969 student publication *Scenario 2: An Eye on the Future,* for which Archigram member Ron Herron acted as editorial adviser (fig. 7).

FIGURE 7.
John V. Mutlow (English-born American).
Ocean Environment collage.
From John Mutlow, Ian Robertson, and Woodie Tescher, eds., *Scenario 2: An Eye on the Future* (Los Angeles: Urban Design Program, School of Architecture & Urban Planning, University of California, Los Angeles, 1969), n.p.

Archigram's presence at UCLA and then at Cal Poly Pomona, USC, and SCI-Arc during subsequent decades would leave an indelible impression on the city's architectural culture. Although still an undergraduate at USC, Thom Mayne was introduced to the group's work through UCLA. In 1972, he formed Morphosis with Michael Brickler, Livio Santini, and Jim Stafford; according to Mayne, Morphosis was "a complete take-off on Archigram."[31]

In 1970, Thomas (Tim) R. Vreeland Jr. came from the University of New Mexico to UCLA to direct a revision of the urban design program, now titled the Department of Architecture and Urban Design. As before, its curriculum was intended to reflect "the University's concern with the escalating problems of the changing urban environment," but with a stronger emphasis on architectural design. It was divided into six integrated areas of study: design method; environmental technology; environment and behavior; architectural and urban analysis; environmental management; and theory, history, criticism. As the program evolved over the next decade, it recruited, among others, Craig Hodgetts, Charles Jencks, and, briefly, Denise Scott Brown, as well as historians Dolores Hayden and Thomas S. Hines—an illustrious faculty that would eventually be joined in various capacities by Charles Gwathmey, Franklin Israel, Barton Myers, and Cesar Pelli. Reflecting the growing idealism of the late 1960s and early 1970s, students were to participate in community-based activities in order to "evolve community serving professions: 'learning to do good competently' should start at the earliest possible moment."[32]

To help implement this goal, Perloff and Mitchell created the Urban Innovations Group (UIG) in 1971. UIG was organized as a nonprofit design laboratory that was intended to augment classroom and studio work with public service projects in urban design. Working hand in hand with the faculty, students were to be exposed to the design, development, and construction supervision encountered in real-world projects.[33] In 1974, Perloff and Mitchell recruited Charles Moore to raise the profile of UIG and further invigorate the young architecture and urban design program, over which he would be named director four years later. Most significantly, perhaps, Moore's evolving postmodern concept of urban "place-making" clearly repudiated the earlier "utopian" modernism of educators such as Gallion and Pereira.

Moore's disdain for this approach to planning is more than evident in his frequent ruminations on public space, in particular his well-known 1965 essay, "You Have to Pay for the Public Life," in which he expresses his love for places such as Disneyland, and his Irvine Ranch lampoon in *The City Observed,* in which he and his coauthors expose their aversion to what they saw as the sterile forms and jargon of modernist planning theory. "Typical of its time," they observe, Pereira's plan for the Irvine Ranch "incorporated the most up-to-the-minute, state-of-the-art urban planning principles. Despite this, it was not wholly vapid in execution."[34] There were residential enclaves, "site-specific within the parameters of the greenscape and the infrastructure of the landscaped, enviromorphic vehicular connectors (streets); industrial parks were systematized sequentially along interurban connectors (freeways) to contain any hyperpenetrable network edge conditions, to interface with the matrix of existing transportation corridors, and not to impact the exurban configurations."[35]

As represented by their widely celebrated Piazza d'Italia in New Orleans (1975–78) and their 1981 design for the Beverly Hills Civic Center, Moore and UIG attempted to present antidotes to the megaplans of the previous decades (fig. 8). While Moore himself would leave for the University of Texas in 1985, UIG continued to operate until 1993. In addition to his impact at UCLA, he left behind the legacy of Moore, Ruble, Yudell, a partnership he formed in 1977 with John Ruble, a former student of his at UCLA, and Buzz Yudell, who had been associated with Moore earlier in Connecticut and had come to Los Angeles to work with UIG and teach at UCLA.[36]

Following Perloff's untimely death, Richard Weinstein became dean of the Graduate School of Architecture in 1985. Previous to this appointment, he had served as director of planning and development for Lower Manhattan in New York City. In 1986, Weinstein established the Harvey S. Perloff Chair at UCLA, and

FIGURE 8.
Charles Willard Moore (American, 1925–93) with Urban Innovations Group (University of California, Los Angeles, 1971–).
Watercolor rendering of the Beverly Hills Civic Center renovation (1981–90), ca. 1980s.
Austin, Charles Moore Foundation.

two years later, he oversaw the founding of the Ralph and Goldy Lewis Center for Regional Policy Studies.[37] Also during this period, Weinstein, working with William Mitchell—an early pioneer in computer-aided design (CAD) who had been on the faculty since the inception of the program—led UCLA early on to the forefront in this area of inquiry with the establishment of a new state-of-the-art computing facility.[38] Weinstein also began to hire new faculty, such as Dana Cuff and Sylvia Lavin, who would dramatically alter the program during the 1990s and early twenty-first century.

CALIFORNIA STATE POLYTECHNIC UNIVERSITY AT POMONA

It was also during the late 1960s that California State Polytechnic University at Pomona (Cal Poly Pomona) began to develop its own plans for a school of environmental design, which they founded in 1970, the same year that Vreeland arrived at UCLA. Ray Kappe was named chairman of the new Architecture Department. Working with Bernard Zimmerman, Kappe established an undergraduate curriculum—because he believed that "architects should understand the land and the environment better"—that combined landscape planning and architecture.[39] Early faculty included Kappe and Zimmerman, as well as recent USC graduates Thom Mayne and Jim Stafford.

During its early years, the program grew rapidly, from some 50 to some 350 students, while moving in January 1971, along with the landscape and urban planning programs, into a new building designed by Carl Maston. Kappe's tenure at Cal Poly only lasted until April 1972, however, when he was dismissed after clashing with William Dale, the dean of the School of Environmental Design, a decision that created considerable controversy among the students and faculty. James Clark, the former chair of the Architecture Department at Pennsylvania State University, replaced Kappe and was joined by Zimmerman and Richard Chylinski (who both stayed at Cal Poly after Kappe's departure), as well as Anthony Lumsden and Marvin Malecha. They developed a curriculum with first- and second-year courses in the humanities and sciences, including the arts, design, graphic communications, and engineering concepts. These classes were followed during the students' subsequent years with a stronger emphasis on design studio, architectural history and theory, and building technology.[40] Robert Mittelstadt and then Malecha followed Clark as chairs of the program, and in 1986, William Adams was named to the position. Additional Cal Poly faculty during the 1980s included Michael Folonis, as well as Craig Ellwood and Raphael Soriano, both of whom had participated in the Case Study Program during the 1950s.[41]

SOUTHERN CALIFORNIA INSTITUTE OF ARCHITECTURE

In response to Kappe's abrupt dismissal from Pomona in 1972, some fifty students and a handful of Cal Poly faculty, including Mayne, Stafford, and Glen Small, followed him to Santa Monica, where they established undergraduate and master of architecture programs in an abandoned industrial building. Much of the interior of what Reyner Banham liked to call "the Big Shed" was gutted to create a large two-story central space (the "main space" as it also came to be known; see fig. 1). This would be used for studios and lectures, and for many years, it was dominated by constantly evolving, Archigram-like scaffolding made of metal pipes and wood panels that functioned as informal gallery space, lecture seating, and crash pad for charrette-weary students.

Other "left-over" spaces functioned as classrooms, offices, and a makeshift library. For many years, a small hamburger joint next door served as school cafeteria and coffee shop. As the institution grew, it expanded into surrounding and nearby buildings and spaces.

Originally called the "New School" by its students, but officially named the Southern California Institute of Architecture (SCI-Arc) by Kappe, this small academy was intended to showcase a radical experiment in architectural education.[42] He and his renegade faculty envisioned "an autonomous self-governing institution based upon the premise that the 200 students and 25 faculty members work together to determine its academic direction."[43] As the 1976 catalog states, this was to embody an "in-process, non-static, responsive educational philosophy with the structured backbone of course material necessary for participation in the profession of architecture."[44] According to Kappe, the school wanted "to encourage invention, exploration, and criticism so that students would create better projects....During the first few years, the school explored social and behavioral aspects of architecture and architectural education."[45]

SCI-Arc also attempted to encourage a "self-motivated" and "open" curriculum, with no prerequisites for admission, tests, grades, or required papers. "The traditional system of letter grades and subsequent grade point averages [were] replaced by the portfolio concept, whereby the student accumulate[d] detailed evaluations and samples of his or her representative work to supplement the transcript of courses completed."[46] With the exception of studios, which more than ever formed the primary focus of student work, much of the "usual curriculum" was initially jettisoned, so, as Kappe observes, he could "see what it would be like if we started wide open."[47]

Taking its place in Los Angeles beside organizations like Beyond Baroque (formed in 1968), California Institute of the Arts (CalArts; 1979) and Womanhouse (1972), this experiment in "open" education was very much a part of SCI-Arc's counterculture era.[48] "With the exception of about 5 percent of the students who were really self-directed," Kappe would later note, "it didn't work....Most of them drifted or wallowed and they began to ask for more structure. They wanted a sense of freedom rather than actual freedom."[49] As a result, a more traditional curriculum began to emerge by the end of the 1970s. Granted initial accreditation in 1976 and full accreditation by the National Architectural Accreditation Board four years later, the school did continue to encourage—through its often-raucous all-school meetings—student participation in administrative decisions and curriculum development.

Design studios, many of which met in the main space, continued to take center stage and were run by their instructors as intense, almost autonomous yet interrelated ateliers that revolved around a rich interchange of ideas between students and faculty. During these early years, recalls Mayne, "we lived there noon to midnight, six, sometimes seven days a week."[50] It was in this "tacky factory shed," observes Peter Cook of Archigram, that "despite physical appearances" Mayne and everyone else indulged "in that game of cajoling, criticism and throwaway dismissal that is the inheritance from the Ecole des Beaux-Arts." So intense was the debate that one had "to listen hard to tell which [was] the Master or Pupil."[51] As "in the big single-volume [design by Mies at IIT] everybody's business was everybody else's business—or could be. The accumulated wisdom and experience of each year above was handily available to each year below, to be tapped by observation, discussion or intellectual osmosis."[52]

By the mid-1980s, under the sway of Mayne and Eric Owen Moss, the pedagogy at SCI-Arc moved away from urban and ecological concerns back toward an interest in "pure" architectural design—what SCI-Arc faculty and students would continually refer to as "making architecture." Architecture sociologist Robert Gutman considered the national shift in architectural pedagogy at the time to the rise of postmodernism, citing Robert Venturi's 1966 manifesto in *Complexity and Contradiction in Architecture,* as an example of this. As Venturi declared:

> I make no special attempt to relate architecture to other things. I have not tried to "improve the connection between science and technology on the one hand, and the humanities and the social sciences on the other and make of architecture a more human social art." I try to talk about architecture rather than around it.... The architect's ever diminishing power and his growing ineffectualness in shaping the whole environment can perhaps be reversed, ironically, by narrowing his concerns and concentrating on his own job.[53]

Around this same time, Kappe began to tire of both the often-contentious atmosphere at SCI-Arc and the direction in which the faculty was moving.

> I thought I had a group that could become interested in the things I cared about: urban issues, number one; technology, of course; and environmental response concerns. And that worked great for about eight years until postmodernism started to dominate architecture. Some of our faculty, Eric Moss and Thom Mayne, jumped ship, and then it became a battle because I wasn't willing to go that way. By the late '80s, I felt I wasn't going to win the fight and didn't want to head a school that I no longer believed in, so I stepped down as director. I continued to teach there and at USC, which was more interested in urban issues than SCI-Arc.[54]

In 1987, Michael Rotondi, who had been a member of the school's original class and had been teaching at SCI-Arc since 1975, took Kappe's place as director of the school and began to make further changes. Rotondi fired many of the original faculty, including Glen Small, who had been the strongest voice for social and environmentally related design, and replaced them with architects whose philosophy was closer to that of Mayne and Moss.[55]

In response to these changes, the earlier discontent and frustration that had, in part, discouraged Kappe seemed to boil over with student protests and strikes and almost ruthless faculty infighting. Rotondi eventually managed to quell much of this mutiny and worked hard to place the institution on a more academic footing. He appointed Robert Mangurian as director of the graduate program and engaged an impressive faculty that included Tom Buresh, Neil Denari, Perry Kulper, Heather Kurze, Norman Millar, Michele Saee, and Gregory Walsh. These instructors—and an impressive and constantly shifting roster of national and international designers such as Merril Elam, Wolf Prix, and Peter Zumthor—exploited this still freewheeling laboratory as both testing ground for their ideas and showcase for their work.

Concurrently, Margaret Crawford, head of the history and theory program, secured a National Endowment for the Humanities grant to develop a humanities curriculum appropriate to a stand-alone architectural academy. She also assembled a history-and-theory faculty that, for a period during the late 1980s, was as strong as that of the area's more established universities; this included Aaron Betsky, Mike Davis, John Kaliski, and Kathryn Smith.[56] Together they formed a robust counterbalance to the often overwhelmingly studiocentric culture of the school. By the late 1980s, SCI-Arc had become a kind of open living room for the city's architectural community; visitors from around the city—and the world—attended the lecture series, crits, and elaborate rites of passage, such as the hugely theatrical final reviews that were introduced by Mangurian.

Betsky has suggested that it may have been the ramshackle and open nature of the school's buildings—"no more than sheds with large doors that opened up to the parking lot where a lot of building and fabricating got done, with skylights and leaks"—almost as much as its faculty that shaped the open and experimental nature of student work during SCI-Arc's early years. As an institution, it

> fostered a notion of architecture as provisional set decoration. What was designed there and sometimes built was as often as not sculptural insertion rather than an object, an act of reuse rather than monument-making. SCI-Arc was an open, contentious place, and the architecture that came out of it had that quality as well. It was not all good, nor was it all very sensible, but the excitement of mining this seemingly endless landscape for new forms of coherence, community, and collage coalescence animated all of us through the 1980s and well into the 1990s.[57]

While all of these Los Angeles architecture schools differed in significant ways, the students, graduates, and faculty during the last three decades of the twentieth century were in a constant state of flux, attending each other's lecture series and final reviews, serving as guest jurors at "rival" institutions, and moving from one program as a student or instructor to another one across town. It is this heterogeneity—especially in the design studios—that helped to form these players, but it was the homogenization of this process that helped to refine what Charles Jencks in 1984 first attempted to identify as a Los Angeles school of design.[58] If, indeed, it is possible to identify such a cohesive phenomenon, it surely owes its existence to the constant and lively interchange of ideas and pedagogies running through Los Angeles's disparate, yet interrelated, schools of design—schools that continue to enrich and enliven the architectural scene in Southern California and the rest of the world.

NOTES

1   Because Woodbury did not graduate its first class until the very end of this period of study, it is not included in this essay. For its formation, see John Sanchez-Chew, "Grading the Schools: Woodbury University," *LA Architect* (September 1985): 6.

2   Dana Cuff, *Architecture: The Story of Practice* (Cambridge, Mass.: MIT Press, 1992), 122.

3   Reyner Banham, "A Black Box: The Secret Profession of Architecture," in idem et al., *A Critic Writes: Essays by Reyner Banham* (Berkeley: University of California Press, 1996), 294–95; and also Reyner Banham, "The Master of Humane Architecture," in Ludwig Mies van der Rohe et al., *Mies van der Rohe: Architect as Educator* (Chicago: Illinois Institute of Technology, 1986), 14–15.

4   Deborah Howell-Ardila, "'Writing Our Own Program': The USC Experiment in Modern Architectural Pedagogy, 1930 to 1960" (MA thesis, University of Southern California, 2010).

5   Howell-Ardila, "'Writing Our Own Program,'" 45.

6   "S.C. Course in Architecture Altered to Fit Defense Needs, Students Will Learn to Design Bomb Shelters, Airports, Hospitals, and Other War Projects," *Los Angeles Times,* 7 September 1941, E3, ProQuest Historical, 4183838591.

7   Howell-Ardila, "'Writing Our Own Program,'" 151–52.

8   For a brief history of this period, see "The School," University of Southern California, School of Architecture, http://arch.usc.edu /Home/TheSchool.

9   Esther McCoy, "*Arts and Architecture* Case Study Houses," *Perspecta: The Yale Architectural Journal* 15 (1975): 72. See also Arthur B. Gallion, "Tomorrow's Architect," *Los Angeles Times,* 14 September 1952, H14, ProQuest Historical, 424546161; Calvin Straub, "Plan: A Flexible House for Family Growth," *Los Angeles Times,* 14 September 1952, H18, ProQuest Historical, 424546191; Garrett Eckbo, "A House with Five Patios," *Los Angeles Times,* 14 September 1952, H16, ProQuest Historical, 424546181; and Howell-Ardila, "'Writing Our Own Program,'" 125–28.

10 James Steele and David Jenkins, *Pierre Koenig* (London: Phaidon, 1998), 9–11, 20–23.

11 Howell-Ardila, "'Writing Our Own Program,'" 108, 113; and Arthur B. Gallion and Simon Eisner, *The Urban Pattern: City Planning and Design* (Princeton, N.J.: Van Nostrand, 1950).

12 Comment by Simon Eisner in George Beal, "The Place of Planning in the Architectural Curriculum," *Journal of Architectural Education* 12 (1956): 21.

13 Philip J. Ethington, "Ghost Neighborhoods: Space, Time, and Alienation in Los Angeles," in Charles G. Salas and Michael S. Roth, eds., *Looking for Los Angeles: Architecture, Film, Photography, and the Urban Landscape* (Los Angeles: Getty Research Institute, 2001), 54n22.

14 "Departments at USC to Merge," *Los Angeles Times,* 30 September 1962, I19, ProQuest Historical, 484493372. Hurst had been a student of Taylor's in the Department of Architecture at the Georgia School (now Institute) of Technology before the war. See Jeffrey Plank, *Crombie Taylor: Modern Architecture, Building Restoration, and the Rediscovery of Louis Sullivan* (Richmond, Calif.: William Stout, 2009), 17, 64–74, 108–9, 293n176.

15 Sam T. Hurst, "Environment and Education: Past, Present, Future," *Journal of Architectural Education* 19, no. 3 (1964): 37.

16 Hurst, "Environment and Education," 37; and Robert Harris, personal communication, 15 October 2011.

17 Jeffrey Kipnis and Todd Gannon, "A Conversation with Thom Mayne," in Thomas Blurock, *Morphosis: Diamond Ranch High School, Diamond Bar, California* (New York: Monacelli, 2001), 9.

18 Alan Maltun, "A. Quincy Jones, Architect, Dies," *Los Angeles Times,* 4 August 1979, B1, ProQuest Historical, 652105742; and Robert Harris, personal communication, 15 October 2011.

19 Kevin O'Shea, "School Expands," *L.A. Architect* (November 1985): 4; and Robert Harris, personal communication, 15 October 2011.

20 See, for example, Gallion and Eisner, *The Urban Pattern,* 313–22, 372–418.

21 "The Land: The Man with the Plan," *Time Magazine,* 6 September 1963, 68, http://www.time.com/time/magazine/article /0,9171,870487-1,00.html; and James Steele, *William Pereira* (Los Angeles: Architectural Guild, 2003), 108–39.

22 "The Land," 71–72; and Steele, *William Pereira,* 90–107, 108–39.

23 Richard Lillard, *Eden in Jeopardy: The Southern California Experience* (New York: Alfred A. Knopf, 1966), 204, 230–45; and David L. Brodsly, *L.A. Freeway: An Appreciative Essay* (Berkeley: University of California Press, 1981), 126–27.

24 Theresa Walker, "Harvey Perloff, Architectural Educator, Dies," *Los Angeles Times,* 31 July 1983, B1, ProQuest Historical, 670500928.

25 Ray Herbert, "Los Angeles—Testing Ground for the Cities of Tomorrow?," *Los Angeles Times,* 5 May 1968, B1.

26 University of California, Los Angeles, *General Catalogue* 9, no. 10 (1969–70): 92–93.

27 Robert Gutman, "Educating Architects: Pedagogy and the Pendulum," in Nathan Glazer and Mark Lilla, eds., *The Public Face of Architecture: Civic Culture and Public Spaces* (New York: Free Press, 1987), 453, 466; and Robert Geddes and Bernard Spring, *A Study of Education for Environmental Design* (Princeton, N.J.: Princeton University Press, 1967), 9–10. Harvard and the University of Pennsylvania had embraced a similar pedagogy in the early 1950s with the establishment of programs in urban design and civic design; the intention was to integrate architectural design with problems associated with housing and urban policy. Gutman estimates that by the late 1970s there were urban design programs at as many as seventy American universities.

28 See University of California, Los Angeles, *General Catalogue* 7, no. 10 (1967–68): 107; and University of California, Los Angeles, *General Catalogue* 9, no. 10 (1969–70): 92–93.

29   William J. R. Curtis, *Modern Architecture since 1900,* 3rd ed. (London: Phaidon, 1996), 539.

30   John V. Mutlow, "Architecture in LA Today," in Derek Walker, ed., *AD/USC Look at LA: Architectural Design Portfolio* (London: Architectural Design, 1981), 96; John Mutlow, Ian Robertson, Woodie Tescher, eds., *Scenario 2: An Eye on the Future* (Los Angeles: Urban Design Program, School of Architecture and Urban Planning, University of California, 1969); and John V. Mutlow, personal communication, 14 October 2011.

31   Kipnis and Gannon, "A Conversation with Thom Mayne," 10; and for Archigram, Curtis, *Modern Architecture,* 538–39.

32   University of California, Los Angeles, *General Catalogue* 11, no. 11 (1971–72): 98; and "Architecture/Urban Design, UCLA," *LA Architect* (January 1980): n.p.

33   Kevin P. Keim, *An Architectural Life: Memoirs and Memories of Charles W. Moore* (Boston: Little, Brown, 1996), 182–86.

34   Charles Moore, Peter Becker, and Regula Campbell, *The City Observed, Los Angeles: A Guide to Its Architecture and Landscapes* (New York: Vintage, 1984), 138.

35   Charles Moore, "You Have to Pay for the Public Life," *Perspecta 9/10: The Yale Architectural Journal* 9/10 (1965): 57–97.

36   Keim, *An Architectural Life,* 182–91, 208–19; and "40 Years of Urban Planning at UCLA," Department of Urban Planning, UCLA School of Public Affairs, http://www.sppsr.ucla.edu/dept.cfm?d=up&s=home&f=history.cfm.

37   "History," UCLA Department of Architecture and Urban Design, http://www.aud.ucla.edu/welcome/history.html.

38   "Schools: UCLA," *LA Architect* (November 1985): 4–5.

39   Robert Ivy, "An Unsung Modernist Master: Ray Kappe," *Architectural Record*, ed. Andrea Oppenheimer Dean (2009): http://archrecord.construction.com/features/0908Kappe/0908Kappe.asp.

40   "Cal Poly Pomona School of Architecture," *LA Architect* (September 1977): n.p.

41   William Trombley, "Ex-Cal Poly Pomona Architect Director Will Open New School," *Los Angeles Times,* 14 September 1972, C1; and "Cal Poly U Names Architecture Dept. Chairman," *Los Angeles Times,* 9 October 1977, SG3.

42   The following is based upon an interview of Ray and Shelly Kappe by Ken Breisch, 27 October 2011; Shelly Kappe, "Ray Kappe and SCI-Arc," typescript, 27 October 2011; Kevin McMahon, personal communication, 10 October 2011; and Joan Hacker, ed., "The LA 12 Revisited: Interview with Bernard Zimmerman; Mark Dillon, Interviewer," *Volume 5* (n.d.): 4, http://www.volume5.com/bz/architect_bernard_zimmerman_in.html.

43   Southern California Institute of Architecture, *SCI-Arc Catalogue* (Los Angeles: SCI-Arc, 1976), n.p. (this quote appears on the page after the cover).

44   Southern California Institute of Architecture, *SCI-Arc Catalogue,* n.p.

45   Ivy, "An Unsung Modernist Master."

46   Southern California Institute of Architecture, *SCI-Arc Catalogue,* 2.

47   Ivy, "An Unsung Modernist Master."

48   According to Bernard Zimmerman, they "were thinking of places like Reed College and Black Mountain, the kind of things they did," when SCI-Arc's educational philosophy was being formulated. Hacker, "Interview with Bernard Zimmerman," 4; and Kevin McMahon personal communication, 10 October 2011.

49   Stacey Peck, "Home Q&A: 'Shelly and Ray Kappe,'" *Los Angeles Times,* 27 April 1980, Q50; and Kevin McMahon, personal communication, 10 October 2011.

50   Kipnis and Gannon, "A Conversation with Thom Mayne," 10; and Michael Folonis, personal communication, 19 October 2011.

51   Peter Cook, "City of Dreams," in Barbara Goldstein and Peter Cook, *Los Angeles Now* (London: Architectural Association, 1983), 4–5.

52   Banham, "The Master of Humane Architecture," 14. Banham is here describing the creative atmosphere in Crown Hall at IIT, but it could just as easily apply to SCI-Arc during this time.

53   Gutman ("Educating Architects," 454), quoting Robert Venturi, *Complexity and Contradiction in Architecture* (New York: Museum of Modern Art, 1966), 14. Venturi is responding to a statement by Robert L. Geddes, which he includes in his quote. For the source of this, see *The Philadelphia Evening Bulletin,* 2 February 1965, 40.

54   Ivy, "An Unsung Modernist Master."

55   Orhan Ayyüce, "Glen Small Interview," *Archinect,* 3 April 2006, http://archinect.com/features/article/36494/glen-small-interview.

56   I was also a member of this group. See Michael Rotondi, *From the Edge: Southern California Institute of Architecture Student Work* (Santa Monica, Calif.: Southern California Institute of Architecture, 1991), n.p.

57   Aaron Betsky, "SCI-Arc: Memories of an Open Architecture," *Architect: The Magazine of the American Institute of Architects,* 4 July 2002, http://www.architectmagazine.com/blogs/postdetails.aspx?BlogId=beyondbuildingsblog&postId=89408.

58   See the review of the Museum of Modern Art exhibition *Los Angeles Now* (29 April–21 May 1988): Charles Jencks, "LA Style/LA School," *AA Files* 5 (1984): 90. See also Charles Jencks, *Heteropolis: Los Angeles, the Riots, and the Strange Beauty of Hetero-Architecture* (London: Academy, 1993).

ACROSS THE PACIFIC
LOS ANGELES AS A CATALYST
FOR ARCHITECTURAL CHANGE IN EAST ASIA

Jeffrey W. Cody

IN 1974, A JOURNALIST WRITING FOR A TRADE JOURNAL about the "changing face of Asian architecture" lamented how "the concrete jungles of the West are devouring the tropical jungles of the East." As evidence, the writer observed how "throughout Asia the trend is for highrise buildings. The traditional Oriental sky-line of the apparently mysterious East is going (or has gone) West. It is being eroded and demystified by those scrutable rectangular boxes of machine-age architecture."[1] Although this journalist—with a penchant for hackneyed clichés—did not single out Los Angeles for being one of those "skyscraper cities" changing Asia's "national and community images, life-styles and social behaviour patterns," the architectural allure of Los Angeles by the mid-1970s was compelling for many Asian architects, urban designers, city planners, and building contractors who were at the vanguard of architectural change throughout the East Asia region.

Two key questions help to anchor a consideration of Southern California's architectural influence across the Pacific in the tumultuous half-century that began in 1940, a year before Japan's attack on Pearl Harbor, and ended in 1990, the year after the calamitous events in Beijing's Tiananmen Square. First, what was it about Los Angeles and its evolving architectural dynamics that was so captivating to certain Asians involved with architecture, property development, and urban design? Second, who or what were the catalysts that ushered in the kinds of changes that this journalist enumerated (as well as many others that he did not name)? In answering these two questions, this essay will highlight a few examples of Southern California's influence in the Pacific Rim and suggest that Asian influences were also significant in Southern California during this time period, just as they had been earlier in the century, when architects such as Charles and Henry Greene, Antonin Raymond, and Frank Lloyd Wright saw their practices transformed by their varying affinities for Japanese architecture, in particular.

Given that this essay is an introductory attempt to understand how, why, and where Los Angeles's architectural and planning innovations had an impact in East Asia, another crucial question follows from the two principal ones: what other kinds of research paths might scholars follow as they try to unravel the knots

FIGURE 1.
Maekawa Kunio (Japanese, 1905–86).
Prou House (completed 1952), Tokyo, n.d.
From Jonathan Reynolds, *Maekawa Kunio and the Emergence of Japanese Modernist Architecture* (Berkeley: University of California Press, 2001), 198.

of influence and inspiration related to Los Angeles's architectural impact throughout the Pacific Rim between 1940 and 1990? As I answer these three questions in this essay, I will broach the vast topic of how Los Angeles's evolving architecture and urbanism influenced Asian architects and designers by placing the exportation of Los Angeles architectural influence within a broader temporal and conceptual framework.[2]

Four aspects of architectural and planning shifts seen in Southern California practice reverberated within certain East Asian urban contexts after World War II, but (as I will discuss further below) there was remarkable variation in the extent to which these reverberations from Los Angeles impacted change abroad. Two of these aspects were related primarily to residential design: spatial fluidity between interiors and exteriors and tendencies to employ modularized and/or standardized building components. The other two aspects of Los Angeles's transformation after World War II that resonated with certain East Asians stemmed from Los Angeles's love affair with the automobile: the creation of retail shopping areas in proximity to residential areas and the proliferation of intraurban highway systems and their spatial implications.

In terms of residential design, the work of the Japanese architect Maekawa Kunio (1905–86) is particularly illuminating because it reflects a bivalent connection to Southern California residential commissions in the late 1940s and early 1950s. Initially, Maekawa was led to Los Angeles via the pivotal work of Richard Neutra, who gave a series of lectures in Japan in 1930, one of which captured Maekawa's keen interest.[3] Twenty-five years old at the time, Maekawa had graduated from the University of Tokyo (Tokyo Daigaku, or Todai) in 1928 and then had worked with Le Corbusier's office in Paris until 1930. When he heard Neutra discuss his work in the context of the modern movement barely two months after Maekawa had returned to Japan, Maekawa was enthralled because it exemplified "the kind of international bridge-building that would be necessary if modern architecture was to achieve its potential."[4] Although no transcript of his talk survives, Neutra would have almost certainly discussed his recently completed Lovell Health House (1927–29) in Los Angeles, where he settled after working briefly with Wright (1924) and with Rudolph Schindler (1925–27). Therefore, one of the vectors connecting Maekawa to Los Angeles came through his ardent admiration for Neutra.

The second, even more tangible way that Maekawa "built a bridge" between his own work and Los Angeles was through some of his residential designs in the early 1950s, most notably his Prou Residence (1952), in Tokyo (fig. 1).[5] Commissioned by Leon Prou, the director of the Japanese office of Agence France-Presse, Maekawa's design employed certain hallmarks of Japanese vernacular design (e.g., rain shutters, or *amado,* and sliding doors, or *shoji*) and had some affinities with the residential work of California architects Charles Warren Callister (1917–2008), Harwell Hamilton Harris (1903–90), Jack Hillmer (1918–2007), and William Wurster (1895–1973).

Maekawa was probably not concerned that Callister, Hillmer, and Wurster were working primarily in the San Francisco Bay Area instead of in Southern California. Instead, he was more likely impressed with the ways that all these architects had found ways to meld modernism with their sensitivity to regional, vernacular traditions and with how some of these designers—particularly Harris—had begun to use Japanese-derived elements in the context of their work. Maekawa was possibly introduced to their designs through the Japanese architectural journal *Shinkenchiku* (New architecture), which began to feature some California

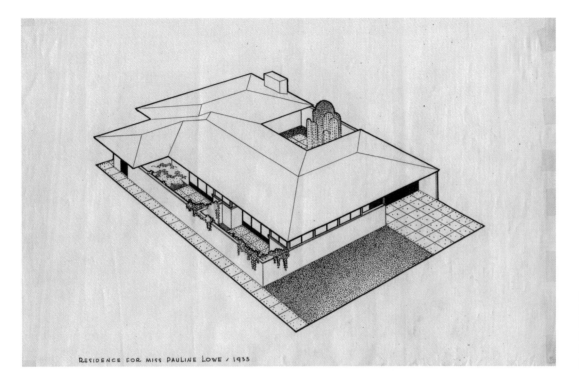

RESIDENCE FOR MISS PAULINE LOWE / 1933

FIGURE 2.
Harwell Hamilton Harris (American, 1903–90).
Lowe Residence (1933–34), Altadena, 1933.
Ink on tracing cloth, 20.3 × 31.8 cm (8 × 12½ in.).
Austin, University of Texas Libraries,
Alexander Architectural Archive.

designs as early as 1950.[6] In 1933, Harwell Hamilton Harris, who had worked with Neutra on the Lovell Health House, designed a house in Altadena for Pauline Lowe that demonstrated rustic simplicity and a Japanese-inspired use of space (e.g., sliding doors, translucent screens, and a merging of interior with exterior) (fig. 2).[7]

All four of the California architects mentioned above

> represented a significant regionalist stream within the modernist movement....Some [had] studied Japanese vernacular design, and many admired Japanese wood craftsmanship. They sought to emulate the direct expression of structure in pre-modern Japanese wood-frame construction and believed that the flowing interior plans and the openness between interior and exterior in some Japanese residential design were especially appropriate in California's mild climate. Maekawa and the Californians were, in effect, dipping from the same well.[8]

One of the other design "elixirs" that all of these architects were taking from that "well" was the use of standardized, modular elements. In this regard, too, the contemporary work of many California architects in the post–World War II period hit a responsive chord with Japanese modernist architects such as Maekawa, who "understood that the similarities between Asian and modern had less to do with influence than confluence."[9] In other words, by the early 1950s, the global "bridge-building" of modern architecture—for example, Maekawa learning from Neutra, who had built his own metaphorical bridge from Europe to Los Angeles—was

FIGURE 3.

Claude Oakland and Associates (1963–ca. 1980s).

A Fairhills tract house developed by Eichler Homes, Inc.
(ca. 1963), Orange, 2005.
Photo by Jim Brown.

making it difficult to discern how a particular innovation in one location, such as Maekawa's Prou Residence, was having a clear influence over a commission in another geographic context.[10]

Two examples help illustrate the "influence-confluence" duality, which is connected to what the Japanese architect Kisho Kurokawa has called "interculturalism, in which cultures of various kinds, both East and West, would develop by means of a symbiotic relationship."[11] Eichler homes in California are the first example, and designs related to prefabrication in Malaysia are the second. Between 1950 and 1974, Joseph Eichler's company built approximately eleven thousand homes for middle-class clients primarily in the San Francisco Bay Area, as well as approximately six hundred homes nearer Los Angeles, in Thousand Oaks, Granada Hills, and Orange (fig. 3).[12] Employing modular elements and standardized construction practices, these homes incorporated many features found in traditional Japanese design: post and beams with nonload-bearing walls; a revealed structure with rhythmic patterns of woodwork, paneling, openings, and light; and a series of linked interior spaces.[13] Eichler homes reflect the convergence of modernist-inspired preferences for modular construction with Japanese-inspired features in California's temperate environment, where indoor-outdoor living and a fluidity of space appealed to a middle-class American clientele.

A key example from Malaysia related to interculturalism, confluence, influence, and the use of pre-fabricated, modular elements is Parliament House, designed, in part, by William Ivor Shipley and completed in 1963 (fig. 4). Sometime in the early 1960s, Shipley, a British architect who worked as state architect prior to Malaya's independence in 1957, had a fortuitous meeting in Penang with Konrad Wachsmann (1901–80), a German architect who had studied with Hans Poelzig in Potsdam.[14] After his formal training, Wachsmann worked for Christoph & Unmack, one of Europe's largest wood construction companies, where in 1925 he developed a prefabricated wood construction system that was used, among other cases, to erect a house for Albert Einstein in Caputh (near Potsdam), Germany. In 1941, with Einstein's help, Wachsmann immigrated to the United States, where, with Walter Gropius, he began a commercial partnership—the General Panel Corporation—which, after the end of World War II, began to use Wachsmann's design for a "wedge connector" to build prefabricated dwellings for clients on both the East and West Coasts.[15] In 1949, Wachsmann began teaching in Chicago; in 1964, he moved to Los Angeles, where he taught architecture for a decade at the University of Southern California, continuing to develop and espouse the use of standardized building systems.

FIGURE 4.
William Ivor Shipley (British, d. 2008).
Parliament House (1962–63), Kuala Lumpur, ca. 1963.
From Lai Chee Kien, *Building Merdeka: Independence Architecture in Kuala Lumpur, 1957–1966* (Kuala Lumpur: Galeri Petronas, 2007), 88.

In Malaysia, the British architect Shipley was heavily swayed by Wachsmann's ideas about modular wood construction. The new country of Malaysia (so named as of 1963) was about to embark on a major national construction program, and "standardization and modularization of materials, designs and building processes took place contemporaneously with the introduction of new building products and systems, as well as efforts to translate and install them locally and logically into the Malaysian environment."[16] Although it was not feasible to apply Wachsmann's component system to a countrywide school building campaign (because of a lack of capacity for producing and transporting the prefabricated elements), Shipley was able to incorporate Wachsmann's ideas into Parliament House.[17] In so doing, the design and construction "genes" conceived by Wachsmann in Germany and then carried with him to the United States (ultimately to Los Angeles) were inherited by Shipley in Malaysia, where they were embedded in an architectural symbol of Malaysia's independence.

FIGURE 5.
Advertisement by Pittsburgh Plate Glass Industries for PPG Solarban Insulating Glass.
From *Asian Building and Construction* (November 1974): opposite p. 62.

The examples cited above demonstrate more than a connecting architectural thread between Southeast Asia and Los Angeles; they also imply some of the complexities associated with defining influence, which is where Los Angeles's role in an increasingly globalizing world during the second half of the twentieth century is concerned. Three dimensions of those "complexities" merit further scrutiny. First, after 1945, larger US construction firms (including Fluor, in Los Angeles) began to expand internationally, which involved the marketing of American building materials and building types in Pacific Rim cities.[18] Some of this intensified marketing stemmed from the Bretton Woods agreements in 1944, which created institutions such as the International Monetary Fund and the World Bank, and some was related to how certain major US companies (such as Sears-Roebuck and Hilton Hotels) were using prototypical structures and materials associated with modernism in their operations abroad (fig. 5).[19]

However, beginning in the 1950s, a second dimension of the complications associated with assigning influence emerged: "depending upon where you look, attitudes in the Far East range[d] from 'why don't you come over?' to 'not much room here,' to 'no Americans need apply.'"[20] This situation was exacerbated by intense competition for architectural commissions in East Asia, where, because of colonialism, clients preferred to work with architects, engineers, and builders who were tethered—conceptually and/or otherwise—to cities such as London or Paris.[21]

Finally, the third dimension of complications involved the vibrant two-way streets of architectural influence/confluence linking several cities of the Pacific Rim—Tokyo connected to Los Angeles just as Kuala Lumpur, Singapore, and Hong Kong[22] connected to cities even more distant from Los Angeles, such as Sydney, where fascination with California architectural developments reached back to the nineteenth century.[23]

Southern California's experiments with the prefabrication of bungalows in the early twentieth century were particularly attractive to property developers and designers in southeastern Australia, where "the sheer number of publications about California houses, West Coast building materials and lifestyle choices that embraced outdoor living—all pouring into Australian newsagents, libraries and bookshops—made it inevitable that Australian architects and developers would discover this kind of bungalow style through printed sources and would adopt these forms from America with alacrity."[24] Although in some instances it becomes possible to follow the heredity of architectural "genes" (e.g., Wachsmann and Shipley, Maekawa and Neutra, or Los Angeles bungalow publications and Australian residential development), in many other cases, those architectural "genes" propagated without a clearly identifiable lineage.

Unfortunately, these complexities of historical attribution become even thornier when one considers the other two aspects of Los Angeles's transformation after World War II that resonated with certain East Asians, both of which are related to Los Angeles's citywide spatial accommodations for the automobile. In one of his recent essays about "architecture and the city," the noted Japanese architect Fumihiko Maki writes that "the 1950s were an exciting time to be part of the architectural world in the United States, particularly in places like New York and California. On a regional level, the practitioners active in a given city and the buildings that provoked discussion were clear indices of the vitality of local architectural schools."[25] Between 1952 and 1956, Maki lived

in four cities on the East Coast and in the Midwest: a suburb of Detroit, a suburb of Boston, New York and St. Louis. A two-year trip through Europe, Southeast Asia, and the Middle East from 1958 to 1960 was followed by a period lasting until 1965 in which I shuttled back and forth between St. Louis, Cambridge (Massachusetts), and Japan. Even after returning more or less permanently to Japan, I made frequent…visits to many North American cities, including several on the West Coast.[26]

Although Maki never lived for a long period in Los Angeles, he was attuned particularly to Los Angeles's accommodation of the automobile. "The freeways of Los Angeles are the ultimate expression of the self," Maki wrote, asserting that

there are three levels to the meaning of the "free" in freeways. The freeways are toll-free, permit freedom of movement, and liberate the self psychologically.…In America the car is seen more as a

FIGURE 6.
Freeway construction in Singapore, n.d.
From Bob Crew, "Changing Face of Asian Architecture,"
Asian Building and Construction (August 1974): 23.

flexible extension of the house. For an American, the house, the garage, the road, and the freeway are metaphorically a linked extension to his body. That is, the equal accessibility roads provide to each house creates an arrangement not unlike that of a 1000-armed Kannon: each arm is a house, and the torso is the main arterial road.... The amenity and tension produced by the contact and friction of self-centered domains form the urban territory distinctive to this country.... In 1978 I spent two months in Los Angeles and used the freeways extensively every day. Gradually, I, too came to see the freeway as a part of my body.[27]

In a larger urban sense, Southern California freeway "templates"—with sweeping cloverleaf exit/entrance ramps, for example—were being adopted more and more by Asian Pacific Rim cities during the latter decades of the twentieth century (fig. 6).[28]

Another result of Asian cities increasingly accommodating the automobile was the proliferation of American-style "convenience centers"—drive-in markets and mini-malls. As one Los Angeles journalist wrote, after 1973 (when many gas stations closed because of oil shortages), "the lack of design and generic bleakness [were] appropriated at tens of thousands of street corners, first in Los Angeles, then southern California, the US and, yes, the world."[29]

A complementary development to this trend, which could be seen in varying degrees throughout East Asia from the 1970s through the 1990s, was the growing number of franchises that originated in the United States but were progressively becoming "localized" in East Asia. McDonald's and 7-Eleven are two of the most popular examples.[30] Neither has corporate roots in Southern California, but both have benefited immeasurably from their symbiotic relationship with the automobile.

Although the convenience center has become a common feature of many East Asian cities, this does not necessarily suggest that so-called Americanization should "be seen as an overly determining force or as merely a negative phenomenon."[31] What the architectural critic Botond Bognar has written about Japan, I would argue, also holds true for other East Asian countries: "American culture and architecture have historically provided...a rich storehouse from which the Japanese could draw and appropriate in various ways and for various purposes, while giving new meanings to the incorporated elements in order to shape and enrich their own complex cultural and urban landscapes."[32] Los Angeles figures prominently in these appropriations and transformations of American architecture and popular culture across the Pacific. One needs only remember, for instance, that Disneyland's first foreign location was in Japan, and that (after EuroDisney), other Disneylands—all derived from but also distinct from the Orange County icon—have sprouted in Hong Kong and mainland China.

In this essay, I have briefly referred to examples of four aspects of Southern California–derived architectural and planning shifts that resonated in Asian contexts: indoor/outdoor spatial fluidity, standardized building components, highway construction, and the creation of retail spaces associated with the automobile. I have also suggested what kinds of agents or catalysts were at play in effecting change. Often, individuals were key to the transfer, as in the case of Maekawa Kunio, Richard Neutra, or Konrad Wachsmann. However, as these examples suggest, architectural and building journals also played a significant role in disseminating news to readers worldwide about Southern California's dramatic changes over the 1940–90 time period. Finally, public and private institutions also facilitated the spread of Southern California approaches to architectural and planning innovation within East Asian contexts. In this regard, federal US aid programs, globalizing US corporations in the architecture/engineering/construction fields, and university programs in architectural design and urban planning figured prominently.

This essay represents an initial attempt at (a) understanding the myriad ways in which changing ideas about architectural form, structure, and space in Southern California rippled across the Pacific for fifty years and (b) clarifying that many of those ripples of influence also originated in Asia, only to metaphorically wash up in Los Angeles in a variety of respects. Much further research is warranted before a cogent synthesis of these architectural dynamics can be provided. For example, it would be fundamental to track the careers of students from Asia who were increasingly able to attend Los Angeles architectural schools in the latter twentieth century. Likewise, it would be fascinating to compare and contrast the impacts of the University of Southern California, the University of California, Los Angeles, and the Southern California Institute of Architecture on these students. Furthermore, given that numerous American architects with Southern California connections began to teach in Asian schools of architecture in the late twentieth century, it would be useful to plot the impressions their instruction had upon their Asian students. More comprehensive analyses of contemporary Asian architectural, planning, and trade journals are also necessary, as are either country- or city-specific studies that delve into these "confluential" situations in greater depth.

As Maki notes, "One thing is certain: we have spent too little time observing the successes of our predecessors with an acute eye. Moreover, we probably do not approach particular parts of our cities with sufficient understanding to extrapolate from them what is useful in human terms. It is one thing to grunt ecstatically in the presence of a significant work. It is another to learn what it can offer for the future."[33] Maki's reflections ring as true for the exhibition related to this catalog as they do for the many places in Asia that this essay has either referred to or neglected. By examining the architecture of Southern California and East Asia with the kind of acuity and social understanding that Maki urges, we are more likely to comprehend the design implications, material innovations, and significant results that stemmed from ideas of architects working throughout the Pacific in the latter twentieth century.

NOTES

1   Bob Crew, "Changing Face of Asian Architecture," *Asian Building and Construction* (August 1974): 21.

2   The "framework" I refer to is related to research I conducted between 1991 and 2002 that resulted in my book *Exporting American Architecture, 1870–2000* (London: Routledge, 2003).

3   Neutra went to Japan at the invitation of Tsuchiura Kameki and his wife, Nobu. The three had known each other when they were working together with Frank Lloyd Wright at Taliesin. Neutra's talk in Tokyo was sponsored by Kokusai Kenchiku Kyokai, publishers of the important architectural journal *Kokusai kenchiku,* which published three short articles about Neutra in its July 1930 issue. See Thomas S. Hines, *Richard Neutra and His Search for Modern Architecture* (Oxford: Oxford University Press, 1982), 93; and Jonathan M. Reynolds, *Maekawa Kunio and the Emergence of Japanese Modernist Architecture* (Berkeley: University of California Press, 2001), 75, 270.

4   Reynolds, *Maekawa Kunio,* 75.

5   *Kokusai kenchiku* 20, no. 9 (1953).

6   Reynolds, *Maekawa Kunio,* 284n6.

7   Harris's Fellowship Park House in Los Angeles (1936), as well as some residential commissions that he completed in the late 1940s (e.g., the Ralph Johnson Residence in Los Angeles [1947–48], and the Clarence Wyle Residence in Ojai [1946–48]), also demonstrated his interest in Japanese traditions. This interest was reinvigorated circa 1944, when Harris returned to California from New York, and when he (and his architectural-historian wife) began to examine the work of Greene & Greene more assiduously. See Lisa Germany, *Harwell Hamilton Harris* (Austin: University of Texas Press, 1991).

8   Reynolds, *Maekawa Kunio,* 199.

9   David Weinstein, "East Meets West: Asian Aesthetic," *Eichler Network,* http://www.eichlernetwork.com/article /east-meets-west-asian-aesthetic.

10   For perceptive commentaries about how what I am calling "global bridge-building" relates to colonialism, empire, modernism, modernization, and postimperial cultural change, see Mark Crinson, *Modern Architecture and the End of Empire* (Aldershot, UK: Ashgate, 2003).

11   Botond Bognar, "Surface above All? American Influence on Japanese Urban Space," in Heide Fehrenbach and Uta G. Poiger, eds., *Transactions, Transgressions, Transformations: American Culture in Western Europe and Japan* (Oxford: Berghahn, 2000), 73; for Kisho Kurokawa, see his *Each One a Hero: The Philosophy of Symbiosis* (Tokyo: Kodansha, 1997).

12   Paul Adamson and Mary Arbunich, *Eichler: Modernism Rebuilds the American Dream* (Layton, Utah: Gibbs-Smith, 2002).

13   Weinstein, "East Meets West."

14   Professor Lai Chee Kien, an architectural historian at the National University of Singapore, kindly informed me of the Shipley-Wachsmann connection. For more about Shipley, see Lai Chee Kien's *Building Merdeka: Independence Architecture in Kuala Lumpur, 1957–1966* (Kuala Lumpur: Galeri Petronas, 2007); and Crinson, *Modern Architecture.*

15   As explained by Jeffrey Head in "Rediscovering a Prefab Pioneer" (*Architectural Record,* http://archrecord.construction.com /features/critique/0810critique2.asp), the wedge connector was "a cast-steel mechanism built into the wood frames of the modular three-foot-four inch plywood panels. Since the horizontal and vertical dimensions of the panels were identical, the connector offered multiple configurations while ensuring a connection that was flush and airtight." Lai Chee Kien further explains in *Building Merdeka* (83) that Wachsmann employed a 40-inch grid system for modular timber construction, "where modular building components could be connected in three dimensions for small houses."

16   Lai, *Building Merdeka,* 10.

17   Lai, *Building Merdeka,* 81–93.

18   For a fuller discussion of these trends, see Cody, *Exporting American Architecture,* 124–40.

19   Annabel J. Wharton, *Building the Cold War: Hilton International Hotels and Modern Architecture* (Chicago: University of Chicago Press, 2001).

20   *Engineering-News Record* 151 (1953): 99.

21   Crinson, *Modern Architecture.*

22   One gets a sense of this intraregional dynamic when perusing contemporary trade publications (which I have done in the context of this essay's research), such as *Asian Architect and Builder* (1974–82), *Asian Building and Construction* (1974–80), or *Asia Pacific Contractor* (1981–82). For a broader synthesis, see William S. W. Lim and Jiat-Hwee Chang, eds., *Non West Modernist Past: Architecture and Modernities beyond the West* (Singapore: World Scientific, 2011).

23   See, for example, Erika Esau, *Images of the Pacific Rim: Australia and California, 1850–1935* (Sydney: Power, 2010).

24   Esau, *Images of the Pacific Rim,* 179.

25   Fumihiko Maki, *Nurturing Dreams: Collected Essays on Architecture and the City* (Cambridge, Mass.: MIT Press, 2008), 21.

26   Maki, *Nurturing Dreams,* 96–97. On page 270 of *Nurturing Dreams,* Maki explains that his essay about American cities, which includes discussion of Los Angeles and freeways, was originally written in 1982 and published in the *Karamu Quarterly* (Japan) in that year.

27   Maki, *Nurturing Dreams,* 103–4.

28   As noted earlier, one impetus for this construction came from desires within Asian cities to be more up-to-date regarding urban infrastructure, while another stemmed from foreign aid money provided by the US government. Regarding the latter case, with particular reference to Cambodia, see Helen Grant Ross and Darryl Collins, *Building Cambodia: "New Khmer Architecture," 1953–1970* (Bangkok: Key, 2006), 160. In Japan, as a result of the US government's War Damage Rehabilitation Plan (1945), "Twenty-four American-style, 100-meter wide boulevards were planned in various Japanese cities." Bognar, "Surface above All?," 57.

29   Mary Melton, "A Brief History of the Mini-Mall," *Los Angeles Times,* 16 November 1997.

30   For McDonald's, see James L. Watson, ed., *Golden Arches East: McDonald's in East Asia,* 2nd ed. (Stanford, Calif.: Stanford University Press, 2006). 7-Eleven, which began in Austin, Texas, in 1927, suffered financial setbacks in the 1980s and is now owned by a Japanese corporation. Thousands of 7-Elevens have been established in Japan, mainland China, Taiwan, South Korea, Thailand, Malaysia, the Philippines, and Australia.

31   Bognar, "Surface above All?," 73.

32   Bognar, "Surface above All?," 73.

33   From Fumihiko Maki and Jerry Goldberg's "Linkage in Collective Form," which originally appeared in *Japan Architect,* no. 16 (1994), and which I quoted from Maki's *Nurturing Dreams,* 59.

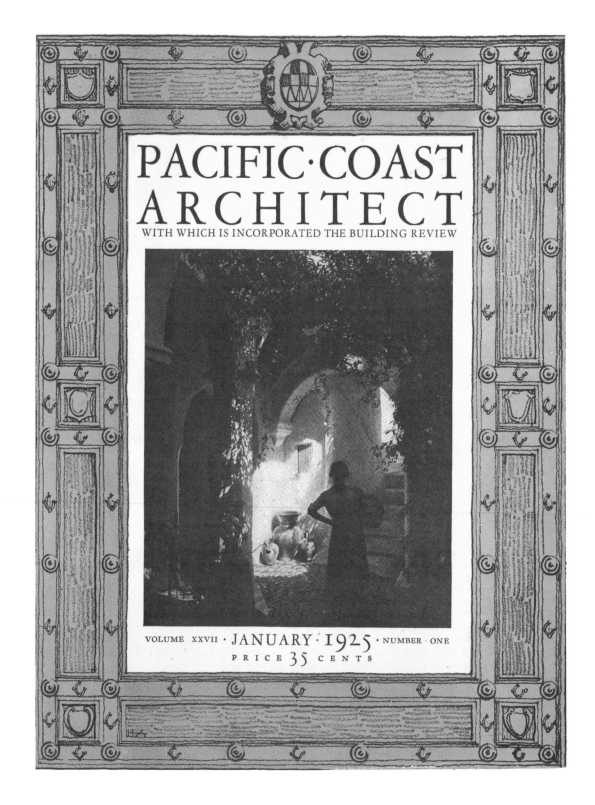

PACIFIC·COAST
ARCHITECT

WITH WHICH IS INCORPORATED THE BUILDING REVIEW

VOLUME XXVII · JANUARY · 1925 · NUMBER · ONE

PRICE 35 CENTS

LATIN AMERICA AND LOS ANGELES
ARCHITECTURAL EXCHANGES

Hugo Segawa and Fernando Atique

THE TWO L.A.S—LOS ANGELES AND LATIN AMERICA—have a long history of exchange and dialogue. When it comes to the field of architecture, the interactions are complex and intertwined. Words such as *assimilation, appropriation, feedback, reception, mixture, adaptation,* and *inspiration,* among others, come to mind, though none of them can provide a satisfactory description of that interaction. Piecing apart such an intricate subject is a difficult task. A cursory examination of buildings designed by Southern California architects seems to suggest an architectural engagement between Los Angeles and Latin America. The Santa Monica Civic Auditorium (1959), by Welton Becket and Associates, for example, shows a similarity with buildings executed by the Venezuelan architect Carlos Raúl Villanueva or the Brazilian architect Affonso Eduardo Reidy. In Palm Springs, the Coachella Valley Savings and Loan building (1961), by E. Stewart Williams, seems to reference some of Brasília's iconic government buildings, designed by the Brazilian architect Oscar Niemeyer. There is also, as has been shown by architectural historian Jean-Louis Cohen, a relationship between the works of John Lautner and those of Niemeyer.[1] And the Theme Building (1965) at the Los Angeles International Airport, by William Pereira, Charles Luckman, Welton Becket, and Paul R. Williams, displays the lightness and curves that one can find in Niemeyer's later work—the arch at the Sambódromo in Rio de Janeiro (1983–84), for example.

Southern California architects such as Richard Neutra often found Latin America a fertile region for ambitious architectural commissions. Hired by the Cultural Cooperation Division of the US State Department in the 1940s, Neutra designed many schools and hospitals in the tropics.[2] He promoted modern architecture though lecture tours in Central and South America and in the Caribbean as a kind of "missionary to the region."[3] There was also an intense dialogue between Neutra and Mexican architects, including Max Cetto and Luis Barragán.[4]

Through an examination of the magazine *Arts & Architecture* between the years 1938 (when John Entenza became its editor and publisher) and 1967 (when the magazine closed), this essay will shed more light on the architectural exchanges between Los Angeles and Latin America. In addition to presenting a

FIGURE 1.
Cover of *Pacific Coast Architect* 27, no. 1 (1925).

fabled collection of issues significant to West Coast cultural history and to the modernization of American residential design, the Los Angeles periodical showcased some of the best Latin American buildings produced in the mid-twentieth century. *Arts & Architecture* was a lighthouse for modern American architecture, art, design, and landscape design; a meeting point for a postwar international dialogue; a guide to a context far greater than the limits of its printed pages; and a venue for professional exchange. The Long Beach architect Edward Killingsworth illuminated the periodical's global character when he recalled "visiting the magazine's office and seeing Entenza's desk 'piled high with goodies'—the work of architects and designers from around the world hoping to be published in its pages."[5]

A WINDOW INTO LATIN AMERICA

Based on a number of architectural publications produced on the West Coast of the United States, one can create a timeline showing this nation's interest in and contact with Latin America. *Arts & Architecture* came out of *Building Review* (founded in 1911), which merged with *Pacific Coast Architect* in 1924 and had a broad circulation both within the United States and throughout the Americas. In general, the editors of *Pacific Coast Architect* (also founded in 1911) paid great attention to Latin America because the magazine explicitly relied upon Latin American architecture—especially Mexican architecture—to foster the so-called mission, California colonial, Spanish, and neocolonial styles in the United States. This position was expressed in an editorial in the March 1926 issue, and then several more issues presented a series of drawings made in Mexico by H. A. Schary: "Not only are these drawings interesting in themselves…but they open up a comparatively new field of opportunity to the California architect [because they reveal] inspiration to be found there for [a] tremendous variety of uses, remarkably adapted for [the] California climate and landscape."[6]

In 1929, the magazine *California Arts & Architecture* arose from the merging of *Pacific Coast Architect* and *California Southland* (founded in 1918). These magazines featured diverse styles such as Tudor, Georgian, Southern colonial, Mediterranean, Spanish colonial, and, later, art deco. Both *Pacific Coast Architect* and *California Arts & Architecture* published reports, notes, and editorials about architectural styles deemed appropriate for California (fig. 1). Foremost among those was the Spanish colonial style, because "the Spanish-Californians had a native talent for pleasant living and joyous gayety, combined somehow with equal natural courtesy, decorum and politeness."[7] This view was shared by architects on the South American continent, such as the Brazilian Christiano Stockler das Neves, who felt that "the American architects had good reason to develop this architecture, which really has beautiful motifs" and was derived from "the trips they made to Spain and Mexico."[8] The Argentine Raúl J. Alvarez proposed in 1919 that his countrymen follow the "examples of the North Americans who have raised, particularly in California, a regional architecture,"[9] an opinion shared by the Uruguayan Raúl Lerena Acevedo, who recommended in 1919 the adherence to the California movement.[10]

This neocolonial Californian style was practiced with intensity throughout the Americas,[11] mostly due to the dissemination of journals published in the United States, such as *House and Garden, Architectural Record,* and, especially, *Pacific Coast Architect* and *California Arts & Architecture.*[12] The search for a neocolonial architecture, although within each country's logic and national discourse, could be seen as an outcome of these magazines. However, the ambiguity between source and reception became evident when passed through the filter of modernity that was being established in Latin America prior to the middle of the century. The Mexican architect Luis Barragán expressed this contradiction in a speech he gave in Coronado, California, in 1951: "We made it clear that we did not understand the term 'modern' to include the so-called California Colonial Style.…In Mexico we have received the unfortunate influence of the California Colonial Style. This is even more absurd since the style came from Mexico in the first place and was taken [from] there to California. Los Angeles and Hollywood re-exported it to Mexico as the California Spanish Colonial style."[13] This quote highlights the two-way exchange capable of producing an architectural style that reached not only Mexico but also other Latin American countries (fig. 2).

When Entenza became the editor of *California Arts & Architecture* in 1938, and especially when he changed the publication's name to *Arts & Architecture* in 1943–44, the character of the magazine changed. While maintaining the regional trend of highlighting California modernism, it also became the voice for the modern movement and began to publish examples of architecture throughout the world. The colophon of *Arts & Architecture* always stated "established in 1911," referring back to the founding of *Building Review*. This shows that the relationship between *(California) Arts & Architecture* and Latin America went through different phases: one that looked to its colonial heritage and another that revealed a cutting-edge vision.

A MAPPING OF LATIN AMERICA

It is possible to single out four publications that together provide a synthesis of the various North American interactions with Latin America during the mid-twentieth century. The first was a book titled *The New Architecture in Mexico* (1938), by Esther Born, a graduate of the School of Architecture at the University of California, Berkeley. She was a remarkable photographer who traveled throughout Mexico in the 1930s and then—together with her husband, architect Ernest Born—produced a book from that experience, essentially creating the first English-language examination of the Mexican architectural movement.[14]

A few years later, the Museum of Modern Art (MoMA) in New York dedicated two catalogs to Latin American architecture. In 1943, the museum published *Brazil Builds: Architecture New and Old, 1652–1942,* by Philip L. Goodwin.[15] Confirming a growing interest in the architecture of the Southern Hemisphere and especially Brazil, the catalog accompanied an exhibition of the same title, which was organized in the context of North America's geopolitical Latin America program or, in other words, Nelson Rockefeller's campaign for the "Good Neighbor" policy established

FIGURE 2.
"Spanish in Design. 'Modern American' in Comfort."
Advertisement for Payne Furnace Company.
From *Arts & Architecture* 63, no. 4 (April 1946): 24.

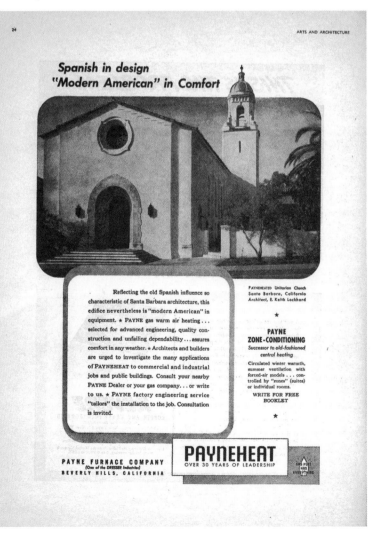

under President Roosevelt during World War II. In 1955, the exhibition and accompanying catalog, *Latin American Architecture since 1945,* by Henry-Russell Hitchcock, offered a panoramic overview of the ongoing modernization in the region.[16]

And lastly, there was *Mexico's Modern Architecture,* written by I. E. Myers in 1952 with a fellowship from the Instituto Nacional de Bellas Artes (INBA). Myers, a graduate of the University of Southern California, had the support of Richard Neutra (who wrote the introduction) and Enrique Yañez (author of the foreword), chief of the Department of Architecture at the INBA.

These four publications—two produced on the East Coast by New York's MoMA and two on the West Coast—were the first books on modern Latin American architecture to be published in the United States and composed the body of knowledge circulated by *Arts & Architecture* during its modern phase. *Arts & Architecture* was thus among the few periodicals of international scope that from the late 1940s onward regularly honored Latin American modern architecture. The experimentation coming out of the region was consistent with the magazine's editorial line. The representation of Latin American countries, architects, and architectural typologies was only inferior when compared to that of North America and included architects from Argentina, Brazil, Chile, Colombia, Cuba, Mexico, and Venezuela.[17] A significant number of these architects and their works were first published in English, thanks to the global perspective of *Arts & Architecture.* We will focus on a few examples.

BRAZIL BLOSSOMS

The launch in 1956 of Brazilian architect Henrique Mindlin's book *Modern Architecture in Brazil* (simultaneously published in Amsterdam, London, Munich, New York, and Paris) was an indication of the prestige of Brazilian architecture prior to the inauguration of the new city of Brasília in 1960. Magazines around the world—including *Arquitectura México, Architectural Forum, Architectural Review, L'architecture d'aujourd'hui, Nuestra Arquitectura, Progressive Architecture,* and *Zodiac*—dedicated special editions to the new developments in this country.[18]

Arts & Architecture, however, did not cover Brazil in the same way that the other magazines did; rather, it focused primarily on individual architects and their work. Two subjects received special attention: Brasília and the Bienal de São Paulo. The magazine began its reports on the new capital one year prior to its inauguration, in its April 1959 issue, by showing some of the buildings designed by Oscar Niemeyer (fig. 3); later on, in the November 1959 issue, it focused on Lucio Costa's "Pilot Plan," which had won the competition for the city's master plan.[19] *Arts & Architecture* highlighted the architecture award at the second Bienal de São Paulo, in January 1954, and during the following decades, the Bienal became an important part of the international art scene.[20] The architecture jury awarded some of the major prizes to North American architects, including Donald Barthelme, Craig Ellwood (in the "collective dwelling" category, for his Courtyard Apartments in the Hollywood district of Los Angeles), Philip Johnson, and Paul Rudolph. It also granted a "special mention" to an exhibition on modern postwar architecture in the United States at the Museum of Modern Art in New York.[21]

The magazine continued to feature Niemeyer's designs; it also dedicated space to the work of Niemeyer's frequent collaborator, the Brazilian landscape architect Roberto Burle Marx. Both were

FIGURE 3.
Oscar Niemeyer in the shack he used for an office while building Brasília, and the Cathedral scale model, February 1960.
Photo by Frank Scherschel.

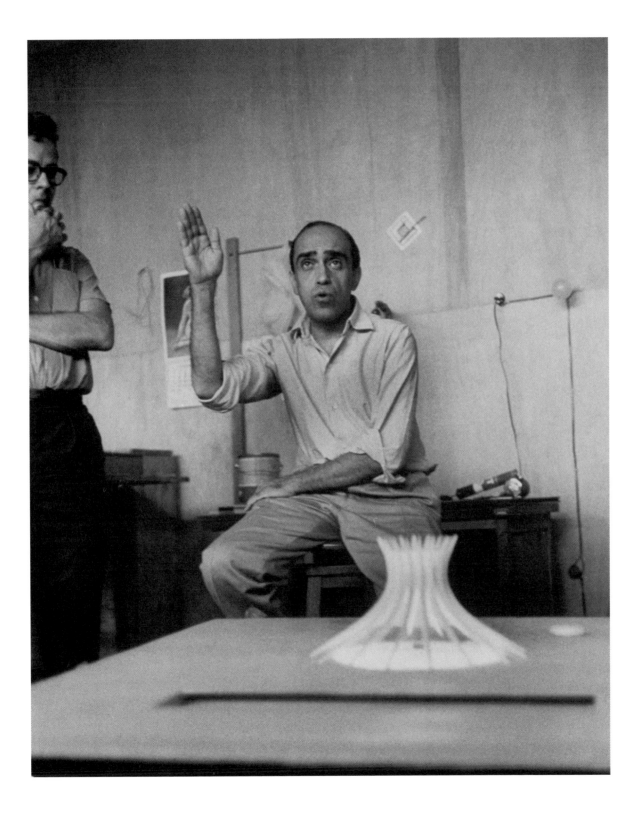

internationally renowned figures, but Niemeyer was especially well known in the United States because of his involvement in the design of the new headquarters for the United Nations (UN), an international collaboration led by the American architectural firm Harrison & Abramovitz. In 1947 and 1948, when Niemeyer was in New York developing his UN proposal, *Time* magazine ran two articles on him.[22] *Arts & Architecture*, however, addressed Niemeyer's work by highlighting his California projects: the unrealized Burton Tremaine Residence in Santa Barbara (designed in 1949) and the Joseph Strick Residence in Santa Monica (1964).[23] The Strick Residence was constructed without the presence of Niemeyer (the United States used his Communist ties as a justification for denying his visa request); instead, construction was supervised by local architect Ulrich Plaut, and the interior design was by Amir Farr, who at that time was an associate editor of *Arts & Architecture*.[24] The September 1964 issue featured a nine-page spread of the project—quite unusual for the magazine at that time—creating a document of great importance for the debates in 2002 over the demolition or preservation of the house. In the end, the house was preserved and declared a Santa Monica architectural landmark.[25]

LATIN AMERICAN ARCHITECTS ON THE VERGE

While Niemeyer was already a recognized global force, a less widely known Brazilian architect, Oswaldo Bratke, was also given the opportunity early in his career to publish one of his houses in the Los Angeles magazine. Bratke was a subscriber of the magazine and an admirer of its editorial mission. On his first trip to the West Coast of the United States in 1948, he went to see the buildings of Richard Neutra and Frank Lloyd Wright and paid a visit to the office of *Arts & Architecture*, which is likely when he arranged for the publication of an article on his house on Avanhandava Street in São Paulo (completed in 1947).[26] Bratke's work has a deep relationship with North American architecture, especially with the West Coast of the United States. Some highlights of his oeuvre, such as his own home and studio (1951) and the Oscar Americano Residence (1952), both in São Paulo, show a sensitive integration of Brazilian and Californian modernism.[27] Bratke was a leading figure in São Paulo in the late 1940s and throughout the 1950s. *Arts & Architecture* continued to have an impact on the Brazilian world of progressive architecture as well. Between 1948 and 1951, a group of architecture students from the Faculdade de Arquitectura Mackenzie in São Paulo (who would become the architecture elite in this city over the following decades) produced the magazine *Pilotis*, for which they used *Arts & Architecture* as a reference in their protest of the school's traditional academic approach.[28]

Chilean Emilio Duhart and Argentine Eduardo Catalano also received early professional exposure in the pages of *Arts & Architecture*, highlighting the magazine's endeavors to showcase the work of young Latino architects and further an international exchange of ideas. Duhart graduated in architecture from the Universidad Católica de Chile in 1941 and continued his studies at the Harvard University Graduate School of Design under the guidance of Bauhaus architect Walter Gropius. He became an assistant to Gropius and Konrad Wachsmann in 1943, when they were developing their prefabricated houses for the General Panel Corporation. In this same year, Duhart began to work in the California offices of another disciple of Gropius's, Ernest J. Kump, with whom Duhart participated in school projects, industrial projects, and prefabricated houses for Kaiser shipyards.[29] He must have become familiar with *Arts & Architecture* during this time. Together with his fellow Harvard student Ieoh Ming Pei, Duhart received in 1943 the second prize in the "Design for Postwar Living" competition, which was promoted by *Arts & Architecture.*[30] The coverage of the contest in the October 1944 issue, which coincided with the period when Duhart was living on the West Coast of the United States, focused on his graduate work for the Universidad Católica de Chile—a design for a commercial fishing village in San Quintín, in the isolated Aisén region of Chile.[31]

Catalano graduated from the Universidad de Buenos Aires in 1940, and from 1944 to 1945, he continued his studies at the University of Pennsylvania and Harvard University, where he first made contact with Marcel Breuer, along with Gropius and Wachsmann. Catalano taught at the School of Design at the North Carolina State University, in Raleigh, and at the School of Architecture and Planning at the Massachusetts Institute of Technology.[32] Spending most of his career outside Argentina, he received recognition both in the United States and Europe. Thanks, undoubtedly, to his contact with Breuer, Gropius, and Wachsmann, Catalano decided to take part in the "Second Annual Competition for the Design of a Small House," sponsored by *Arts & Architecture* in 1944.[33] The interaction between the architect and the magazine became even more important in the 1950s, when Catalano became a member of the editorial advisory board of *Arts & Architecture.* He wrote two articles for the magazine, one titled "Auditorium for the City of Buenos Aires," which he had designed in 1947, and the other "Structures of Warped Surfaces," a study on hyperbolic paraboloids that was inspired by the work of Félix Candela in Mexico and that Catalano had applied in his famous house in Raleigh in 1954.[34]

DIALOGUE AMID A WORLD IN TRANSFORMATION

Arts & Architecture did not comprehensively report on the overall breadth of Latin American architectural manifestations, unlike larger architectural magazines, notably, *L'architecture d'aujourd'hui.* The different iterations of this American publication—*Pacific Coast Architect, California Arts & Architecture,* and *Arts & Architecture*—provide a more refined lens through which one can see the evolution of the view of Latin America during the twentieth century. A host of Latin American building trends—from the Spanish style to the Brazilian avant-garde—ran through its pages either as sources of inspiration, transformative manifestos, or references to other modernities (fig. 4).

Entenza's discriminating eye for exceptional new talent and his professional eagerness to feature global pioneers in his publication helped launch the careers of many Latin American architects. The magazine's bet on this region's modernist leaders was clearly prophetic. Years after their initial introduction in *Arts & Architecture,* most of these architects were

FIGURE 4.
Ray Eames (American, 1916–88).
Collage showing the many architectural characters of modernity, including the Ministry of Education and Health building, by Lucio Costa's design team, in Rio de Janeiro, Brazil.
From *California Arts & Architecture* 60, no. 8 (September 1943): 16.

FIGURE 5.
**Cover of *Arts & Architecture* 68, no. 8 (August 1951),
showing the deck of the Casa Luis Barragán in Tacubaya,
Mexico City, 1951.**

featured in monographs written in their homelands and abroad, attesting to the accuracy of the magazine's editorial choices. All four modern Latin American monuments on the United Nations Educational, Scientific and Cultural Organization World Heritage List—the city of Brasília (listed in 1987), Ciudad Universitaria de Caracas (listed in 2000), the Casa Luis Barragán in Tacubaya (listed in 2004), and the Ciudad Universitaria at the Universidad Nacional Autónoma de México (UNAM; listed in 2007)—were published in *Arts & Architecture* as early as the 1950s (fig. 5). As scholars continue to explore this magazine's international impact and legacy, it is certain that this publication will remain an important resource for future in-depth investigations regarding the complex architectural engagements between L.A. and L.A.

NOTES
This essay was translated from Portuguese by Simone Osthoff.

1   Jean-Louis Cohen, "John Lautner's Luxuriant Tectonics," in Nicholas Olsberg, ed., *Between Earth and Heaven: The Architecture of John Lautner* (New York: Rizzoli, 2008), 19.

2   Richard Neutra, *Architecture of Social Concern* (São Paulo: Gerth Todtmann, 1948).

3   Catherine R. Ettinger, "Architectural Colonialism: Richard Neutra and Latin America" (working paper, Universidad Michoacana de San Nicolás de Hidalgo, Morelia, Mexico: 2011); and Catherine R. Ettinger, "Richard J. Neutra: Visión par las Américas" (working paper, Universidad Michoacana de San Nicolás de Hidalgo, Morelia, Mexico, 2011).

4   Keith Eggener, *Luis Barragán's Gardens of El Pedergal* (New York: Princeton Architectural Press, n.d.).

5   Barbara Goldstein, ed., *"Arts & Architecture": The Entenza Years* (Cambridge, Mass.: MIT Press, 1990).

6   "Editorial," *Pacific Coast Architect* 29, no. 3 (1926): 37. The sketches appear in the following issues: "Original Sketch in Mexico," *Pacific Coast Architect* 29, no. 4 (1926): 41; "Sketch in Mexico," *Pacific Coast Architect* 29, no. 5 (1926): 35; "Sketch in Mexico," *Pacific Coast Architect* 30, no. 1 (1926): 33; "Sketch in Mexico," *Pacific Coast Architect* 30, no. 2 (1926): 39; "Sketch of San Juan de Dios, Mexico City," *Pacific Coast Architect* 30, no. 3 (1926): 45.

7   Marion Parks, "The Art of Living in California," *California Arts & Architecture* (January 1933): 11–15, 22.

8   Christiano Stockler das Neves, "Architectura Colonial," *Revista de Engenharia do Mackenzie College,* no. 19 (July 1919): 41.

9   Aracy Amaral, *Arquitectura Neocolonial: América Latina, Caribe, Estados Unidos* (São Paulo: Memorial; Fondo de Cultura Económica, 1994), 69.

10   Amaral, *Arquitectura Neocolonial,* 71.

11   Fernando Atique, *Arquitetando a "Boa Vizinhança": Arquitetura, cidade e cultura nas relações Brasil-Estados Unidos, 1876–1945* (Campinas: Pontes; FAPESP, 2010); Ramón Gutiérrez, "Una entusiasta introspección: El neocolonial em el Río de La Plata," in Aracy Amaral, *Arquitectura Neocolonial: América Latina, Caribe, Estados Unidos* (São Paulo: Memorial; Fondo de Cultura Económica, 1994), 61–78; and Francisco Ramírez Potes, Jaime Gutiérrez Paz, Rodrigo Uribe Arboleda, *Arquitecturas Neocoloniales: Cali 1920–1950* (Cali: CITCE, 2000).

12   In Brazil, the Escola Politécnica de São Paulo subscribed to both of these magazines, whereas the oldest school of architecture, the Escola Nacional de Belas Artes, subscribed to *Architectural Digest* and *Architectural Record.*

13   Luis Barragán, "Secret Gardens" lecture, California Council of Architects and the Sierra Nevada Regional Conference, Coronado, Calif., 6 October 1951, reproduced in Raul Rispa, ed., *Barragán: The Complete Works* (New York, 1996), 33–34, as cited in Marc Treib, "To End a Continent: The Courtyard of the Salk Institute," *Journal of the Society of Architectural Historians* 65, no. 3 (2006): 427.

14   José Villagrán García, "Foreword," in Clive Bamford Smith, *Builders in the Sun: Five Mexican Architects* (New York: Architectural Book Publishing, 1967), 9; and "Ernest & Esther Born," Environmental Design Archives, University of California, Berkeley, http://www.ced.berkeley.edu/cedarchives/profiles/born.htm.

15   See also Zilah Quezado Deckker, *Brazil Built: The Architecture of the Modern Movement in Brazil* (New York: E. & F.N. Spon, 2000).

16   Patricio del Real, "Building a Continent: MoMA's *Latin American Architecture since 1945* Exhibition," *Journal of Latin American Cultural Studies* 16, no. 1 (2007): 95–110.

17   Due to space limitations, we list here the architects who were published in the magazine, but we will not refer to them in the essay: Mario Roberto Alvarez (Argentina); Affonso Eduardo Reidy, Lucjan Korngold, Plínio Croce, Roberto Aflalo, and Gian Carlo Gasperini (Brazil); Horacio Acevedo (Chile); Jorge Arango (Colombia); Mario Romañach and Emilio Fernández (Cuba); Juan Sordo Madaleno, Augusto H. Alvarez, Jorge Creel, and Teodoro González de Leon (Mexico).

18   Hugo Segawa, *Arquiteturas no Brasil 1900–1990,* 3rd. ed. (São Paulo: Edusp, 2010): 107.

19   "Brasília, a New National Capital," *Arts & Architecture* 76 (April 1959): 15–21; and "Brasília, Pilot Plan—Lucio Costa," *Arts & Architecture* 76 (November 1959): 21–23.

20   "The São Paulo Award," *Arts & Architecture* 71 (March 1954): 12–16.

21   "Prizes in Architecture; Second Biennial of the São Paulo Museum of Modern Art," *Arts & Architecture* 71 (March 1954): 15–16.

22   "On Stilts," *Time,* 5 May 1947; and "Gentleman, Very Timid," *Time,* 26 January 1948.

23   "Santa Barbara, Project for a House: O. Niemeyer, Arch; Detailing and Execution, Lutah Maria Riggs and Arvin Shaw III," *Arts & Architecture* 66 (March 1949): 26–29; and "Landscape Design for House in Santa Barbara," *Arts & Architecture* 66 (March 1949): 26–29.

24   Nikolai Ouroussoff, "A House at Stake, an Attitude in Flux: The Battle over Preservation of an Oscar Niemeyer Home Shows a Region Waking Up to Cultural Needs," *Los Angeles Times,* 23 October 2002, http://articles.latimes.com/2002/oct/23/entertainment /et-ouroussoff23.

25   "Project for a House in Santa Monica, California," *Arts & Architecture* 81 (September 1964): 20–28. Ouroussoff, "A House at Stake"; Kimberly Stevens, "Santa Monica House at Risk: Niemeyer-Designed Modernist House May Be Razed," *Chicago Tribune,* 3 November 2002; and "Strick House, 1964," Santa Monica Landmark Properties, http://www.santamonicalandmarks.com/landmk58.html.

26   "São Paulo House and Studio," *Arts & Architecture* 65 (October 1948): 32–33.

27   Hugo Segawa and Guilherme Mazza Dourado, *Oswaldo Arthur Bratke* (São Paulo: ProEditores, 1997), 106–47.

28   Marlene Milan Acayaba, *Branco & Preto: Uma história do design Brasileiro nos anos 50* (São Paulo: Instituto Lina Bo e P.M. Bardi, 1994), 48–49. For more on the São Paulo connection to California, see Adriana Irigoyen, "Da Califórnia a São Paulo: Referências norte-americanas na casa moderna paulista 1945-1960" (PhD diss., University of São Paulo, 2005).

29   "Ernest J. Kump, Jr. (1911–1999)," *A Guide to Historic Architecture in Fresno, California,* http://historicfresno.org/bio/kumpjr.htm; and Alberto Montealegre Klenner, *Emilio Duhart Arquiteto* (Santiago: Ediciones ARQ, 1994), 203.

30   "Post-War House," *Arts & Architecture* 60 (August 1943); see also Hugo Mondragón, "Chile en el debate sobre la forma de la arquitectura moderna," *ARQ,* no. 64 (December 2006): 17–19.

31   "Commercial Fishing Village in Chile," *Arts & Architecture* 61 (October 1944): 23–26. The design was presented as Duhart's graduate work for the Universidad Católica de Chile.

32   Fernando Aliata, "Catalano, Eduardo," in Jorge Francisco Liernur and Fernando Aliata, eds., *Diccionario de arquitectura en Argentina* (Buenos Aires: Clarín, 2004), 1:47–48.

33   "*Arts and Architecture*'s Second Annual Competition for the Design of a Small House," *Arts & Architecture* 62 (February 1945): 28–41.

34   "Auditorium for the City of Buenos Aires," *Arts & Architecture* 67 (January 1950): 27–29; Eduardo F. Catalano, "Structures of Warped Surfaces," *Arts & Architecture* 80 (December 1963): 22–24; "Professor Emeritus of Architecture Eduardo Catalano Dies at Age 92," *MIT News,* 2 February 2010, http://web.mit.edu/newsoffice/2010/catalano-obit.html; and Jonathan Glancey, "Eduardo Catalano Obituary," *The Guardian,* 15 February 2010.

PRESERVING MODERN ARCHITECTURE IN LOS ANGELES

Susan Macdonald

AS TIME PASSES, SOCIETIES REFLECT ON PAST ACHIEVEMENTS—assessing successes and failures and celebrating their contributions to current understandings of culture and the environment. Historic preservation contributes to this reflection by identifying those places that represent aspects of our past that we now cherish and wish to sustain for the benefit of future generations.

Internationally, the architectural heritage of the modern era began to be recognized, protected, and conserved beginning in the late 1980s, as the seminal works of the modern movement turned fifty and became eligible for heritage protection. As of July 2011, there were twenty-three twentieth-century places inscribed on the UNESCO World Heritage List for a variety of cultural values.[1] Auschwitz Birkenau German Nazi Concentration and Extermination Camp (1940–45), Poland, is recognized as a place of painful memory and a symbol of past brutalities and human cruelty. Individual houses such as the Luis Barragán House and Studio (1949) in Mexico City and the Rietveld Schröderhuis (Gerrit Rietveld, 1924) in Utrecht, the Netherlands, represent new forms of architectural expression associated with modernism that changed the face of the built environment. The Sydney Opera House (Jørn Utzon, 1973) in Australia is inscribed on the World Heritage List as a work of outstanding creative genius—a building that marked the cultural coming of age of a nation seeking to create its identity and shake off its colonial past. Architect Oscar Niemeyer and planner Lucio Costa's city of Brasília (1956) demonstrates new theories for urban living and the modern movement's use of architecture as a tool in social reform.

Despite recognition that the architecture of the early twentieth century is worthy of attention, conserving places from the second half of the century has been a slow and sometimes difficult process. The fact that the construction of such buildings took place in the living memory of much of the population prompts questions of value. Common refrains include "That's not old" and "I remember when that was built; everyone hated it, and now you want to save it!" The scale, character, and materiality of modern architecture from this era also raise new and complex problems for preservationists. Many of these buildings have

FIGURE 1.
Minoru Yamasaki and Associates (1949–2009).
Century Plaza Hotel (1961–66), Century City, 2011.
Photo by Holly Brobst.
Los Angeles, Getty Conservation Institute.

not stood the test of time well, and the way they age is challenging traditional approaches and techniques and raising new conservation issues.

Angelenos, however, have generally been comfortable with a recent built heritage. Los Angeles boasts a large building stock that postdates 1950, as well as a culture that is at ease with innovation and experimentation and is not overly bound by tradition and history. Los Angeles's collection of modern architecture is extraordinarily rich; it celebrates California's forgiving climate, a ready access to a vast array of new materials, a need to meet the demands of a rapidly expanding city, and a crop of influential architects, many of whom came to the United States to flee the turmoil of Europe between and after the World Wars.

In many countries, the identification of heritage places has been led by government agencies, which has necessitated concerted efforts to change public opinion about post–World War II architecture before its most emblematic buildings are lost or changed beyond recognition. In Los Angeles, community advocacy has led the way. In 1979, a group of Angelenos concerned about the loss of a number of historic buildings formed the Los Angeles Conservancy with a mandate to advocate for, advise on, and act on preserving the heritage of Los Angeles. With over six thousand members, it is now the largest local preservation group in the United States.[2] Today, over 60 percent of the conservancy's work is related to preserving modern heritage. The Sixties Turn Fifty initiative attracted huge interest in the preservation of architecture from the second half of the twentieth century. Other organizations, such as the National Trust for Historic Preservation, with its Modernism + Recent Past Program, have also played a significant role in raising awareness about the preservation of heritage of this era.

Initially, the interest in preserving modern heritage focused largely on the quirky Googie commercial architecture from the 1950s and, more recently, on midcentury modern residential architecture. The work of photographers such as Julius Shulman, whose iconic images of Los Angeles's houses have been hugely influential in generating attention and appreciation for midcentury modern architecture, has also influenced the approach to conservation (see Isenstadt, this volume, fig. 10). Today, these houses are much sought after; they appear in films and TV shows as the chosen style of the young, hip, and glamorous. Midcentury modern is a selling point for real estate agents; there are copies of Eames sofas and tables, Nelson lamps, and Cherner chairs everywhere.

However, while there is growing awareness for midcentury residential architecture, iconic buildings such as the LAX Theme Building (Pereira & Luckman, Welton Becket and Associates, and Paul R. Williams, 1961; see pl. 29), and the work of celebrated architects such as Gregory Ain, John Lautner, and Richard Neutra, there are still challenges for broader recognition of commercial, educational, and other building types. Furthermore, wider interest in buildings from the 1970s and later is yet to develop. Large government agencies have yet to appreciate the legacy of their own buildings from this period, often seeing them purely from a utilitarian perspective or merely as real estate.[3] Once modern structures are obsolete, few recognize potential for their adaptation to contemporary needs. The battle to preserve Minoru Yamasaki's Century Plaza Hotel (1966) after it was threatened with demolition has been described as a turning point in attitudes toward this period.[4] The efforts of community advocacy groups, the Los Angeles Conservancy, and the National Trust for Historic Preservation secured a solution to the building's future as the centerpiece of a new development (fig. 1).

FIGURE 2.
Jones and Emmons, Architects (1950–72).
A Balboa Highlands tract house developed by Eichler Homes, Inc. (ca. 1963–64), Granada Hills, 2008.
Photo by Emile Askey.
Los Angeles, Getty Conservation Institute.

Heritage surveys are an important first step in the conservation process; they help determine what is important and why. A lack of recognition of and appreciation for modern heritage means many important buildings are not protected in the way buildings from previous eras have been. Questions remain about how we select what is worth keeping given the limited passage of time between construction and conservation. Can we use the same criteria for selecting what gets conserved, when the performance, use, and relevance of these buildings are yet to be fully tested?

The five-year SurveyLA project by the Los Angeles Office of Historic Resources, with support from the Getty Conservation Institute, is an ambitious and large-scale attempt to recognize the rich and diverse heritage of the city; it is one of the largest such heritage surveys ever attempted. The survey seeks to identify Los Angeles's historic resources on a geographic information system (GIS) database linked to the city's planning system. It is organized, as are most studies, thematically and historically, and it includes a specific study of modernism. Spanning the development of the city from 1781 to 1980, SurveyLA assesses over 880,000 land parcels to determine if and how places contribute to our understanding of the city, with the aim of identifying those places that are of value and worthy of recognition as cultural resources.[5]

There are already a number of individual buildings and areas of the city from this era that have been identified for legal protection. These include the Gregory Ain Mar Vista Tract of 1948 and Joseph Eichler's Balboa Highlands tract.[6] Balboa Highlands, a development of about one hundred houses in Los Angeles's San Fernando Valley, was one of three areas that Eichler developed in Southern California during the 1950s and 1960s using well-known architects. Aimed at middle-income families, the houses feature compact and efficient open plans, creating a relationship between inside and outside through the use of atriums, skylights, and high-level glazing. In Balboa Highlands, residents worked to raise awareness of the significance of the collective value of the houses. A tour in 2000 was the catalyst for widespread local appreciation and for the formation of an action group that lobbied for recognition and protection of the area as a Historic Preservation Overlay Zone (HPOZ); it was so designated in 2007 (fig. 2). These houses, and other California Eichler developments,

are now highly sought after; there are a number of dedicated websites and at least two real estate firms that specialize in the sale of these homes and that provide information for their care and conservation. The community's appreciation of the houses has resulted in a practical, needs-driven approach to their maintenance.

As time passes, enthusiasm for buildings from the modern era will undoubtedly grow. However, there is another significant challenge in the preservation of architecture from this period: physical conservation. Modern architecture broke with traditional forms, materials, and planning. The abandonment of proven materials for experimental materials and construction techniques has created problems of life span and replacement. Conservators usually attempt to do the minimum amount of work possible to prolong the life of the historic fabric. Typically, buildings are conserved as found; the removal of historic fabric is avoided and replacement materials that closely match those that have come to the end of their natural life are used when possible. But how, for example, do you replace mass-produced components of buildings that are now no longer made? There are limited repair techniques available for newer materials, and an approach to conservation similar to what exists for older historic buildings is yet to be developed.

The materiality of modern architecture creates a different frequency of intervention. Evidence suggests that modern buildings deteriorate in half the time of older structures,[7] which means there are a huge number of buildings from the postwar boom of the 1950s and '60s that will need their first major conservation intervention. As a result, this area of conservation is urgent.

Materials during this period were sometimes experimental; the use of materials now known to be toxic, such as asbestos and formaldehyde, was common. Replacing materials constructed with these components is therefore problematic. The replacement of the white vinyl flooring of the living room at Case Study House #8, the residence designed by Charles Eames for himself and his artist wife, Ray, is a typical case (fig. 3). The flooring contained asbestos, an exact match is no longer made, and it is difficult to assess its true original color. The new material also had to be tested to ensure it did not off-gas (release chemicals that may over time damage the house's contents). A special-order tile, in a color that approximates a cleaned original tile, was eventually identified. All of these issues make replacement in a way that retains the authenticity of the material difficult.[8]

Buildings from this era also face the problems of obsolescence and adaptation. Sustaining heritage buildings requires them to have a use, an idea also found in the underlying tenets of modernism, such as the familiar principle "form follows function." There are a huge number of quite specific new building types that emerged over the past seventy years; these can be difficult to adapt for other uses without major impact to their significance. And the innovative designs and materials of modern architecture—the thin concrete walls, large expanses of glass, and flat roofs—all create specific environmental challenges made more difficult by new imperatives for energy conservation and green building standards, which do not take into account the needs of cultural heritage conservation.[9]

Advancing knowledge about the breadth of architecture from the 1940s to the 1990s (the subject of this exhibition) is a vital first step in identifying the heritage of this era. Conservation is, in effect, breaking new ground, in terms of both developing criteria for selecting what we want to keep and how we deal with some of the physical challenges resulting from the materiality of buildings from this period of history.

FIGURE 3.
The living room of the Eames Residence in Pacific Palisades, 1958.
Photo by Julius Shulman.
Los Angeles, Getty Research Institute.

The Getty Conservation Institute's Conserving Modern Architecture Initiative, launched in 2012, attempts to advance some of these issues so that the cultural resources of the modern era can be sustained and enjoyed by a new generation of enthusiasts.[10]

Dealing with the cultural resources of the modern era allows us to touch the past. There are many people for whom these creations are a living memory. It is rare in conservation to have access to this primary knowledge about the object or place you are conserving—in some cases, the creators or patrons may even be available for help. This brings a new level of understanding and raises interesting philosophical questions about authenticity. This is an area of conservation where the past, present, and future collide, bringing new and difficult challenges, and that is what makes it interesting.

NOTES

Thanks to Linda Dishman, executive director of the Los Angeles Conservancy, and Ken Bernstein, manager, and Janet Hansen, deputy manager, of the City of Los Angeles Office of Historic Resources, who were interviewed to assist in preparing this paper. Thanks to Sarah Macdonald, Gail Ostergren, and Luann Manning.

1   The United Nations Educational, Scientific, and Cultural Organization (UNESCO) World Heritage List can be accessed online at http://whc.unesco.org/en/list. Information on the World Heritage Center's Modern Heritage Programme can be found at http://whc.unesco.org/en/modernheritage/.

2   For information on the Los Angeles Conservancy, see http://www.laconservancy.org.

3   Per the author's experience and gleaned from discussion with Los Angeles professionals such as Ken Bernstein, from the City of Los Angeles Office of Historic Resources and Linda Dishman, from the Los Angeles Conservancy.

4   Linda Dishman, interview by Susan Macdonald, 2011.

5   For information on SurveyLA, see http://preservation.lacity.org/survey.

6   For further information on the Mar Vista Tract, see http://preservation.lacity.org/hpoz/la/gregory-ain and http://preservation.lacity .org/node/466. For more information on Balboa Highlands, see http://www.balboahighlands.com and http://preservation.lacity.org /node/466.

7   Robert Thorne, "Quality, Longevity, and Listing," in Michael Stratton, ed., *Structure and Style: Conserving 20th Century Buildings* (London: E. & F. N. Spon, 1997), 199.

8   In 2012, the Getty Conservation Institute and the Eames Foundation began collaborating on the conservation of the Eames House. As work progresses, information will be available at http://www.getty.edu/conservation/our_projects/field_projects/eameshouse /index.html.

9   For a listing of bibliographic references on the conservation of modern architecture, including sustainability and adaptive reuse, see Susan Macdonald and Gail Ostergren, eds., *Conserving Twentieth-Century Built Heritage: A Bibliography* (Los Angeles: Getty Conservation Institute, 2011), http://www.getty.edu/conservation/publications_resources/pdf_publications/mod_arch_bib _aug11.pdf.

10   For information on the Getty Conservation Institute's Conserving Modern Architecture Initiative, see http://www.getty.edu /conservation/our_projects/field_projects/cmai/.

DEVELOPING COMMUNITIES

SUBURBAN LANDSCAPES OF LOS ANGELES

Becky Nicolaides

IN 1940, LOS ANGELES STOOD POISED between two suburban visions. Coming of age as an urban place
in the early twentieth century, Los Angeles embraced the promise of suburbia from its beginnings, offer-
ing in the spread-out paradigm a better way to live. At the heyday of industrial urbanization in America, Los
Angeles was intent on learning from the mistakes of big eastern cities. It would not build densely and gritty.
It would build out. And it would fold its communities into nature—into the lovely green and golden acres of
Southern California, amid the orange groves and oak trees, and along the ridges rimming the majestic Pacific.
This would be a better city. A suburban city.[1]

To an impressive degree, Los Angeles fulfilled this aspiration in its early years.[2] From 1890 to 1940,
suburban communities gradually multiplied. They were spaced at comfortable distances, enough to allow for
a palpable feeling of nature as well as appropriate social distance. They spanned the gamut of suburban types.
At one end were the elite picturesque enclaves that took their place in the very best locations—the rolling hills
overlooking the vast Pacific, the scenic foothills of the San Gabriel Mountains, the hillsides of the Santa Monica
Mountains. At the other end were streetcar suburbs and modest subdivisions. Los Angeles's early massive
streetcar system stimulated suburban build-outs along its pathways, creating the sinews of the region's
sprawling form. The automobile opened up new opportunities for infill development. After 1920, modest subdivisions for the working and middle classes proliferated. Yet still, suburbia in Los Angeles retained a palpable
city-country balance. Settlement was sparse enough to allow it. As historian Robert Fishman has observed,
the streetcar era was the most successful period of suburbanization in L.A. history.[3] Suburbs were small,
coherent villages of modest bungalows surrounded by citrus groves and irrigated fields and linked to a vibrant
downtown through an efficient, far-flung rail system. Los Angeles before 1940 had achieved the optimal suburban vision. It was a paradigm of metropolitan success, a model for America.

The postwar years were game changers. As new suburban forms emerged, spreading like wild-
fire across the region and nation, suburbanization transformed from solution to problem. The scale of

FIGURE 1.
**Lakewood construction showing the innovative
truck-mounted shingle delivery system, 1950.**

development reached beyond the imagination, even as the character of suburban places changed. Gone was the communion with nature. In its place was technology and its capacity to transform suburbia into a mass-produced—and mass-consumed—enterprise.

THE SITCOM-SUBURB ERA

Technology may have facilitated the change, but federal policy and housing shortages caused it. During and after World War II, the federal government committed gargantuan subsidies to private builders to construct single-family homes on vast suburban tracts to meet the voracious housing demand that had been swelling since 1930. Urban historian Dolores Hayden has labeled developments built during the postwar years "sitcom suburbs": "model houses on suburban streets held families similar in age, race, and income whose lifestyles were reflected in the nationally popular sitcoms of the 1950s and 1960s."[4] During this phase, suburbia experienced a transformation both qualitative and quantitative. It became a built landscape of mass production. In an assembly-line fashion, large-scale builders churned out homes that were of similar architectural design, to both lower costs and speed production (fig. 1). The results were visible in the repetitive landscapes of places such as Lakewood, Westchester, and large swaths of the San Fernando Valley (see Cuff, this volume, fig. 1).

As in all cities, sitcom suburbs added to a diversified suburban landscape already in place. Yet they quickly overshadowed what had come before, bulldozing their way toward dominance. The number of structures built in Los Angeles during this era eclipsed that in all others (fig. 2). Sitcom suburbia covered acres and acres of open space and infill areas in older towns. This mass proliferation of housing satiated a booming market driven by rapid population growth. From 1950 to 1970, Los Angeles County's population jumped from about four million to seven million.

Los Angeles played a key role in the national history of postwar suburbanization, as historian Greg Hise has shown. Key builders in the area—Fritz Burns and Fred Marlow, in particular—pioneered

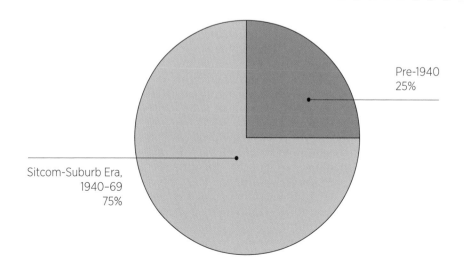

FIGURE 2.

Housing snapshot in 1970: The proportion of structures built in Los Angeles County prior to 1940 and during the sitcom-suburb era.
Source: US Census of Housing, 1970.

mass-production building methods during the war that would be emulated in more famous suburbs such as Levittown, New York.[5] The workplace-residence link was crucial to postwar development as well. According to Hise, "Proximity to employment remained a central development tenet. Postwar dispersion was not an inchoate sprawl."[6] The tale of Kaiser Community Homes was exemplary. During the war, Kaiser became committed to community planning to serve the needs of its defense workers. In the postwar period, it expanded into community building, constructing master-planned developments of homes, schools, recreation centers, medical clinics, and shopping centers, all sited in proximity to industries and regional job centers. Kaiser partnered with Fritz Burns on several L.A. projects, including developments in North Hollywood, Panorama City, and Monterey Park and the completion of Westchester.[7]

The sitcom suburbs began as landscapes of standardization. Guided by the Federal Housing Administration's minimum house standards, homes were very modest in size (typically nine hundred square feet), with two bedrooms and one bath—smaller than the typical prewar home.[8] Many looked alike, apart from some small exterior variations (figs. 3, 4). Most developers anticipated that homeowners would embellish the original house with add-ons and cosmetic changes. As such, local building regulations usually allowed for such alterations. These suburbs were designed for the automobile, with gridiron or curving street patterns (the curves usually had nothing to do with the natural terrain). In the early years, the land looked barren once the bulldozers cleared the area for construction; saplings were planted along parkways to bring nature back to the landscape, but it took years for this artificial vegetation to mature. If early suburbia folded communities into nature, sitcom suburbia denuded it and then tried to replant it.

FIGURE 3.
Model home in Lakewood, early 1950s.

FIGURE 4.
The sitcom suburb of Carson, located just west of Lakewood, 2009.
Photo by Michael Salvatore Tierney.

FIGURE 5.
Carson home showing the owner's design customizations, 2009.
Photo by Michael Salvatore Tierney.

Sitcom suburbia was also a class democratizer. It often housed blue- and white-collar workers side by side. Builders such as Kaiser Community Homes programmed this into their plans by offering housing in a range of prices; they believed it helped prevent un-American social stratification.[9] This pattern was apparent in a variety of suburban towns, from Lakewood to South Gate. But the ideal of inclusivity did not extend to race. Most sitcom suburbs tightly excluded African Americans, although Latinos and Asian Americans were gradually gaining a foothold in the postwar years.[10]

The modest nature of this suburban landscape, combined with fairly permissive building regulations and the developers' invitation to renovate, created the potential for change, both physical and social. Homes could be remodeled or expanded. Figure 5 shows how one Carson homeowner put an indelible stamp of defensive individuality on his property. In subsequent years, after legal barriers to racial housing segregation fell, the affordability of homes in sitcom suburbs made them natural destination points for upwardly mobile Latinos, Asians, and African Americans. Ironically, a landscape once reviled for its physical and social homogeneity became remarkably diverse, thanks to the original affordable designs of these homes.

One vivid example is Lakewood. This iconic sitcom suburb, famous for its massive scale and mass-produced feel, drew the national spotlight in the 1950s when it became the largest development in the country—with 17,500 homes—surpassing even Levittown. The repetitive landscape conjured Lewis Mumford's nightmarish view of postwar suburbia, where "a multitude of uniform, unidentifiable houses, lined up inflexibly, at uniform distances, on uniform roads, in a treeless communal waste" were churning out people as monotonous as the landscape itself.[11] Yet within twenty years, history flipped. Like many sitcom suburbs, lily-white Lakewood became a town of whites, Latinos, Asians, and blacks. Sitcom suburbia, once the incubator of the white American mainstream, had become the staging ground of neighborhood diversity.[12]

EDGE CITIES AND CORPORATE SUBURBIA

After 1970, the texture of the suburban landscape changed once again. It became a kind of extreme landscape, where the pattern of sitcom suburbia—the mass production of homes around regional hubs—was exaggerated by an order of magnitude. If postwar suburbs in Los Angeles were often anchored by industrial hubs, suburbs after 1970 were anchored by more mature economic centers known as "edge cities"—clusters of corporate offices, industrial parks, shopping centers, cineplexes, chain hotels, and fast-food restaurants. Surrounding these nodes were more residential tracts built at unprecedented scales. People could contain all aspects of their everyday lives in these peripheral hubs without dealing much at all with the rest of the metropolis.

This was the era of the edge city/corporate suburb. In the historical evolution of the edge city, Los Angeles looms large. Writer Joel Garreau considers Los Angeles "the birthplace of the American landscapes and life styles that are the models for Edge Cities worldwide."[13] While development in L.A. County was important during this time—the second-largest building period after the sitcom-suburb era (fig. 6)—the greatest growth occurred in the four outlying counties of Orange, Riverside, San Bernardino, and Ventura. In Los Angeles, this phase began in the 1960s and accelerated in the 1970s and 1980s. A key turning point was 1957, when the height restriction on buildings in the City of Los Angeles was eliminated (it had been limited to 150 feet). This unleashed the construction of tall buildings in dispersed hubs, in places such as new, gleaming Century City, built on an old 20th Century Fox backlot.[14]

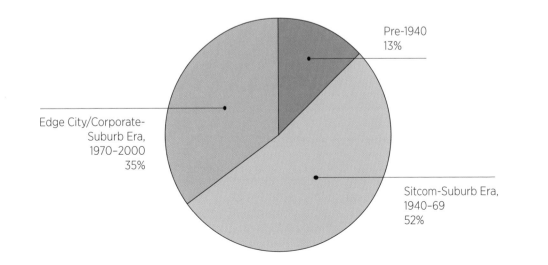

Pre-1940
13%

Edge City/Corporate-
Suburb Era,
1970–2000
35%

Sitcom-Suburb Era,
1940–69
52%

FIGURE 6.
Housing snapshot in 2000: The proportion of structures built in Los Angeles County prior to 1940, during the sitcom-suburb era, and during the edge city/corporate-suburb era.
Source: US Census of Housing, 2000.

Edge cities are a great example of suburban change. Several of these centers evolved from older suburban towns, such as Pasadena, Burbank, and Beverly Hills. Some had their roots as postwar industrial nodes, such as North Hollywood. In these instances, the economies of these towns diversified as redevelopment introduced new offices and housing. In other cases, as with Warner Center in the West Valley and, more famously, Irvine, the edge city and its surrounding suburbs were built on virgin greenfields—one massive-scale conurbation plunked down in the middle of nowhere. In these areas, the whole feel was new and nonlocal, with chain restaurants and movie theaters, bulk housing, nondescript office parks, and shopping malls.[15]

In areas of new development, the landscape that emerged is what I term "corporate suburbia." This landscape was produced by corporate enterprises, even global conglomerates—entities far larger than postwar community builders such as the Levitts. An excellent example was KB Home, which had become the leading builder in California by 1968. KB Home was especially active in exurbs such as Lancaster, Palmdale, and Santa Clarita. Corporate America, in fact, was entering real estate in profoundly new ways. Historian Andrew Wiese has dubbed this "the era of corporate real estate development," a period when the scale of home production spiked radically. Even at the height of the sitcom-suburb era, Wiese writes, "the average 'large home-builder' in the U.S. built between 200 and 300 homes annually, on a total of just 70–100 acres." That changed

FIGURE 7.
The uniform landscape of corporate suburbia in Santa Clarita, 2009.
Photo by Michael Salvatore Tierney.

in the 1960s, when a series of structural alterations in real estate finance allowed for access to much greater stores of capital, via new real estate investment trusts (REITS), pension funds, and a host of large corporate and Wall Street investors. California was the favored benefactor of these ventures.[16]

Pumped up by this new steroidal capital, the scale of suburban development swelled, making once-record-breaking tracts such as Lakewood (3,400 acres) look small by comparison. Land developments in Westlake Village and Simi Valley hit the 11,000- to 12,500-acre range.[17] And the mass-produced feel of these places became stronger than ever. To achieve profitable economies of scale, corporate builders standardized multiple aspects of home production while offering consumers a wide variety of choices on interior amenities. The emphasis was on "domestic bling" inside the home, such as high ceilings, bigger walk-in closets, and larger kitchens with professional-style appliances; there was less concern for what was on the outside.[18] The end result was a terrain of even starker visual uniformity (fig. 7). Moreover, developers discouraged alterations to home exteriors through mind-numbing lists of covenants, conditions, and restrictions (CC&Rs) enforced by homeowners associations. In this way, the original mass-produced feel of these suburbs was frozen into place (fig. 8).

In corporate suburbia, the landscape was sprawling, car dependent, and monotonous. Land uses were usually segregated into large-scale clusters accessible only by car. Single-family homes were isolated

FIGURE 8.
A condominium complex in Santa Clarita, 2009.
Photo by Michael Salvatore Tierney.

into sprawling residence-only tracts that were distant from services. Houses were bigger and occupied larger lots compared to earlier times.[19] This distinctive landscape made it a favored target of suburban critics, from New Urbanists to social commentators ruminating on the causes of school shootings. They homed in on this built topography, with its placeless and faceless feel, its lack of accessible and authentic public spaces, and its utter dependency on cars.[20]

———

If Los Angeles is a mosaic of historic suburban landscapes, the gargantuan footprint left by sitcom and corporate suburbia is hard to overstate. Sitcom suburbia created an immense panorama of modest housing. It began as a democratic landscape, so conceived by its builders, and stayed as such in ways they could have never foreseen. Moderate regulations created an openness in both the physical and social character, securing a dynamic future for these places that would blow out every conceivable stereotype the TV sitcoms ever created. Ozzie and Harriet bolted without looking back. And they probably settled down in corporate suburbia, the booming towns in the far reaches of the metropolis that represent the last, perhaps most recognizable suburban form. These are townscapes of contemporary standardization, with a new fixedness of place enforced by private regulation. This is the far frontier of suburbia, the fringe destination of urban flight for ever-succeeding generations chasing the American dream. At the same time, it represents the ultimate fodder for those seeking to build a more sustainable, livable metropolis.

NOTES

This work was created with the generous support of the John Randolph Haynes and Dora Haynes Foundation. The author would like to thank Andrew Wiese for his valuable comments.

1   On the early roots of this suburban vision, see Robert Fogelson, *Fragmented Metropolis* (Berkeley: University of California Press, 1993); and Robert Fishman, *Bourgeois Utopias* (New York: Basic, 1987).

2   Much of this essay is drawn from Becky Nicolaides, *On the Ground in Suburbia: A Chronicle of Social and Civic Transformation in Los Angeles since 1945* (forthcoming), chap. 1.

3   Fishman, *Bourgeois Utopias,* 160–61.

4   Dolores Hayden, *Building Suburbia* (New York: Pantheon, 2003), 128.

5   Many historians recognize Levittown, New York—built by Abraham Levitt and his two sons, William and Alfred—as the most significant postwar suburban development for its massive scale and innovative production techniques. See Kenneth T. Jackson, *Crabgrass Frontier* (New York: Oxford, 1985), 234–45.

6   Greg Hise, *Magnetic Los Angeles* (Baltimore: Johns Hopkins University Press, 1997), 159.

7   Hise, *Magnetic Los Angeles,* chs. 5 and 6.

8   Hise, *Magnetic Los Angeles,* 66–71, 137–38; Hayden, *Building Suburbia,* 190.

9   Hise, *Magnetic Los Angeles,* 204.

10   Hise, *Magnetic Los Angeles,* 203–5; D. J. Waldie, *Holy Land* (New York: W. W. Norton, 2005); Becky Nicolaides, *My Blue Heaven* (Chicago: University of Chicago Press, 2002); Josh Sides, *L.A. City Limits* (Berkeley: University of California Press, 2006); and Charlotte Brooks, *Alien Neighbors, Foreign Friends* (Chicago: University of Chicago Press, 2009).

11   Lewis Mumford, *The City in History* (New York: Harcourt, Brace, & World, 1961), 486.

12   Rich Connell, Doug Smith, and Teresa Watanabe, "Local Suburbs More Diverse," *Los Angeles Times,* 9 December 2008, A1.

13   Joel Garreau, *Edge City* (New York: Doubleday, 1991), 269.

14   "Huge Century City Project Will Begin This Spring," *Los Angeles Times,* 29 January 1961, CSA5; "Sound Stage Making Way for Century City," *Los Angeles Times,* 10 April 1961, 23; and "Bulldozers to Topple Make-Believe World," *Los Angeles Times,* 16 July 1961, WS1.

15   Garreau, *Edge City,* 262–63; and Hayden, *Building Suburbia,* 172–75.

16   Andrew Wiese, "'The Giddy Rise of the Environmentalists': 'Corporate Real Estate Development' and Environmental Politics in San Diego, California, 1969–1973" (working paper, September 2011, in author's possession); Mike Davis, *City of Quartz* (London: Verso, 1990), 130–34; and Ned Eichler, *The Merchant Builders* (Cambridge, Mass.: MIT Press, 1982).

17   Wiese, "Giddy Rise," 12.

18   Paul Knox, *Metroburbia, USA* (New Brunswick, N.J.: Rutgers University Press, 2008), 76–78.

19   Hayden, *Building Suburbia,* 190.

20   Andres Duany, Elizabeth Plater-Zyberk, and Jeff Speck, *Suburban Nation* (New York: North Point, 2000); and Christopher Caldwell, "Levittown to Littleton: How the Suburbs Have Changed," *National Review* 51, no. 10 (1999): 30–32.

DOMESTIC SPECULATION
ARCHITECTS AND BUILDERS IN POSTWAR LOS ANGELES

Dana Cuff

INTRODUCTION

ALTHOUGH SUBURBS HAVE EXISTED at least since Ancient Rome, no city is more strongly associated with the invention and exportation of postwar emblematic sprawl than Los Angeles.[1] The origins of the city's midcentury domestic landscape are located in the histories of its architects and builders. Common wisdom holds that the suburbs represent the American dream: they look as they do because that is what people want. The data are inarguable that Americans in vast numbers bought suburban houses after World War II, the quick sale of the houses does not confer desire. It is more accurate to say that pent-up demand in the mid-1940s satisfied the dream of sellers rather than that of buyers. These sellers were themselves at a critical juncture between their prewar identities as small general contractors or merchant builders and what they would become by the 1960s: developers within an articulated building industry.

Beginning in the late 1940s, new subdivisions opened to long lines of prospective homeowners who could evenly trade monthly rent for mortgage payments on newly structured government-insured loans. Because buyers had few options, it is possible that their dream came by default, but even this default option had its origins. Los Angeles was at the very center of a perfect storm for housing. Builders, lenders, government agencies, buyer demand, available land, and, not least, architects were all primed to go into production. Pioneers of contemporary design such as Gregory Ain, Charles and Ray Eames, and Richard Neutra were experimenting with every aspect of the house in an effort to make it the site of "modern living." How is it possible, then, that postwar suburbia could be invented in Los Angeles but have so little design to show for it?

The early postwar years represent a sea change in the domestic landscape, with the stick-built detached dwelling as its seemingly inevitable genetic code. In fact, the standard wood-frame house was not inevitable; there was a wide range of architect-designed alternative homes that were more modern, flexibly planned, and experimental. Likewise, there were innovative alternatives to the standard, repetitious subdivision land platting that aggregated individual houses into creative collective arrangements. Imagine what the

FIGURE 1.
William A. Garnett (American, 1916–2006).
Lakewood, California, construction series, 1950.
Six gelatin silver prints, each approximately
20.3 × 25.4 cm (8 × 10 in.).
Los Angeles, J. Paul Getty Museum.

oceanic proportions of Los Angeles tract-home developments might have looked like under other circumstances: if Henry Kaiser's plastic house had triumphed over the balloon-frame alternative; if Richard Neutra's plans for Levittown had gotten any traction; if Gregory Ain's Mar Vista housing had been more competitively priced; if *Arts & Architecture* magazine had built its multifamily competition winners rather than the single-family Case Study Houses; or if Crestwood Hills had met with less resistance.[2] If any of these modernist models had prevailed, then Los Angeles and the sites that imported its housing styles and land patterns, in suburbs as far flung as Las Vegas and Shanghai, might be very different today. In a photograph taken by William A. Garnett as he flew over Lakewood in 1950, we see what Los Angeles hath wrought (fig. 1). Current explanations are hardly robust enough to explain such a significant outcome. Repetitive, builder-designed houses seem to float in space because they are situated on individual pieces of property without regard to specific site conditions — laid out on flat terrain with few if any shared spaces.

WARTIME HOMEBUILDING IN LOS ANGELES

Los Angeles led the nation's cities into suburbia. In the years following the Great Depression, government programs restructured the lending industry so that renters could become buyers; experiments in construction and delivery meant that housing could be mass-produced; and the housing supply nationwide at the end of the war was low. These conditions were exaggerated in Los Angeles. The defense industries had pulled the region out of the Depression ahead of other cities and were now prepared to repurpose the production facilities, labor, and techniques for homebuilding. In addition, the area's advanced auto-oriented infrastructure (the first freeway opened in 1940) made inexpensive outlying land viable for home sites.[3]

Demand for housing in the West was intense, but because Los Angeles was in one of the most productive agricultural counties in the United States, there was plenty of relatively flat land to convert to residential use. One distinctive element of Los Angeles's homebuilding capability was the fact that low-cost mass-produced housing had been built and tested at least five years before the war ended.[4] Given the influx of defense workers to the area, builders were anxious to meet their housing needs. In 1939, the first of almost eight hundred houses was sold in Westside Village, just two miles from Douglas Aircraft in Santa Monica.[5] In 1941, the builder of those houses, Fritz Burns, produced four hundred more at Toluca Woods, where Burbank meets North Hollywood; the location was convenient to jobs at Lockheed and Vega Aircraft as well as the Hollywood studios. Already, houses could be customized within a limited range of options, and curbs and sidewalks were part of the package.[6] Although Levittown, New York, is the caricature of ticky-tacky mass housing, it was preceded by Westside Village, Toluca Wood, and more than three thousand homes for defense workers built in Los Angeles's Westchester between 1941 and 1944. Levitt and Sons would not even purchase land in Long Island until 1946.

There were important ways defense housing laid the groundwork for the explosion of homes produced after the war. For example, Westside Village was the first housing project with more than forty units to be issued a loan. Financing large housing developments was a complicated process undertaken by Depression-wary lending institutions, so such trials were essential to jump-start later projects. In an effort to build lender confidence, Burns surveyed one thousand potential buyers about their needs and tastes, resulting

in more bedrooms, more storage space and larger garages.[7] Such market research was new to homebuilding, setting the stage for a consumer logic that placed mass housing among other commodities. In the first
decades of the housing boom, the long-term, low-down-payment mortgage created a mass of potential buyers; the house as a speculative venture was beginning to take hold. This radical restructuring of the home into
single-family housing meant that use value grew subordinate to exchange value: a house was an investment
and a tax write-off for the occupants rather than a dwelling that met their specific needs. This critical transformation only appeared after the war.

Captains of defense production, armed with multiple forms of government sponsorship, moved into
homebuilding. The federal government had infused the local economy with more than $150 million by 1942,
through contracts for the construction of aircraft and shipbuilding plants, refineries, and military bases, as
well as the housing that went with it.[8] A construction industry of giants capable of working with government
bureaucracy was already in place when the war ended. The premier example is Kaiser Community Homes, a
partnership between industrialist Henry Kaiser and Burns, the latter of which was by then Los Angeles's biggest residential builder. At its height in 1947, Kaiser Community Homes would churn out twenty houses a day,
making it the world's largest homebuilder.[9]

Kaiser's Housing Research Division, located in San Francisco, took part in the widespread prepara-
tions to convert defense industries into homebuilding after the war, focusing its attention on the Southern
California region. They considered a number of potential housing models, the most radical of which was
an all-plastic house. The research team was charged with evaluating the costs of each model compared to
those of conventional construction. The all-plastic lost out, and while it was rendered in a strikingly modern
aesthetic compared to its ranch-style counterpart, the question of form was never raised because cost alone
determined the winner.[10] The stripped-down ranch house of Toluca Woods origins would be deployed to
expand Westchester and build Panorama City, among other communities. Kaiser and Burns's great experiments reinvented not materials but rather on-site building practices. They tested various prefabrication
efficiencies, the most audacious of which was a factory in Westchester with two full production lines. The
houses were criticized for their economy and homogeneity, but marketing brochures tried to suggest this
was intentional architectural restraint.[11] It appears that restraint was so extensive that no architects were
even involved.

ARCHITECTS AND EXPERIMENTATION

Prior to the war, architects were engaged in the design of large custom homes for the wealthy and in
projects across the entire metropolitan area, from the city center to the garden suburbs. But simultaneous
with the push to construct a bona fide middle class came an emphasis in American city planning on
decentralization, which threatened to leave architects on the margins of the greatest restructuring of the
American landscape since the Civil War. Los Angeles maps how this transpired and with what results for
the built environment.

In the nation's midcentury migration toward the American Southwest, the region at the campaign's leading edge was Southern California. Architects watched the first stick-built houses roll out over

the farmlands and were determined to change the course of events. They were convinced that the popular house was malleable rather than inevitable, and that these early tracts were imperfect models for the soon-to-be-transformed postwar household.[12] To guide residential building, architects undertook two types of experiments: first, in the house itself, and, second, by testing out new roles for architects.

Los Angeles architects thought they were prepared for "194X," as the projected postwar period's onset was called by *Architectural Forum* magazine. Such magazines were filled with creative ideas about the modern mass house, the homebuyers who would demand new houses for new lifestyles, and cautions to homebuilders who would get left behind if they tried to conduct business as usual. Architects tested new materials such as plywood, plastic, aluminum, and gunite for family rooms, open kitchens, flat roofs, carports, and patio living. Critic and historian Thomas Hine argues that principles of modernism in the 1950s translated less into the architecture of the house and more directly into its modern accoutrement, from dishwashers and built-in televisions to radiant heat systems that extended from the interior of the house onto the patio slab.[13] But Hine broadly portrays the American postwar home; when it comes to Los Angeles, another overlay is visible. Here, homebuilders turned their craft into a veritable industry, innovating amenities but also architectural features and, perhaps more importantly, home delivery. Mass housing flirted with new means of production, new forms of the decentralized community, and, finally, with new packaging of the home itself.

The postwar house was variously called the "small house," the "low-cost house," or the "mass-housing solution." To create this new entity, architects experimented with modular systems, prefabrication, assembly-line manufacturing, structural innovation, and new materials that wartime production made feasible. The question was this: who were the clients for mass modern housing? The likely implementers would be large-scale contractors, whose taste for experimentation was small and further lessened by the regulatory and lending preferences for conventional construction. Indeed it was this situation that motivated John Entenza, the editor of *Arts & Architecture* magazine, to launch the Case Study House Program. Renowned architecture historian Esther McCoy described the motivation:

> Unless there were clients who could wait patiently until an architect had succeeded in getting plans through a building department without compromising his design, and unless there were loan agencies who would finance experimental work, many of the creative ideas on the drawing boards and in the minds of architects would be lost. In 1945, Entenza abandoned his passive role as editor to play a dynamic one in postwar architecture. He announced that the magazine itself had become a client. Eight offices were commissioned to design eight houses.[14]

While the Case Study House Program was significant in many ways (and further described in other chapters of this volume), here it is relevant to call attention to its reactionary stance toward the regulatory and lending agencies.

BUILDER-ARCHITECT COLLABORATIONS

Develop a relationship with a builder, do good work, and you won't need to go ringing doorbells to get new clients.

   —William Krisel[15]

Of all the Case Study House architects, only A. Quincy Jones would follow Krisel's advice and develop a lasting relationship with a builder. Jones took this route in 1950, teaming for more than two decades with Joseph Eichler.[16] Eichler would go on to build over ten thousand houses, primarily in Northern California but also in three developments in the Los Angeles region: Granada Hills, Orange, and Thousand Oaks. As home construction mutated from the small-time operations of builders who would make a few residences each year into the mass production of housing, it was unclear just who would control this new market. The "building industry" was taking shape, but the specialized roles we now take for granted did not exist. Builders, architects, residents, product manufacturers, furniture stores, magazines, department stores, banks, corporations, and government agencies were just some of the players. Architects and builders together forged a variety of collaborations during this period.

  One good example of these collaborations is the model home, an evolving agent in the homebuilding process. Prior to the war, builders would participate in home exhibitions by building a full-scale house to show their construction capabilities. This was a demonstration of craft rather than design, since standard practice was to purchase an empty lot from a subdivider and then search for an independent builder as well as house plans. The exhibition house expanded as a popular means to market home design, architects, builders, and furniture, and even lifestyle. Wurdeman and Becket's design for Fritz Burns's Postwar House (1946) was displayed in the middle of the city, on Wilshire and Highland Boulevards; it was later converted into the Home of Tomorrow and featured Barker Brothers furniture. Cliff May's Magic-Money House was built on the rooftop of W. & J. Sloane Furniture Company in Beverly Hills.[17] The exhibition house evolved into the more common model home, which sat within a new subdivision as a marketing demonstration for the entire development. Prospective home buyers could tour models that displayed the different house types and interiors for the Alexander Houses by architects Dan Palmer and William Krisel in the Corbin Palms development of Woodland Hills (fig. 2).[18]

  Shelter magazines promoted house styles along with the architects who would make them.

FIGURE 2.
Palmer and Krisel, Architects (1949–66).
Model home in Corbin Palms (1953–55),
Woodland Hills, ca. 1954.
Photo by Douglas M. Simmonds.
Los Angeles, Getty Research Institute.

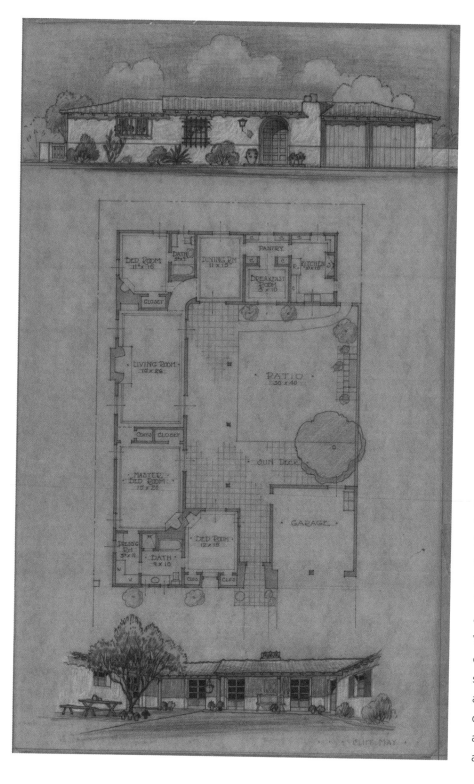

The *Arts & Architecture* Case Study House Program was overshadowed in the popular media by both *House Beautiful* and *Sunset* magazine's promotion of the ranch-style home. *Sunset* published books and house plans by its favorite California son, Cliff May. His successful career designing custom homes first led him to try to become his own merchant builder. He entered the homebuilding market by buying property that he called Riviera Ranch along a canyon off Sunset Boulevard. There, he subdivided and sold lots and built his own house to serve as a model home, which was published in *House Beautiful.* The Pace-Setter House was on its cover in February of 1947; three years earlier, the magazine had featured another May house on the cover. May's informal ranch-house plan bore similarities to modern houses in its interior openness and connections to the outdoors (fig. 3). According to historians Sally Woodbridge and Daniel Gregory, the California-ranch-style house was positioned as a populist alternative against the abstract modernism promoted by Philip Johnson and Henry-Russell Hitchcock in their "international style" exhibition organized at the Museum of Modern Art in 1932. *House Beautiful*'s editor, Elizabeth Gordon, wrote about the ranch style: "A house can be modern and not look it."[19]

While Palmer and Krisel and Jones and Emmons had long-term relationships with individual builders (the Alexander Construction Company and Eichler, respectively), May tested a wider range of collaborative structures. Along with his architect-partner Chris Choate, he generated a stripped-down version of the ranch house that they successfully marketed to builders across California and the Southwest through the Ranch House Supply Corporation, which they formed in 1953.[20] In contrast to the larger and prototypical ranch-style homes, such as those sold in Riviera Ranch or featured in *House Beautiful,* the small house does not have much ranch style or form. These plans are telling: the standard small house—whether in Cupertino, Westchester, or Levittown, New York—left little room for architectural invention. Variations in plan withered away, leaving a thin surface of market differentiation created by mere styling, such as a long porch for "ranch" and shutters for "Cape Cod." There was not enough room for modern living, as an ideal, in the one-thousand-square-foot home. Only Gregory Ain contrived a distinctly modern plan for such a very small space, including an open and flexible room arrangement, connections between inside and outside, and a lack of distinct circulation space (figs. 4–6).

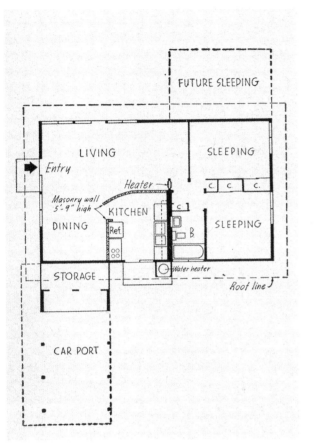

FIGURE 4.

**Cliff May (American, 1908–89) and
Chris Choate (American, 1908–81).**
Plan for a ranch-style tract house in Cupertino, ca. 1952.
From "More Living Space," *Sunset: The Pacific Monthly*
(November 1952): 46.

FIGURE 5.

Alfred Levitt (American, 1912–66).
Plan for a Levittown Long Island Cape Cod house
developed by Levitt and Sons, 1947.

FIGURE 6.

Ain, Johnson and Day, Architects (1947–51).
Plan for a Modernique home, 1946–48.
Ink, zip-a-tone, and correction fluid on paper,
59.1 × 82.6 cm (23¼ × 32½ in.).
Santa Barbara, Art, Design & Architecture Museum
at the University of California, Santa Barbara.

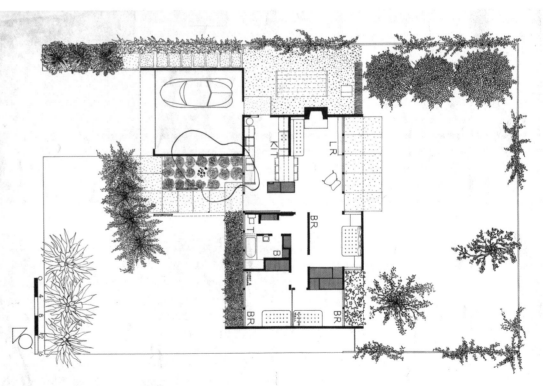

FIGURE 3. *(OPPOSITE PAGE)*
Cliff May (American, 1908–89).
Unidentified house: plan, perspective,
and elevation, ca. 1932.
Pencil and colored pencil on paper,
101.6 × 38.1 cm (40 × 15 in.).
Rendering by Starling Watson.
Santa Barbara, Art, Design & Architecture Museum
at the University of California, Santa Barbara.

There were other California experiments in homebuilding while postwar conventions were gestating. One of the most radical propositions was Crestwood Hills, planned and executed by a cooperative of future residents whose political and aesthetic agendas set them apart.[21] They formed the Mutual Housing Association and hired the modernist design team of Edgardo Contini, A. Quincy Jones, Whitney Rowland Smith, and landscape architect Garrett Eckbo. Jones and Smith were, in 1945, among the first of eight architects commissioned by Entenza for the Case Study House Program. Strongly influenced by Frank Lloyd Wright, the Crestwood Hills team designed what they hoped would be five hundred houses in the Brentwood hills that would be priced competitively with the low-cost tract houses being built at the time. But the designers struggled to get approvals from "the antimodernist FHA" for the first cluster of homes breaking ground in 1949.[22] As with Ain's Modernique homes at the Mar Vista Tract (fig. 7; see fig. 6), modernism was associated at Crestwood Hills with political progressivism if not socialism. To prospective residents, this was the point; to the general public with the McCarthy era on the horizon, this verged on anti-Americanism. Political hostility slowed the project in many ways, as did complications with stepping outside convention. Builders were unfamiliar with

FIGURE 7.
Gregory Ain (American, 1908–88).
Modernique home in Mar Vista Tract (1946–48), 2012.
Photo by Octavia Leclerc-Jones.

modernist construction details and engineering, and lenders were accustomed to working with merchant builders rather than cooperatives. Finally, the cost of houses at Crestwood Hills more than tripled and the number of units built was just over one hundred.

CONCLUSIONS

By 1962 it had become clear that the battle for housing had been won by the developers, with more drafting services involved than architects.
—Esther McCoy[23]

Mass-produced housing erupted in Los Angeles after the war, and the urban geography would never recover. Los Angeles pioneered the tract home and then exported it across the globe. It was also in Los Angeles that builders became developers, real estate became an industry, and architects experimented in myriad ways to engage what was considered the new American landscape. During the postwar era, the merchant builder, or production homebuilder, would assume a role that was equivalent to the director in a movie: the person who would bring all the actors together and orchestrate their efforts toward a final production. Eventually, this role solidified into the developer. McCoy states that the "developers" had taken the primary role in housing by 1962, but she could only make this statement in 1977, with hindsight. In 1962, these same individuals were still identified as "homebuilders," "merchant builders," or "contractor-designers."[24]

In the early postwar years, a practical utopia seemed imminent. Every middle-class family could own its own home, garden, and car. The scarcity that permeated the war years was over; a resurgent economy was producing what appeared to be an endless abundance of buildable land, resources such as water and energy, and leisure time. Los Angeles, more than any other city, grew to be governed by the hinterlands rather than the center, undermining the established belief put forward by the Chicago School urbanists that the city was shaped in concentric rings rippling out from the core. The older East Coast city might follow this pattern, but the newer city of the Southwest was not structured so rigidly around a nineteenth-century downtown. Without the latter generating urban structure, the postwar metropolis effectively liberated everyday life from its heretofore hierarchical relationship as "sub"-urban to work and culture. Now the home was its own center, leisure its own pursuit, the patio as important as the theater. While sprawl is guilty of environmental assault, in some ways that early vision was more sustainable than it might at first seem: households had just one car, houses were small and thus more efficient, the work commute of one wage earner was relatively short. And in Los Angeles, as the suburbs came unhinged from the city, what actually happened was the erasure of those very distinctions—urban and suburban no longer pertained. In Los Angeles, the metropolis mutated into a new beast, one for which terminology remains inadequate. Los Angeles is the poster child for what Michael Dear, planner and geographer, calls "postmodern urbanism," and architect Albert Pope classifies as the "city of space."[25]

Among those shaping this new geography in midcentury, architects, true to their disciplinary nature, experimented with materials, design, floor plans, indoor-outdoor connections, and program of the 194X house. As McCoy said of the Los Angeles modernist architects in her introduction to the second edition of *Case Study*

Houses, "They had demonstrated that a good house can be of cheap materials; outdoor spaces are as much a part of design as enclosed space; a dining room is less necessary than two baths and large glass areas; a house should be turned away from the street toward a private garden at the back, etc."[26] These same ideas permeated the drawings by architects working directly with production homebuilders, creating innovations ranging from the evolving ranch-style home to the more radical removal of the traditional wall between the kitchen and the rest of the house. These changes were not insignificant, but they were dwarfed by the transformation of home production on the whole. To deliver a house to every family, a housing industry replaced homebuilders. Rather than selecting a site and then finding a banker and a builder, a family visited a model home that would be exactly like their own, which, upon move-in, would be replete with blinds, sprinklers, trees, cabinets, and appliances. Modern tract houses like those of Ain and Palmer and Krisel turned their backs on the street to open to their own backyards (see fig. 7). Houses were built to Federal Housing Administration (FHA) standards so that loans were pro forma. The design of the neighborhood was little more than efficient property subdivision, commensurate with the emphasis on the individual house. Designers such as Jones and Emmons, May and Choate, and Palmer and Krisel waded into the development industry by extending the architect's role past a one-to-one relationship with a client. But the tract house was so small that in all but a few instances, efficiencies crowded "modern living" out of the plans, leaving only the vestiges of styling.

The conventional suburban postwar pattern might have turned out differently had ideas such as those of Ain in Mar Vista or the Mutual Housing Association at Crestwood Hills taken hold. But as those projects uncovered, the architecture and the community planning were caught in a web of constraints that only the most conventional housing escaped. Breaking free incurred costs in time and money that undermined the basic project of housing for the masses. Those significant departures from the prevailing practices now stand as important testimony that together, designers, residents, and builders invented more than one American dream for the house, the neighborhood, and the city. With criticism of the suburban norms mounting on all fronts—from the foreclosure crisis that began in 2008 to greenhouse gas emissions—the time is ripe for a new era of architect-builder experimentation.

NOTES

1   For histories of suburbs, see Dolores Hayden, *Building Suburbia: Green Fields and Urban Growth, 1820–2000* (New York: Pantheon, 2003); and the long view is described by Robert Bruegmann, *Sprawl: A Compact History* (Chicago: University of Chicago Press, 2005).

2   Among other features, Kaiser's plastic house incorporated full walls of windows and flat roofs; Neutra's proposals for an East Coast version of Levittown showed open plans and clean elevations that might have shaped a different domestic imaginary had they ever been built en masse; Ain's Mar Vista is illustrated in figures 6 and 7. As neighborhood plans, Crestwood Hills in Los Angeles include shared facilities along with private, modern houses that are built into an articulated topography, while the multifamily Case Study Houses show benefits of collective site planning. Many of these examples are included in Dana Cuff, *The Provisional City: Los Angeles Stories of Architecture and Urbanism* (Cambridge, Mass.: MIT Press, 2000); to learn more about Crestwood Hills Village, see Harold Zellman and Roger Friedland, "Broadacre in Brentwood? The Politics of Architectural Aesthetics," in Charles G. Salas and Michael S. Roth, eds., *Looking for Los Angeles: Architecture, Film, Photography, and the Urban Landscape* (Los Angeles: Getty Research Institute, 2001), 167–210.

3   Greg Hise, *Magnetic Los Angeles* (Baltimore: Johns Hopkins University Press, 1997).

4   Cuff, *The Provisional City,* 242–45.

5   James Thomas Keane, *Fritz B. Burns and the Development of Los Angeles* (Los Angeles: Loyola Marymount University, 2001), 75.

6   Keane, *Fritz B. Burns,* 75–77.

7   Keane, *Fritz B. Burns,* 73–75.

8   Merry Ovnick, *Los Angeles: The End of the Rainbow* (Los Angeles: Balcony, 1994), 256.

9   Kaiser and Burns are described in Cuff, *The Provisional City;* Hise, *Magnetic Los Angeles;* and Keane, *Fritz B. Burns.*

10 Kaiser's plastic house is documented in the following report: Housing Division, Henry J. Kaiser Company, *Prefabricated Plastic Houses* (Oakland, Calif.: January 1945), Kaiser Papers, file 315 19, Bancroft Library, University of California, Berkeley.

11 Keane, *Fritz B. Burns,* 157.

12 See, for example, the series of articles on the postwar house in the 1944 issues of *Architectural Forum,* and the whole issue "New Building for 194X," *Architectural Forum* 78, no. 5 (1943).

13 Thomas Hine, "The Search for the Postwar House," in Elizabeth A. T. Smith, ed., *Blueprints for Modern Living: History and Legacy of the Case Study Houses* (Cambridge, Mass.: MIT Press, 1989), 167–81.

14 Esther McCoy, *Case Study Houses, 1945–1962,* 2nd ed. (Los Angeles: Hennessey & Ingalls, 1977), 9.

15 Krisel speaking in 2009 about working with the homebuilder Robert Alexander in Palm Springs in the 1950s; Morris Newman, "Masters of Modernism—The Butterfly Effect," *Palm Springs Life,* February 2009, http://www.palmspringslife.com /Palm-Springs-Life/February-2009/Masters-of-Modernism-The-Butterfly-Effect/.

16 A. Quincy Jones, Frederick E. Emmons, and John L. Chapman, *Builders' Homes for Better Living* (New York: Reinhold, 1957). Eichler would also work with Edward Fickett, another prolific architect of postwar houses from Los Angeles.

17 Mary A. van Balgooy, "Designer of the Dream," *Southern California Quarterly* 86, no. 2 (2004): 127–44.

18 These houses and their neighborhood, often referred to as the Alexander Tract, were named after the builder, the Alexander Construction Company, in Palm Springs. See Dave Weinstein, "The Elite Modern of Corbin Palms, Woodland Hills," *Eichler Network,* http://www.eichlernetwork.com/article/elite-modern-corbin-palms-woodland-hills?page=0,2.

19 This quote is from the article "A House Can Be Modern and Not Look It," *House Beautiful,* October 1945, 109–15. See Daniel P. Gregory, *Cliff May and the Modern Ranch House* (New York: Rizzoli, 2008); and Sally Woodbridge's review of Gregory's book: "Book Review: *Cliff May and the Modern Ranch House* by Daniel P. Gregory," *Design by the Bay,* http://designbythebay.com/2009/01 /cliff-may-modern-ranch-house/.

20 Van Balgooy, "Designer of the Dream," 137.

21 Zellman and Friedland, "Broadacre in Brentwood?" The essay describes the socialist cooperative that sought to create a community open to artists, progressives, Jews, blacks, and all income groups.

22 Zellman and Friedland, "Broadacre in Brentwood?," 193.

23 McCoy, *Case Study Houses,* 5.

24 McCoy, *Case Study Houses,* 5. In the introduction to the second edition (1977), McCoy reflects on the first edition, which appeared fifteen years earlier. In the later text, she uses the new terminology.

25 Michael Dear, *The Postmodern Urban Condition* (Oxford: Blackwell, 2000); and Albert Pope, "From Form to Space," in Dana Cuff and Roger Sherman, eds., *Fast-Forward Urbanism: Rethinking Architecture's Engagement with the City* (New York: Princeton Architectural, 2011), 143–75.

26 McCoy, *Case Study Houses,* 4.

They papered their walls with the view

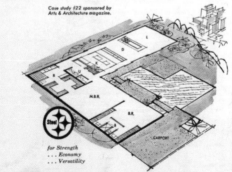 

EXPERIMENTAL JET SET
AEROSPACE AND THE MODERN HOUSE IN LOS ANGELES

Dana Hutt

During the war many architects and engineers…were preparing plans for a future house
that was to be brilliantly engineered, furnished with gadgets and clothed in pastoral garb—
a marriage between Walden Pond and Douglas Aircraft.
　　　—Esther McCoy[1]

WITH CHARACTERISTIC WIT AND BLUNTNESS, architectural historian Esther McCoy forged a vivid image of the dual design aspirations of Los Angeles's postwar architects—aspirations shaped in part by the exponential growth of the city's aircraft and aerospace industries and the accompanying technological and material innovations. From Le Corbusier to Frank Gehry, architects have been fascinated by the design and technology of aircraft. Aircraft design and modern architecture share common goals of lightness, thinness, modernity, and defiance of gravity. Charles Eames avidly read catalogs of aviation equipment and wrote, "In the airplane, one feels strongly the appropriateness of its streamed lines and they seem healthy and good."[2] R. Buckminster Fuller brought together the two design disciplines in the Dymaxion House, his solution for a strong, lightweight mass-produced house. Following the principles of aircraft design, Fuller sought to maximize the house's industrial efficiency while minimizing material and weight based on his belief that in industry the basic accounting unit is the pound.[3] In 1946, a full-scale prototype of the Dymaxion House was built with the sponsorship of Beech Aircraft of Wichita, Kansas.

　　　During the war, the aircraft industry in Los Angeles engaged quite a number of architects. Gregory Ain helped to invent the "Kazam! machine," which produced the molded plywood nose and other aircraft parts for Consolidated Vultee Aircraft. Charles and Ray Eames, who famously gave the Kazam! its sobriquet, used the machine to fabricate plywood aircraft parts, leg splints, and stretchers. Esther McCoy and Rodney Walker both worked in engineering drafting in the Experimental Shop at Douglas Aircraft; he was her immediate supervisor.[4] Engineers and others in the fields of aircraft, aerospace, and science advanced experiments

FIGURE 1.
**Advertisement for Bethlehem Steel showing
Pierre Koenig's Case Study House #22 (Stahl Residence).**
From *Arts & Architecture* 79, no. 8 (August 1962):
back cover.

in modern architecture through patronage and collaboration. Before the war, Richard Neutra attracted prominent clientele in the world of technology and science, including two professors at the California Institute of Technology (Caltech) in Pasadena. He designed the innovative all-metal Beard Residence (1934) for an engineering professor and the Richter Residence (1936) for a renowned seismologist.[5] After World War II, many clients in Southern California were receptive to architectural innovation and material experimentation in residential architecture, and this open-mindedness was particularly true for individuals whose livelihoods involved aviation, research, testing, and technological progress.[6]

This essay will review key interactions between architecture and the aircraft and aerospace industries and explore technological advancements and experimental uses of materials in the custom-built house. Topics to be examined include how architects deployed crossover materials—steel, aluminum, fiberglass, synthetic resins, plastics—and, critically, how individuals and manufacturers from aircraft/aerospace and ancillary industries fostered innovation in modern residential design through patronage and partnership.

STEEL

The story of one of the most prominent steel-framed houses in Los Angeles begins appropriately enough at an airport. The couple who commissioned the house initially met through a mutual friend who introduced them at the Flight Deck restaurant at LAX.[7] Buck Stahl was then a purchasing agent with Hughes Aircraft, his future wife, Carlotta, a secretary at North American Aviation. Unlike Case Study House projects in which a client was paired with a speculative house, it was the Stahls who bought the site, determined the program, and selected the architect. And unlike other architects they interviewed, Pierre Koenig agreed without hesitation to their request for no solid walls facing the view. He accomplished it through steel: a minimal structural frame covered by a roof of steel decking and enclosed by panels of glass or steel for privacy, creating a balance of "house, pool, sky and view."[8] Advertising copywriters for a steel company cast the Stahls' wide-open vistas in a more conventional light: "They papered their walls with the view" (fig. 1).[9] In the celebrated Julius Shulman photograph, a wing of Case Study House #22 (1960) projects out over the nighttime urban grid of Los Angeles, the streetlights below forming dotted lines like so many airport runways.

As wartime shortages gave way to peacetime prosperity, steel assumed a fresh postwar identity as the material of distinction for modern architecture. It especially appealed to architects who participated in the Case Study Program, launched in 1945 by *Arts & Architecture* magazine. Steel manufacturers enlisted Koenig, Craig Ellwood, Raphael Soriano, and others to tout the benefits of steel in print advertisements in the late 1950s and early 1960s. Steel, they suggested, was superior to wood for its strength, durability, precision, speedy construction, flexibility, and ability to frame large, open spaces and enable construction on difficult hillside sites without first leveling. Steel was essential to architects' increasing interest in prefabrication, standardization, and use of off-the-shelf parts, as exemplified by Case Study House #8 (1945–49), designed by Charles and Ray Eames. Thin beams and columns of steel made possible the openness, lightness, and transparency of the new modern house, its large panels of glass and sliding glass doors the outcome of wartime innovation.

The industrial connotations of structural steel posed a formidable obstacle to the public's acceptance of the material for houses. Steel suppliers such as Bethlehem Steel, U.S. Steel, and Truscon Steel attempted to soften its character in advertisements in order to arm architects with reasons to give potential clients for using it, including steel's ability to withstand an earthquake and the ease of configuring rooms with movable walls within a fixed frame—but to little avail.[10] Esther McCoy later observed, "It appears now that the steel-framed house answered no long-lived social need; the average family sooner or later sought the wood-framed tract house."[11] It clearly took an exceptional family to commission Case Study House #22.

Metal-framed sliding glass doors were critical to the transparency and openness of Case Study House #22 as well as other modern houses of the period. Koenig even appeared in an advertisement for Bellevue steel doors to say: "One of the most important trends today in the construction of homes is the use of sliding glass doors."[12] As the aerospace industry continued to expand and consolidate in the postwar years, the heavily promoted trend drew the notice of Northrop Corporation. In 1961, the Southern California–based aircraft company announced its acquisition of Arcadia, one of the original manufacturers of sliding glass doors.[13] Arcadia's cofounder had, in fact, previously worked at Douglas Aircraft developing lightweight aircraft.[14] A full-page ad in *Arts & Architecture* presents the new company, renamed Northrop Architectural Systems, as an example of synergistic thinking: "Brand names long associated with quality and technological progress, now combined and coordinated to bring a new systems approach to architectural product development."[15] An illustration in a later ad for Arcadia Series 800 Sliding Glass Doors implies the dual expertise of the company. From the interior of a restaurant, we look through floor-to-ceiling plate glass windows to a balcony overlooking an airport. On the right, a man gestures to a helicopter hovering above, while, to the left, a jet lands. The caption suggests a market ambition larger than either discipline: "Another project to build the face of a city … from Northrop Architectural Systems" (fig. 2).

FIGURE 2.
Advertisement for Arcadia Series 800 Sliding Glass Doors.
From *Arts & Architecture* 79, no. 5 (May 1962): 2.

ALUMINUM

Marketed as the "metal of the future" since the late nineteenth century, aluminum became synonymous with lightness, abundance, beauty, resistance to corrosion, and progress—characteristics that made it ideal for modern aircraft and, later, modern design.[16] World War II forced a radical reconfiguration of the US aluminum industry. To meet the huge wartime demand for strong lightweight metal with which to fabricate airplanes, the US government broke up a veritable monopoly by the Aluminum Company of America (Alcoa) by subsidizing the industry's expansion and increasing production by 600 percent.[17] After the war, the government deemed it necessary for America's defense to maintain aluminum's increased production capacity. By 1945, industry analysts were arguing that new uses for aluminum must be found, and designers outside the industry were encouraged to imagine new applications for the metal.[18]

In Southern California, as wartime factories were converted to peacetime uses, the pressing housing demand led to nascent efforts in housing prefabrication. One such prototype was the Vultee House, designed in 1947 by industrial designer Henry Dreyfuss and architect Edward Larabee Barnes "in collaboration with top aircraft engineers."[19] Units of the prefabricated two-bedroom house were built in a Consolidated Vultee Aircraft factory in Los Angeles. The house's walls and roof were constructed of sandwich panels in which sheets of high-strength aluminum encased "lumicomb," a lightweight cardboardlike honeycomb core primarily used for airplane bulkheads. Two prototypes were constructed, but the house never went into mass production.[20]

Raphael Soriano recognized the design potential of aluminum as early as the "House 194X" competition, sponsored by *Architectural Forum* in 1942. The competition challenged architects to speculate on how wartime industrial innovations would reshape houses. Soriano's fascination with airplanes provided the inspiration for his entry, a mobile home. He returned to aluminum, after years of designing for steel, when he began to work with Alcoa in 1950.[21] He developed what he called the "all-aluminum" building system in the early 1960s, which he later introduced as "Soria Structures." Aluminum, for Soriano, represented technological progress and greater economy than steel: aluminum was easier to fabricate and ship because of its light weight, and it required no painting. The first all-aluminum residence was built in 1964 in Studio City, California. Al Grossman, an aluminum subcontractor and cousin of the inventor of Glide aluminum sliding windows, was intrigued by the idea of a house to display his products. The one-story 3,200-square-foot house, with twenty-eight sliding glass doors, featured integral color on beams and columns anodized in jewel-like hues of purple, bronze, and blue. The temperamental and exacting Soriano walked off the job two-thirds of the way through completion and was never involved in any published articles on the house.[22] He used the all-aluminum system to build only one other project, which he also considered unsuccessful; nevertheless, he continued to promote the system for both residential and commercial buildings.[23]

Previously, Soriano's brusque and uncompromising attitude had ended another trailblazing aluminum project. Several years before Dreyfuss and Barnes's Vultee House, Soriano had approached Consolidated Vultee Aircraft about developing a light-metal house. Soriano told the company president that fabricating his "beautiful house of metal like an airplane" would stimulate the industry.[24] But, according to the architect, the talks derailed when Vultee's chairman of the board—a scientist at Caltech—asked him,

"Mr. Soriano, can we put [on] some colonial type of an entrance, porches?" Soriano responded: "Why do you want to do that? Do you do that to your planes?"[25]

PLASTICS

Of all the materials developed during World War II, plastics underwent the most rapid transformation from wartime to peacetime use. Plastics of various formulations replaced light metals during wartime shortages and performed other critical roles in aeronautics. In the postwar spirit of invention and innovation, architects and manufacturers experimented with crossover applications of these materials, and some gained widespread usage in the building industry.

Synthetic resins, together with adhesives and new processes, significantly strengthened and improved wood products during the war. Plywood with added strength, water resistance, and durability was used for aircraft wings and fuselages.[26] Wooden pieces could now form laminated trusses and arches as strong as metal ones in large factories, such as Hughes Aircraft in Culver City.[27] Resin-enhanced wood products, used singly or as laminates in a sandwich application, became indispensable for postwar ranch and post-and-beam houses. An outstanding example was Buff, Straub, and Hensman's Case Study House #20 (1958) in Altadena, built for graphic designer Saul Bass and biochemist Dr. Ruth Bass, with panels of stressed-skin, plastic-impregnated Douglas fir plywood for the walls, and an experimental barrel-vaulted roof. Structural glued laminated timber, or glulam, made possible the long-span beams and uninterrupted space in Ray Kappe's own house in Pacific Palisades (1967).

Acrylic resins, with their exceptional clarity, strength, and ability to be molded, became preferred materials for the nose cones of bombers and for the complex shapes of fighter-plane cockpit canopies.[28] These materials were then easily adapted for domestic use in skylights and skylight domes (fig. 3). In Los Angeles, Swedlow Plastics—a pioneering manufacturer of acrylics and laminated plastics for aerospace, including complex transparent systems for the Lockheed Hudson bomber and fuel cells for military aircraft—developed a material called Plyon for domestic use.[29] This translucent glass-cloth laminated sheeting, which *Arts & Architecture* described as a "very new and versatile wall covering," was used on sliding diffusion screens in the upper portion of the living room of the Eameses' Case Study House #8.[30] Featured as a "merit-specified" material in the magazine, Plyon appears to have had a short shelf life, while the use of other plastics, especially fiberglass, expanded.[31]

Fiberglass became synonymous with progress and was the principal material for the Monsanto House of the Future, erected at Disneyland Park in Anaheim in 1957. The composite, also known as glass fiber–reinforced plastic, is lightweight, strong, and water-resistant. During wartime, fiberglass was used for aircraft radomes, as it fully protected radar technology while allowing radio-wave penetration.[32] At the war's end, Charles and Ray Eames and Eero Saarinen created chairs of fiberglass, working with Zenith Plastics of Gardena, California, which had fabricated radomes during the war.[33] Fiberglass swiftly gained a place in the Southern California building industry as insulation, built-up roofing, and fabric for drapery or curtains. A. Quincy Jones, Frederick Emmons, and Soriano exploited its translucence for screens, garden walls, and patio coverings. Demand for fiberglass grew throughout the 1950s. *Sunset* magazine presented

FIGURE 3.
Advertisement for Plexiglas.
From *Architectural Record* 124, no. 9 (1958): 344–45.

do-it-yourself applications for the low-cost material, available in various hues and either flat or corrugated. For outdoor use, *Sunset* recommended "blue, soft green and yellow."[34]

Rudolph Schindler seized upon the expressive qualities of fiberglass. Even before his unbuilt design for Aline Barnsdall's Translucent House (1927), he was interested in how lighting and translucency affected the shaping of space. The effects of color also began to fascinate Schindler.[35] In 1952, he wrote, "The ultimate and revolutionary aim will be to create a feeling of color throughout the atmosphere of the room, rather than to be satisfied with static areas of color on the walls."[36] To achieve translucency and a "feeling of color," he proposed blue fiberglass panels in a vaulted ceiling to Adolf Tischler, a client whom Schindler sensed would be open to experimentation. The client, an artist and silversmith, worked as head of the graphics department at the Aerospace Corporation in El Segundo. Years later, Tischler described the experience:

[Schindler] liked to experiment and some of his experiments were not revealed until the client saw them in place. One such experiment was proposed for our house—a translucent blue fiberglass material on part of our roof. We were concerned, but Schindler assured us it would be fine. We decided to reserve judgment until we saw the material…. The fiberglass roof was a disaster. Everything inside the house looked blue, including people, and the heat came through with a vengeance.

Several years later, Tischler reduced the amount of fiberglass by covering the top portion with plywood (fig. 4). He later wrote that, despite early heartaches caused by cost overruns, leaks, and the blue fiberglass, the house was "something really special…a strong architectural statement with timeless beauty."[37]

The Merwyn C. Gill Residence (1967) in Pasadena, designed by Buff and Hensman for the inventor, more subtly manifested its material innovation. The M. C. Gill Corporation, originally named the Peerless Plastics Products Company, developed composite plastics for the aircraft industry, including the cargo compartment liner for the DC-6.[38] The post-and-beam house features panels of plastic and other materials by the manufacturer, including resins, fiberglass, and laminates of polyurethane, paper, and balsa wood.[39] Sandwich panels containing cores of honeycomb paper, polyurethane foam, or fiberglass, depending on load and function, were used for skylights, wall panels, and roofing.[40] The client continued to test and upgrade building materials as an ongoing project of research and development.

FIGURE 4.
Rudolph M. Schindler (Austrian-born American, 1887–1953).
Tischler Residence (1949–50), Westwood, 1997.
Photo by Grant Mudford.

FIGURE 5.
Cover of *Home* (*Los Angeles Times* magazine), 1 July 1962, showing Bernard Judge's "Triponent" House.
Photo by Julius Shulman.
Los Angeles, Getty Research Institute.

Another unexpected test for plastics was Bernard Judge's "Triponent" House (1960) in the Hollywood Hills, a variation on the geodesic domes of R. Buckminster Fuller (fig. 5).[41] To Judge, the dome was a research house for how to build lightly on the ground. It was designed and constructed with the help of professors and his fellow students in the School of Architecture at the University of Southern California (USC). A colleague of Fuller's gave Judge the structural system of aluminum pipe and stainless steel wire for the fifty-foot dome, but Judge needed to determine the best material for the envelope—something waterproof that would expand and contract. After months of testing plywood, glass, and plastics in the Mojave Desert without success, he read about the National Aeronautics and Space Administration's Echo satellite, a communications balloon launched in 1960 and made of a flexible, semitransparent polyester film invented in the early 1950s called Mylar.[42] Judge contacted the manufacturer, DuPont, for a sample to test, and the company agreed, perceiving a new market for the material. Judge enclosed the dome with sheets of clear Mylar attached to bowstring-like mechanisms inside to allow expansion and contraction. Hendrik de Kanter, a student in industrial design at USC and a designer for Douglas Aircraft, helped build it, supported the project financially, and later owned the dome. According to a 1962 *Los Angeles Times* article, De Kanter worked on "structures to house the first expeditions on the moon!"[43] Subsequently sold, the dome was dismantled.[44]

SPACE

In late-1950s Los Angeles, architects increasingly conducted spatial experiments in residential designs and explored how architectural space itself could be considered a material. Schindler had posited as much in a 1914 manifesto: "The architectural design concerns itself with 'Space' as its raw material and with the articulated room as its product.... The architect has finally discovered the medium of his art: SPACE."[45] John Lautner respected the work of Schindler, and for him it was also space that mattered most in architecture: "To me [space is] one of the biggest contributions to joy in life, to human welfare. So, when you contribute this kind of space, you're giving life...to the environment."[46]

Postwar advances in engineering, technology, and material science allowed new spatial fluidity in Lautner's work—for example, in the Chemosphere (Malin Residence), in the Hollywood Hills (fig. 6), and in Silvertop (Reiner Residence), in the Silver Lake neighborhood of Los Angeles. The risk-taking, forward-looking clients, both of whom had worked in the aerospace industry, were crucial to these experimental projects.[47] Leonard Malin and Kenneth Reiner both became integral collaborators with Lautner in the design and construction of their homes.

The Chemosphere (1960), the best known of Lautner's houses, demonstrates how an improbable design can be achieved through an unlikely but ideal convergence: an architect who envisions how to build on an impossibly steep hillside without disturbing it; a client, an aerospace mechanical engineer, who is, according to Lautner, "open to new ideas and imaginative designs" and who leaves his job at the age of twenty-eight to work on the house's construction full-time; and a sponsor, Chem Seal Corporation (manufacturer of epoxies, sealants, and coating compounds used in the aerospace industry), who is eager to promote architectural applications of its products.[48] The *Los Angeles Times* lauded the epoxies, which are "only a fraction of an inch thick, work on surfaces of any shape and thickness, and need not be concealed," as alternates to nails

Sunday *Los Angeles Times* April 30, 1961

Home

Julius Shulman

PEDESTAL HOUSE

A radical plan for hillside living

The beauty of diamonds ● Palos Verdes homes tour

FIGURE 6.
Cover of *Home* **(***Los Angeles Times* **magazine),
30 April 1961, showing John Lautner's Malin Residence
(Chemosphere).**
Photo by Julius Shulman.
Los Angeles, Getty Research Institute.

and bolts in homebuilding.[49] This mix of solutions—a steel-and-wood structure resting on a central concrete column—would be unorthodox for most modernists, but it was a rational solution to Lautner, whose primary objective was "keeping a clear span roof with no center column, and creating a maximum of livable space."[50] Scholar Jon Yoder observes how Lautner borrowed the central plan and central mechanical core of Fuller's Dymaxion House and notes that "Lautner was disappointed that aircraft companies never mass-produced the Dymaxion house, and the Chemosphere was partially his attempt to fulfill the promise of Fuller's design."[51] The plan and elevation of the Chemosphere, much like an air traffic control tower, provide a sense of spatial freedom, and one's gaze is guided skyward.[52]

Silvertop (1956) represents the epitome of midcentury architectural experimentation in Los Angeles. Client Kenneth Reiner, an inventor and engineer, asked Lautner to design a research house for his family to test "new materials and techniques for the market."[53] The inventor and the architect collaborated for nearly ten years; they created and tested new custom designs—from electrically operated skylights and doors to new light switches—in a "machine shop behind Mr. Reiner's factory kept entirely for our use."[54] Reiner had trained as an electrical engineer and worked briefly at Lockheed Aircraft before starting his own business inventing products for the aircraft industry, most notably, the Kaylock self-locking nuts.[55] He was Lautner's ideal client: "an engineer with a constantly inventive and inquisitive mind" who was "willing to explore any idea I presented to him."[56] As with the Chemosphere, Silvertop was designed to leave the hillside intact. A thin, cantilevered ramp for the driveway preserved the hill, but city building inspectors challenged Lautner's innovative structure, which combined prestressed vertical block and prestressed, horizontal cast concrete, and Reiner sued the city to allow it.[57] The heart of the house is a three-thousand-square-foot living area under a low-arched, formed-in-place concrete roof. The vast living space extends outward, from frameless hanging sheets of glass held by clips made in Reiner's machine shop to an unimpeded view of nature, sky, and the silvery basin below.

The exploration of "space" took a new turn two decades later. In 1980, the California Council of the American Institute of Architects (CCAIA) Foundation commissioned Ray Kappe to develop concepts for an Advanced Technology House (ATH). The house would use the latest research from NASA. In contrast to other prototypes of the "future house," the ATH would embody multidisciplinary solutions to address critical concerns of the time: namely, increasing energy costs, environment degradation, and "diminishing space on the planet."[58] Kappe designed for the ATH a flexible modular system that attached horizontally or vertically. A car could easily pull each unit. His concept, as requested by the CCAIA Foundation, included a traveling prototype accompanied by a technology fair (see pl. 72).[59] But Kappe says, in the end, NASA never understood how its technology, materials, and methods could transfer to housing. A prototype was yet to be built when, in 1981, the initiative was terminated.[60]

CONCLUSION

Architecture is an act of optimism and ingenuity, as are aviation and aerospace. Postwar experimental houses in Los Angeles manifest the optimistic spirit and the booming economy of the United States in the years after World War II. Conditions coalesced in an ideal environment for invention. With the great demand for housing, architects and their clients were especially receptive to new building materials, new relaxed ways of living, and more openness and transparency in houses. Experimentation was in the air.

Southern California had gained a large pool of engineers and inventors in aircraft and aerospace who possessed perseverance, a penchant for risk taking, and, most important, a passion for discovery—all vital traits for clients and architects of experimental houses.

Architects in Los Angeles never lost their special fascination with aircraft and aerospace design. In the next two decades, a new nexus of aircraft/architecture innovation emerged as Frank Gehry drew upon CATIA, an early CAD program developed by a French aerospace company, allowing the next generation of architectural innovation in Los Angeles to take flight.[61]

NOTES

I would like to express my appreciation to Wim de Wit and Christopher James Alexander for the opportunity and encouragement to undertake this research. Special thanks also to Kenneth Breisch, John Crosse, Bernard Judge, and Ray Kappe.

1   Esther McCoy, "West Coast Architects V: John Lautner," *Arts & Architecture* 82 (August 1965): 22. The "marriage" McCoy performs is a tantalizing blend of literary reference and literal reference, the latter both autobiographical and synecdochical. McCoy worked at Douglas Aircraft during World War II.

2   Beatriz Colomina, "Reflections on the Eames House," in Donald Albrecht, ed., *The Work of Charles and Ray Eames: A Legacy of Invention*, exh. cat. (New York: Harry N. Abrams, 1997), 138; and Charles Eames, "Design Today," *California Arts & Architecture* 58 (September 1941): 18.

3   Edward R. Ford, *The Details of Modern Architecture, 1928 to 1988,* vol. 2 (Cambridge, Mass.: MIT Press), 251.

4   Susan Morgan, "Being There, Esther McCoy, the Accidental Architectural Historian," *Archives of American Art Journal* 48, nos. 1–2 (2009): 23; Kimberli Meyer and Susan Morgan, *Sympathetic Seeing: Esther McCoy and the Heart of American Modernist Architecture and Design* (West Hollywood, Calif.: MAK Center for Art & Architecture, 2011), 41.

5   Thomas S. Hines, *Richard Neutra and the Search for Modern Architecture* (New York: Oxford University Press, 1982), 119, 120. In 1977, Neutra designed the Singleton Residence in Bel Air for an engineer/cofounder of the aeronautics conglomerate Teledyne (Ruth Ryon, "Windows of Opportunity," *Los Angeles Times,* 25 April 2004).

6   Ray Kappe, for example, observed that at the beginning of his career in the mid-1950s, "aeronautical engineers were especially good clients"; Michael Webb, *Themes and Variations: House Design; Ray Kappe; Architects/Planners* (Mulgrave, Victoria: Images, 1998), 10.

7   Mary Melton, "Shot in the Dark," *Los Angeles* 46 (2001): 68.

8   "Case Study House No. 22," *Arts & Architecture* 77 (June 1960): 15.

9   "They Papered Their Walls with the View" (Bethlehem Steel advertisement), *Arts & Architecture* 79 (August 1962): back cover.

10   "Would Your Client Like Living in a Steel-Framed House?" (Bethlehem Steel advertisement), *Arts & Architecture* 80 (February 1963): 38.

11   Elizabeth A. T. Smith, ed., *Blueprints for Modern Living: History and Legacy of the Case Study Houses,* exh. cat. (Los Angeles: Museum of Contemporary Art, 1989), 33.

12   Bellevue Metal Products advertisement, *Arts & Architecture* 75 (May 1958): 38.

13   "Northrop Corp. to Buy Arcadia Metal Products," *Wall Street Journal,* 13 April 1961; and "New Offshoot for Northrop," *Los Angeles Times,* 29 September 1961.

14   See "Henry Emerson North Jr., '39," *Stanford Magazine* (2000): http://www.stanfordalumni.org/news/magazine/2000/mayjun /classnotes/obituaries.html.

15   Northrop Architectural Systems advertisement, *Arts & Architecture* 78 (October 1961): back cover.

16   Eric Schatzberg, "Symbolic Culture and Technological Change: The Cultural History of Aluminum as an Industrial Material," *Enterprise & Society* 4, no. 2 (2003): 226–71. Special thanks to Gregory Dreicer for bringing this article to my attention.

17   John Lauber, "And It Never Needs Painting: The Development of Residential Aluminum Siding," *APT Bulletin* 31 (2000): 17–18; and Dennis Doordan, "Promoting Aluminum: Designers and the American Aluminum Industry," *Design Issues* 9, no. 2 (1993): 45–46.

18   Doordan, "Promoting Aluminum," 46.

19   Henry Dreyfuss, "House in a Factory," *Arts & Architecture* 64 (September 1947): 31.

20   Jeffrey Head, "Snatched from Oblivion," *Metropolis* 26 (2006): 56.

21   Wolfgang Wagener, *Raphael Soriano* (New York: Phaidon, 2002), 58, 61, 67, 157.

22   Katherine Salant, "A 1963 Home Framed and Clad in Aluminum Is Still Virtually Maintenance-Free Today," *Los Angeles Times,* 2 April 2000; and Neil Jackson, *The Modern Steel House* (London: E. & F. N. Spon, 1996), 114. Thanks to Sian Winship for discussing aspects of the Grossman House with me.

23   Soriano's only other all-aluminum houses were built in Maui in 1965. According to Wagener, the houses were poorly constructed and soon after were altered by a new owner; Wagener, *Raphael Soriano,* 162, 163.

24   Quoted in Wagener, *Raphael Soriano,* 67.

25   Raphael Soriano, interview by Marlene L. Laskey, *Substance and Function in Architecture* (Los Angeles: Oral History Program, University of California, 1988), 120, 121.

26   Robert Friedel, "Scarcity and Promise: Materials and American Domestic Culture during World War II," in Donald Albrecht, ed., *World War II and the American Dream: How Wartime Building Changed a Nation,* exh. cat. (Cambridge, Mass.: MIT Press, 1995), 59.

27   Jean-Louis Cohen, *Architecture in Uniform: Designing and Building for the Second World War* (Paris: Editions Hazan, 2011), 59.

28   Friedel, "Scarcity and Promise," 51.

29   See "Swedlow, David A.," *Plastics Academy's Hall of Fame,* http://www.plasticshalloffame.com; and "Merit Specifications for 1949 Case Study House," *Arts & Architecture* 66 (December 1949), 14. Many thanks to John Kishel for bringing to my attention Plyon, Swedlow Plastics, and their connection to the Eames House.

30   "Case Study House for 1949, Designed by Charles Eames," *Arts & Architecture* 66 (December 1949): 35.

31   Plyon is commonly misspelled as "Pylon" in histories of the Eames House, which may add to its obscurity. See National Park Service, National Historic Landmark Nomination, *Eames House* (2005), 5; James Steele, *Eames House, Charles and Ray Eames* (London: Phaidon, 1994), 10; and Amelia Jones and Elizabeth A. T. Smith, "The Thirty-Six Case Study Projects," in Elizabeth A. T. Smith, ed., *Blueprints for Modern Living: History and Legacy of the Case Study Houses,* exh. cat. (Los Angeles: Museum of Contemporary Art, 1989), 52.

32   Stephen Phillips, "Plastics," in Beatriz Colomina, Annmarie Brennan, and Jeannie Kim, eds., *Hothouses, Inventing Postwar Culture, from Cockpit to Playboy* (New York: Princeton Architectural, 2004), 94.

33   Donald Albrecht, "Evolving Forms," in idem, ed., *The Work of Charles and Ray Eames: A Legacy of Invention,* exh. cat. (New York: Harry N. Abrams, 1997), 86. At Zenith Plastics, they worked specifically with a researcher who, while previously with Owens-Corning Fiberglas, had developed airplane wings for the US Air Force. See Kaitlin Handler, "The History of the Eames Molded Plastic Chairs," *Eames Designs,* http://www.eamesdesigns.com/library-entry/molded-plastic-chairs/.

34   "How to Roof a Patio with Corrugated Plastic," *Sunset* 109 (1952): 65.

35   Richard Guy Wilson, "Schindler's Metaphysics: Space, the Machine, and Modernism," in Elizabeth A. T. Smith and Michael Darling, *The Architecture of R. M. Schindler,* exh. cat. (Los Angeles: Museum of Contemporary Art, 2001), 133.

36   Rudolph M. Schindler, "Visual Technique," 1952, as quoted in Wilson, "Schindler's Metaphysics," 133, 136.

37   Adolph Tischler, "Faith Pays Off: Home Designed by Rudolph Schindler Is a Monument," *Los Angeles Times,* 18 July 1993. In 1963, Lloyd Wright deployed corrugated blue fiberglass as a flamboyant roof trim for the Bowler ("Bird of Paradise") Residence in Rancho Palos Verdes.

38   "History," *M. C. Gill Corporation,* http://www.mcgillcorp.com/about/history.html.

39   Merwyn C. Gill House, National Register of Historic Places registration form, 4 April 2008, 6.

40   Merwyn C. Gill House, National Register form, 6.

41   For a more complete history, see John Crosse, "Living Lightly on the Land: Bernard Judge's 'Triponent' and 'Tree' Houses," *Southern California Architectural History,* 25 August 2011, http://so-cal-arch-history.com/archives/2609.

42   Bernard Judge, interview by Dana Hutt, 31 October 2011; "Scientists Say Balloon Has No Leak," *Los Angeles Times,* 18 August 1960, pt. 1, 32; and "L.A. to See Echo 3 Times in 3 Days," *Los Angeles Times,* 12 September 1960, 2.

43   Dan MacMasters, "A Bubble on a Hilltop," *Los Angeles Times,* 1 July 1962, 21.

44   Judge, interview, 2011.

45   R. M. Schindler, "Modern Architecture: A Program," in August Sarnitz, *R. M. Schindler, Architect, 1887–1953* (New York: Rizzoli, 1988), 42.

46   John Lautner and Marlene L. Laskey, *Responsibility, Infinity, Nature* (Los Angeles: Oral History Program, University of California, 1986), 84.

47   Lautner attracted a specific kind of client: scientific and/or artistic, inventive, and independent in spirit. Of Malin and Reiner, Jon Yoder writes, "It is no accident that Lautner's architectural practice started to take off in the early part of the decade; his success relied partly on the aircraft industry"; see Jon Yoder's review "Vignette Films for *Between Earth and Heaven: The Architecture of John Lautner* by Murray Grigor; *Infinite Space: The Architecture of John Lautner* by Murray Grigor," *Journal of the Society of Architectural Historians* 68, no. 2 (2009): 287.

48   Frank Escher, ed., *John Lautner, Architect* (London: Artemis, 1994), 113; Frank Escher, "Structuring Space," in Nicholas Olsberg, ed., *Between Earth and Heaven: The Architecture of John Lautner,* exh. cat. (New York: Rizzoli International, 2008), 175; and Dan MacMasters, "A Home Built on a Pedestal," *Los Angeles Times,* 30 April 1961, K24.

49   MacMasters, "A Home Built on a Pedestal," K24.

50   Jean-Louis Cohen, "John Lautner's Luxuriant Tectonics," in Nicholas Olsberg, ed., *Between Earth and Heaven: The Architecture of John Lautner,* exh. cat. (New York: Rizzoli International, 2008), 30; and Escher, *John Lautner, Architect,* 113.

51   Jon Yoder, "Vignette Films," 286.

52   About the Chemosphere, Lautner said, "I purposely sloped the glass in so when you stand up against it you can't look straight down. You are forced to look at the magnificent view"; quoted in Yoder, "Vignette Films," 288n6, which cites *John Lautner: Architect, Los Angeles—An Exhibition on the Occasion of His 80th Birthday* (Vienna: Ludolf von Alvensleben, 1991), 25.

53   Nicholas Olsberg, "Shaping Awareness," in idem, ed., *Between Earth and Heaven: The Architecture of John Lautner,* exh. cat. (New York: Rizzoli International, 2008), 91.

54   Escher, *John Lautner, Architect,* 137.

55   Harry Saltzgaver, "Inventor, Philanthropist Reiner Dies," *Gazettes,* 21 September 2011, http://gazettes.com/news/inventor-philanthropist-reiner-dies/article_8da78f6c-e485-11e0-bca7-001cc4c002e0.html.

56   Escher, *John Lautner, Architect,* 136.

57   Alan Hess, *The Architecture of John Lautner* (New York: Rizzoli International, 1999), 106.

58   Brochure, *The Advanced Technology House* (1980), Ray Kappe papers, 1954–2000, acc. no. 2008.M.36, box 41, folder 7, Getty Research Institute, Los Angeles.

59   Ray Kappe, interview by Dana Hutt, 2 November 2011.

60   Kappe, interview, 2011.

61   CATIA is an acronym for Computer Aided Three-Dimensional Interactive Application, and CAD is an acronym for "computer-aided design" program. CATIA was developed by Dassault Systèmes.

The car that's going places with the Young in Heart!

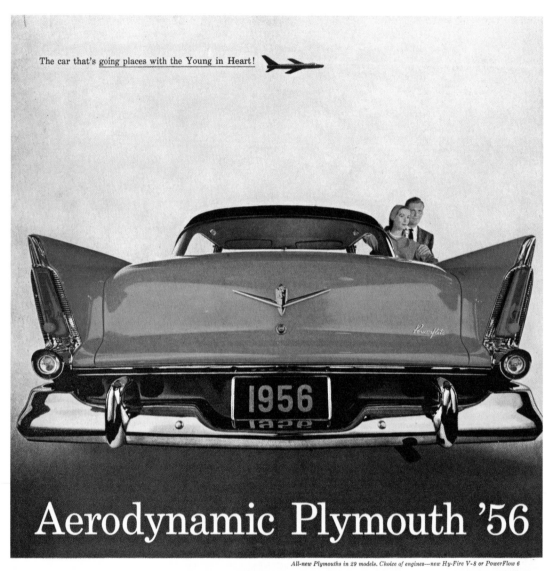

1956

Aerodynamic Plymouth '56

All-new Plymouths in 29 models. Choice of engines—new Hy-Fire V-8 or PowerFlow 6.

Driving Takes Wings

Settle yourself behind the Push-Button controls of the <u>all-new Plymouth '56</u>. Look proud, because every eye is turned on this big, beautiful triumph of jet-age design.... Then a gentle toe-touch on the throttle! Feel that forward push against your back... see how Plymouth leaves other cars behind?

That's Plymouth's magnificent new Hy-Fire V-8... plus *90-90 Turbo-Torque* getaway and PowerFlite, for top thrust at take-off... swift, safe passing. Or, for maximum economy, choose the new, increased-horsepower PowerFlow 6.

Get the news: PLYMOUTH NEWS CARAVAN with John Cameron Swayze, NBC-TV, SHOWER OF STARS and "CLIMAX!" CBS-TV.

PUSH-BUTTON DRIVING

<u>*What it means to you.*</u> First on Plymouth in the low-price 3! A touch of a button selects your driving range. Easy as pressing a light switch. Then PowerFlite fully automatic transmission takes over. Here's new driving ease!

ENGINEERED AUDACITY

LAX
DESIGNING FOR THE JET AGE

Vanessa R. Schwartz

AS PART OF THE PREPARATION FOR HIS 1967 BOOK profiling contemporary Los Angeles, *New Yorker* staff writer Christopher Rand went right to one of the region's most prolific and influential planners and architects, William Pereira, to seek a description of the seemingly incomprehensible city. The interviewee boiled it down to this: "The growth of Los Angeles coincided with a great deal of gadgetry. The airplane did more for this city than for any other because it ended our isolation—first our isolation from the rest of America, by the deserts, and then our isolation by the Pacific."[1] Mechanized transportation—the train, car, and plane—played an unusually important role in the development of both the state of California and what would become its largest city, Los Angeles.[2] The train may have joined the West to the East, but the automobile is usually credited as the most influential of the trio of transport forms that changed the region. The ubiquitous freeways, which now double as parking lots at rush hour, have become the city's most indelible icon.[3]

Yet it was aviation that redrew national and global geography from the 1930s onward as planes moved mail, cargo, and people the long distances to and from Los Angeles, lifting the city out of its geographic remoteness. In the process, the nation's western edge became host to a series of transport hubs, the most significant of which would become Los Angeles International Airport (LAX). Once merely a stretch of bean fields in Inglewood sandwiched between the ocean and the oil refineries of El Segundo, Mines Field became one of three tiny municipal airports in 1928.

Airplanes did not just come and go from Los Angeles. Many were also "born" there, as manufacturers settled in a place with clear weather for 350 days a year. The aviation industry developed into one of the cornerstones of the regional economy. By the end of the 1930s, Douglas Aircraft, Lockheed Corporation, Northrop Aircraft, and North American Aviation had established manufacturing headquarters in the Los Angeles area. The California Institute of Technology (Caltech) provided a research center for government projects, such as the Jet Propulsion Lab, and also spun off private rocket-building initiatives, such as the firm Aerojet. Southern California alone accounted for 45 percent of the nation's airframe-manufacturing facilities.[4] World

FIGURE 1.
Advertisement for the 1956 Plymouth, with Powerflite push-button automatic transmission.
From *Life,* 26 December 1955, 32.

War II stepped up aviation manufacturing, and by 1960, aerospace provided approximately one third of the region's employment.[5] A confident report from the Los Angeles Department of Airports (DOA) explained that the aerospace industry employed more than half a million people and assured that Los Angeles would "remain the acknowledged air capital of the world."[6]

Indeed, the DOA had reason to boast. After nearly ten intensive years of planning and building, Los Angeles opened the first American jet-age airport in 1961. Only six years earlier, one journalist expressed concern about the region's airport problem: "It seems incredible…that Los Angeles, which is perhaps the greatest center of American aviation—the largest industry in the nation and the state—should in the year 1955 still be operating with interim airport facilities."[7] Those interim facilities lasted through the planning process that ultimately resulted in Los Angeles's highly successful solution to the challenges faced by all airports at the dawn of the jet age: to accommodate the new planes and, especially, the vast increase in passengers that followed in the wake of the arrival of jet service in 1958.

Although architectural historians have begun to study these distinctly twentieth-century features of the built environment, they have, for the most part, concentrated on the terminal buildings by classifying them as building types. They have considered them in the context of the work of such celebrated architects as Eero Saarinen, Paul Andreu, and Norman Foster.[8] Special attention to the moment of jet-age construction reveals, however, that architects and planners had much more on their minds than terminal buildings. We cannot study airports by treating them as the cathedrals of the mid-twentieth century. Instead, we must consider them as functional places whose meanings can be grasped by concentrating as much on the design of the spaces in between the terminals as on the buildings themselves.

Jet-age airport planners conceived spaces to enhance the fluid motion of passengers. They sought to extend the jet's experience of "high speed and comfort"—that is to say, sensationless and effortless travel through space—to passengers while they were still on the ground.[9] The planners primarily sought to attend to the passengers' movements, and, especially, to getting them through space with little physical effort, in an extension, one might say, of the logic of the jet plane. Driven by the rapid expansion of travel the jet would inevitably stimulate and the belief that industrial society and its technologies favor the consumer, the planners built airports around people rather than around terminal buildings and jet planes.

LAX became the quintessential jet-age airport for two reasons: the radical changes to the travel experience made possible by the jet and the local commitment to incorporating a functional aesthetic found in many of Southern California's midcentury designs. LAX planners insisted that the success of such a huge infrastructural project would depend on preparing for its own obsolescence. Reyner Banham, the well-known British design critic with a background in aviation, observed in his 1962 essay "The Obsolescent Airport" that airports had become like "demented amoebas" that had turned inside out, to the point of "the disintegration of buildings."[10] The compact clustering associated with early airport design disappeared in the new decentralized airport plan, creating a form that would be imperceptible to its users. Banham remarked that airports reflected the logic of a techno-pop culture: "Like all monuments in a technological culture, they were by definition dead, superseded before they were designed."[11] The planners of LAX embraced the idea of getting beyond monumental culture. They accepted that planning meant designing flexibly and knowing that obsolescence was inevitable.

Los Angeles International Airport was not the only jet-age airport. Between 1958 and 1962, new airports (or redesigned and expanded ones) opened in many places: Algiers, Bordeaux, Brussels, Copenhagen, London (Gatwick), Marseilles, Montego Bay, Montreal, New York (Idlewild, renamed John F. Kennedy International in 1963), Nice, Paris (Orly), Rome, and Vienna, among others. Dulles, sited outside the US capital in Chantilly, Virginia, became the first brand-new airport built to welcome the jet age. Observers commented on the airports' lack of grand aesthetic. As a special section of *Time* magazine dedicated to jet-age airports notes, "Many of the new airports boast functional rather than beautiful buildings."[12]

While LAX and its functional design were not alone among projects oriented to meet the jet, it is fair to say it was well ahead of the others through its planners' bold willingness to make thinking ahead the key measure of a successful plan. As the 1960 DOA annual report explained, "An airport system is never completed. Constant change is routine in airport operations; maintaining the status quo is synonymous with being 'out of date.'"[13] The innovations that made the airport a model for others included planning for obsolescence and expansion, decentralization of the terminals, and the focus on "breaking the ground barrier" to passenger movement (prioritizing speed on land as well as in the air). Prescient site planning meant the airport could physically handle remarkable increases in both the numbers of planes and passengers well into the half-century after its initial jet-age redesign.

What the planners of LAX did not envision, however, was that the optimism evoked by jet travel in the late 1950s and early 1960s would quickly change to complaint as the jet age became a way of life. William Pereira, one of the designers of the LAX Master Plan, summarized the situation in 1974: "No industry has ever been as successful in achieving more criticism than praise, more opponents than proponents, in such an unprecedented short span of time."[14] For LAX, this shift in attitude also paralleled a series of unrealized expansion plans (including scrambles to find other sites in the region), large-scale housing expropriation programs, and endless lawsuits over noise. By the time of the 1984 Olympics, when the pressure was on Los Angeles to welcome millions of visitors no matter the impact on the area adjoining LAX, airport renovation consisted of merely a sufficient but piecemeal final fleshing out of aspects of the jet-age Master Plan. Despite the constant attempts by the DOA to renovate and rethink the airport, the original plan was so prescient that it had not yet outdated itself, as planners in the 1950s had envisioned. Remarkably, the flexible plan has meant that LAX still bears the stamp of the jet-age redesign. The irony of such foresight is that today's airport remains very much in the image of its jet-age debut, seemingly poised for a future that is now well past.

ENTERING THE JET AGE

The term *jet age* initially came into currency in relation to the military jets that entered service during World War II.[15] But *jet age* did not become a common phrase until the mid-1950s, when journalists were already asking if it had come too soon because of several spectacular crashes of the De Havilland Comet, the first commercial jet to go into service, in 1952.[16] Optimism prevailed when Pan American Airways inaugurated the Jet Clipper America, a Boeing 707 that provided trans-Atlantic service between New York and Paris starting in October 1958. The first transcontinental jet flight to Los Angeles arrived from New York, cutting the travel time from seven hours and forty-five minutes to four hours and fifteen minutes, with speeds reaching six hundred miles per hour. Flown by American Airlines on 5 January 1959, it arrived at an airport that was more than two years away from opening permanent facilities designed to cater to this new aircraft and travel experience.

But such dissonance was characteristic of the jet age—aviation officials simultaneously announced the future as they struggled to keep pace with it. Many simply conceived of the period as one of complete turmoil. C. E. Woolman, president of Delta Airlines, observed, "We are buying airplanes that haven't been fully designed, with millions of dollars we don't have, and we are going to operate them off of airports that are too small, in an air traffic control system that is too slow, and we must fill them with more passengers than we have ever carried before."[17] Despite such challenges, air travel increased tremendously during the new era of jet service. For example, in 1959, there were an additional 5 million travelers by air at LAX, of whom 250,000 flew on jets. The next year, more than 1 million LAX passengers flew on jets, and by 1963, the 8 million passengers arriving at LAX were seen by airport authorities as evidence of "the rapid acceptance by the travelling public of the jet age way of life."[18] By the end of the 1960s, approximately 89 percent of aircraft passenger miles consisted of travel by jet. There was a remarkable expansion of air travel more generally from 1945 to 1970; domestic air travel went from 6.6 million to 153.4 million passengers, and international travelers increased from a few thousand to nearly 16.2 million, attributable primarily to the arrival of jet service.[19]

Once it became apparent that jets would become the boom mode of travel, *jet age* became a descriptor for a style and a way of life as much as for a mode of travel. When used as an adjective, *jet-age* came to denote objects considered fast and aerodynamic. Thus, advertisers promoted the 1956 Plymouth, with its fins deliberately evoking the wings of a jet, as the "triumph of jet-age design" (fig. 1). The term also started pertaining to the technological cutting edge. For example, a 1955 ad for a General Electric transistor radio declared that it "belongs in the jet age."[20] By using the word *in* rather than *to,* the ad emphasized the immanence of the moment—the jet age, like the new radio, suggested that the future had already arrived in the present.[21] The ubiquity of the term can also be measured by the name of the popular animated television series *The Jetsons,* which debuted in 1962. Set during an age in which families live in sky-high apartments that resemble the Theme Building at LAX and travel by flying car, the series embraced a vision of technology that kept people on the move, in the sky, and thereby living a better life.

Jets ushered in an era of major expansion of air travel, because of both their speed and the quality of the ride. Flying in jets, as a 1954 *Newsweek* article noted, can "seem like slipping through space. No vibrations, no lurches, and no sense of speed."[22] Once faster speeds made flying at a higher altitude possible, jet flights were less turbulent. Without the piston-operated engine, the ride was quiet and had little of its characteristic vibration. In short, the trip was less of a physical experience. Taking the cue from the speed and smoothness of jet travel, a 1968 report for the preparation of LAX summarized what an airport should be: "The airport...is dedicated to moving people in an orderly manner in the shortest time possible," just like the jet itself.[23]

Such was not always the vision of the airport. At the dawn of aviation, a simple landing field was all that was needed for leaving and returning to terra firma. Despite the presence of aviation manufacturing in Southern California in the early 1920s, it was not until 1928 that the city leased the land on the site known as Mines Field for an airport; a grander plan to buy three sites eventually came to pass.[24]

Rapid postwar economic growth in Los Angeles, even before the jet, set the pace of change. The airport became an international facility in 1949, and LAX was born. Between 1947 and 1952, the number of travelers using or passing through the airport increased by 80 percent.[25] Even before the end of the war, the DOA had begun to ponder postwar expansion, which included moving several major carriers from Burbank's airport, expanding west of Sepulveda Boulevard (the major north-south thoroughfare to the airport), and building a tunnel (completed in 1953) for car traffic under the south runway along Sepulveda. The period's major challenge, however, became passing a bond issue that would help pay for further expansion, since LAX's budget had become separate from that of the municipality as part of the airport's growing administrative autonomy. The newly independent DOA went to the voters in 1951 and in 1953 to approve a $14.5 million bond issue, which failed both times because local voters believed they were shouldering the cost of an institution that represented the interests of the entire region, not just their city.[26]

These setbacks did not discourage the determined leadership of the DOA, who pressed ahead by commissioning the firm of Pereira & Luckman to conceive a master plan, despite the fact that no funds yet existed for the envisioned expansion. By 1953, William Pereira, whose eventual contributions to the architecture and planning of the Southern California region are vast, had already left his work as a movie theater architect for Balaban and Katz and as an art director for the film industry (begun when Barney Balaban became head of Paramount Pictures) for a life of running an architectural practice and teaching at the University of Southern California (USC), where he further developed his interest in regional master planning. In 1950, Pereira invited Charles "Boy Wonder" Luckman, with whom he had gone to architecture school and who had been the president of both Pepsodent and Lever Brothers, to join his practice. The team had been commissioned to design CBS Studios when Pereira had his USC students create a new master plan for LAX as an assignment, with little consideration for how jets might change the airport experience.[27] The first iteration of the Pereira & Luckman plan, completed for the DOA in March 1953, based many of its ideas on those generated by Pereira's USC students, including a central circular terminal building housed in a glass dome, with fingers leading out to the parked aircraft. An alternative scheme involved tunnels, rather than fingers, which left open space on the apron for planes to maneuver and allowed planes to circle the satellite where the tunnels emerged, shortening the walking distances for passengers. This element would develop into one of the most important and original aspects of the final plan: decentralized terminals (fig. 2).

The DOA moved forward with Pereira & Luckman and added new members in 1955, creating a joint venture with the firms of Welton Becket and Associates and Paul R. Williams. In the meantime, the DOA went back to the city with a bond issue of almost $60 million and a proposal for the airport to raise the money and pay its debts at no risk to the taxpayer. The measure passed with 86 percent of the vote, and the design plans firmed up—just in time to rethink the initial plan in response to the advent of the jet.

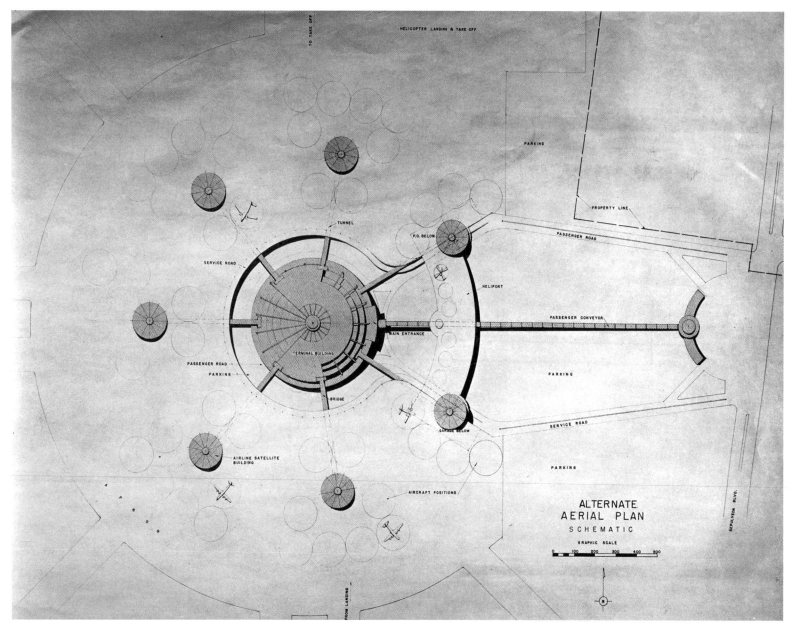

FIGURE 2.
Pereira & Luckman, Architects, Engineers and Planners (1950–58).
Alternate aerial plan schematic for Los Angeles
International Airport (unrealized), 1953.
From Pereira & Luckman, *Master Plan for Los Angeles
International Airport with Preliminary Studies
for Proposed Terminal Building* (1953).
Los Angeles, LAX Flight Path Learning Center Museum.

THE DESIGN

Although the Pereira and Luckman partnership did not last very long in the scheme of two very important careers, both men shared a commitment to research and planning as fundamental aspects of architectural practice and design, and both specialized in large-scale projects. Between the two, Luckman had the more matter-of-fact approach. He noted, "I believe only in the common sense master plan. To put it simply, I am opposed to the 'dream-table' [*sic*] plans. I am in favor of do-able plans."[28] At the same time, though, he found the challenge of the airport to be centered on anticipating growth and change, and thus dreaming the future became a preoccupation of his working life. In a retrospective explanation of the design framework for LAX, he explained, "We were then, in 1955, planning an airport to be constructed by 1960, which was to be large enough for 1980."[29]

The airport Pereira & Luckman proposed diverged from typical airport structures and kept operations on the functional rather than the flamboyant side. Specifically, the 1957 Master Plan broke with the idea of a main terminal building, in part because the airlines preferred to operate their own terminals. At New York's JFK, that concept had already led to elaborate architectures that created a distinction between airlines. Critic Michael Brawne called this the "Penn Station–St. Pancras stage" (otherwise known as monumentalism), in which tangible symbols were used as a form of advertisement to "create differences between airlines."[30] Brawne looked forward to a time when the "architecture of passenger-handling buildings [would]...become more rational, perhaps less memorable or possibly except for a vestigial space, disappear altogether." He might as well have been talking about LAX. In the Master Plan, all ticketing terminals looked alike. Additionally,

FIGURE 3.
Pereira & Luckman, Architects, Engineers and Planners (1950–58), Welton Becket and Associates (1949–88), and Paul R. Williams (American, 1894–1980).
Version of Los Angeles International Airport Master Plan, 1956.
Los Angeles, LAX Flight Path Learning Center Museum.

the plan separated ticketing from passenger loading through a system of underground tunnels that led to satellite terminals. As Luckman put it, "The only way to solve the complex problem of a modern airport is to separate the people from the planes."[31] This early vision is seen in figure 3: the satellites are already sited and the domed central building would determine the eventual placement of the Theme Building.

Decentralization of the airport terminals functioned as the linchpin in a vision of better continuity between ground and air for the new masses of travelers. According to Grant Anderson, the chief engineer for the DOA during the era of expansion, with such decentralization, planners could better manage the anticipated increase in passenger growth especially: "There is a limit to how many people can be processed in a single building," he explained. The idea was to see greater proliferation in the number of buildings; check-in would be separated from departure. Terminals would be imagined as interchanges rather than holding places.[32] Thus they gave particular attention to building tunnels that were between 375 and 575 feet wide, with "color, special lighting and decoration."[33] The tunnels used lighting effects to make them appear to be shorter (fig. 4). Some members of the LAX project also recommended installing moving sidewalks within these tunnels to further automate and speed the process, and in 1964, the Astroway opened in the American Airlines tunnel.[34]

The satellites themselves were elliptical in shape, which enabled the planes to taxi right up to the edge of the building (fig. 5). Each satellite boasted ten plane-loading positions; the removal of the fingers not only decreased walking distances for passengers but also gave the planes greater maneuverability. Passengers accessed planes in the two-story satellites by climbing a circular staircase lit from above by a glass dome (fig. 6). In the original Master Plan, each satellite was designed with a possible 50 percent expansion that included the addition of a mezzanine. All the satellites had restaurants with California themes, such as "Old Hollywood" and "California Desert Flowers," and were managed by Interstate Host, a food supplier that specialized in concessions on toll roads and steamship shopping centers.[35] A 1967 plan, designed by Pereira after his split from Luckman, even proposed a space in the satellites for enplaning passengers to assemble, which he

FIGURE 4.
Passengers walk through the underground channels at Los Angeles International Airport with its new lighting system, 1961.
Los Angeles, LAX Flight Path Learning Center Museum.

FIGURE 5.
Aerial view of Los Angeles International Airport with elliptical satellites, 1962.
Los Angeles, Los Angeles Public Library, Herald Examiner Collection.

FIGURE 6.
Charles Luckman Associates (1958–79), Welton Becket and Associates (1949–88), and Paul R. Williams (American, 1894–1980).
Rendering showing the interior view of the satellite rotunda, Los Angeles International Airport, 1961.
Los Angeles, LAX Flight Path Learning Center Museum.

called a "holding gate." It was to attach to rather than act as a structural part of the satellite building. He called this a form of "mobile architecture" and was clearly influenced by the mobile lounge concept that had been introduced at Dulles in 1962.[36] For Pereira, the less permanent and durable the building structure, the better.

The designers of LAX explicitly sought to create continuity in the travel experience from ground to air. Of airport design during the period, Reyner Banham observed, "The emphasis lies increasingly on the continuity of the process of transport, rather than the monumental halting places along the way."[37] To wit, the most important innovations consisted of tunnels, Jetways, blast walls, viewing platforms, and walls of glass—all designed to move the passengers through space rather than have them stop in their tracks. One of LAX's unrealized schemes was the coin-operated Skylift (which was contracted out to Lockheed Aircraft Service to build); it would have carried cabs of four passengers on overhead cables, providing automated airborne movement around the entire airport (fig. 7).[38]

Although Pereira explained that architecture was a "series of contrasting spaces which solve specific functional and aesthetic problems," his work really focused almost exclusively on creating functional spaces. For the airport, he and Luckman defined that challenge as moving people rather than planes. The "movement of people can be intercepted and diverted by architecture, just as a dam affects a river," he observed. If a particular space required a passenger slow down, Pereira simply proposed to put a rough surface on the floor.[39] Signs were located at the sides of throughways in order to divert confused people off of the main paths. In other words, not only did form follow function; it would expressly shape use and passenger mobility.

If the lion's share of the design effort went into the work of moving passengers from their cars to their planes in as seamless a way as possible, such priorities made for poor symbolism. Public transport monuments may have been evolving past the St. Pancras phase, but critics and visitors still wanted an emblem to "see" the otherwise diffuse and mobile experience of LAX. Although today the landmarked Theme Building appears to have been designed for just that role, airport planners did not initially envision it as the airport's main symbol, because they imagined such a symbol would have to be explicitly tied to actual airport operations in a functional way.

The DOA and the joint venture of architects selected the airport's new control tower—which would be the nation's tallest such tower and would house not only the air

FIGURE 7.
Proposal for Los Angeles International Airport Intra-terminal Transportation System, by Lockheed Aircraft Service, Inc., 1960.

and ground control operations but also the DOA's administrative offices—as the airport's central symbolic structure. Its location at the airport's eastern, and main, entrance (the Century Boulevard entrance) meant it greeted the majority of passengers and visitors. The control tower was even represented on the covers of the DOA's 1958 and 1959 annual reports. The 1958 report predicted that the "tower [would] be the identifying landmark of the airport and [would] serve a dual function."[40] The Flame of Freedom and a court of flags were positioned in front of the 172-foot building at the newly named address of #1 World Way. When the City of Los Angeles selected LAX to represent it in the 1962 Tournament of Roses Parade, the float featured both the control tower and the Theme Building (figs. 8, 9). When the airport put up its Christmas decorations that year, both buildings were transformed: the tower was lighted with a cross and the Theme Building, its whimsical partner, was adorned with a Christmas tree (figs. 10, 11).

For the design team, the Theme Building remained the alternative to the central building found in earlier iterations of the plan. Many people had a hand in the final details of the design of the structure; the 135-foot-high parabolic arches were initially scheduled to be clad in aluminum for an even more futuristic look, but budget concerns determined the use of stucco instead. Having imagined the space occupied by a building, the DOA encouraged the designers to give the structure some purpose, but even the persistence of its generic name, the Theme Building, suggests its lack of mission. Ever mindful of shouldering the burden of paying their own bills, they turned it into a revenue-generating source: it would house a restaurant and an observation deck (which charged admission until the cost of maintaining the deck as a ticketed space was no longer worth the effort). The building would also house Host's enormous food kitchen, which serviced all the

FIGURE 8.
Tournament of Roses Parade float for the City of Los Angeles featuring the Los Angeles International Airport Theme Building, 1962.
Los Angeles, LAX Flight Path Learning Center Museum.

FIGURE 9.
Aerial view of Los Angeles International Airport showing the control tower and Theme Building, 1973.
Los Angeles, Los Angeles Public Library, Herald Examiner Collection.

FIGURE 10.
Control tower, Los Angeles International Airport, Christmas 1962.
Los Angeles, LAX Flight Path Learning Center Museum.

FIGURE 11.
Theme Building, Los Angeles International Airport, Christmas 1962.
Los Angeles, LAX Flight Path Learning Center Museum.

satellite restaurants and offered a commissary for employees; it was located on the ground level behind the perforated concrete wall surrounding the building's circular base.

The Theme Building eventually outshone its more pragmatic control tower partner in several ways. It was opened to visitors who could look out over the airport from the 81-foot-high observation deck (fig. 12). In its first month of operation, three thousand people visited the deck alone.[41] It remained open seven days a week and would often host one thousand visitors a day during vacation months and on weekends. With its "Court of Stars" panels—backlighted color transparencies of the heavens taken at the Mount Palomar Observatory—the entrance played to the jet age's broader interest in the skies and the final frontier: outer space. The restaurant became a destination for those flying as well as those who simply wanted to visit what they imagined as the life of the future. Because not everyone could actually travel by plane, the restaurant offered a taste of the world now reachable by jet: international tourist sites were represented on murals; hostesses dressed in costumes from France, Japan, Scandinavia, and Spain; and the menu included fare such as Swedish meatballs. At the Theme Building, the world became smaller, effectively expanding the horizons of geographically constrained Angelenos.

Most significant, the building's lack of apparent purpose put pressure on the idea that it should have "style," under the assumption that style attracts visitors. The chosen style links the building to the broader landscape of Southern California "fantasy architecture" and to its greatest contributor: Walt Disney. The fantasy architecture of Los Angeles had multiple ties to the movies (Pereira's film link is always summoned in connection to the Theme Building), but the tight group of designers and their connections to

FIGURE 12.
**Observation deck atop the Theme Building,
Los Angeles International Airport, 1963.**
Los Angeles, LAX Flight Path Learning Center Museum.

Disney shed light on the relations between entertainment culture and urban infrastructural projects such as the airport.[42]

The Theme Building drew a circle of connections between Welton Becket, Pereira, Luckman, and Disney, whose career in the movies had been just recently eclipsed by the phenomenal success of his major planning project, Disneyland. The theme park opened in July 1955 and was responsible for a great deal of the traffic increase at LAX. The airport and Disneyland became linked in public discourse. In a preview article, the *New York Times* called the airport a "Disneyland for adults."[43] When the airport opened in 1961, Federal Aviation Administration (FAA) chairman and native son Najeeb Halaby quipped, "You will have the first airport terminal area specifically designed for the jet age and it well may achieve some of the world-wide renown, some of the international acclaim as—who knows?—Disneyland."[44]

By the time of the creation of the Theme Building, Becket was already known for his "total design" concept that characterized such projects as the Bullock's Pasadena store and the Capitol Records Tower. The Theme Building's flying-saucer look was designed the year Disneyland opened. Becket and Disney knew each other well as neighbors in the Los Angeles community of Holmby Hills. Becket and Pereira, linked in the LAX joint venture, had already worked together on the flagship theater of the Pan Pacific movie theater chain in the 1940s. Disney, in the initial design phase for Disneyland, commissioned Pereira & Luckman to offer a

FIGURE 13.
Disneyland Hotel, with hotel tram and decorative iron beams, 1957.

FIGURE 14.
Disneyland Hotel, showing the new extension of the Disneyland Alweg Monorail to the hotel, 1961.

preliminary study that he eventually dismissed out of hand in favor of doing the park himself with his animators and art directors turned Imagineers, many of whom were also trained in architecture.[45] Luckman, in turn, was responsible for introducing Disney to the Stanford Research Institute engineer Harrison Price, who eventually helped him locate the park site in Anaheim.[46] Despite his rejection of their theme park plan, Disney hired Pereira & Luckman to design the Disneyland Hotel in Anaheim from 1954 to 1955, the same period in which they worked on the airport. The two projects share a design dedicated to people moving rather than to monumental architecture (figs. 13, 14).[47]

For reviewers and patrons eager to interpret the airport, the Theme Building reinforced the association of fantasy architecture with futuristic design. Praising California's many "free-wheeling shapes with a feel for the future," a *Life* magazine article about the state concluded that the Theme Building at LAX is "all future, no past."[48] Airport public relations material showcased the building as part of a "futuristic theme" for the airport.[49] Thus, despite the fact that airport planners were attached to the control tower as a symbol of the future rather than the functionality of the present, the Theme Building became the airport's icon, precisely because it lacked a function. In fact, its lack of functional role assured that it was also destined to last. The original control tower became so outdated that it was closed, with only the DOA offices remaining, while a new air traffic control tower, located much closer to the Theme Building and in the middle of the field of operations, was opened in 1996.

OPEN AND OUTDATED

On 25 June 1961, seventy-five thousand people greeted Vice President Johnson, who stood on the ticketing Terminal 7 observation deck, with the control tower and Flame of Freedom behind him. He used the occasion to address Cold War tensions in Berlin, hardly the peaceful globalism the jet age promised to usher in. The opening was more of a rollout, however, that lasted until well into 1962, when construction of the international terminal was finished. But the presence of FAA chairman Halaby symbolized the benefit of the airport expansion: bringing Los Angeles closer to the rest of the country and the world beyond it. The airport would stand in for the progress the city itself had undergone in the past fifty years, nicely summarized in a special supplement to the *Los Angeles Examiner* that announced, "Your airport grows from beanfield to jet age terminal."[50] Uniformed airport guides in "snappy World Way blue uniforms" led tours of the facilities to about five thousand monthly visitors, who took pride in the cutting-edge quality of the new gateway to Los Angeles (fig. 15).[51] For twenty-five cents a passenger, a tram transferred travelers between terminals and offered visitors the chance to tour the new

FIGURE 15.
Airport tour guides, 1962.
Los Angeles, LAX Flight Path Learning Center Museum.

facilities.[52] The DOA, determined to create effective public relations, also made the film *#1 World Way* (1963). The film's viewers were treated to a vision of the efficient operations of the airport, including the arrival of a plane via precision radar; the one thousand "u drive cars" rented daily; the helicopter service to downtown; the Japanese American tenant farmers picking flowers on airport lands, remaining undisturbed by the jets overhead; the airport's five hundred employees; and the "greatest show on earth"—sunset at the Theme Building. The film emphasized that the remarkable accomplishments of the modernized airport were made possible with no expense to the taxpayers.[53]

LAX no sooner opened than it was outpaced by its own success, as it struggled to keep up with the heavy use of the facilities. In the wake of the completion of the last of the new terminals in 1962, the expanded number of travelers (approximately 10 million by 1964) coupled with the anticipated arrival of both jumbo jets and supersonic transport (SST) resulted in a new planning phase.[54] The DOA went back to Pereira in 1965 with the hope of maximizing the capacity of LAX as originally planned and with a special determination to "break the ground barrier"—the time it took getting to and from the airport.[55] Pereira obliged by giving shape to a vision advanced by the DOA for a regional airport system defined by a 150-mile perimeter.

What had initially been 2,000 acres at LAX had grown to 3,500. To that, the DOA added 17,000 acres in Palmdale, adjacent to 6,000 acres of an already functional military air base. In a document titled "What About Tomorrow? Let's Face It Today," the DOA presented the new plan to break the ground barrier. Palmdale would function as an "intercontinental airport" that would receive the SST planes and have a capacity of 120 million passengers, nearly twice the capacity of LAX.[56] Los Angeles would be redrawn by air culture. "City limits, county and state lines…lose their importance in the air age….From the air, it is virtually impossible to tell where one political subdivision ends and another begins."[57] The DOA touted the idea of such physical decentralization.

The move to decentralize across the region imitated the way LAX decentralized functions at the airport. The DOA envisioned a series of "metroports," including one at Union Station (fig. 16), where passengers could park, check luggage, and then be transported to the airport via monorail or "skylounge"—a vehicle that was both helicopter and mobile lounge designed to pass over the streets, which had become so occluded that people reportedly abandoned their cars on the roads leading directly to the airport in order to make their flights. The skylounges and a helicopter service would provide short-haul travel around the region.

At LAX, the DOA proposed a second stage of expansion: the building of another terminal (the West Terminal—part of the original plan), a second-level roadway (also part of the original plan but not built until 1984), and bridges from the parking lots to the terminals. The new terminal would be sited entirely underground, and passengers would be automatically loaded into the waiting planes. Pereira also experimented with radio broadcasts about parking conditions at the airport and concentrated his intellectual energy less on designing spaces that maximized ease of movement and more on disseminating information, which would be gathered via sensors placed around the airport as well as from flight data.[58] Information would be transmitted via a simplified and universal set of pictographic signs, closed-circuit television, and public announcements. With the move to computerization, Pereira reconsidered the centrality of the built environment to planning and instead began to envision the immaterial sphere of information as the key to improving air travel.

FIGURE 16.
**William L. Pereira and Associates, Planning
and Architecture (1958–85).**
Los Angeles Union Station Terminal Annex Heliport
(unrealized), 1967.
Los Angeles, LAX Flight Path Learning Center Museum.

The cost of expansion, the complexity of finding ways to transport people to Palmdale, as well as the generally successful operation of LAX based on the jet-age Master Plan meant that only piecemeal elements of the 1967 plan came to fruition. Although Pereira's thinking suggests he had entered a planning realm of immaterial and informational elements, the very material problem of noise has also shaped the development of LAX since the late 1960s.

Despite the generally optimistic attitude toward air travel in the jet age, there were new challenges from people concerned with the effects of increased air travel. The problem of noise at airports was not new in the late 1960s, but the community's tolerance decreased due to the quality of the jet "whine," the fear of pending sonic booms from the SST (which would never materialize), greater environmental awareness, and the familiarization with jets that made people simply less tolerant as the bloom fell off the rose of air travel. As early as 1959, LAX established a Noise Abatement Division, but the airport operators also had a basic calculation for providing the greatest good for the greatest number of people. As General Manager Francis Fox explained in 1977, the airport counted about twenty thousand local people affected daily by the noise but had sixty to seventy thousand travelers daily.[59] In another strange and peculiarly Los Angeles twist, price values around the airport actually increased during the period, and many of those who complained had moved in after the arrival of the jets.[60] During the 1960s, the airport began a land expropriation program. Between 1965 and 1986, the program cost the DOA more than $145 million.[61]

As LAX became stretched to capacity in the late 1970s, the Board of Airport Commissioners finally approved further expansion of an airport that by then needed temporary building space in the form of air-supported fabric buildings (air-pressure kept the balloonlike roofs and walls firm) simply to receive and process international arrivals.[62] It was during this over-capacity condition that the International Olympic Committee announced the good news: Los Angeles would host the Twenty-Third Summer Olympics. For those in favor of expansion, there could have been nothing as invaluable. Aside from runway reconstruction and the renovation of the central utility building, the Olympic-ready LAX would require the final elements of the 1957 plan: a second-level roadway that would separate arriving and departing traffic and the building of what is today Terminal 1 (already sited in 1957) by none other than Welton Becket and Associates.

By the symbolically rich year of 1984, the airport designed in 1957 was finally completed. The remarkable achievement of the jet-age Master Plan can perhaps be best appreciated in hindsight, since we can evaluate the extent to which the plan anticipated change and provided flexibility for responding to the rapidly changing nature of air travel in the period of great expansion that resulted from jet travel. Armed with a vision that airports would always be obsolescent, the team led by Pereira and Luckman succeeded in moving their planning past the monumental Penn Station–St. Pancras phase, while also creating an icon, the Theme Building, that would stand as a beacon of the once-optimistic moment when Los Angeles would dream the future as it opened the first airport in the United States redesigned to welcome the jet age.

NOTES

The author wishes to thank the Haynes Foundation, the University of Southern California's Dornsife College, and the Provost's Office of the University of Southern California for generous funds in support of the research for this essay. I wish to acknowledge Sammy Goldenberg, my USC research assistant, and Ethel Pattison, of the Flight Path Learning Center at LAX, for their aid.

1   Christopher Rand, *Los Angeles: The Ultimate City* (New York: Oxford University Press, 1967), 23.

2   See William Deverell, *Railroad Crossing: Californians and the Railroad, 1850–1910* (Berkeley: University of California Press, 1994).

3   Ed Dimendberg, "The Kinetic Icon: Reyner Banham on Los Angeles as Mobile Metropolis," in Phil Ethington and Vanessa Schwartz, eds., "Urban Icons," *Urban History* 33 (2006): 106–25.

4   Paul David Friedman, "Fear of Flying: The Development of Los Angeles International Airport and the Rise of Public Protest over Jet Aircraft Noise" (MA thesis, University of California, Santa Barbara, 1978), 2–3.

5   Steven P. Erie, *Globalizing L.A.: Trade, Infrastructure, and Regional Development* (Stanford, Calif.: Stanford University Press, 2004), 96.

6   LA DOA, *Annual Report* (1962), 6, LAX Flight Path Learning Center Museum, Los Angeles.

7   Marvin Miles, "LAX," *New Frontiers* (1955): 5.

8   Hugh Pearman, *Airports: A Century of Architecture* (New York: Harry N. Abrams, 2004); John Zukowsky, ed., *Building for Air Travel: Architecture and Design for Commercial Aviation* (Munich: Prestel, 1996); Thomas S. Hines, *Architecture of the Sun: Los Angeles Modernism 1900–1970* (New York: Rizzoli, 2010); Deyan Sudjic, *Norman Foster: A Life in Architecture* (London: Weidenfeld, 2010); and Brian Edwards, *The Modern Airport Terminal: New Approaches to Airport Architecture,* 2nd ed. (London: Taylor & Francis, 2005). For a general history of the airport, see Alastair Gordon, *Naked Airport: A Cultural History of the World's Most Revolutionary Structure* (Chicago: University of Chicago Press, 2008). Sammy Goldenberg also wrote an undergraduate honors thesis in the History Department at the University of Southern California, "Rejecting Futurama: Los Angeles International Airport and the American Turn against Growth" (2010), based on the research he did under my direction.

9   J. G. Borger, "Meeting the Jet Transport Challenge," 5 March 1953, Pan American World Airways, Inc. Archives, I (B), box 6, Special Collections, University of Miami Library.

10   Reyner Banham, "The Obsolescent Airport," *Architectural Review* (October 1962): 252–53. He would also go on to write one of the most important interpretations of Los Angeles: Reyner Banham, *Los Angeles: The Architecture of Four Ecologies* (New York: Harper & Row, 1971). Banham worked at Bristol Aeroplane Company. Nigel Whiteley, *Reyner Banham: Historian of the Immediate Future* (Cambridge, Mass.: MIT Press, 2002), 4.

11   Banham, "The Obsolescent Airport," 252.

12   "Airport Cities: Gateways to the Jet Age," *Time,* 15 August 1960.

13   LA DOA, *Annual Report* (1960), LAX Flight Path Learning Center Museum, Los Angeles.

14   William Pereira, "Architecture, Nature, and the City," in James Steele, ed., *William Pereira* (Los Angeles: Architectural Guild, 2002), 54–55.

15   See, for example, "Jet Propulsion Launches a New Era in Man's Locomotion," *Life,* 27 November 1944, 47–53. See also Rhodri Windsor-Liscombe, "Usual Culture: The Jet," *Topia* 11 (Spring 2004): 83–99.

16   William D. Perreault and Anthony Vandyk, "Did the Jet Age Come Too Soon?," *Life,* 25 January 1954, 51–52. The De Havilland Comet was operated by the British Overseas Airways Corporation (BOAC).

17   Charles D. Bright, "The Heartbreak Market: Airliners," *The Jet Makers: The Aerospace Industry from 1945 to 1972,* http://www .generalatomic.com/jetmakers/chapter7.html; original citation from "Special Report: Jet Planes," *Business Week,* 21 July 1956, 170.

18   Numbers are from the LA DOA annual reports of 1959, p. 4; 1960, p. 12; and 1963, p. 6, all held at the LAX Flight Path Learning Center Museum, Los Angeles.

19   Douglas Karsner, "Leaving on a Jet Plane: Commercial Aviation, Airports, and Post-Industrial American Society, 1933–70" (Ph.D. diss., Temple University, 1993), 119. See also Jenifer Van Vleck, "No Distant Places: Aviation and the Global American Century" (Ph.D. diss., Yale University, 2009). Other important studies for contextualizing the history of aviation are Roger E. Bilstein, *Flight in America, 1900–1983: From the Wrights to the Astronauts* (Baltimore: Johns Hopkins University Press, 1984); Joseph J. Corn, *The Winged Gospel: America's Romance with Aviation* (Baltimore: Johns Hopkins University Press, 2002); and Tom D. Crouch, *Wings: A History of Aviation from Kites to the Space Age* (Washington, D.C.: Smithsonian, 2003).

20   G.E.'s new three-way portable radio ad, *Boys' Life,* May 1955, 59.

21   For more on architecture and the future, see Donna Goodman, *A History of the Future* (New York: Monacelli, 2008).

22   "12-Hour World: First American Jet Airline," *Newsweek,* 8 March 1954, 48–51.

23   William L. Pereira, *A Journey to the Airport* (1968), 13, William L. Pereira Associates Records, 0326, box 107, Special Collections, University of Southern California Library, Los Angeles.

24   Erie, *Globalizing L.A. Trade,* especially 45-77. Erie is my principal source on the history of the economic and political development of the airport in the earlier period and provides excellent context on the governing structures of L.A. transportation and infrastructure.

25   Friedman, "Fear of Flying," 64.

26   Friedman, "Fear of Flying," 56.

27   Victor Cusack, *A Symbol of Los Angeles: The History of the Theme Building at Los Angeles International Airport, 1952-1961* (Virginia Beach: Donning, 2005), 21.

28   Charles Luckman, "1952 Speech to California Real Estate Association," 1952, Charles Luckman Papers, CSLA-34 2006.65, series 10, box 6, folder 27, Loyola Marymount University, Los Angeles.

29   Charles Luckman, *Twice in a Lifetime* (New York: Norton, 1988), 299.

30   Michael Brawne, "Airport Passenger Buildings," *Architectural Review* (November 1962): 348. For the branding by virtue of the unit terminal system, see Thomas Leslie, "The Pan Am Terminal at Idlewild/Kennedy Airport and the Transition from the Jet Age to the Space Age," *Design Issues* 21, no. 1 (2005): 63-80.

31   Charles Luckman, "Luckman Talk at the Seagram Sales Meeting," July 1954, Charles Luckman Papers, series 10, box 1, folder 9, Loyola Marymount University, Los Angeles.

32   Grant Anderson, interview by Paul Friedman at LAX, 28 March 1997, LAX Flight Path Learning Center Museum, Los Angeles.

33   LA DOA, *Master Plan for LAX* (1957), 18, 20.

34   LA DOA, *Master Plan* (1957), 18.

35   LA DOA, *Facts about Interior Treatment of New Terminal Area Buildings, 1961,* Public Relations Files, LAX Flight Path Learning Center Museum, Los Angeles.

36   *Master Plan Development for LAX, 1966-67,* William Pereira Archives, 61, Special Collections, University of Southern California, Los Angeles. According to Thomas Hines, Dulles planner Eero Saarinen consulted the Pereira and Luckman LAX Master Plan as he designed Dulles, taking the concept of decentralization so far as to eliminate the satellite terminals in favor of the "mobile lounge" that would detach from the ticketing building and load people directly onto planes in the field. I have not found evidence of that in the Saarinen archives at Yale. In any event, LAX and Dulles represent the fundamental jet-age concern of reducing passenger distances in order to ensure that fluidity of the journey began on the ground.

37   Banham, *Obsolescent Airport,* 258.

38   Lockheed Air Service, *Proposal for LAX Intra-Terminal Transportations System* (1960), 11, LAX Flight Path Learning Center Museum, Los Angeles; and "Work Advances on Los Angeles Jet Airport," *Aviation Week,* 3 July 1961, 41.

39   William Pereira, *A Journey to the Airport,* 27-28.

40   LA DOA, *Annual Report* (1958), 5, LAX Flight Path Learning Center Museum, Los Angeles.

41   LA DOA, *Annual Report* (1962), 22. Admission to the deck initially cost ten cents, but the DOA decided the effort and resources needed to collect the fee were not worth it, so the charge was abandoned early on.

42   Hines, *Architecture of the Sun.* And see Philip J. Ethington, "Los Angeles and the Problem of Urban Historical Knowledge," *American Historical Review* 105, no. 5 (2000), n.p., available online at http://www.usc.edu/dept/LAS/history/historylab/LAPUHK/. By the time the Theme Building was being constructed, Pereira was already off the project, having split with Luckman, who took over the LAX project in the split.

43   Gladwin Hill, "A Disneyland for Adults," *New York Times,* 28 May 1961, XX4.

44   "Speech by Najeeb Halaby at Airport Dedication, 25 June 1961," Public Relations Files, Press Release, LAX Flight Path Learning Center Museum, Los Angeles.

45   Karal Ann Marling, "Imagineering the Disney Theme Parks," in idem, ed., *Designing Disney's Theme Parks: The Architecture of Reassurance* (New York: Flammarion, 1997), 58. In this way, we can better understand and contextualize the career of someone such as William Pereira.

46   Neal Gabler, *Walt Disney: The Triumph of the American Imagination* (New York: Vintage, 2006), 604.

47   Donald W. Ballard, *The Disneyland Hotel: The Early Years, 1954-1988* (Self-published, 2005).

48   "California Spectacle: Pleasures and Palaces of a Golden Land," *Life,* 19 October 1962, 17.

49   Memo from Peggy Hereford, public relations director, to Erwin Baker, Editorial Department, *Los Angeles Examiner,* 25 September 1961, LAX Flight Path Learning Center Museum, Los Angeles.

50   Supplement, *Los Angeles Examiner,* 15 November 1961, 36.

51   LA DOA, *Annual Report* (1962), 5. The airport tour guide program at LAX began in 1956 and was the first of its kind.

52   LA DOA, *Annual Report* (1961), 11, LAX Flight Path Learning Center Museum, Los Angeles.

53   The film is held by the LAX Flight Path Learning Center Museum, Los Angeles. Such was the renown of the airport and the film, that I found a script of it in the archives of the Aeroports de Paris, which wanted to screen the film that year, because they were making one of their own about Orly.

54   LA DOA, *Annual Report* (1964), 2, LAX Flight Path Learning Center Museum, Los Angeles.

55   LA DOA, *Annual Report* (1966), 4, LAX Flight Path Learning Center Museum, Los Angeles.

56   LA DOA, *What About Tomorrow? Let's Face it Today!,* 1967, 14, LAX Flight Path Learning Center Museum, Los Angeles.

57   LA DOA, *What About Tomorrow?,* 4.

58   Pereira, *A Journey to the Airport,* 90–93.

59   Francis Fox, interview by Paul Friedman, 20 July 1977; see the transcription, pp. 34–35, LAX Flight Path Learning Center Museum, Los Angeles.

60   Fox, interview, 1977. I have not independently verified this as it seems highly plausible.

61   Tom Moran, *Los Angeles International Airport: From Lindbergh's Landing Strip to World Air Center* (Canoga Park, Calif.: CCA, 1993), 67.

62   Moran, *Los Angeles,* 73.

ARCHITECTURE INDUSTRY
THE L.A. TEN

Stephen Phillips

FROM 1977 TO 1978, THE RELATIVELY UNKNOWN Los Angeles architect Frank Gehry enclosed a nondescript 1920s two-story pink bungalow on the corner of Twenty-Second Street and Washington Avenue in Santa Monica within a staged fortress of industrial "debris" of "outrageous appearance" that, in the words of *Progressive Architecture* (*P/A*) magazine, "distort[ed] and shift[ed] perspective while dramatizing views" (fig. 1).[1] Gehry's use of materials reminiscent of "light industrial buildings"—chain-link fencing, plywood, and aluminum siding—according to *P/A* magazine, "violate[d]" the "conventions" of "domestic architecture." Recalling a troubling image of industry set within a suburban context, Gehry's "carefully ramshackle construction," *P/A* argued, "summon[ed]...painful remembrances of the built environment the profession ha[d]...*not* been able to control." "Stripped, then swathed in tin clothes," forming a "tougher-than-nails jagged carapace of aluminum siding," Gehry's industrialized shell protected the delicate nature of residential life. Proving more than a simple representation of a confused world inhabiting a collage city, or the haphazard play of cheap industrial materials constructed with inane humor, or irony (as other critics and architects have surmised),[2] the "tension posed by the emergence of the pink house from the jagged shell," as *P/A* well observed, expressed domesticity in a state of extreme vulnerability.

With new industry expanding into older residential communities and new residences sprawling into outmoded industrial territories, normative separation between housing and industry in Los Angeles by the 1970s was becoming blurred. Thus, through building forms of disfigured, Janus-faced expression, Gehry, alongside a group of younger L.A. architects at the time, seemed to confront, if not critique, the impact industry was having on the changing physical and psychological character of the city, among other ideas. Although it is uncomfortable in retrospect for this group of L.A. architects to admit to any kind of cultural regionalism embedded in their formative work, together their designs posed a highly responsive critical assessment of urbanity that radically confronted the roles of domesticity and industry within an evolving postmodern metropolis.

FIGURE 1.
Frank O. Gehry and Associates (1962–2001).
Gehry Residence (1977–78), Santa Monica, 1979.
Photo by Tim Street-Porter.

THE L.A. TEN

Characterized by an expansive network of manufacturing, industrial, and warehouse communities situated alongside trucking facilities, ports, rail yards, freeways, waterways, and endless parking lots, Los Angeles's infrastructure supports a sublime manufactured landscape that has had a powerful influence on the cultural imagination of a generation of postmodern architects.[3] Postmodernism, in general, had a radicalizing impact on architects who aimed to challenge the lack of historical precedent demonstrated in the didactic industrial building forms of the modernist period. Exemplifying the postmodern shift away from the more unequivocal forms of modern space and organization characterized by Fordist assembly-line systems and factories of mass production was the work of this young generation of L.A. architects experimenting with industrial sites and the relationship of those sites to domesticity.[4] Similar to the fracturing of large Hollywood film studios from the 1950s to the 1970s into disperse production and distribution facilities, such spaces of outmoded modernist forms of mass production were converted into more fragmented, diverse, and flexible spatial operations. These L.A. architects invented new forms of postmodern space while repositioning ubiquitous industrial materials such as concrete, aluminum, chain-link, and rigid container sheet (RCS) products in rebellious and innovative ways.

By 1980, Los Angeles proved an incubator for experimental post-Fordist practices, which critic and writer Olivier Boissière surmised to be a movement surrounding the L.A. Ten—a loosely affiliated cadre of architects associated with the University of California, Los Angeles (UCLA) and the Southern California Institute of Architecture (SCI-Arc), formatively including Frederick Fisher, Gehry, Craig Hodgetts, Coy Howard,

FIGURE 2.
L.A. architects at Venice Beach, left to right: Frederick Fisher, Robert Mangurian, Eric Owen Moss, Coy Howard, Craig Hodgetts, Thom Mayne, and Frank Gehry, 1980.
Photo by Ave Pildas.

Robert Mangurian, Thom Mayne, Eric Owen Moss, James Stafford, Thane Roberts, and Michael Rotondi (fig. 2).[5] These architects exhibited their work locally at the Architecture Gallery in Venice Beach and hosted a series of lectures at SCI-Arc that garnered local attention through sensational write-ups by John Dreyfuss of the *Los Angeles Times.* Affiliation with this group ebbed and flowed, and later included Neil Denari, Ming Fung, Franklin Israel, Wes Jones, Eugene Kupper, and Michele Saee.[6]

Tim Street-Porter, primarily a photographer and an important champion for this emerging group, notoriously deemed Gehry to be the "Father of Them All," for not only was Gehry the most mature in age but his Santa Monica house of 1977–78 arguably initiated the aesthetic and material direction for their burgeoning postmodern style.[7] Although other formative members of the L.A. Ten were equally active during the 1970s—for example, Mayne and Rotondi of Morphosis, like Gehry, investigated corrugated aluminum materials when they designed and built their Delmer Residence from 1976 to 1977 (fig. 3)—none of this work garnered the same international attention as that of Gehry, who a decade later was heralded as one of the most formative deconstructivist architects of the twentieth-century.[8]

For better or worse, "deconstructivism" became the official label applied to this school of L.A. architects, for certainly as early as 1980, *de-construction* was a noun unwittingly used to describe Gehry's fragmented designs.[9] It was not, however, until 1988 that Mark Wigley and Philip Johnson, in their exhibition *Deconstructivist Architecture* at the Museum of Modern Art (MoMA), first associated deconstruction, the literary movement, with the contemporary field of architecture design.[10] Hoping to encapsulate and understand a new global form of innovative design practice and package it to an international, interdisciplinary audience, the deconstructivist exhibition at MoMA included several mid- to late-1980s projects by the New York and European architects Zaha Hadid, Rem Koolhaas, Daniel Libeskind, Wolf Prix, and Bernard Tschumi alongside Gehry's designs from Los Angeles. So as to avoid Gehry's appearing too distant from these later deconstructivist designers, the Gehry house was redated "1977–87" in the exhibition fact sheet and the catalog, in effect glossing over the preceding decade of postmodern L.A. architecture that Gehry had already contributed.[11]

From the late 1970s to the late 1980s, the L.A. Ten (sometimes referred to as the Santa Monica Group or the L.A. School) experimented with local opportunities, demonstrating innovation that had very little, if anything, to do with deconstruction, the literary movement. More earnestly, on the Westside of Los Angeles, these young architects took advantage of a relative canvas for experimentation created by the detritus left in the wake of the oil, manufacturing, and aerospace industries in and around Playa del Rey, Venice Beach, and Culver City that deflated land values and attracted a strong local art community amid a casual and liberal beach culture. If by the 1920s, Hollywood had produced a fertile environment of sunshine, opportunity, talent, and land value for the film industry to attain critical mass, then by the 1970s,

FIGURE 3.
Morphosis (1979–).
Delmer Residence (1976–77), Venice Beach, 1977.
Photo by Daniel Zimbaldi.

the Westside offered a similarly compelling geographical, political, cultural, and economic landscape. Los Angeles supported the birth of an emerging architecture industry that was catapulted to fame in the 1980s through the powerful reach of international media and an association with the East Coast and European deconstructivist movements in architecture.[12]

The official breakout project for the L.A. Ten proved to be Gehry's house, which posed a character truly unlike anything Gehry had done before. Prior to the late 1970s, Gehry was predominantly a modernist whose domestic work, similar to that of architects Joseph Esherick and Charles Moore of Northern California, had formally used shedlike roof forms with creatively exposed interior wood structures that elegantly conformed to the natural rural topography. Expressing taut surfaces that carefully extruded the floor plan clear to the roof, these modern buildings produced simple figures through clear and appropriate, if imaginative, uses of industrial materials typically found in agricultural buildings, storage facilities, warehouses, and barns. Gehry, for the most part, remained reservedly modern prior to the construction of his Santa Monica house. The clashing corner skylights, angular windows, and canted walls used in his home—reminiscent of the precarious angular spaces of Robert Wiene's expressionist film *Dr. Caligari's Cabinet* (1920)—constructed a new perspective on architecture, one in which industry was seen crashing headfirst into domestic life.

The Ellen and Jay McCafferty Studio, designed and built by Coy Howard in San Pedro from 1979 to 1980, most explicitly recognized the same latent need as the Gehry Residence to respond to the onslaught of industry impacting everyday life in Los Angeles. Reacting most specifically to the ecology of the San Pedro port only blocks away, Howard's renovation of this three-story home presented a staged gabled facade armored with shiny new RCS aluminum siding. A stern material image was posed to the street facing the port, only to be countered by a lyrical series of variegated window systems beside an asymmetrical line of fenestration that broke up the symmetrical window pattern (fig. 4). As one critic described at the time, the McCafferty Studio exploited "jarring juxtapositions and formal incompleteness to create a sense of wonder and mystery" through eroding elements that suggest "an enigmatic sense of 'abandonment and rehabilitation' to relate to the tough and dilapidated character of the area."[13] The McCafferty Studio was artistically rendered with an industrialized skin to contextualize domesticity within the neighboring port infrastructure, if not to harmonize with it.

The Gagosian Studio (built 1980–81), by Hodgetts and Mangurian of Studio Works Architects; the Lawrence Residence (1981–84), by Mayne and Rotondi of Morphosis; and the Culbertson Residence, or Petal House (1982–84), by Moss also presented similarly stark, if aggressive, industrial exteriors to confront otherwise seemingly harsh urban sites (figs. 5–7). However, unlike Howard's more normative contextualism, the Lawrence Residence and Petal House hardly warranted their extreme industrial facades; they were located on fairly provincial streets adjacent to single-family homes or apartments. Predominantly drawing views toward the top floor, these houses effectively

FIGURE 4.
Coy Howard and Company, Architects (ca. 1977–).
Ellen and Jay McCafferty Studio (1979–80),
San Pedro, 2010.
Photo by Orhan Ayyüce.

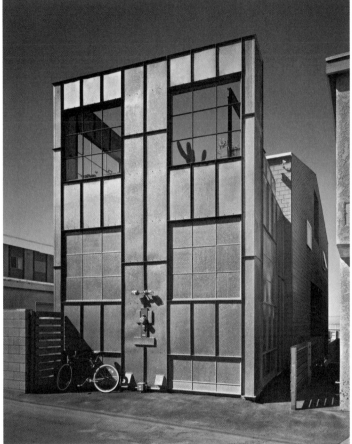

FIGURE 5.
Studio Works Architects (1969–84).
Gagosian Studio (1980–81), Venice Beach, 1980.
Photo by Robert Mangurian.

FIGURE 6.
Morphosis (1979–).
Lawrence Residence (1981–84), Venice Beach, 1984.
Photo by Peter Aaron.

FIGURE 7.
Eric Owen Moss Architects (1973–).
Culbertson Residence (Petal House; 1982–84),
West Los Angeles, 1984.
Photo by Tim Street-Porter.

turned their backs to the residential street life, as if in response to a more dehumanizing landscape than was actually there. The Petal House, for example, had a roof that peeled apart into four eccentric petals that made way for a rooftop pool while misappropriating fixtures from the marine industry—railings, light fixtures, and ladders—outside of any meaningful context, ultimately transforming an existing midcentury two-story wood-frame tract home in West Los Angeles into a quirky postmodern piece of art. With asphalt roof shingles adapted similarly to those used on Morphosis's 2-4-6-8 House (1978) sheathing the facade and steel rebar surrounding the residence as reconstituted fence and gate materials, the Petal House ceased to be a suburban tract house per se and instead, similar to the Lawrence Residence, supported a dystopian view of an industrialized future yet to come. As Moss argued at the time, "careful effort was made to understand and extend the essential qualities of both the existing house and the immediate neighborhood," where the house served as a "counter-point to the tract vocabulary."[14] Culturally specific, it radically poked fun at the standard postwar suburban housing condition, here riffing on the fact that this house was located almost too close to the Santa Monica (10) Freeway to function as a quiet suburban home. The city, with its extreme kinds of infrastructure, posed a new ecological condition, one in which industry was imagined as expanding cheek by jowl with residential life, producing a new hybridized paradigm: the postmodern industrial-domestic urban form.

Able to seamlessly operate between varied building types and settings, both industrial and domestic, Moss had garnered a keen understanding of Los Angeles's evolving urban character from one of his earliest commissions, a thirteen-thousand-square-foot office building and warehouse at 1140 South Main Street in the Garment District (fig. 8). Presented with an enormous opportunity to rethink the urbanity of a typical Los Angeles industrial neighborhood, Moss recognized how the local conditions were "very introverted

FIGURE 8.
Eric Owen Moss Architects (1973–).
Morgenstern Warehouse (1977–79), Garment District,
Los Angeles, 1979.
Photo by Daniel Zimbaldi.

and defensive"; the industrial buildings were "mostly masonry and mostly barred up." In somewhat satirical response, he thought to innervate this barren industrial neighborhood with what he described as a "conceptual hypodermic to the life of the street."[15] Bringing a touch of art to an otherwise hard-edged neighborhood (and possibly paying homage to the Centre Pompidou in Paris, completed by Richard Rogers and Renzo Piano that same year), Moss created an artful composition he described tongue in cheek as "utility exhibitionism."[16] As the warehouse was visible from both nearby office towers and the city street, Moss painted bright yellow patterns on the roof and facade, and he creatively positioned industrial ventilators, register grills, conduit lines, meters, lights, mechanical ducts, and signage to ornament the building. Moss's industrial motifs served not only to inspire a critique of the banality of normative industry but also to entice a new clientele to occupy these outmoded industrial territories.

Becoming the exemplar of an emerging postmodern urban aesthetic, described locally at the time as "industrial chic," Moss took advantage of the opportunities produced by a shift in economic practices in the workforce to popularize a new architectural language.[17] By cutting, opening, and operating within failing manufacturing territories, Moss formed a new hybridized aesthetic: one that was both institutional and domestic and that appealed, as he said at the time, to a "new proletariat—going from punch-press industry to computer industry." At a series of urban sites in and around downtown and particularly in Culver City, where a new digital-film and media-tech community was thriving as a condition of an evolving post-Fordist studio industry, Moss created "funky atmosphere[s]" with "witty stuff going on in the architecture" that tantalized and made more palatable the mundane reality of going to work among old abandoned warehouses. For this "new proletariat" service industry, Moss staged dynamic urban settings that provided fashionable, casually domestic style and character, creating workplaces where one might feel more at home wearing a cool T-shirt and jeans.

Culver City, in many ways, still exemplifies this evolving industrial-domestic condition where outmoded factories are next to affordable working-class neighborhoods located among an expanding film industry; together they provide the setting for many of Moss's best interventions. Over the years in and around Hayden Street, Moss experimented with reconstructing industrial environments that at one time were vacant and fairly unsafe, only to become the experimental centers for not only Moss's own artistic and architectural expertise but also a thriving new high-tech-media business culture. Moss's most important commission within this emerging industry was the reconfiguration of a group of five warehouses formerly used for plastics manufacturing at 8522 National Boulevard, which he turned into a "hip" work space. In over sixty thousand square feet of available area owned by Frederick Norton Smith, Moss made a series of interventions that appealed to graphic design, computer software, hardware, and music companies interested in an industrial space transformed through creative and artistic uses of fairly standard building materials (glass, aluminum, wood, concrete, and various metals) that suggested a new and "edgy" industrialized aesthetic.[18]

Such post-Fordist film and media-tech communities fostered a new architectural expression, which Franklin Israel, an architect and faculty member at UCLA working along lines similar to Moss', was able to develop into a complex proportional and material sensibility with very fashionable high-industrial style. One of Israel's most significant works, the studio for Limelight Productions, for example, delivered strong architectural qualities of light, color, and spatial materiality through the use of a design aesthetic reminiscent of

FIGURE 9.
Franklin Israel (American, 1945–96).
Limelight Productions (completed 1991), Los Angeles, 1991.
Photo by Grant Mudford.

Rudolph Schindler's angular, tatami-inspired proportional systems (fig. 9). Israel, perhaps more than any other L.A. Ten architect, demonstrated the region's legacy of technological and formal innovation and its emerging "California-fusion" style. In his Limelight Productions design, Israel advanced a new palette of materials and methods—ripping, tilting, bending, and folding brightly stained or naturally finished plywood materials and aggregating them with metals, Italian plaster, glass, and fiberglass to give sensational atmospheric character to his building. In keeping with the rhythms of a high-pressure 24/7 media culture, Israel's diverse series of fragmented formal and material techniques were lit up during the day and at night, creating a high-design image and aesthetic desired by film industry professionals within the space of a contemporary administrative network. By dividing the original Hollywood warehouse into a progressive clustering of office and in-house consulting units, Israel developed a more fluidly organized, flexibly divided, and readily adaptable workplace.

As Gehry observed, Israel possessed the personal and political skills necessary to work within the film community.[19] Inspired by "the products and personalities of 'The Industry,'" Israel created staged environments that expressed the tensions between the media image of L.A. as an urban car culture of unbounded freedom and the contradictory reality of Los Angeles as a city of fortified homes, gated communities, and closed office parks.[20] L.A. architecture for Israel, as it had been for Gehry, revealed this Janus-faced media image of a city that celebrates creative freedom within the confines of high-profile, heavily guarded, pristine residential neighborhoods set among gritty industrial territories.

In developing a fashionable style based on proportion, materials, and fragmentation, these postmodern L.A. architects challenged the artistic and cultural assumptions embedded in traditional modern approaches to industry and its components, setting off a new avant-garde aesthetic. As such, "industrial chic" came to be desired by a very high-end, artistically oriented clientele for their Westside and Hollywood homes, almost counterintuitively to their otherwise privileged upper-class lifestyles. For instance, similar to Israel's designs, Hodgetts + Fung's Viso House (1990), in the Hollywood Hills, fragmented and reconfigured the spaces of the typical modern residence through a cacophonous arrangement of multicolored interlocking spatial units (fig. 10). Commanding views were choreographed between still moments upon interior landings, balconies, and rooms and then seamed together along a path of circulation. Such creative spatial arrangements generated the effect of a moving filmic narrative that remained hidden from street view behind a stark, virtually windowless, stucco box facade. The glamour of the movie industry found architectural translation in the internal psychological spaces of a new form of industrial-domestic architecture.

Inspired by perhaps edgier forms of L.A. industry outside Hollywood culture, Moss's quite stunning Lawson-Westen Residence, built in Brentwood, housed domesticity in a large industrial drum similar to the conical central figure of his 8522 National building, or perhaps more an aerospace fuselage. Client Linda Lawson placed her trust in Moss: "When we walked into the National building that Eric renovated in Culver City, I knew that if Eric could transform an abandoned old warehouse…Eric could create a house that would reflect our own beliefs, attitudes, aesthetics."[21] With the clients accepting, if not desiring, the image of industry for their new home, Moss was free to apply a number of formally based geometric explorations (similar to the earliest postmodern methodologies of Peter Eisenman in his House series)—a conical surface, cylindrical shape, and spiraling stair—to form intricate spatial figures appropriate to the complexities of postmodern life (fig. 11).

The interior of the Lawson-Westen Residence provided a convoluted network of spaces that Moss sheathed within an unapproachably solid concrete facade—a powerful industrial image to confront an otherwise pleasant suburban neighborhood. Recalling the heavy industrial construction typically unimaginable along this beatific, tree-lined street of Brentwood, the concrete silo and harsh facade with a touch of humor

FIGURE 10.
Hodgetts + Fung Design and Architecture (1984–).
Rear facade of Viso House (completed 1990),
Hollywood, 1990.
Photo by Tim Street-Porter.

FIGURE 11.
Eric Owen Moss Architects (1973–).
Lawson-Westen Residence (1988–93), Brentwood, 1993.
Photo by Tom Bonner.

FIGURE 12.
Eric Owen Moss Architects (1973–).
Interior view of the Lawson-Westen Residence (1988–93),
Brentwood, 1993.
Photo by Tom Bonner.

elicited curiosity, criticism, and debate. The brushed stainless steel details, the carefully constructed concrete masonry unit (CMU) walls, and the guarded concrete facade were all counterbalanced in jest with an obliquely placed corner window, curved roofs with cylindrical and castlelike forms, and a cut-off conical structure, all of which made the industrialized architecture more palatable. Moss seemed to agree with Adolf Loos's declaration that ornament is a crime; he had stripped the building down to a simple, solid shell, which he compared to Henry Moore's 1950 *Helmet Head* sculptures.[22] But unlike Loos, who argued that modern domestic exteriors should be hardened to protect against the traumatic shock of living in an industrial city, while the interiors should be comfortable and artistic, Moss designed an interior for the Lawson-Westen Residence that provided little place for the habitants to hide from the onslaught of industrial high-tech culture; the house instead persuaded the residents to evolve their character and style toward a new industrialized point of view. Every detail in the Lawson-Weston Residence was so exquisite, yet hardened and machinelike, that there was little room left for art beyond the architecture itself (fig. 12). As client Tracy Westen well observed: "Eric changed our aesthetic. We probably expected something tamer. Now, we pull out paintings we planned to hang in the house and see that we've changed our minds. I'd often read about the power of art to transform a person and it didn't mean anything until this house. We are different people from what we were…and it's the house that is doing it."[23] Postmodern habitants were hardly provided with a place of refuge from a difficult day of work or a harsh city commute. Through the disarming pretext of architecture in the form of an industrialized work of art, they were forced to confront industry from within their high-fashion homes.

The L.A. Ten architects thus repositioned the image of industry within varied residential frameworks throughout the city. Thom Mayne's Sixth Street House (1988) was perhaps the best example of an architect's attempt to stylize this evolving role of industry. Through the use of outmoded machinery in the home, Mayne established the setting for a new form of cultural revolution. According to Mayne at that time, "The Sixth Street Project continues our investigation of the impacted or imploded building, a metaphor for the veils or walls with which we protect ourselves from the world and from the secrets and mysteries that are so much a part of the human condition. This project, part of the diffused Los Angeles metropolis, accepts the suburban context as a point of departure. Present are the traditional concerns of shelter, structure, use, and materiality, order, beauty and meaning."[24]

Mayne addressed culturally specific architectural concerns and challenged the local suburban condition by subtracting, adding, and repositioning ten industrial fragments within the interior of his home. He was engaged in a cryptic and somewhat critical reassessment of the nature of machine artifacts: "The house explores the ground between these ten found objects and building. The pieces (parts of discarded machinery or dead tech) impart decay, tension, risk, balance—a world between utopia and atopia."[25] In the Sixth Street House, Mayne deployed the industrial machine as a trope to alter and redefine notions of domestic life. He posited "dead tech" machinery outside its cultural context, like a Duchampian ready-made, by suspending it within his home—providing a display for personal use, analysis, and critique and a forum for the habitant's body to engage with obsolete industrial works (fig. 13).

Forming, in effect, a technology museum, the Sixth Street House served as a training ground to simultaneously acclimatize the viewer to the tectonics of a superseded machinic past and the unimpeded onslaught of an aggressive technological future. Through miniaturization and domestication, Mayne set industry on exhibit like a wild animal caged up in a zoo, giving habitants the opportunity to experience the wonder and curiosity of these outmoded forms of technology. Foreshadowing a seamless future between domestic and industrial life, the aim of the Sixth Street House was to provide the habitant time and position to gain authority over past technology, ultimately acclimatizing humanity to a more robust technological future. For Mayne, "the Sixth Street Project is about objects and building, the one self-sufficient and uninhabitable, the other integrated, accommodating, and occupiable."[26] The interrelationship between domesticity and the machine, as constructed by Mayne, encouraged an enchanted image, an industrial mystique or fetish, of rusting metal, aged concrete, and dilapidated machines (i.e., the relics of everyday modern industry housed within an inner world or the imagined psyche of the domicile) sharing a home with the habitants, who would intellectualize an authoritative position over them. The machines were captured, splayed, and demoralized—tortured, if you will, to personal intrigue and amusement—in order for the viewer to overcome any latent fears that technology might one day replace us and any discomfort with its inorganic materiality. Mayne still argues today that his home, with its industrial character and aggressive displacement of dead-tech machinery, feels to him quite "cozy."[27] Similar to Morphosis's early restaurants and later institutional buildings, Mayne's home demonstrated a desire to overcome the repressed modern psyche associated with the imagery of an industrial past. Through their architecture, Morphosis reimagined humanity's relationship to the machine and prepared society for the coming future—that of a hypertechnological, posthuman condition.

From the late 1980s through the 1990s, aerospace facilities, mechanical plants, and even shipping containers further inspired the industrial imaginary of high-postmodern L.A. fetish—a style best demonstrated in the souped-up, hypertech projects of young architects Wes Jones and Neil Denari. Although a latecomer to the L.A. scene, Jones—originally a partner of Holt Hinshaw Pfau Jones (HHPF), in San Francisco, and a prior collaborator with Peter Pfau on several innovative speculative design projects—envisaged reality in the 1980s to be

FIGURE 13.
Morphosis (1979–).
Sixth Street House (1987–92), Santa Monica, 1990.
Screen print with metal foil on paper,
101.6 × 76.2 cm (40 × 30 in.).
Los Angeles, Getty Research Institute.

"inescapably mechanical."[28] According to Jones, machines were not "asked to look like something else," so neither should buildings; architecture should develop "its own expressive potential."

HHPF's Chiller/Cogeneration plant (1991–94) for UCLA embodied this paradigm with hypertechnological mechanical systems that, similar to Howard's residence or Moss's warehouse projects, maintained a direct correlation between context, program, and industrial aesthetic. The building didactically expressed its mechanical systems, whereas the design for a Pfau Jones tract house (1986) in Manhattan Beach more provocatively located domestic life within a Corbusian *machine à habiter* unlike any modern architecture previously imagined. Jones did not simply use industrial motifs in unique or confrontational ways, as done by his postmodern predecessors; rather, he designed the roof, ceiling, and walls to actually expand or contract space, move along tracks, and react with overt machinic expression to the needs of everyday suburban life. In this suburban "house," industry and domestic life were integrated within one overt technological operation (fig. 14).

Exploring this allegory one step further at an altogether different size and scale was Denari's entry for the "West Coast Gateway" competition of 1988. Aiming to commemorate the pride and achievements of Los Angeles's immigrant population, the city formatively posed a competition for the design of a landscaped pedestrian bridge deck to serve as a symbolic yet physical multicultural gateway and connector over the Hollywood (101) Freeway at Spring and Main Streets. Denari's design, originally deemed by one *Los Angeles Times* critic as "a hard-edged, high-tech harvester parked above the freeway," challenged the cultural relationship being presented by the L.A. Ten: the correlation between humanity, industry, and their machines.[29] Responding to the image of Los Angeles as it one day might become—a vast city of industry with an expansive and dynamic all-invasive infrastructure—Denari retrospectively positions how he understood Los Angeles at that time:

> The industrial landscape, ranging from the local condition of the parking lot to the more visible industrial infrastructure and the imagined world of the military complex, always seemed the subtext to analyzing L.A. on the historical level and of how it was created, whether the movie industry or the heavy industry surrounding aerospace. You couldn't think about L.A., at least conceptually, if you did not invoke or understand the larger landscape at that level.[30]

Industry on a expansive and compelling infrastructural scale became integral to what Los Angeles was and might inevitably be. For his competition entry, Denari created goliath forms of experimental architecture to express his curiosity surrounding the underpinnings of economic land use on such a vast urban scale. The type of dystopian megastructure he proposed, one that was reminiscent of Archigram's Walking City or Japan's Metabolists' proposals of the 1960s, produced a "friendly monster" of immense technological construction.[31] With its extreme megalomaniacal shape and form, industry had grown in the imagination of Denari and inspired some of the most sublimely dehumanizing forms of architecture yet conceived (figs. 15A, 15B). Although Denari would argue in retrospect that his work was never intended to be imperious, the "West Coast Gateway" competition design, like his "Tokyo International Forum" competition entry to follow, affords us an understanding of our predilection toward an extreme posthuman society where architecture might

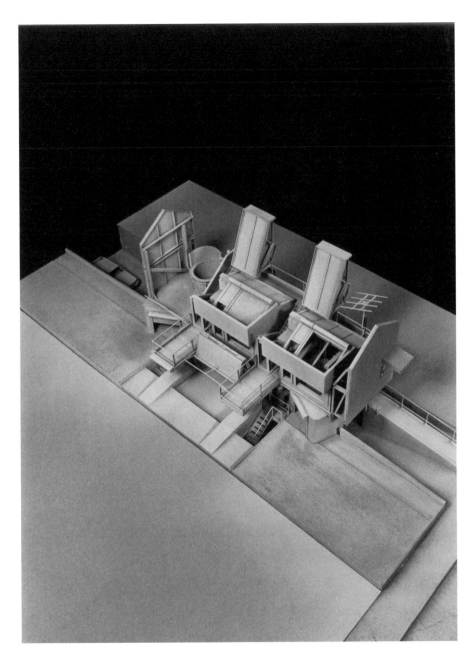

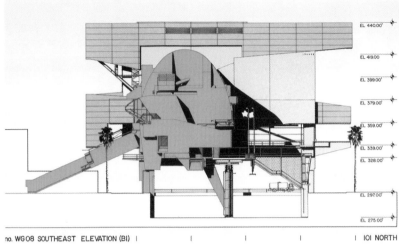

no. WG08 SOUTHEAST ELEVATION (BI)   IOI NORTH

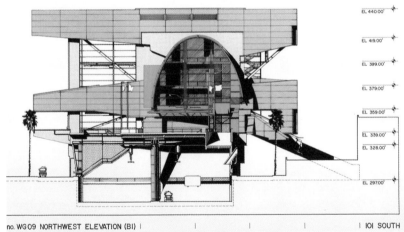

no. WG09 NORTHWEST ELEVATION (BI)   IOI SOUTH

FIGURE 14.
Wes Jones (American, b. 1958),
for Holt Hinshaw Pfau Jones (1986–92).
Model for tract house in Manhattan Beach
(unrealized), 1987.
Chipboard, basswood, corrugated cardboard,
and paint, 50.8 × 76.2 × 40.6 cm (20 × 30 × 16 in.).
San Francisco, Offices of Pfau Long Architecture.

FIGURES 15A, 15B.
Neil M. Denari Architects (1988–).
Southeast elevation and northwest elevation for
"West Coast Gateway" competition entry, 1988.
Ink on paper, sheet: 77.5 × 104 cm (30½ × 41 in.).
Los Angeles, Neil M. Denari Architects.

expand into the perverse realms of infrastructural engineering, beyond the confines of any one cultural expression, domestic region, dwelling, or viable function. Architecture taken to this extreme hyperpostmodern position supports an industrial production of global proportion that exceeds the known limits of human construction. It does not belong to any one localized culture or economy, citizenship, gender, or race, but it is consequent of a multifarious understanding that speaks to perhaps a greater, more intimate expression of all humankind: that our most basic instinct for survival and shelter prompts our desire to exceed (for better or worse), through science or otherwise, the sustainable limits of our planet and our own delicate human form. The technophilic proposition underlying our drive to be surrounded in a carapace of industrial materials and machines—whether outmoded, radically new, fashionable, kindred, or chic—speaks to our insatiable need to extend life beyond the limits of the human body within an architecture that doubles as a harbinger for a new prosthetic life.

NOTES

1   "Out of the Rage for Order: Frank Gehry House," *Progressive Architecture* 61, no. 3 (1980): 81–85. Emphasis in original.

2   Frank O. Gehry, *Frank O. Gehry: Individual Imagination and Cultural Conservatism,* ed. Charles Jencks (London: Academy Editions, 1995). See also Charles Jencks, *The New Paradigm in Architecture: The Language of Post-Modern Architecture* (New Haven, Conn.: Yale University Press, 2002).

3   Postmodernism was an international movement forged within the architecture community by East Coast architect Robert Venturi through his book *Complexity and Contradiction in Architecture* (1966) and then later in the eclectic forms of historical pastiche promoted by architects Michael Graves, Charles Jencks, Philip Johnson, Charles Moore, James Sterling, and Venturi, among others. Postmodern urbanism similar to what I am describing in this essay was first introduced to architecture in 1945 by Joseph Hudnut, American architect and dean of the Harvard Graduate School of Design, in his essay "The Postmodern House," *Architecture Record* 97 (1945): 70–75. Postmodern urbanism was then later advanced in the writing of Frederick Jameson surrounding his analysis of the Bonaventura Hotel in "Postmodernism or the Cultural Logic of Late Capitalism," *New Left Review* I/146 (1984).

4   "Fordism" refers to the system of mass production associated with Henry Ford: car manufacturing, factories, and assembly-line standardization. "Post-Fordism" is characterized by the development of computer information and fabrication systems that afford more flexible, disperse, and networked production facilities and operations, giving rise to multidisciplinary consulting teams and the outsourcing of labor.

5   Olivier Boissière, "Ten California Architects," *Domus,* no. 604 (1980): 17–31. My use of the L.A. Ten is based on a similar name from the MoMA exhibition on five New York architects in 1969 and the movement surrounding them. See *Five Architects: Eisenman, Graves, Gwathmy, Hejduck and Meyer* (New York: Museum of Modern Art, 1975). Similarly, there was the Chicago Seven exhibition in 1976. See *Seven Chicago Architects: Beeby, Booth, Cohen, Freed, Gagle, Tigerman, Weese,* exh. cat. (Chicago: Richard Gray Gallery, 1976).

6   John Dreyfuss, "Gallery Stirs Up Architects," *Los Angeles Times,* 12 December 1979, E26.

7   Tim Street-Porter, "Houses Now," *House & Garden* (February 1982), 136.

8   Philip Johnson and Mark Wigley, *Deconstructivist Architecture: The Museum of Modern Art* (New York: Little Brown, 1988).

9   "Out of the Rage for Order," 82.

10   Jacques Derrida introduced the concept of deconstruction in his three 1967 publications: *Writing and Difference, Speech and Phenomena,* and *Of Grammatology.* Deconstruction, the literary movement, soon centered around Yale University, after Paul de Man joined the faculty in 1970 and wrote the defining deconstructivist text *Blindness and Insight: Essays in the Rhetoric of Contemporary Criticism* in 1971. Bernard Tschumi and Derrida began collaborating on architecture and deconstruction in 1985. Peter Eisenman joined this collaboration soon after, prior to Wigley and Johnson's deconstructivist exhibition in 1988. See Mark Wigley, *The Architecture of Deconstruction: Derrida's Haunt* (Cambridge, Mass.: MIT Press, 1993).

11   See "Fact Sheet, Exhibition: *Deconstructivist Architecture*" (March 1988), Press Archives, Museum of Modern Art, New York; available at www.moma.org/docs/press_archives/6526/releases/MOMA_1988_0029_29.pdf?2010. See also Johnson and Wigley, *Deconstructivist Architecture,* 22.

12   Although John Dreyfuss initiated media discussions surrounding the L.A. Ten, it was European articles such as those written by Charles Jencks and Olivier Boissière that provided notoriety and international support to the L.A. school of architects. See the exhibition review of *Los Angeles Now* (29 April–21 May 1988): Charles Jencks, "LA Style/LA School," *AA Files* 5 (1984): 90.

13   "Citation: Architectural Design; Coy Howard," *Progressive Architecture* 61, no. 1 (1980): 110.

14   Eric Owen Moss, "Petal House (Culbertson House), Los Angeles, California, 1981–83," in Eric Owen Moss, Pilar Viladas, and Yukio Futagawa, eds., *California Architecture,* GA Houses, Special 1 (Tokyo: A.D.A. Edita, 1985), 128.

15   Eric Owen Moss, *Eric Owen Moss: Buildings and Projects* (New York: Rizzoli, 1991), 17–18.

16   "Design Accents Utilities," *Los Angeles Times,* 29 May 1977, Real Estate, Homes-Industry, Part II, 5.

17   Rick Cziment, "Industrial Chic," *Santa Monica Outlook,* 4 April 1989.

18   John Hartmire, "Architect Brings CC New Look," *Culver City News,* 1 June 1989.

19   Frank Gehry, "Introduction," in Franklin D. Israel, *Franklin D. Israel: Buildings + Projects,* ed. Thomas S. Hines (New York: Rizzoli, 1992), 9.

20   Franklin Israel, *Franklin D. Israel* (London: Academy, 1994), 7.

21   Linda Lawson, "Westen House: The House and the Building Process as It Means to the Client," *L.A. Architect* (October/November 1993).

22   Adolf Loos, "Ornament and Crime" [1908], in Ulrich Conrads, ed., *Programs and Manifestoes on 20th-Century Architecture,* trans. Michael Bullock (Cambridge, Mass.: MIT Press, 1975), 19–24.

23   Ziva Freiman, "Into the Uncharted," *Progressive Architecture* 74, no. 5 (1993): 68–77.

24   Thom Mayne, "Detritus and Flotsam," in idem, *Thom Mayne: Sixth Street House,* ed. George Wagner (Cambridge, Mass.: Harvard University Graduate School of Design, 1989), 50.

25   See Rolf Steinberg, *Dead Tech: A Guide to the Archaeology of Tomorrow,* trans. Michael Stone (San Francisco: Sierra Club, 1982).

26   Mayne, "Detritus and Flotsam," 50.

27   Thom Mayne, interview by Stephen Phillips, 10 November 2011.

28   Peter Pfau and Wes Jones, "Pfau/Jones—Holt & Hinshaw," in Robert McCarter, ed., *Building Machines,* Pamphlet Architecture, no. 12 (New York: Princeton Architectural, 1987), 55, 58.

29   Sam Hall Kaplan, "Unlocking Gateway Competition," *Los Angeles Times,* 28 August 1988, Real Estate, 8.

30   Neil Denari, interview by Stephen Phillips, 9 December 2011.

31   Neil Denari, "Four Statements on Architecture 1990," *A+U: Architecture and Urbanism,* no. 246 (1991): 26.

EVERYDAY ENTERTAINMENT
POST-POSTWAR LIFE IN THE SAN GABRIEL VALLEY

Chris Nichols

SOUTHERN CALIFORNIA IN THE DECADES immediately following its midcentury boom was littered with the detritus of a world created anew and instantly forgotten. The architectural wonders of the postwar generation were deteriorating and mysterious, like totems of a lost civilization. By the 1980s, they began to rapidly disappear in favor of fashionably muted architecture. A style that was once full of energetic optimism had become a garish embarrassment to the generation that created it.[1] However, in towns such as Azusa and West Covina, it was as if time had stood still; many of the prime monuments remained. Today, Southern Californians live life at the scale of eighty-eight cities and the speed of ten-lane freeways, and amid this massive push of people and growth, the architectural history of the suburban valleys seems forgotten.

Both the San Gabriel and the San Fernando Valleys have a history dating back to the eighteenth century and their own Spanish missions. From 1900 to 1920, downtown Los Angeles was the beginning and end of the city, and the valleys were equidistant; but when people in Los Angeles speak colloquially about "The Valley," the San Fernando Valley reigns supreme. Before the 1920s, Western Avenue was the western boundary of Los Angeles, but as the city expanded, the center of thinking moved west; that shift escalated in the 1950s and spiked exponentially after the Watts Riots of 1965. As this nascent suburban metropolis headed for the coast, western neighborhoods became more convenient. In the 1960s, this convenience led to the development and redevelopment of the San Fernando Valley, which, in turn, led to a higher densification that, by the 1990s, had erased most traces of the midcentury commercial strip there. Stagnant real estate values in the San Gabriel Valley, however, led to preservation through neglect, leaving the ruins for future explorers.

The San Gabriel Valley covers more than two hundred square miles east of downtown Angeles—between the San Gabriel Mountains to the north and the Puente Hills to the south. The Tongva people had a civilization there for more than twelve hundred years before the Spanish Franciscan Junípero Serra built a large mission near the San Gabriel River in 1771, a decade prior to the Spanish settlement of Los Angeles. In fact, the eleven founding families (Los Pobladores) left from Misión San Gabriel Arcángel on their march

FIGURE 1.
John Lautner (American, 1911–94).
Googie's on Sunset Boulevard
(1949; demolished in 1989), 1952.
Photo by Julius Shulman.
Los Angeles, Getty Research Institute.

to the area near what is now the historic El Pueblo district to create the city of Los Angeles. A century later, San Gabriel Valley settlements were among the first incorporated cities in Los Angeles County; Pasadena was established in 1886, Monrovia in 1887, and Azusa and Whittier in 1898.

Scattered among the backyards of modern, storybook, and ranch houses were countless fruit trees, remnants of the orange groves left behind by developers as free landscaping. In 1970, one could purchase a three-bedroom tract home for less than the cost of a smaller rental in Los Angeles.[2] A generation of home-owners settled into a comfortable life of shopping centers, bowling alleys, and coffee shops. Surrounded by plenty of land and a growing infrastructure, and possessing an endless optimism, these "settlers" had found a new suburban dream—one that would redefine the way the world eats, sleeps, plays, and works.

West Covina became America's fastest-growing city of the 1950s, with the population increasing 1,000%—from five thousand to more than fifty thousand—by the end of the decade.[3] The Eastland Shopping Center became the city center. When Richard Nixon made a campaign stop there in 1960, nearly twenty-five thousand residents came out to support him. Nixon noted that when he was first elected to Congress in 1946, "The city of West Covina did not exist."[4]

It was the giant roads that brought people to Covina. Thanks to the ten-lane freeways and Azusa Avenue, a designated six-lane state highway, even today, one can zip the five miles from Azusa to West Covina a lot faster than the same mileage between Beverly Hills and Santa Monica. But the roadside culture did not end at the roads. Commuting quickly between home, work, and play required a car-friendly environment; mandatory were acres of convenient parking right in front, gigantic signs, and flashy architecture that caught a driver's eye with enough time to pull in.

John Lautner designed the original Googie's on Sunset Boulevard in 1949 (fig. 1). Through a feature in *House and Home* magazine, this small glass-and-steel restaurant would provide a name to an emerging style of commercial architecture. The electric and aggressive form was an inspiration for a generation of flam-boyant buildings from Armet & Davis, Honnold & Rex, Martin Stern Jr., and other designers who understood the power of dynamic architecture to attract customers. Critic Philip Langdon observes that the buildings stood out with "planes, angles, juttings, textures and colors [that] couldn't possibly coincide or blend with anything else about them."[5] Alan Hess's groundbreaking book *Googie: Fifties Coffee Shop Architecture* (1985) was the first to explore the style in detail. Even today, Hess struggles to explain some of the more complex geometry: "The best Googie" he says, "cannot be described with words."[6]

Many of the structures, businesses, and demographics remained in a state of suspended animation through the end of the century. Well into the 1990s, radio station KGRB in West Covina played exclusively big-band music directly off 78 rpm albums. To this day, a visitor can enjoy a steak in a sprawling Yukon cabin with glittering snow on the roof or drive through two enormous fiberglass donuts for a cup of coffee (fig. 2). But twenty years ago, it was even easier to use landmarks and signs from this "valley of the giants" to navi-gate. Just behind the neon-laced ten-gallon cowboy hat of Arby's and across from the big cartoon beaver atop Builder's Emporium sat an epic city of bowling: an alley with fifty lanes, a barbershop, beauty parlor, cocktail lounge, nightclub, billiard hall, pro shop, coffee shop, and endless banquet halls. The centerpiece of the Covina Bowl (designed by Powers, Daly, DeRosa, 1955) is a giant origami pyramid of folded stucco at the

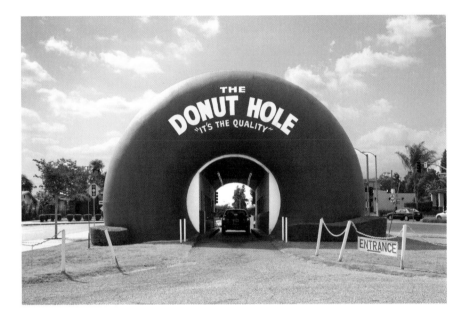

end of a zigzag porte cochere supported by rugged flagstone columns (fig. 3). "The more forms you used the better," Pat B. DeRosa told the *Los Angeles Times,* "especially if [the building] looked like it was just floating there, if you couldn't see how it could stand up. That was the trick of it."[7] The composition is complimented by a stylized modernist representation of an Egyptian ankh for a sign, a sixty-foot key glowing with rings of multicolored neon spelling "BOWL," a verb like *eat* and *shop* that motivated a generation to leave their homes in search of the good life.[8] At the center of the entire complex was a sumptuous cocktail lounge called the Pyramid Room, which featured dancing and entertainment nightly.

    Although the sport of bowling dates to at least the Middle Ages, for the first half of the twentieth century, American alleys were still pretty primitive and often in a saloon setting.[9] Pins were set by hand, and balls were returned to the player via a young workforce dubbed "pinboys." The era of modern bowling took off after supplier American Machine and Foundry introduced a reliable mechanical pinsetter in 1952. Automation allowed the centers to grow without additional labor costs.[10] The lack of brusque pinsetters and the addition of amenities like beauty shops and child care (as well as a registered nurse at Covina Bowl)[11] opened the traditionally male sport to a new family audience. By 1964, one in four Americans considered themselves bowlers.[12] Architects Gordon Powers, Austin Daly, and DeRosa built seventy-two of these palaces.[13] Inspiration came from fantasy—and the booming aerospace industry unfolding around them. "I just dreamed about them," remembered DeRosa. "Everyone was space conscious."[14] "The eye-popping décor seemed to strike a chord among suburban bowlers," says critic Andrew Hurley, "many of whom were experiencing material affluence for the first time."[15]

    Powers, Daly, and DeRosa's work was as eye-catching as any of the Googie coffee shops and incorporated many of the same design features. One has to appreciate these buildings as choreography. First, the sign comes into view, flashing in sequence from blocks away. Then, as one's car goes rollicking up and down

FIGURE 2.
Edmund C. Foerstel (American, b. 1923).
Donut Hole (1968), La Puente, 2012.
Photo by John Kiffe.
Los Angeles, Getty Research Institute.

FIGURE 3.
Powers, Daly, DeRosa (1955–64).
Covina Bowl (1955), Covina, 1956.
35 mm color slide.

FIGURE 4.
Lee Linton (American, 1922–2006).
The Huddle (completed 1958), West Covina, ca. late 1950s.
Photo by Gordon Ayers.

into the driveway, the neon dances around the curves of the hood and fenders, growing larger as one pulls up under the sign, near a sheltering roof (perhaps a jutting prow or a curving arc) and an exotic garden of foliage—the primitive and the futuristic clashing in harmony. "Here Fred Flintstone and George Jetson," says Hess "could meet over a cup of coffee."[16]

Louis Armet and Eldon Davis created several landmarks in the San Gabriel Valley, from Catholic churches to their better-known coffee shops. Their chief designer in the 1950s was Lee Linton, who in decades to come would become best known for a collection of outrageous Las Vegas casinos such as remodels of the Aladdin and Circus Circus. In 1958, he broke away from Armet & Davis and began working directly for restaurant owner Paul Cummins. That year, Linton designed a particularly lavish restaurant called The Huddle next to the Eastland shopping center (fig. 4). The most prominent element was the dynamic floating roofline, which Linton and Armet & Davis were famous for. It could be found across the country at numerous locations for Bob's Big Boy and Denny's, which were responsible for spreading the style nationwide. Emerging from underneath the roof was a row of multicolored beams, reaching out like tentacles toward the San Bernardino (10) Freeway, beckoning motorists to pull off and have a cup of coffee.

Eastland was a large modern shopping center anchored by the May Company department store. Centers like these started arriving soon after World War II, as shopping moved from downtown stores to exciting new arrangements in the suburbs. One of the first was Broadway-Crenshaw Center in 1947. This complex is considered the oldest regional shopping center in operation in the United States.[17] North Hollywood became home to Valley Plaza, a regional center anchored by Sears and designed by Stiles O. Clements in 1951. The instant community of Lakewood, near Long Beach, was anchored by the Lakewood Center in 1952. The San Gabriel Valley greeted the ultramodern Eastland Center, designed by A. C. Martin and Associates, in 1957 (fig. 5). The firm was founded in 1913 and was a partner on the design of the Los Angeles City Hall; the West Adams headquarters of the Automobile Club of Southern California; and major department stores, including the May Company at Wilshire Boulevard and Fairfax Avenue. The firm also designed significant aerospace facilities in the 1950s. "I suppose the 'space frame' of Eastland," says current A. C. Martin chairman David Martin, "reflected some of this experience."[18]

Eastland was long, low, and sleek, with parking for 5,500 cars. The mall featured sixty-five stores of the type that continue to fill malls today. Kay Jewelers and See's Candies were among the first tenants.[19] The May Company alone had an auditorium and tearoom, as well as departments for books, televisions, and even

pianos.[20] The shopping center was modular and built to be expanded if demand arose for more department stores. Eastland combined the middle-class glamour of the May Company with more practical notions from dime-store retailers such as W. T. Grant and the homespun comfort food of Clifton's Cafeteria (designed by McAllister & Wagner, 1957), a new outpost of the venerable downtown chain.[21] This modernist interior was a vast departure from Clifton's earlier restaurants, which were lavish tropical or woodland fantasies.

Erupting from the center of Eastland was an enormous tower, an Eames-like space-frame assemblage of steel girders and multicolored triangles that rose fifty feet above the acres of parking and became a beacon seen from miles away (fig. 6).[22] The *Los Angeles Times* described the May Company store as "imposing," and, at four stories, it was likely the tallest building in the entire valley.[23] It was finished in "yellow face brick, Swedish blue-pearl granite and mellow cream concrete." The architects described the mall as split-level, as there were shops opposite the upper, north-facing elevation and the lower, south-facing level that could be seen from the San Bernardino (10) Freeway.[24] Stairs and escalators framed by lush landscaping led to an inner courtyard shielded by a horizontal space frame and housing even more shops amid benches, trees, and a steel sunshade.

As more amenities began to arrive in the San Gabriel Valley, landmarks like Wallichs Music City were relocating to the suburbs. By the early 1960s, Capitol Records founder Glen Wallichs had built a small

FIGURE 5.
A. C. Martin and Associates (1945–ca. 1970).
Eastland Shopping Center (1955–57), 1957.
Photo by Howard D. Kelly, Kelly-Holiday Aerial Photography.

FIGURE 6.
Postcard showing the color sign for the Eastland Shopping Center, ca. 1960.
Photo by David M. Mills.

chain of the supermarket-sized record shops known for their innovative listening stations and revolving credit accounts.[25] In 1964, he closed his downtown Los Angeles store and moved it to Eastland in West Covina.[26]

Cinematic entertainment came to the San Gabriel Valley as early as 1911, when the Clune's Pasadena Theatre opened.[27] In the 1920s, there was a small boom of more theaters opening in Pasadena and farther east in Azusa, Covina, and Glendora. The Eastland Theatre was designed by Case Study House architects Whitney Rowland Smith and Wayne Williams; it opened in 1961 a block west of the shopping center (fig. 7).[28] The Eastland Theatre, along with the Capri theater nearby (opened in 1963), brought celebrity appearances, wide-screen presentations, and roadshow-type productions to the area.[29]

FIGURE 7.
Smith & Williams, Architects (1946–73).
Eastland Theatre (built 1961; demolished 2006), n.d.
Rendering by Stan Repp.
San Luis Obispo, California, Sanborn Theater Archives.

FIGURE 8.
Postcard of Norbert Pieper's Carousel Theatre,
West Covina, November 1965.

Across the parking lot from the powerhouse mall was the Carousel Theatre (designed by Norbert Pieper, 1965), a 3,300-seat theater-in-the-round[30] advertised as the largest venue of its kind in the world, with performances ranging from Rodgers and Hammerstein to the Doors (fig. 8).[31] Producers Danny Dare and Sammy Lewis sought to "merchandise good theater to suburban areas,"[32] ultimately building three similar entertainment complexes in the state, including the Circle Star in San Carlos and Melodyland in Anaheim.[33] Children's acting classes, ballet, and opera were planned for the venue. "Of course," Lewis remarked at the time, "we also have rock 'n' roll nights, closed circuit TV for fights and auto races. We're even thinking of putting in an ice show one of these days."[34] The producers called the Carousel a "Magic Circle of Entertainment," and it opened with a sold-out performance by Liberace.[35]

After a promising start, audiences failed to return. In retrospect, theater staff blame the decline on unfamiliarity with the circular arrangement, both by audiences used to a traditional stage and performers who did not adapt to the unique constraints of the venue.[36] Another reason cited was the lack of high-end restaurants in the area associated with a night out on the town. Audiences paying top dollar for a Broadway show wanted more than hamburgers for their date night.[37]

Norbert Pieper led the architecture division of the Sheldon L. Pollack Corporation, which built the venue. His own firm was described as a "wholly owned subsidiary" of the Pollack Corporation.[38] Pieper had previously designed post offices and hospitals before joining the company. Pieper and Pollack's strength was coming in on time and on budget, not architectural theory.[39] The theater closed after only three years and was demolished soon after.[40]

Before Los Angeles's well-known theme parks were developed in the 1950s and '60s, leisure activities included roadside amusements such as the reptile farms along Route 66—a road that knitted together a string of valley towns, luring travelers off the highway on their way to Santa Monica and the terminus of the so-called Main Street of America. Early in 1990, *Entertainment Weekly* profiled a Tulsa writer who had traveled Route 66 and was publishing a new book called *Route 66: The Mother Road.* Azusa was featured, so a grassroots coalition persuaded author Michael Wallis, who was traveling the route in a red Corvette that summer on a publicity junket, to stop in Azusa on his way to the end of the road. Assisted by the city council, they organized a parade, a police escort, and a big party at City Hall; included in the festivities were some authentically road-weary Model Ts and the senior citizen junkyard band. This coalition was the beginning of the California Historic Route 66 Association, which marked the route with the first new signage in decades, created maps and guides, and still thrives today.[41]

Azusa's stretch of Route 66 was a checklist of classic roadside architecture that lasted well into the 1980s: drive-in restaurants, motels, a bowling alley with a big neon pin, and an epic drive-in theater anchoring the most prominent stretch. According to *Architectural Record* in 1963, "Growing numbers of people, with increased leisure and income, [were] spending more time and money on travel and recreation than ever before."[42] It is difficult from our perspective of uniform chains and online reservations to imagine how important the appearance of a motel was in making the selection of where to stay. "The success of motels," wrote the editors of *Record,* "depends almost entirely on the attraction (and retention) of customers." One of the most eye-catching was the outer space–themed Stardust Motel (architect unknown, 1961). The building had a zigzag porte cochere at its entrance and a concrete screen with three-dimensional stars. The lobby was a sparkling glass box showcasing the clean and modern lodging within. The animated sign featured a font lifted directly from its predecessor in Las Vegas and was many times larger than the building itself.

The Azusa-Foothill Drive-In Theater (designed by Roland Decker Pierson, 1961) was built during the peak of the drive-in era (in 1955, there were more than five thousand so-called Ozoners in the United States)[43] and featured a large snack bar and playground equipment under its massive canted screen tower. Drive-ins often advertised their family-friendly policies, encouraging the new suburbanites to bring their kids to the movies, something the previous generation could not easily do.

The A&W Drive-In restaurant, with its wedge-shaped signboard bursting through the roof, was located at the center of the strip. These small carhop drive-ins were descendants of lost giants such as Tiny Naylor's in Hollywood, architect Douglas Honnold's jet-shaped landmark that defined its corner of Sunset and La Brea Boulevards from 1949 to 1984. In the early years of A&W, frosty mugs of root beer were served from programmatic buildings shaped like giant barrels.[44] By the 1950s, stands like the one in Azusa sported a long, low modern steel car canopy that shaded the row of finned behemoths ordering banana splits and floats below.

Though they are popularly associated with the 1950s, drive-ins were on their way out; coffee shops and fast food ruled the roadside.[45] The fast-food industry was born in 1948 when the McDonald brothers,

Richard ("Dick") and Maurice ("Mac"), turned their San Bernardino barbecue drive-in into the first version of the restaurant we know today. That same year, Harry and Esther Snyder opened In-N-Out Burger in the San Gabriel Valley city of Baldwin Park.[46] Four years later, Neil Baker opened Baker's near the original McDonald's in San Bernardino. Carl Karcher opened his first Carl's Jr. in Anaheim in 1956 after operating hot dog stands in Los Angeles for fifteen years.[47] By the early 1960s, Southern California had perfected the formula, as Del Taco, Pioneer Chicken, Der Wienerschnitzel, and Taco Bell were born.

Dick and Mac sold the chain in 1961 to Raymond "Ray" Kroc and retired. The path they took from movies to hamburgers is a true California success story. Hoping to work in the film industry, the brothers moved from New Hampshire to Hollywood in the 1930s and became studio grips. They next operated a theater, where they learned that the profits were in concessions. They bought the adjoining candy shop, which led to operating an orange juice stand and eventually to restaurants. After nearly twenty years of experimentation, the McDonald brothers designed and manufactured the equipment, tools, and methods that allowed a new type of food service to emerge. Dick and Mac were visionaries; they took drive-in restaurants, which were the hot new thing of the 1930s, and used their innovations to become early pioneers in fast food the following decade. All the fast-food chains had a distinctive appearance, but none were as innovative as McDonald's.

Architect Stanley Clark Meston designed an iconic 1952 prototype for McDonald's: the red-and-white tiled stand was a glass-and-steel modernist sculpture with a sloping roof and canted windows framed by a stainless steel counter and aluminum mullions; the whole composition was pierced by thirty-foot-tall

FIGURE 9.
Stanley Clark Meston (American, 1910–92).
Restaurant rendering for the McDonald brothers, 1952.
Water-based tempera on white illustration board.
Rendering and design by Charles W. Fish.

steel arches (fig. 9). The tension of the parabolas, their yellow color, and the way they came to animated life at night through row after row of flashing pink neon forced drivers to take notice. Most of them also bought a hamburger and fries. Soon the restaurant design was copied by as many competitors as their menu was. Burger King's Florida version had steel handlebars on the roof; the Carroll's chain transformed the arches into sharp boomerangs.

      One of the earliest McDonald's was #7 in Azusa, where Route 66 met Cerritos Avenue. The Azusa location opened on 17 September 1954, the year before founders Dick and Mac would offer Kroc his first franchise. When it closed thirty years later, not many noticed. Most patrons appreciated that the newer location down the street offered Chicken McNuggets, air conditioning, and indoor seating. The McDonald's lot in Azusa decayed over time, like modern Mayan ruins collapsing into disarray. By 1968, when a new store design was introduced, there were more than a thousand McDonald's based on Meston's design; today there are maybe six.

      At the beginning of the 1960s, the San Gabriel Valley still seemed new, but just a decade later, things were starting to fray. Philip Langdon described it as the "'Browning of America,' buildings trying to blend into the environment with bricks and wood and earth tones."[48] As chains such as McDonald's retired their early units, others followed, and the entire species became endangered. In 1984, city planners in Azusa forced the owners of the Stardust to apply brick, sawn lumber, heavy-texture stucco, and a Spanish-style parapet to mask the Googie facade.[49]

      When Tiny Naylor's and Ship's coffee shop in Westwood were demolished in 1984, the Los Angeles Conservancy formed a group now known as the Modern Committee dedicated to preserving midcentury landmarks.[50] This group redefined the field by dedicating as much effort to homes by Rudolph Schindler and Richard Neutra as to a drive-in theater along Route 66. The group has honored prolific but little-known architects and firms such as Wayne McAllister and Armet & Davis with lectures, exhibitions, and tours. They fought for the preservation of Welton Becket's Santa Monica Civic Auditorium and the world's oldest McDonald's in Downey, and they continue to advocate for significant architecture, large and small. The lost wonders of the postwar generation have earned their place in history and will not be forgotten.

NOTES

1   The pioneering research of authors such as Alan Hess gave insight into a whole species that was already going extinct less than a generation after it was built. See, for example, the following books by Hess: *Googie Redux: Ultramodern Roadside Architecture* (San Francisco: Chronicle, 2004), *Palm Springs Weekend: The Architecture and Design of a Mid-Century Oasis* (San Francisco: Chronicle, 2001), and *Viva Las Vegas: After-Hours Architecture* (San Francisco: Chronicle, 1993).

2   Display ad 235, *Los Angeles Times,* 6 November 1966, ProQuest Historical, E6.

3   "Historical West Covina," *City of West Covina,* http://www.westcovina.org/about/history/default.asp.

4   Jack Smith, "Nixon Winds Up Southland Tour with Whirlwind 18-Hour Drive," *Los Angeles Times,* 15 October 1960, ProQuest Historical, A1.

5   Steve Harvey, "'Coffee Shop Modern' Architecture: Googie—History Closing the Menu on a 1950s Style," *Los Angeles Times,* 9 June 1986, 1.

6   Alan Hess, interview by Chris Nichols, 4 January 2012.

7   Maria L. La Ganga and Steve Harvey, "'Coffee Shop Modern' Architecture: Googie—History Closing the Menu on a 1950s Style," *Los Angeles Times,* 9 June 1986.

8   Thank you to Gordon Powers for pointing out the similarity of the sign to an Egyptian ankh: Gordon Powers, interview by Chris Nichols, 4 January 2012. H. M. Raphaellian and Felix Marti-Ibanez, *Signs of Life: A Pictorial Dictionary of Symbols* (Whitefish, Mont.: Kessinger, 2006), 12.

9   Gideon Bosker and Bianca Lenc ek-Bosker, *Bowled Over: A Roll Down Memory Lane* (San Francisco: Chronicle, 2002).

10 Gordon Powers, telephone interview by Chris Nichols, 6 January 2012.

11 "San Gabriel Valley Pictorial," *Los Angeles Examiner,* 18 March 1956, 8.

12 Bosker and Lenc ek-Bosker, *Bowled Over;* and US Census Bureau, "Characteristics of the Population, Part A: Number of Inhabitants," vol. 1, http://www2.census.gov/prod2/decennial/documents/10107945v1pA.zip.

13 Powers, interview, 2012.

14 Ganga and Harvey, "'Coffee Shop Modern' Architecture."

15 Andrew Hurley, *Diners, Bowling Alleys, and Trailer Parks: Chasing the American Dream in the Postwar Consumer Culture* (New York: Basic, 2001).

16 Alan Hess, *Googie: Fifties Coffee Shop Architecture* (San Francisco: Chronicle, 1985), 15.

17 "Home Goods Get Big Share of Coast Chain's New Link," *Retailing, Home Furnishings Edition,* 24 November 1947, http://www.hagley.lib.de.us/libimages/LoewyScrapbooks/0062.jpg; and "About BHCP," *Baldwin Hills Crenshaw Plaza,* http://www.baldwinhillscrenshawplaza.com/about.

18 David C. Martin, personal communication, 4 January 2012.

19 "West Covina to Welcome May Co.," *Los Angeles Times,* 12 September 1957, ProQuest Historical, B1.

20 *Your Guide to May Co. Eastland in West Covina,* brochure, 1957, Chris Nichols Collection, Los Angeles.

21 Chris Nichols, *The Leisure Architecture of Wayne McAllister* (Salt Lake City: Gibbs Smith, 2007), 109.

22 Martin, personal communication, 2012.

23 "West Covina to Welcome May Co.," B1.

24 David C. Martin, personal communication, 6 December 2011.

25 John Sippel, "Integrity Opens 2 Largest Calif. Big Bens Stores," *Billboard,* 3 December 1977, 16; and "Wallichs New Look Spurs Music City Chain's Profits," *Billboard,* 18 December 1971, 66.

26 "Music City to Shutter Its Downtown LA Branch," *Billboard,* 18 July 1964, 4.

27 "Clune's: Pasadena's First Movie House, Photo Essay," *Pasadena Star News,* 7 October 2001, A2.

28 Bruce Sanborn, personal communication, 6 January 2012. Photo Standalone 25, *Los Angeles Times,* 12 November 1961, ProQuest Historical, N32.

29 "Statewide to Open Theater in West Covina," *Los Angeles Times,* 17 June 1963, ProQuest Historical, D11; and "Capri Theatre," *Cinema Treasures,* http://cinematreasures.org/theaters/19063. And Sanborn, personal communication, 2012.

30 "$3 Million Showplace Planned in West Covina," *Los Angeles Times,* 30 October 1964, ProQuest Historical, A3.

31 Stan Bernstein, "Rodgers and Hammerstein 'Sound of Music' in Round," *Los Angeles Times,* 4 May 1967, ProQuest Historical, E14; and "Doors: Jack Jones and Doors Booked at Carousel," *Los Angeles Times,* 28 December 1967, ProQuest Historical, C8.

32 John Scott, "Melodyland Operators Branch Out," *Los Angeles Times,* 21 May 1965, ProQuest Historical, D14.

33 "$3 Million Showplace Planned in West Covina."

34 Scott, "Melodyland Operators Branch Out."

35 "New Theater Will Open in West Covina," *Los Angeles Times,* 11 June 1965, ProQuest Historical, C24.

36 Carousel usher (1965–68) Cheryl Pease, interview by Chris Nichols, 2 January 2011.

37 Pease, interview, 2011.

38 "Sheldon Pollack Again Running His Old Firm," *Los Angeles Times,* 28 April 1974, ProQuest Historical, G19.

39   "He Sticks to His Estimates," *Los Angeles Times,* 4 September 1966, ProQuest Historical, D1.

40   "Carousel Dark Month of July," *Montclair Tribune,* 3 July 1968; and Joseph H. Furman, "The Spectrum," *Progress Bulletin,* 15 February 1970. Regarding its demolition, Pease, interview, 2011.

41   "Who We Are," *California Historic Route 66 Association,* http://www.route66ca.org/chr66a/whoweare.html.

42   *Motels, Hotels, Restaurants, and Bars,* 2nd ed. (New York: F. W. Dodge, 1960), v.

43   Don Sanders and Susan Sanders, *The American Drive-In Movie Theater* (Osceola, Wis.: Motorbooks International, 1997), 130.

44   Philip Langdon, *Orange Roofs, Golden Arches: The Architecture of American Chain Restaurants* (New York: Knopf, 1986).

45   Jim Heimann, *Car Hops and Curb Service: A History of American Drive-In Restaurants, 1920–1960* (San Francisco: Chronicle, 1996).

46   Stacy Perman, *In-N-Out Burger: A Behind-the-Counter Look at the Fast-Food Chain That Breaks All the Rules* (New York: Collins Business, 2009).

47   Carolyn B. Knight, *Making It Happen: The Story of Carl Karcher Enterprises* (Anaheim, Calif.: C. Karcher Enterprises, 1981).

48   Ganga and Harvey, "'Coffee Shop Modern' Architecture."

49   Document 2, resolution no. 7578: A resolution of the city council of the city of Azusa granting a zone variance to Sankukh Bhakta for property located at 666 East Foothill Blvd., Azusa, California, variance case no. V-846, City of Azusa Department of Building and Safety.

50   "Home Page," *Los Angeles Conservancy Modern Committee (ModCom),* http://modcom.org/.

PLATES

URBAN NETWORKS

PLATE 1. | **Will Connell (American, 1898–1961).** *Electrical Transmission Towers,* ca. 1935. Gelatin silver print, 50.8 × 40.6 cm (20 × 16 in.). Studio City, collection of Stephen White.

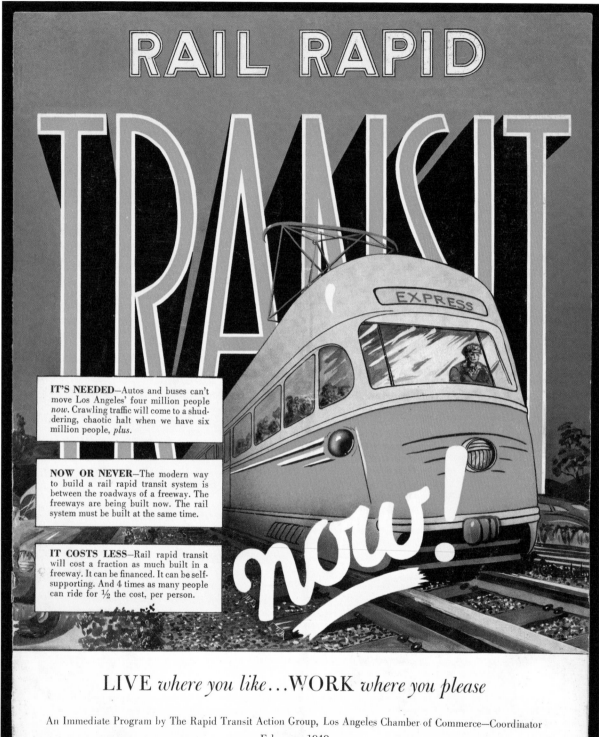

PLATE 2. | *Rail Rapid Transit*, **February 1948.** Print on paper, 25.4 × 20.3 cm (10 × 8 in.). Los Angeles, Dorothy Peyton Gray Transportation Library and Archive.

PLATE 3. | **Kahn, Kappe, Lotery, Boccato Architects/Planners (1973–78).** People mover at a bus intercept in downtown Los Angeles (designed 1975; unrealized), 1975. Print, 38.5 × 89 cm (15⅛ × 35⅛ in.). Los Angeles, Getty Research Institute.

216

PLATE 4. | **View looking north toward Vineland Avenue, December 1956.** Los Angeles, Los Angeles Public Library.

PLATE 5. | **Contact sheet of photographs showing freeway construction, 1964.** Photos by Harry Drinkwater. Los Angeles, Getty Research Institute.

8667-6

PLATE 6. | **Golden State (I-5) Freeway extension, March 1962.** Los Angeles, Los Angeles Public Library, Herald Examiner Collection.

PLATE 7. | **Aerial view of construction of the Four-Level Interchange, looking west across the Civic Center, 1950.** Photo by Delmar Watson. Los Angeles, Los Angeles Public Library.

PLATE 8. | **Aerial view of the Four-Level Interchange, n.d.** Los Angeles, Los Angeles Public Library.

PLATE 9. | **William A. Garnett (American, 1916–2006).** *Smog, Los Angeles,* 1949. Gelatin silver print, 25.2 × 34 cm (9¹⁵⁄₁₆ × 13⅜ in.). Los Angeles, J. Paul Getty Museum.

CAR CULTURE

PLATE 10. | **John P. Aiken (American, b. 1934).** Ford automobile design concept, 1960s. Pencil, colored pencil, marker, chalk, and gouache on colored paper, 49.8 × 62.3 cm (19⅝ × 24½ in.). Los Angeles, Getty Research Institute.

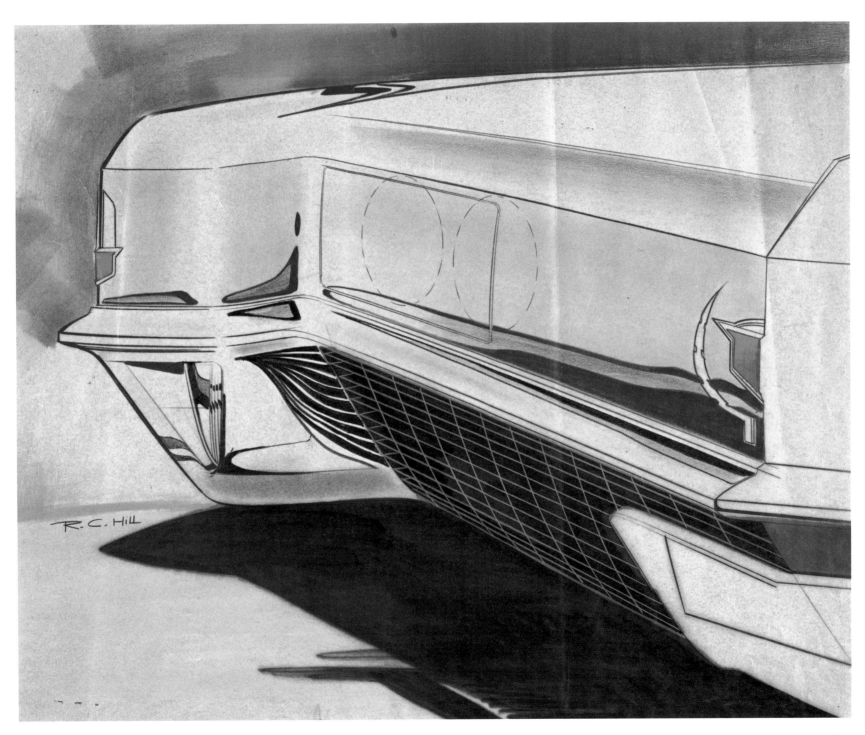

PLATE 11. | **Ron Hill (American, b. 1934).** Pink Cadillac, ca. 1960s. Pencil, colored pencil, pastel, and crayon on vellum with black-tape border, 34.9 × 42.2 cm (13¾ × 16⅝ in.). Los Angeles, Getty Research Institute.

PLATE 12. | **Studio of Richard Arbib (1949–94).** Packard concept car, 1959. Pencil on paper, 21.6 × 27.9 cm (8½ × 11 in.). Los Angeles, Getty Research Institute.

PLATE 13. | **Mobil gas station, 1956.** Photo by Julius Shulman. Los Angeles, Getty Research Institute.

PLATE 14. | **Ray Kappe (American, b. 1927).** Parking garage (unrealized), 1950s. Pencil and crayon
on tracing paper, mounted on board, 51 × 76.5 cm (20⅛ × 30⅛ in.). Los Angeles, Getty Research Institute.

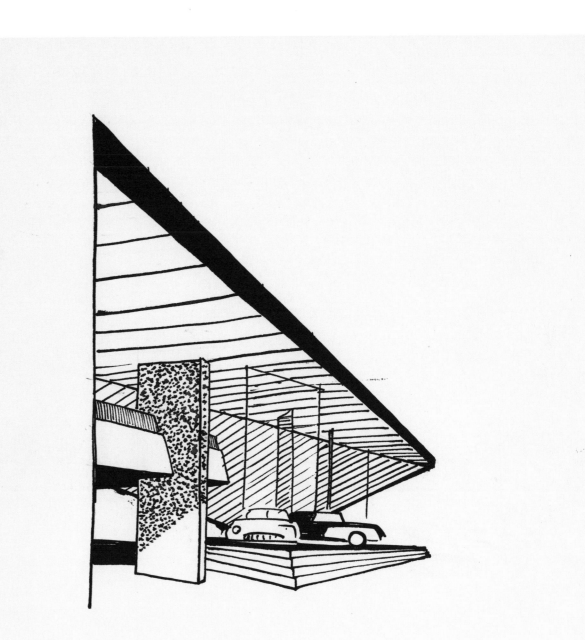

PLATE 15. | **John Lautner (American, 1911–94).** Lincoln Zephyr showroom (completed 1948), Glendale, 1948. Ink on paper, 30.6 × 24.1 cm (12⅛ × 9½ in.). Los Angeles, Getty Research Institute.

PLATE 16. | **Killingsworth, Brady, Smith and Associates (1953–64).** Perspective of the new showroom of Duffield Lincoln-Mercury for the Bixby Land Company (1962–63), Long Beach, 1962. Ink and zip-a-tone, matted, 76.2 × 101.6 cm (30 × 40 in.). Santa Barbara, Art, Design & Architecture Museum at the University of California, Santa Barbara.

PLATE 17. | **Killingsworth, Brady, Smith and Associates (1953–64).** Duffield Lincoln-Mercury showroom (1962–63), Long Beach, 1963. Photo by Julius Shulman. Los Angeles, Getty Research Institute.

PLATE 18. | **Armet & Davis, Architects (1947–72).** Romeo's Times Square restaurant (completed 1955),
Los Angeles, 1955. Pencil on paper, 73.7 × 175.3 cm (29 × 69 in.). Los Angeles, Armet Davis Newlove Architects.

PLATE 19. | **John Lautner (American, 1911–94).** Googie's sign (completed 1949), West Hollywood, 1949.
Gouache on sepia print, sheet: 47 × 86.5 cm (18½ × 34⅛ in.). Los Angeles, Getty Research Institute.

PLATE 20. | **Carl Maston (American, 1915–92) and Richard Banta.** Proposed restaurant for U.P.T. (unrealized), 1953. Pencil on vellum, 55.9 × 66 cm (22 × 26 in.).

ENGINES OF INNOVATION

PLATE 21. | **Daniel, Mann, Johnson and Mendenhall (1946–2000).** American Cement Building (1960–64), Los Angeles, 1960. Photo by Julius Shulman. Los Angeles, Getty Research Institute.

PLATE 22. | **Will Connell (American, 1898–1961).** Union 76 refinery at night (1926), Wilmington, 1950. Gelatin silver print, 39.4 × 49.5 cm (15½ × 19½ in.). Studio City, collection of Stephen White.

235

PLATE 23. | **Austin, Field, and Fry, Architects (1953–58).** Union Oil Company of California research building (ca. 1952), Brea, ca. 1952. Photo by Maynard L. Parker. San Marino, California, Huntington Library.

PLATE 24. | **Pereira & Luckman, Architects, Engineers and Planners (1950–58).** Firestone Tire and Rubber
Company Headquarters (1958), Los Angeles, 1958. Photo by Julius Shulman. Los Angeles, Getty Research Institute.

PLATE 25. | **Cleared Bunker Hill redevelopment project area, 1971.** Photo by Julius Shulman. Los Angeles, Getty Research Institute.

238

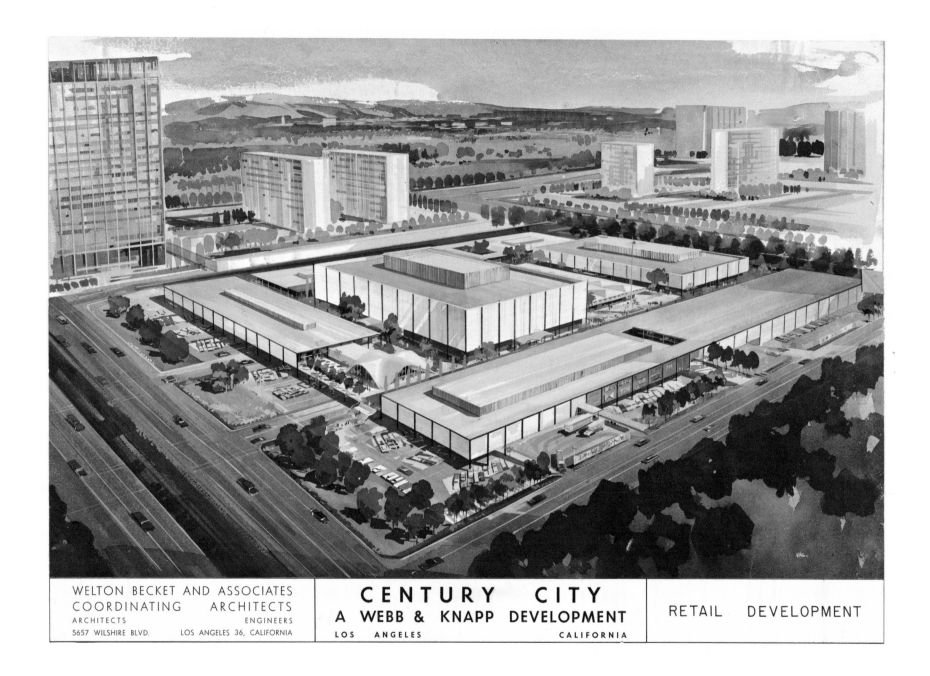

WELTON BECKET AND ASSOCIATES
COORDINATING ARCHITECTS
ARCHITECTS   ENGINEERS
5657 WILSHIRE BLVD.   LOS ANGELES 36, CALIFORNIA

CENTURY CITY
A WEBB & KNAPP DEVELOPMENT
LOS   ANGELES   CALIFORNIA

RETAIL   DEVELOPMENT

PLATE 26. | **Welton Becket and Associates (1949–88).** Rendering of a retail development design for Century City, ca. 1962. Watercolor and gouache on paper, mounted on cardboard, mount: 76.4 × 101.8 cm (30⅛ × 40⅛ in.); drawing: 48.5 × 69.7 cm (19⅛ × 27½ in.). Los Angeles, Getty Research Institute.

PLATE 27. | **Carlos Diniz (American, 1928–2001).** Melrose elevation of Pacific Design Center, by Cesar Pelli for Gruen Associates (completed 1975), West Hollywood, 1973. Ink on vellum, 47 × 106.7 cm (18½ × 42 in.). Los Angeles, Edward Cella Gallery.

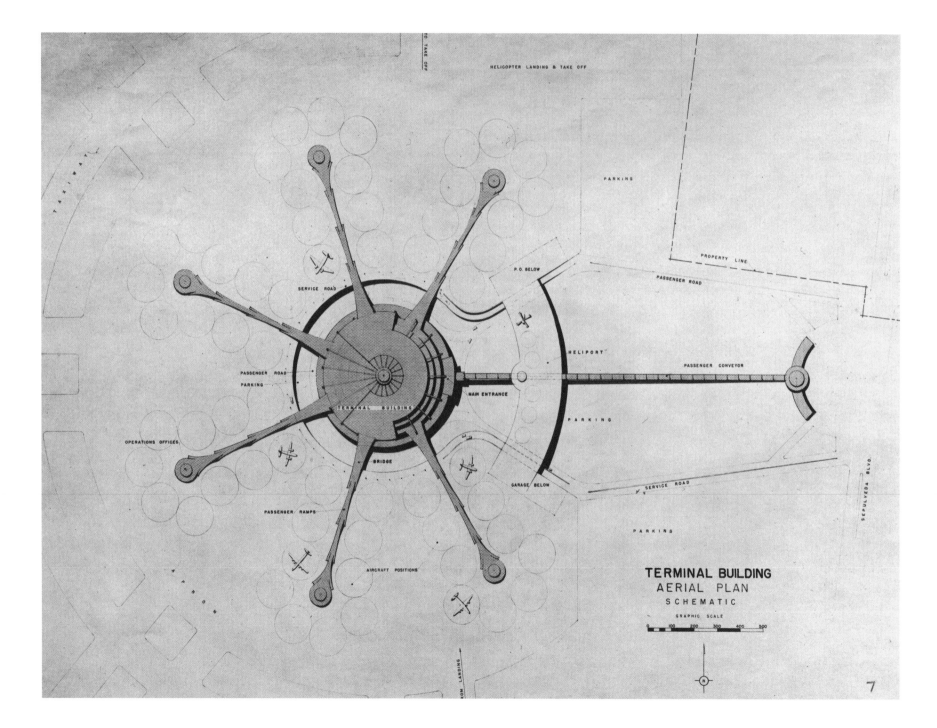

PLATE 28. | **Pereira & Luckman, Architects, Engineers and Planners (1950–58).** Roof plan for preliminary design of the Los Angeles International Airport Terminal Building (unrealized), 1953. From Pereira & Luckman, *Master Plan for Los Angeles International Airport with Preliminary Studies for Proposed Terminal Building* (1953). Santa Barbara, Art, Design & Architecture Museum at the University of California, Santa Barbara.

PLATE 29. | **William Pereira, Welton Becket, Charles Luckman, and Paul R. Williams.** Theme Building at Los Angeles International Airport (completed 1961), 1958.
Pencil, watercolor, and gouache on board, mount: 76.2 × 101.6 cm (30 × 40 in.); drawing: 60 × 87.6 cm (23⅝ × 34½ in.). Los Angeles, Alan E. Leib Collection.

56.29

SCALE

DATE 2.26.60

PLATE 30. | **Maynard Lyndon (American, 1907–99).** Perspective view of Social Sciences Building, Bunche Hall, University of California, Los Angeles (completed 1964), 1960. Pencil on tracing paper, 22.5 × 30 cm (8⅞ × 11¹³⁄₁₆ in.). Santa Barbara, Art, Design & Architecture Museum at the University of California, Santa Barbara.

PLATE 31. | **Edward Durell Stone and Associates (1936–76).** The Von KleinSmid Center at the University of Southern California (completed 1966), 1966. Photo by Julius Shulman. Los Angeles, Getty Research Institute.

KTLA
STUDIO PLANT

1. ENTRANCE
2. SWITCH BOARD
3. SALES MANAGER
4. SECRETARIES
5. MANAGER
6. CLIENTS
7. CONTROL
8. EQUIPMENT ROOM
8A. RELAY TRANSMITTING ABOVE.
9. STUDIO "B"
10. ANNOUNCE BOOTH
11. STUDIO "A"
12. DRESSING ROOMS
13. WASH ROOMS
14. PROGRAM DIRECTOR
15. PROGRAM DEPARTMENT
16. NEWS & FILM DEPARTMENT
17. SALES & PROMOTION
18. PRODUCTION
19. ACCOUNTING DEPARTMENT
20. ART DEPARTMENT
21. PROPERTIES
21A. STORAGE ABOVE.
22. LABORATORY
23. REMOTE EQUIPMENT ROOM
24. SERVICE
25. PASSAGE BACK TO OFFICES

PARAMOUNT TELEVISION PRODUCTIONS INC.
KLAUS LANDSBERG - WEST COAST DIRECTOR.
721 NORTH BRONSON AVE. HOLLYWOOD, CALIF.

THORNTON M. ABELL - ARCHITECT

JOB 148 - 9-6-48

PLATE 32. | **Thornton M. Abell (American, 1906–84).** Axonometric drawing of the KTLA Studio Plant (ca. 1949), 1948. Ink and pencil on tracing paper, 52.7 × 102.6 cm (20¾ × 40⅜ in.). Santa Barbara, Art, Design & Architecture Museum at the University of California, Santa Barbara.

PLATE 33. | **Kem Weber (German, 1889–1963).** Perspective of Disney Studios (1939–40), Burbank, 1939. Pencil, watercolor, and gouache on board, 14 × 19.1 cm (5½ × 7½ in.). Santa Barbara, Art, Design & Architecture Museum at the University of California, Santa Barbara.

PLATE 34. | **Frank O. Gehry and Associates (1962–2001).** Preliminary sketch of elevation and plan for Chiat/Day offices (completed 1991), Venice, ca. 1985. Ink on paper, 22.9 × 30.5 cm (9 × 12 in.). Santa Monica, Gehry Partners, LLP.

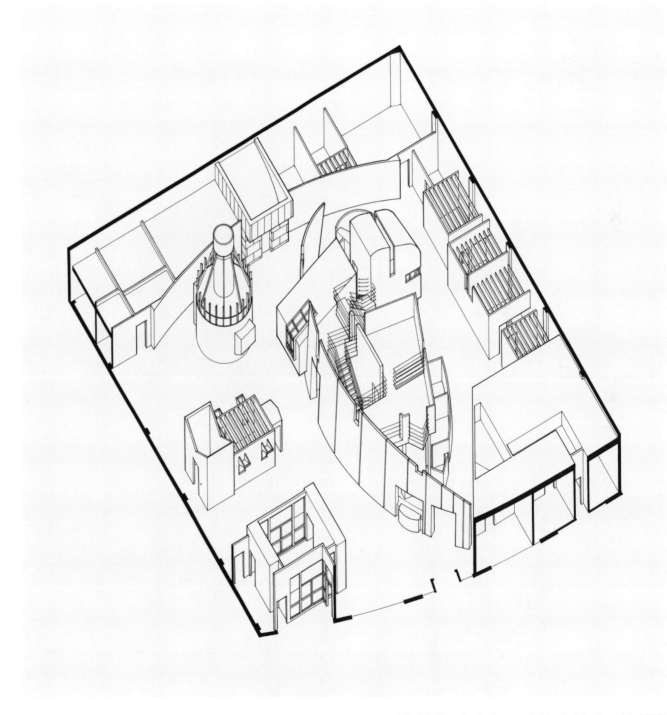

PLATE 35. | **Franklin Israel (American, 1945–96).** Floor plan for Propaganda Films building (completed 1988), Hollywood, 1988. Ink on mylar, 61 × 91.4 cm (24 × 36 in.). Los Angeles, Getty Research Institute.

COMMUNITY MAGNETS

PLATE 36. | **Aerial view of Dodger Stadium, n.d.** Photo by Ralph Morris. Los Angeles, Los Angeles Public Library.

AXONOMETRIC

ELEVATION.

ENTRANCE TOWER

PLATE 37. | **John Spohrer (American, b. 1939), Archisystems International (1983–).** Entrance tower on Vermont Boulevard to the 1984 Olympics (completed 1984), Los Angeles, 1983. Color pencil, crayon, and ink on tracing paper, 46.2 × 40.3 cm (18³⁄₁₆ × 15⅞ in.).

PLATE 38. | **View of Simon Rodia's Watts Towers, Los Angeles, n.d.** Los Angeles, Getty Research Institute.

PLATE 39. | **Lloyd Wright (American, 1890–1978).** Wayfarers Chapel (1949–51), Palos Verdes Estates, 1949. Photo by Julius Shulman. Los Angeles, Getty Research Institute.

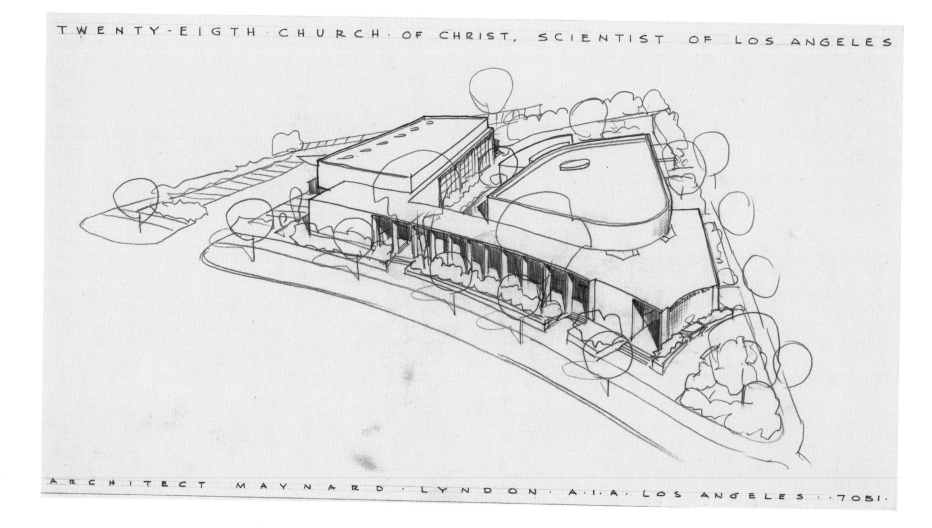

TWENTY·EIGTH·CHURCH·OF CHRIST, SCIENTIST OF LOS ANGELES

ARCHITECT MAYNARD·LYNDON·A·I·A·LOS ANGELES··7051·

PLATE 40. | **Maynard Lyndon (American, 1907–99).** Twenty-Eighth Church of Christ, Scientist of Los Angeles (1954–55), Westwood, 1954.
Pencil on tracing paper, 37.3 × 67.5 cm (14 11/16 × 26 9/16 in.). Santa Barbara, Art, Design & Architecture Museum at the University of California, Santa Barbara.

PLATE 41. | **Sidney Eisenshtat (American, 1914–2005).** Sinai Temple (1956–1960), Westwood, 1959. Pencil, watercolor, and gouache on paper, 61 × 90.2 cm (24 × 35½ in.). Los Angeles, University of Southern California.

PLATE 42. | **Gruen and Krummeck, Architects (1941–51).** Rooftop parking ramp of Milliron's Department Store (1947–49), Westchester, 1949. Photo by Julius Shulman. Los Angeles, Getty Research Institute.

PLATE 43. | **Thornton M. Abell (American, 1906–84).** Perspective of Valley Center (unrealized), 1947. Conte crayon and adhesive on board, 50.8 × 102.2 cm (20 × 40¼ in.). Santa Barbara, Art, Design & Architecture Museum at the University of California, Santa Barbara.

RESIDENTIAL FABRIC

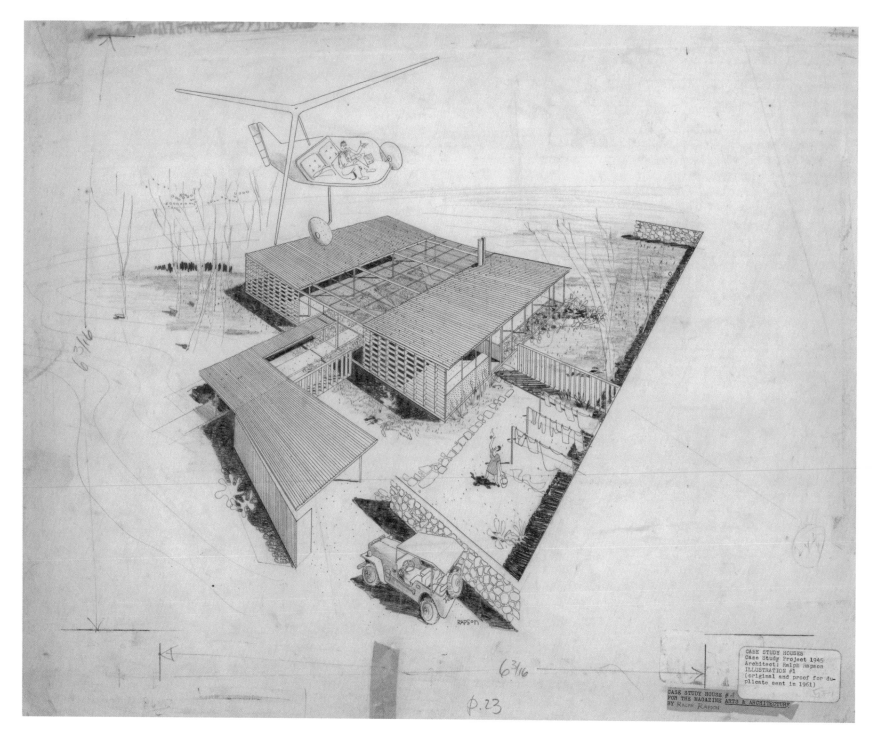

PLATE 44. | **Ralph Rapson (American, 1914–2008).** Case Study House #4, Greenbelt House (unrealized), 1945. Pencil on tracing paper, 53.3 × 63.5 cm (21 × 25 in.). Santa Barbara, Art, Design & Architecture Museum at the University of California, Santa Barbara.

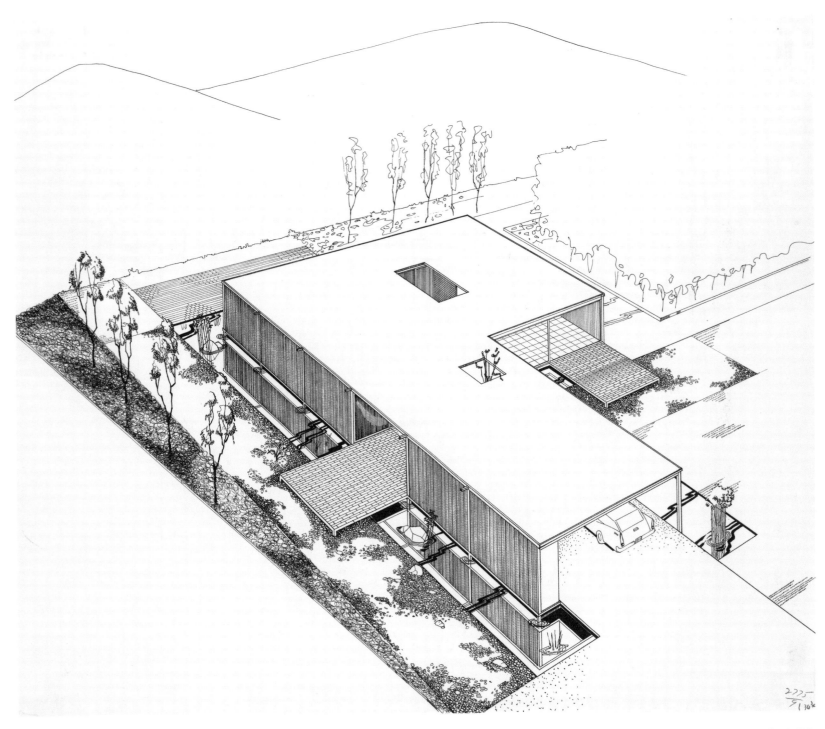

PLATE 45. | **Pierre Koenig (American, 1925–2004).** Bird's-eye-view drawing of Case Study House #21, Bailey Residence (completed 1958), Los Angeles, 1957–58. Ink on vellum, 53.3 × 63.5 cm (21 × 25 in.). Los Angeles, Getty Research Institute.

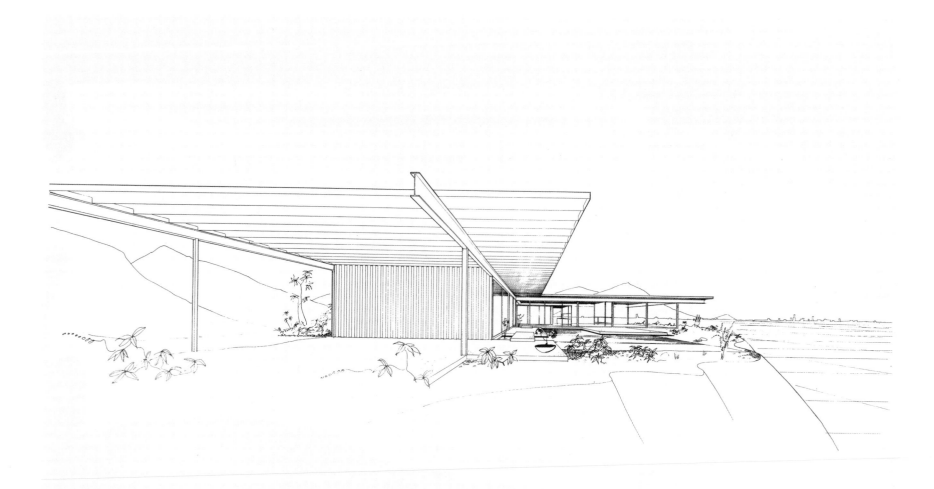

PLATE 46. | **Pierre Koenig (American, 1925–2004).** Perspective view (from carport) of Case Study House #22, Stahl Residence (1959–60), Los Angeles, 1960. Ink on vellum, 50.9 × 76.4 cm (20⅛ × 30⅛ in.). Los Angeles, Getty Research Institute.

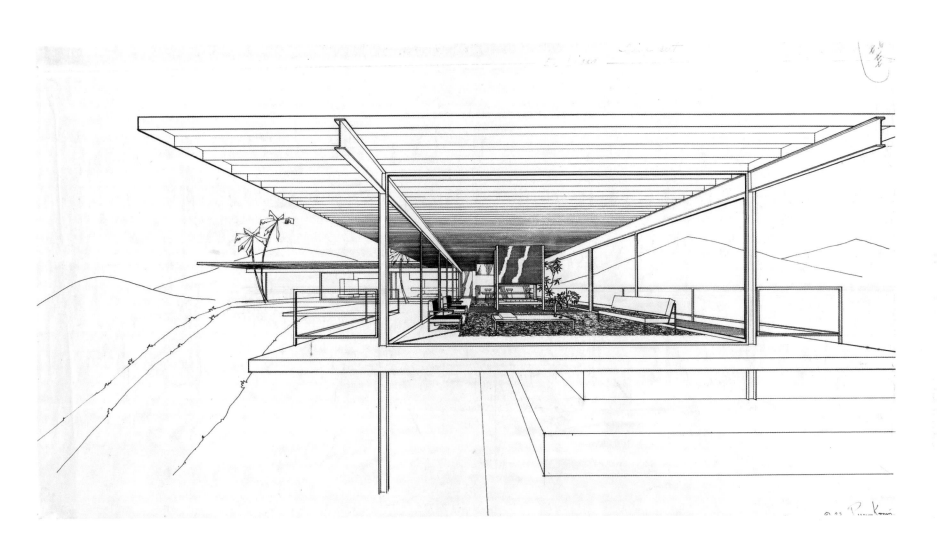

PLATE 47. | **Pierre Koenig (American, 1925–2004).** Perspective view (from hillside) of Case Study House #22, Stahl Residence (1959–60), Los Angeles, 1960. Ink on vellum, 39.6 × 71.1 cm (15⅝ × 28 in.). Los Angeles, Getty Research Institute.

PLATE 48. | **Gordon Drake (American, 1917–52).** Drake Residence (completed 1946), Beverly Glen Canyon, 1946. Photo by Julius Shulman. Los Angeles, Getty Research Institute.

PLATE 49. | **Frederic P. Lyman (American, 1927–2006).** Model for Lyman Residence (1958–61; destroyed by fire, 1993), ca. late 1980s. Wood, 88.9 × 50.8 × 50.8 cm (35 × 20 × 20 in.). Los Angeles, Getty Research Institute.

PLATE 50. | **Buff, Straub, and Hensman, Architects (1957–62).** Case Study House #20, Bass Residence (completed 1958), Altadena, 1958. Photo by Julius Shulman. Los Angeles, Getty Research Institute.

PLATE 51. | **Richard O. Spencer (American).** Spencer Residence (completed 1955), Malibu, 1955. Photo by Julius Shulman. Los Angeles, Getty Research Institute.

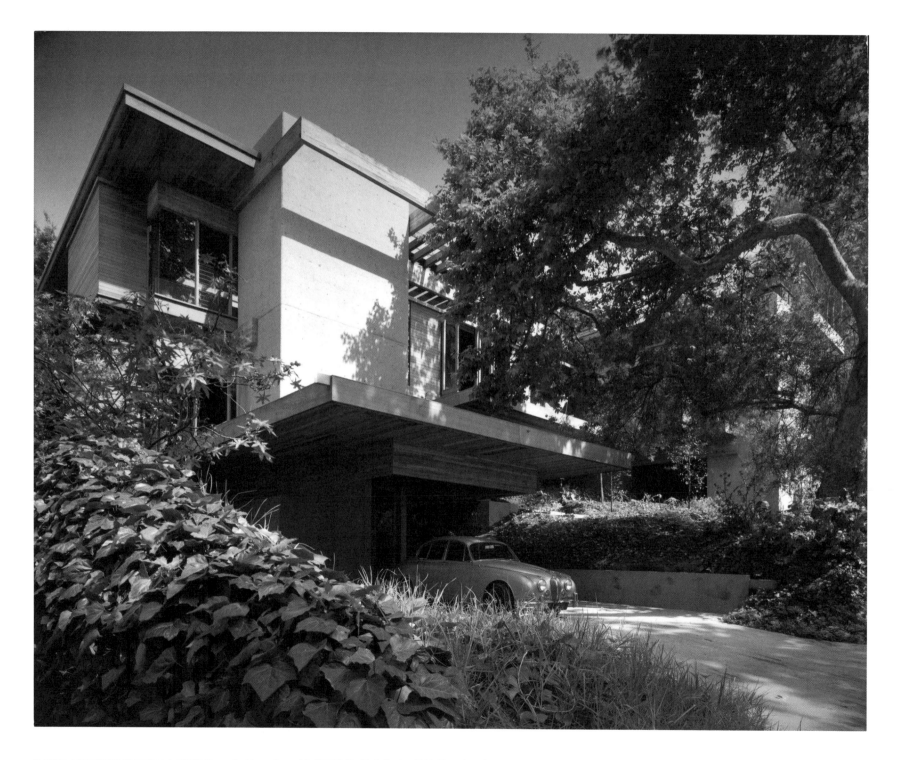

PLATE 52. | **Ray Kappe (American, b. 1927).** Kappe Residence (completed 1967), Pacific Palisades, 1968. Photo by Julius Shulman. Los Angeles, Getty Research Institute.

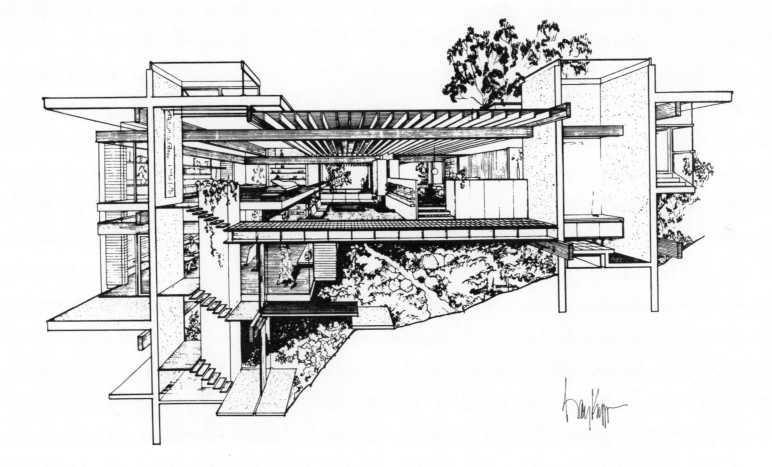

PLATE 53. | **Ray Kappe (American, b. 1927).** Section of Kappe Residence (completed 1967), Pacific Palisades, 1967. Photocopy on vellum, 45.5 × 55.5 cm (18 × 21⅞ in.). Los Angeles, Getty Research Institute.

PLATE 54. | **John Lautner (American, 1911–94).** Malin Residence (Chemosphere) (1958–60), Los Angeles, n.d. Pencil on vellum, 76.1 × 77 cm (30 × 30⅜ in.). Los Angeles, Getty Research Institute.

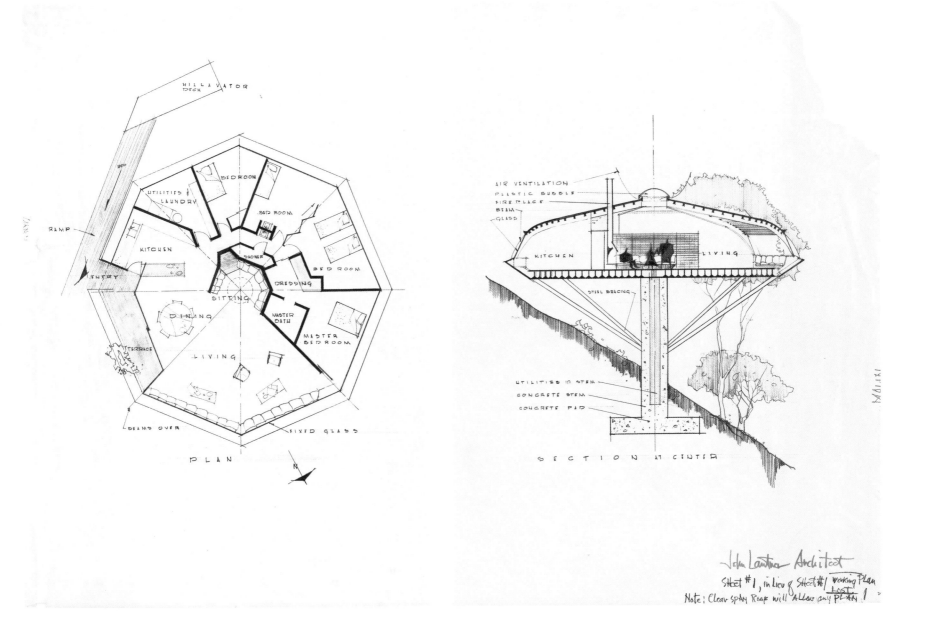

PLATE 55. | **John Lautner (American, 1911–94).** Floor plan and section drawing of the Malin Residence (Chemosphere) (1958–60), Los Angeles, n.d. Pencil on vellum, sheet: 76.9 × 107.2 cm (30¼ × 42¼ in.). Los Angeles, Getty Research Institute.

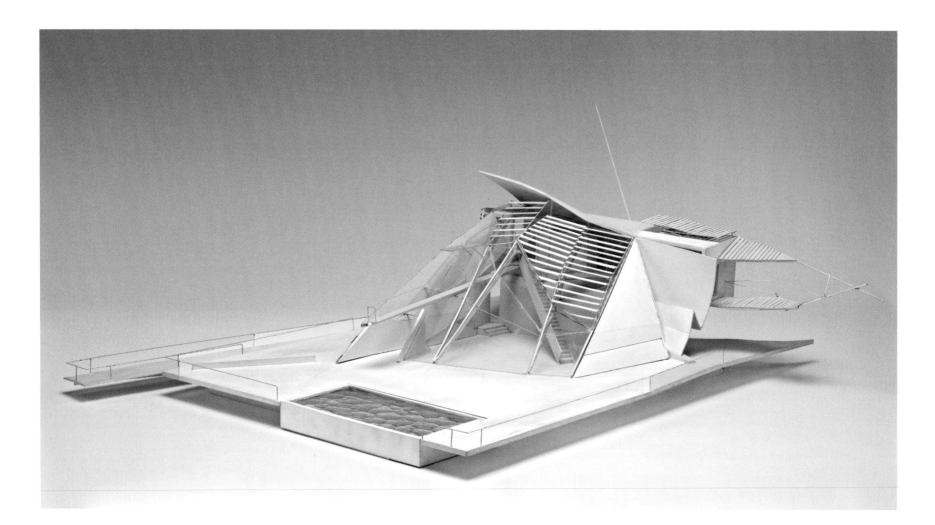

PLATE 56. | **Coop Himmelblau (1968–).** Model for Open House (unrealized), 1983–ca. 1990. Boards, cardboard, corrugated board, polystyrene sheets, hard foam, iron rod, wood, glass, and spray paint, 31.8 × 91.4 × 63.5 cm (12½ × 36 × 25 in.). Los Angeles, Getty Research Institute.

PLATE 57. | **Coop Himmelblau (1968–).** Model for Rehak Residence (unrealized), ca. 1990. Paper, wood, and mylar on wood base, 36.8 × 48.9 × 101 cm (14½ × 19¼ × 39¾ in.). Los Angeles, Getty Research Institute.

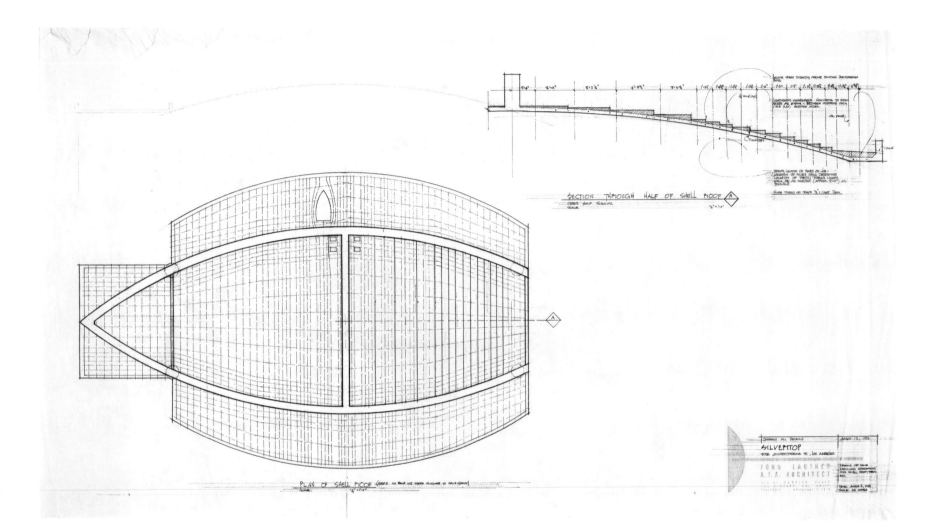

PLATE 58. | **John Lautner (American, 1911–94).** Plan of shell roof and section for Reiner Residence (Silvertop) (1956–77), Los Angeles, 1958. Ink on vellum, 60.5 × 107 cm (23⅞ × 42⅛ in.). Los Angeles, Getty Research Institute.

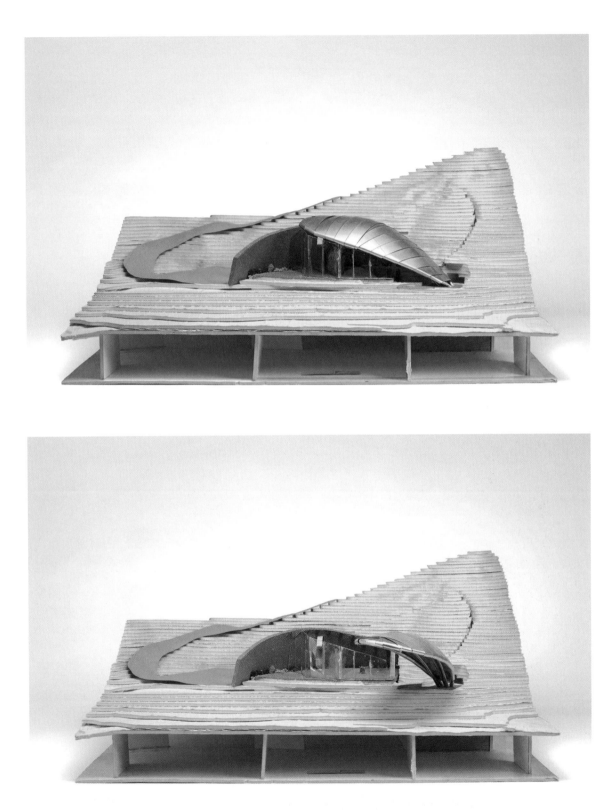

PLATES 59A, 59B. | **John Lautner (American, 1911–94).** Model for Haagen Beach Residence (unrealized), views of the house with roof in closed and open positions, 1988. Paper, plastic, wood, metal, foam core, and paint, 40 × 82.6 × 62.2 cm (15¾ × 32½ × 24½ in.). Los Angeles, Getty Research Institute.

PLATE 60. | **Richard Neutra (Austrian-born American, 1892–1970).** Chuey Residence (1956), Los Angeles, 1956. Photo by Julius Shulman. Los Angeles, Getty Research Institute.

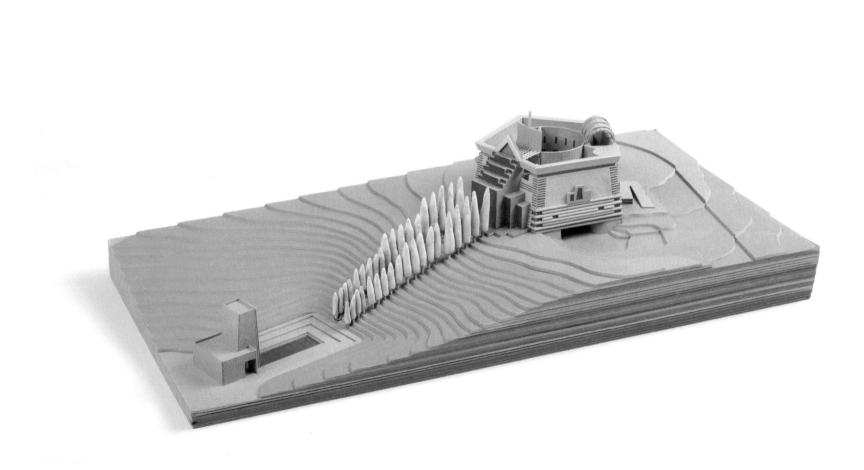

PLATE 61. | **Franklin Israel (American, 1945–96).** Model of Clark Residence (unrealized), 1980.
Wood, modeling clay, and cardboard, 15.2 × 54.6 × 27.3 cm (6 × 21½ × 10¾ in.). Los Angeles, Getty Research Institute.

From across the street, Aliso Village--
bathed in the freshness of a morning
rainfall-is a hope to the slum-dweller
and a promise of the future.

On a clear day, when the industrial
smog does not corrode the air over
Los Angeles, the mountains can be
seen in the distance. Aliso's two
and three story structures were designed to afford a maximum exposure
to the sun.

PLATE 62. | **Housing Group Architects (1940–42), led by Ralph Flewelling and including Lloyd Wright.** Aliso Village (designed 1942), Boyle Heights, ca. 1949.
From Leonard Nadel, "Aliso Village U.S.A." (unpublished manuscript, 1949). Photo by Leonard Nadel. Los Angeles, Getty Research Institute.

PLATE 63. | **Southeast Housing Architects (1940–42), including Richard Neutra, Gordon Kaufman, Adrian Wilson, Paul R. Williams, and the firm of Wurdeman and Becket.**
Pueblo del Rio (1940), South Central Los Angeles, ca. 1948. From Leonard Nadel, "Pueblo del Rio: The Study of a Planned Community"
(unpublished manuscript, ca. 1948). Photo by Leonard Nadel. Los Angeles, Getty Research Institute.

PLATE 64. | **Witmer and Watson (1919–46).** Wyvernwood Garden Apartments (completed 1939), Boyle Heights, ca. 1939. Photo by Dick Whittington. Los Angeles, Getty Research Institute.

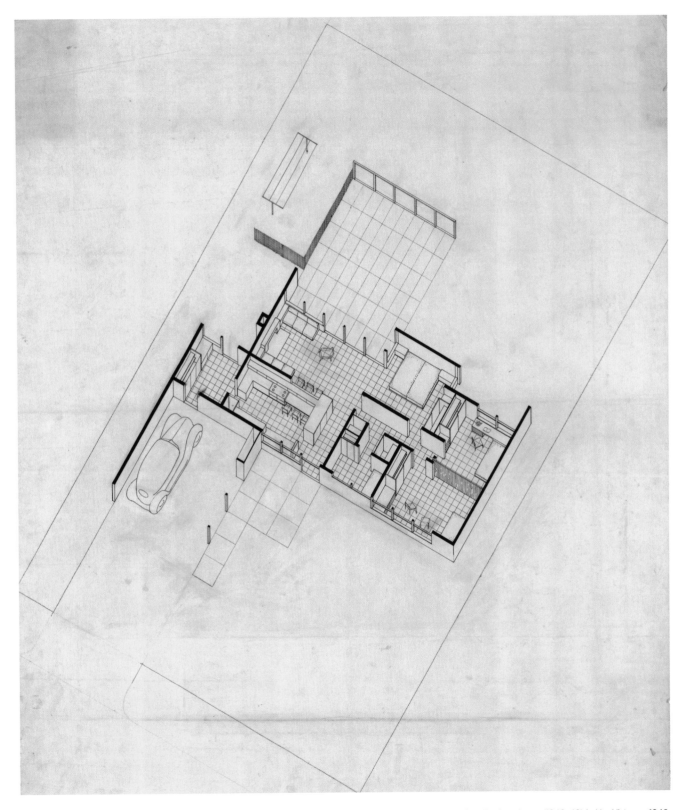

PLATE 65. | **Ain, Johnson and Day, Architects (1947–51).** Axonometric view of Modernique home (1946–48) in Mar Vista, ca. 1948. Pencil and ink on paper, 101.6 × 91.4 cm (40 × 36 in.). Santa Barbara, Art, Design & Architecture Museum at the University of California, Santa Barbara.

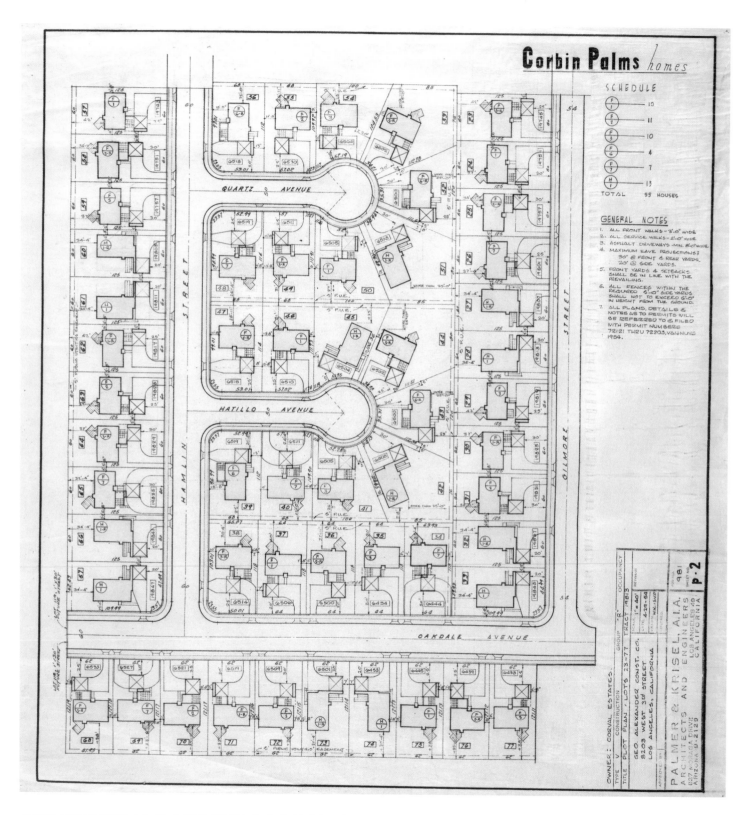

PLATE 66. | **Palmer and Krisel, Architects (1949–66).** Plot plan for Corbin Palms (1953–55), Woodland Hills, ca. 1954.
Pencil and pen on vellum, sheet: 66.2 × 61 cm (26⅛ × 24 in.); drawing: 61 × 56 cm (24 × 22 in.). Los Angeles, Getty Research Institute.

PLATE 67. | **Palmer and Krisel, Architects (1949–66).** Elevation drawings of tract house models B-1, B-2, and A-4 for Murray Strauss, Palm Gardens (unrealized), 1954. Pencil on vellum, sheet: 60.8 × 60.5 cm (24 × 23⅞ in.); drawing: 57.5 × 50.7 cm (22⅝ × 20 in.). Los Angeles, Getty Research Institute.

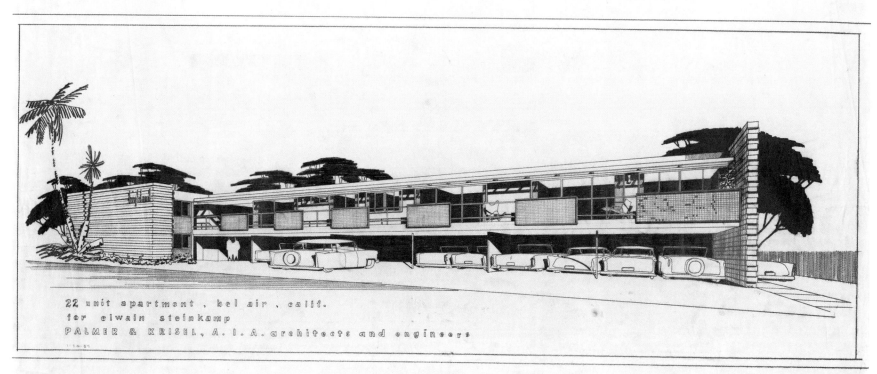

22 unit apartment , bel air , calif.
for elwain steinkamp
PALMER & KRISEL, A. I. A. architects and engineers

PLATE 68. | **Palmer and Krisel, Architects (1949–66).** Twenty-two-unit Bel Air apartment building for Elwain Steinkamp (unrealized), 1955.
Pencil on vellum, sheet: 52.5 × 107.5 (20⅝ × 42⅜ in.); drawing: 39 × 103.5 cm (15⅜ × 40¾ in.). Los Angeles, Getty Research Institute.

APARTMENT BUILDING FOR MR. & MRS. P. KAPPE . . . .

PLATE 69. | **Ray Kappe (American, b. 1927).** Apartment building for Mr. and Mrs. P. Kappe (completed 1956), Culver City, 1954. Pencil on tracing paper, 68.3 × 96.8 cm (26⅞ × 38⅛ in.). Los Angeles, Getty Research Institute.

36/RD/038

PLATE 70. | **Raphael Soriano (Greek-born American, 1904–88).** Apartment house for Lucile Colby (completed 1952), Los Angeles, 1948–49.
Pencil and ink on vellum, 34.3 × 41.9 cm (13½ × 16⁷⁄₁₆ in.). Pomona, Cal Poly Pomona, College of Environmental Design Library.

PLATE 71. | **Edward Fickett (American, 1923–99).** Forty-unit apartment building for M. Baker (1952–54), South Pasadena, 1954. Pencil and crayon on tracing paper, 61 × 94 cm (24 × 37 in.). Los Angeles, University of Southern California.

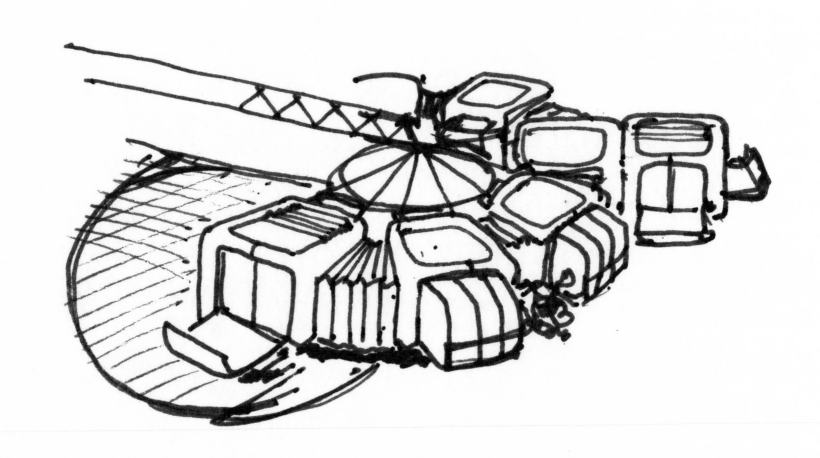

PLATE 72. | **Ray Kappe (American, b. 1927).** Advanced Technology House (unrealized), 1980. Ink on tracing paper, sheet:
35.5 × 22.1 cm (14 × 8¾ in.); image: 6 × 8 cm (2⅜ × 3⅛ in.). Los Angeles, Getty Research Institute.

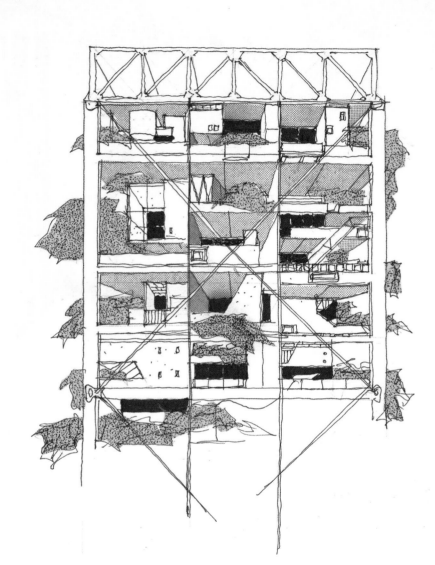

PLATE 73. | **Haralamb Georgescu (Romanian, 1908–77).** Perspective view of Skyloft (unrealized), late 1960s.
Ink and zip-a-tone on vellum, 25.4 × 20.3 cm (10 × 8 in.). Los Angeles, Getty Research Institute.

CONTRIBUTORS

CHRISTOPHER JAMES ALEXANDER is the assistant curator of architecture and design at the Getty Research Institute. Since arriving at the Getty in 2004, he has co-curated the touring exhibitions *Julius Shulman's Los Angeles* (2007–12); *Julius Shulman, Modernity and the Metropolis* (2005–6); *Bernard Rudofsky: What Would Intrigue Him Now?* (2007–8); and the GRI's installation of *Lessons from Bernard Rudofsky: Life as a Voyage* (2008). He is the author of *Julius Shulman's Los Angeles* (2011).

FERNANDO ATIQUE is an architect and an associate professor of history at the Universidade Federal de São Paulo. Among his books are *Arquitetando a "Boa Vizinhança": Arquitetura, cidade e cultura nas relações Brasil-Estados Unidos, 1876–1945* (2010) and *Memória moderna: A trajetória do Edifício Esther* (2002), both of which received awards from the Brazilian Institute of Architects. He was a researcher for Docomomo Brazil and a visiting scholar at the University of Pennsylvania.

ERIC AVILA is an associate professor of history, Chicano studies, and urban planning at the University of California, Los Angeles. He is the author of *Popular Culture in the Age of White Flight: Fear and Fantasy in Suburban Los Angeles* (2004) and *The Folklore of the Freeway: Highway Construction and the Making of Race in the Modernist City* (forthcoming).

KEN BREISCH is an assistant professor in the School of Architecture at the University of Southern California. He has a PhD from the University of Michigan and currently serves as first vice president of the Society of Architectural Historians. He is the author of *Henry Hobson Richardson and the Small Public Library in America* (1997) and the forthcoming *The Library in America: Images from the Library of Congress.*

JEFFREY W. CODY is a senior project specialist at the Getty Conservation Institute. From 1995 to 2004, he taught architectural history at the Chinese University of Hong Kong. He is the author of *Building in China: Henry K. Murphy's "Adaptive Architecture," 1914–1935* (2001) and *Exporting American Architecture, 1870–2000* (2003), and the coeditor of *Chinese Architecture and the Beaux-Arts* (2010) and *Brush and Shutter: Early Photography in China* (2011).

DANA CUFF is a professor of architecture and urban design at the University of California, Los Angeles, and director of the design/research center cityLAB. In 2006, she founded cityLAB to explore the challenges facing the contemporary metropolis beginning with her home city, Los Angeles. Her current research explores the nature of public architecture, emergent pervasive computing technologies, design opportunities leveraged from infrastructure, and infill housing.

WILLIAM DEVERELL is the director of the Huntington-USC Institute on California and the West. He is the author of *Whitewashed Adobe: The Rise of Los Angeles and the Remaking of Its Mexican Past* (2004). With Greg Hise, he coedited *Land of Sunshine: The Environmental History of Metropolitan Los Angeles* (2005) and *A Companion to Los Angeles* (2010). He is currently at work on a book exploring the post–Civil War American West.

WIM DE WIT is an architectural historian and the head of the Department of Architecture and Contemporary Art at the Getty Research Institute in Los Angeles. He has organized numerous exhibitions, including *Julius Shulman: Modernity and the Metropolis* (2005–6), and made contributions to catalogs about various topics in the history of twentieth-century architecture, including *Lessons from Bernard Rudofsky: Life as a Voyage* (2007).

PHILIP J. ETHINGTON is a professor of history and political science at the University of Southern California. He is the multimedia editor of the journal *Urban History* and a member of the board of editors of the *American Historical Review.* He is currently completing a geohistorical narrative titled *Ghost Metropolis: Los Angeles since 13,000 BP.*

DANA HUTT is an architectural historian whose essays and writing have appeared in the books *Open House: Architecture and Technology for Intelligent Living* (2006), *Symphony: Frank Gehry's Walt Disney Concert Hall* (2003), *L.A. Now: Volume One* (2002), and *Lloyd Wright: The Architecture of Frank Lloyd Wright Jr.* (1998). A native Angeleno, she holds a master of science in architectural studies, history, and theory from the University of Texas, Austin.

SANDY ISENSTADT teaches the history of modern architecture at the University of Delaware. He is the author of *The Modern American House: Spaciousness and Middle-Class Identity* (2006), and he is the coeditor of *Modernism and the Middle East: Architecture and Politics in the Twentieth Century* (2008). He is currently researching the luminous spaces introduced by electric lighting in the twentieth century.

SUSAN MACDONALD is the head of field projects at the Getty Conservation Institute (GCI), where she oversees the Conserving Modern Architecture Initiative. Susan trained as an architect and planner, has a master's degree in conservation studies from the University of York/International Centre for the Study of the Preservation and Restoration of Cultural Property (ICCROM), and has worked as a conservation practitioner in her native Australia and in England. She has a particular interest in the conservation of twentieth-century heritage and has written widely on this subject.

CHRIS NICHOLS is a native of the San Gabriel Valley and has been involved in historic preservation for over twenty years. He is an editor at *Los Angeles* magazine, where he writes the popular "Ask Chris" column, and he is the author of *The Leisure Architecture of Wayne McAllister* (2007). He is chairman emeritus of the Los Angeles Conservancy Modern Committee and currently serves on the board of directors of Hollywood Heritage.

BECKY NICOLAIDES is a research scholar at the Center for the Study of Women at the University of California, Los Angeles. She is the author of *My Blue Heaven: Life and Politics in the Working-Class Suburbs of Los Angeles, 1920–1965* (2002), and coeditor, with Andrew Wiese, of *The Suburb Reader* (2006). She is currently writing a book on the history of social and civic life in Los Angeles suburbia since 1945.

STEPHEN PHILLIPS is director of the Los Angeles Metropolitan Program in Architecture and Urban Design and associate professor of architecture at California Polytechnic State University, San Luis Obispo. He is design principal in the award-winning firm Stephen Phillips Architects (SPARCHS) and visiting faculty at the Southern California Institute of Architecture (SCI-Arc). His PhD in history and theory is from the School of Architecture at Princeton University, and his current book projects include studies on Austrian-American architect Frederick Kiesler, the new Los Angeles public schools, and the L.A. Ten architects.

VANESSA R. SCHWARTZ is a professor of history, art history, and film at the University of Southern California. Her books include *Spectacular Realities: Early Mass Culture in Fin-de-Siècle Paris* (1998), *It's So French: Hollywood, Paris, and the Making of Cosmopolitan Film Cultures* (2007), and *Modern France: A Very Short Introduction* (2011). She is the coeditor of *Cinema and the Invention of Modern Life* (1995) and *The Nineteenth-Century Visual Culture Reader* (2004). She is currently writing a book about the dawn of the jet age in a global context.

HUGO SEGAWA is an architect and a professor of architecture and urbanism at the Universidade de São Paulo. He is dedicated to studies on modern and contemporary Latin American architecture within an international context. He is the author or coauthor of a number of books, including *Arquitectura Latinoamericana Contemporánea* (2005), *Arquiteturas no Brasil, 1900–1990* (1998), and *Oswaldo Arthur Bratke* (1997). He is a former member of the advisory board of Docomomo International and an active member of the Observatorio de Arquitectura Latinoamericana Contemporánea.

ILLUSTRATION CREDITS

Photographs of items in the holdings of the Getty Research Institute are courtesy the Research Library. Every effort has been made to identify and contact the copyright holders of images published in this book. Should you discover what you consider to be a photo by a known photographer, please contact the publisher. The following sources have granted additional permission to reproduce illustrations in this book:

FOREWORD
Figs. 1, 2. Photos by Spence Air Photos, Inc. Getty Research Institute, Aerial photographs of Los Angeles, 2011.R.12, box 1. UCLA Department of Geography, Benjamin and Gladys Thomas Air Photo Archives, The Spence Collection.
Figs. 3a, 3b. Getty Research Institute, 86-B19486. © Ed Ruscha.
Fig. 4. California Division of Highways. Neg 10892-1. Santa Monica and San Diego Freeway interchange. Reproduced by permission of the California Department of Transportation, Library and History Center.

INTRODUCTION
Figs. 1, 2, 4. Photos by Spence Air Photos, Inc. Getty Research Institute, Aerial photographs of Los Angeles, 2011.R.12, box 1. UCLA Department of Geography, Benjamin and Gladys Thomas Air Photo Archives, The Spence Collection.
Fig. 3. Photo by C. C. Pierce & Co., Los Angeles/Title Insurance and Trust Company Collection of Historical Photographs. Getty Research Institute, J. Paul Getty collected photographs and postcards of Los Angeles, California, and vicinity, 1986.IA.29, box 2.
Fig. 5. Los Angeles Times Staff. © 1926, Los Angeles Times. Reprinted with permission. Image: Courtesy of The Huntington Library, San Marino, California.

ETHINGTON
Figs. 1, 4. © 2013 Philip J. Ethington.
Fig. 2. Photograph by Max Bruensteiner. University of Southern California, California Historical Society Collection, image ID# chs-m8002.
Fig. 3. Library of Congress, Geography and Map Division.

DEVERELL
Fig. 1. Courtesy of The Huntington Library, San Marino, California.
Fig. 2. "Dick" Whittington Studio. Courtesy of The Huntington Library, San Marino, California.
Fig. 3. © U.S. National Park Service. Courtesy of the Santa Monica Mountains Nat. Rec. Area Museum, National Park Service.
Figs. 4a, 4b. Courtesy Tree People.
Fig. 5. Courtesy William Preston Bowling.
Fig. 6. Courtesy Gary Leonard.

AVILA
Fig. 1. Courtesy of University of Southern California, on behalf of the USC Libraries Special Collections. Courtesy, California Historical Society Collection at the University of Southern California, CHS-48579.
Fig. 2. California Division of Highways. 1965 LA Area Map. California Freeway and Expressway System map. Reproduced by permission of the California Department of Transportation, Library and History Center.
Fig. 3. Los Angeles Public Library Photo Collection.
Fig. 4. © Julian Wasser, all rights reserved. Courtesy Julian Wasser and Craig Krull Gallery, Santa Monica.
Fig. 5. © 1984 Judith F. Baca. Photo courtesy of SPARC (sparcmurals.org).
Fig. 6. © 1994 Lalo Alcaraz, laloalcaraz.com. Original drawing appeared in *L.A. Weekly.*

ISENSTADT
Fig. 1. Copyright © The University of Southern California.
Fig. 2. Washington, D.C., Library of Congress, Prints & Photographs Division, FSA/OWI Collection, LC-USZ62-60071.
Fig. 3. Los Angeles Public Library Photo Collection.
Fig. 4. Los Angeles Public Library Photo Collection.
Fig. 5. Courtesy the CBS Photo Archives.
Fig. 6. Los Angeles Public Library Photo Collection. Photo: Rob Brown.
Fig. 7. Los Angeles Public Library Photo Collection.
Fig. 8. Art © 2013 Bruce Nauman / Artists Rights Society (ARS), New York. Image © Tate, London 2012.

Fig. 9. Los Angeles Public Library Photo Collection. © James Ruebsamen.
Fig. 10. Getty Research Institute, Julius Shulman photography archive, 2004.R.10. © J. Paul Getty Trust. Used with permission.

DE WIT
Fig. 1. Photo of drawing: Otto Rothschild. Los Angeles Public Library Photo Collection.
Fig. 2. Getty Research Institute, Julius Shulman photography archive, 2004.R.10, box 6, folder 5. © J. Paul Getty Trust. Used with permission.
Fig. 3. CBS Photo Archive / CBS / Getty Images. © 1958 CBS Photo Archive.
Fig. 4. Photo by Pacific Air Industries. Getty Research Institute, Welton Becket architectural drawings and photographs, 2010.M.83, box T45. Gift of Mr. & Mrs. Welton McDonald Becket—Laguna Beach, CA. Courtesy Regents of the University of California.
Fig. 5. © David Travers, used with permission. Courtesy David Travers.
Fig. 6. Getty Research Institute, Julius Shulman photography archive, 2004.R.10, box 1056, folder 28. © J. Paul Getty Trust. Used with permission. Los Angeles Times Staff. Copyright © 1951, Los Angeles Times. Reprinted with permission.
Fig. 7. Getty Research Institute, William Krisel papers, 2009.M.23. Gift of William and Corinne Krisel, William Krisel Architectural Archive. © J. Paul Getty Trust.
Fig. 8. From Brandow & Johnston, Inc.
Fig. 9. Getty Research Institute, Welton Becket architectural drawings and photographs, 2010.M.83**, flatfile T10**. © J. Paul Getty Trust.
Fig. 10. Getty Research Institute, Julius Shulman photography archive, 2004.R.10, box 315, folder 1. © J. Paul Getty Trust. Used with permission.
Fig. 11. Courtesy Diniz Family Archive and Edward Cella Art + Architecture.
Fig. 12. Getty Research Institute, Julius Shulman photography archive, 2004.R.10, box 326, folder 5. © J. Paul Getty Trust. Used with permission.
Fig. 13. Courtesy of the Arkansas Architectural Archives, Special Collections, University of Arkansas Libraries.
Fig. 14. Image Courtesy of Gehry Partners, LLP.

BREISCH
Fig. 1. Photograph by Morton Neikrug.
Figs. 2, 3. Courtesy Gregory Walsh.
Fig. 4. Getty Research Institute, Julius Shulman photography archive, 2004.R.10, box 44, folder 1. © J. Paul Getty Trust. Used with permission.
Fig. 5. Image: Baukunstarchiv, Akademie der Künste, Berlin. Courtesy Ray Wachsmann.
Fig. 6. Courtesy Ralph Knowles and *Sunset* magazine.
Fig. 7. Courtesy John Mutlow.
Fig. 8. Courtesy the Charles Moore Foundation.

CODY
Fig. 2. Harwell Hamilton Harris Papers, 1903–1990, The Alexander Architectural Archive, The University of Texas Libraries, The University of Texas at Austin.
Fig. 3. © Jim Brown, atomic ranch. Courtesy Jim Brown.
Fig. 5. © PPG Industries, Inc.

SEGAWA AND ATIQUE
Fig. 1. Getty Research Institute, NA1.A79.
Fig. 2. Printed with permission of Carrier Corporation.
Fig. 3. Frank Scherschel / Time & Life Pictures / Getty Images. © Time Life Pictures.
Fig. 4. Getty Research Institute, NA1.A79. Art © 2012 Eames Office, LLC (eamesoffice.com). Magazine © David Travers, used with permission.
Fig. 5. © David Travers, used with permission. Courtesy David Travers.

MACDONALD
Figs. 1, 2. Photo © J. Paul Getty Trust.
Fig. 3. Getty Research Institute, Julius Shulman photography archive, 2004.R.10, box 200, folder 5. © J. Paul Getty Trust. Used with permission.

NICOLAIDES
Figs. 1, 3. Photo by Rothschild Photo. Image courtesy City of Lakewood Historical Collection.
Figs. 4, 5, 7, 8. Image © Michael Salvatore Tierney.

CUFF
Fig. 1. J. Paul Getty Museum, 2000.32.24–2000.32.29. © Estate of William A. Garnett.
Fig. 2. Getty Research Institute, William Krisel papers, 2009.M.23. Gift of William and Corinne Krisel, William Krisel Architectural Archive. © J. Paul Getty Trust.
Fig. 3. Clifford Magee May Papers, Architecture and Design Collection, Art, Design & Architecture Museum, UC Santa Barbara.
Fig. 4. Courtesy *Sunset* magazine. © The Cliff May Trust.
Fig. 5. Plan redrawn by Dan Oprea Design, 2012. Courtesy John Stuart Levitt.
Fig. 6. Gregory Ain Papers, Architecture and Design Collection, Art, Design & Architecture Museum, UC Santa Barbara.
Fig. 7. Courtesy Octavia Leclerc-Jones.

HUTT
Fig. 1. Courtesy National Museum of Industrial History, Bethlehem, PA. Getty Research Institute, NA1.A79.
Fig. 2. Courtesy of Arcadia Architectural Products, Inc. Getty Research Institute, NA1.A79.
Fig. 3. Provided courtesy of The Dow Chemical Company. Used by permission of Arkema Inc. Plexiglas is a registered trademark of Arkema. Getty Research Institute, NA1.A79.
Fig. 4. © Grant Mudford.
Fig. 5. Los Angeles Times Staff. Copyright © 1962, Los Angeles Times. Reprinted with permission. Courtesy Bernard Judge.
Fig. 6. Getty Research Institute, John Lautner papers, 2007.M.13, box 20. Los Angeles Times Staff. Copyright © 1961, Los Angeles Times. Reprinted with permission.

SCHWARTZ
Fig. 1. Courtesy of Chrysler Group LLC. Getty Research Institute, AP2.L547.
Fig. 2. LAX Photo Archives. Image courtesy of and © The Luckman Partnership, Inc. | a Salas O'Brien Company.
Fig. 3. LAX Photo Archives. Image courtesy of and © The Luckman Partnership, Inc. | a Salas O'Brien Company. Used with permission of AECOM. The Paul R. Williams Collection.
Figs. 5, 8, 10–12, 15. LAX Photo Archives.
Figs. 5, 9. Los Angeles Public Library Photo Collection.
Fig. 6. LAX Photo Archives. Image courtesy of and © The Luckman Partnership, Inc. | a Salas O'Brien Company. Used with permission of AECOM. The Paul R. Williams Collection.
Fig. 7. Courtesy Lockheed Martin Aeronautics.
Figs. 13, 14. Photo: The Wrather Family, courtesy Donald W. Ballard.

PHILLIPS
Fig. 1. © Tim Street-Porter / ESTO. Image courtesy of Gehry Partners, LLP.
Fig. 2. Courtesy Ave Pildas.
Fig. 3. Courtesy Daniel Zimbaldi.
Fig. 4. Orhan Ayyüce.
Fig. 5. Courtesy Studio Works Architects.
Fig. 6. Peter Aaron/OTTO.
Fig. 7. © Tim Street-Porter.
Fig. 8. Courtesy Daniel Zimbaldi.
Fig. 9. © Grant Mudford.
Fig. 10. © 1990 Tim Street-Porter.
Figs. 11, 12. © Tom Bonner.
Fig. 13. Getty Research Institute, 97.DA.16. Courtesy of Morphosis Architects.
Fig. 14. Image courtesy Holt Hinshaw Pfau Jones.
Figs. 15a, 15b. Courtesy Neil M. Denari Architects.

NICHOLS
Fig. 1. Getty Research Institute, Julius Shulman photography archive, 2004.R.10, box 59. © J. Paul Getty Trust. Used with permission.
Fig. 2. Photo © J. Paul Getty Trust.
Fig. 3. Charles Phoenix Collection.
Fig. 4. Courtesy Gordon Ayers. Digital image courtesy Victor Stapf and the Cummins family.
Fig. 5. Courtesy Howard Kelly. Courtesy A. C. Martin and Associates.
Fig. 6. Courtesy Chris Nichols.

Fig. 7. Image courtesy Sanborn Theater Archives. Courtesy Paula Williams.

Fig. 8. Courtesy Chris Nichols.

Fig. 9. Courtesy Charles W. Fish.

PLATES

Pls. 1, 22. Stephen White, Collection II. © Will Connell.

Pl. 2. Transportation Library & Archives—Los Angeles County Metropolitan Transportation Authority.

Pl. 3. Getty Research Institute, Ray Kappe papers, 2008.M.36, box 82*, folder 6. Gift of Ray Kappe. © J. Paul Getty Trust.

Pl. 4. Los Angeles Public Library Photo Collection.

Pl. 5. Getty Research Institute, Harry Drinkwater photography archive, 2011.R.23, box T1. © Harry Drinkwater.

Pl. 6. Los Angeles Public Library Photo Collection.

Pl. 7. Los Angeles Public Library Photo Collection. Watson Family Photo Archive.

Pl. 8. Los Angeles Public Library Photo Collection. © Modernage Photo Service.

Pl. 9. J. Paul Getty Museum, 2000.32.23. © Estate of William A. Garnett.

Pl. 10. Getty Research Institute, American automobile design concept drawings, 2011.M.16. Courtesy John P. Aiken.

Pl. 11. Getty Research Institute, American automobile design concept drawings, 2011.M.16. © Ron Hill.

Pl. 12. Getty Research Institute, American automobile design concept drawings, 2011.M.16. Courtesy of Richard Arbib (son of the designer).

Pl. 13. Getty Research Institute, Julius Shulman photography archive, 2004.R.10, box 135, folder 21. © J. Paul Getty Trust. Used with permission.

Pl. 14. Getty Research Institute, Ray Kappe papers, 2008.M.36, box 82. Gift of Ray Kappe. © J. Paul Getty Trust.

Pl. 15. Getty Research Institute, John Lautner papers, 2007.M.13, flatfile 558. Gift of The John Lautner Foundation. © The John Lautner Foundation.

Pl. 16. Edward C. Killingsworth, FAIA Papers, Architecture and Design Collection, Art, Design & Architecture Museum, UC Santa Barbara.

Pl. 17. Getty Research Institute, Julius Shulman photography archive, 2004.R.10, box 290, folder 9. © J. Paul Getty Trust. Used with permission.

Pl. 18. Collection of Armet Davis Newlove Architects.

Pl. 19. Getty Research Institute, John Lautner papers, 2007.M.13, flatfile 264. Gift of The John Lautner Foundation. © The John Lautner Foundation.

Pl. 20. From the collection of Brian Lane and Lucy Gonzalez.

Pl. 21. Getty Research Institute, Julius Shulman photography archive, 2004.R.10, box 526. © J. Paul Getty Trust. Used with permission.

Pl. 23. Maynard L. Parker, photographer. Courtesy of The Huntington Library, San Marino, California.

Pl. 24. Getty Research Institute, Julius Shulman photography archive, 2004.R.10, box 888. © J. Paul Getty Trust. Used with permission.

Pl. 25. Getty Research Institute, Julius Shulman photography archive, 2004.R.10, box 341. © J. Paul Getty Trust. Used with permission.

Pl. 26. Getty Research Institute, Welton Becket architectural drawings and photographs, 2010.M.83. © J. Paul Getty Trust.

Pl. 27. Courtesy Diniz Family Archive and Edward Cella Art + Architecture.

Pl. 28. Pereira & Luckman Papers, Architecture and Design Collection, Art, Design & Architecture Museum, UC Santa Barbara. Image courtesy of and © The Luckman Partnership, Inc. | a Salas O'Brien Company.

Pl. 29. From the Alan E. Leib Collection. Image courtesy of and © The Luckman Partnership, Inc. | a Salas O'Brien Company.

Pls. 30, 40. Maynard Lyndon Papers, Architecture and Design Collection, Art, Design & Architecture Museum, UC Santa Barbara.

Pl. 31. Getty Research Institute, Julius Shulman photography archive, 2004.R.10, box 311, folder 10. © J. Paul Getty Trust. Used with permission.

Pls. 32, 43. Thornton Montaigne Abell Papers, Architecture and Design Collection, Art, Design & Architecture Museum, UC Santa Barbara.

Pl. 33. Kem Weber Papers, Architecture and Design Collection, Art, Design & Architecture Museum, UC Santa Barbara.

Pl. 34. Sketch Courtesy of Frank O. Gehry.

Pl. 35. Getty Research Institute, Frank Israel papers, drawings, and models, 2009.M.6. © J. Paul Getty Trust.

Pl. 36. Los Angeles Public Library Photo Collection.

Pl. 37. Collection of John Spohrer, Los Angeles.

Pl. 38. Getty Research Institute, Reyner Banham papers, 910009, box 7.

Pl. 39. Getty Research Institute, Julius Shulman photography archive, 2004.R.10, box 166. © J. Paul Getty Trust. Used with permission.

Pl. 41. © Sidney Eisenshtat Estate. Image courtesy of the USC Helen Topping Architecture and Fine Arts Library.

Pl. 42. Getty Research Institute, Julius Shulman photography archive, 2004.R.10, box 221, folder 34. © J. Paul Getty Trust. Used with permission.

Pl. 44. Gregory Ain Papers, Architecture and Design Collection, Art, Design & Architecture Museum, UC Santa Barbara. Copyright Rapson Architects.

Pl. 45. Getty Research Institute, Pierre Koenig papers and drawings, 2006.M.30, box 63. © J. Paul Getty Trust.

Pls. 46, 47. Getty Research Institute, Pierre Koenig papers and drawings, 2006.M.30, flatfile 22**. © J. Paul Getty Trust.

Pl. 48. Getty Research Institute, Julius Shulman photography archive, 2004.R.10, box 214. © J. Paul Getty Trust. Used with permission.

Pl. 49. Getty Research Institute, Frederic Lyman papers, 2011.M.31. Gift of Katherine Starke Lyman. © J. Paul Getty Trust.

Pl. 50. Getty Research Institute, Julius Shulman photography archive, 2004.R.10, box 186. © J. Paul Getty Trust. Used with permission.

Pl. 51. Getty Research Institute, Julius Shulman photography archive, 2004.R.10, box 249. © J. Paul Getty Trust. Used with permission.

Pl. 52. Getty Research Institute, Julius Shulman photography archive, 2004.R.10, box 322, folder 10. © J. Paul Getty Trust. Used with permission.

Pl. 53. Getty Research Institute, Ray Kappe papers, 2008.M.36, flatfile 56. Gift of Ray Kappe. © J. Paul Getty Trust.

Pl. 54. Getty Research Institute, John Lautner papers, 2007.M.13, flatfile 401**. Gift of The John Lautner Foundation. © The John Lautner Foundation.

Pl. 55. Getty Research Institute, John Lautner papers, 2007.M.13, flatfile 399. Gift of The John Lautner Foundation. © The John Lautner Foundation.

Pls. 56, 57. Getty Research Institute, Coop Himmelblau architectural models and drawings for five projects, 2002.M.2**. © J. Paul Getty Trust.

Pl. 58. Getty Research Institute, John Lautner papers, 2007.M.13, flatfile 460. Gift of The John Lautner Foundation. © The John Lautner Foundation.

Pls. 59a, 59b. Getty Research Institute, 2010.M.30. Gift of Helena Arahuete. © The John Lautner Foundation. Photo © J. Paul Getty Trust.

Pl. 60. Getty Research Institute, Julius Shulman photography archive, 2004.R.10, box 84. © J. Paul Getty Trust. Used with permission.

Pl. 61. Getty Research Institute, Frank Israel papers, drawings, and models, 2009.M.6. © J. Paul Getty Trust.

Pl. 62. Getty Research Institute, Leonard Nadel photographs and other material relating to housing and urban redevelopment in Los Angeles, 2002.M.42, box 10. © J. Paul Getty Trust.

Pl. 63. Getty Research Institute, Leonard Nadel photographs and other material relating to housing and urban redevelopment in Los Angeles, 2002.M.42, box 11. © J. Paul Getty Trust.

Pl. 64. Getty Research Institute, Photographs documenting the Wyvernwood Garden Apartments, 2011.R.11, box 1. Copyright © The University of Southern California.

Pl. 65. Gregory Ain Papers, Architecture and Design Collection, Art, Design & Architecture Museum, UC Santa Barbara.

Pl. 66. Getty Research Institute, William Krisel papers, 2009.M.23. Gift of William and Corinne Krisel, William Krisel Architectural Archive. © J. Paul Getty Trust.

Pl. 67. Getty Research Institute, William Krisel papers, 2009.M.23. Gift of William and Corinne Krisel, William Krisel Architectural Archive. © J. Paul Getty Trust.

Pl. 68. Getty Research Institute, William Krisel papers, 2009.M.23. Gift of William and Corinne Krisel, William Krisel Architectural Archive. © J. Paul Getty Trust.

Pl. 69. Getty Research Institute, Ray Kappe papers, 2008.M.36, flatfile 1. Gift of Ray Kappe. © J. Paul Getty Trust.

Pl. 70. Raphael Soriano Collection, ENV Archives—Special Collections, Cal Poly Pomona.

Pl. 71. Copyright © The University of Southern California. Courtesy of University of Southern California, on behalf of the USC Libraries Special Collections.

Pl. 72. Getty Research Institute, Ray Kappe papers, 2008.M.36, flatfile 244**. Gift of Ray Kappe. © J. Paul Getty Trust.

Pl. 73. Getty Research Institute, Haralamb H. Georgescu papers, 2008.M.35, box 6*. Gift of Christopher Georgesco. © J. Paul Getty Trust.

ACKNOWLEDGMENTS

AN EXHIBITION AND CATALOG THAT COVER FIFTY YEARS OF ARCHITECTURE, numerous influential architects, and countless innovative buildings constructed in a region of more than four thousand square miles can only be realized thanks to the support of a large number of colleagues and advisers. We are most grateful to Thomas Gaehtgens, director of the Getty Research Institute (GRI), who, from the moment of his arrival at the GRI in late 2007, began to promote the idea of an exhibition about Los Angeles's influential post–World War II architecture. Andrew Perchuk, deputy director of the GRI, also played a crucial role in the ongoing development of the project from its inception. Within the J. Paul Getty Trust, we owe a debt of gratitude to James Cuno, president and CEO, who gave the project his full support, and to Ron Hartwig, vice president of Communications, and everyone in his office, including Julie Jaskol, Maureen McGlynn, Amy Hood, and Maria Velez—all of whom worked very hard to promote the exhibition within the United States and abroad.

During the exhibition preparation, we received invaluable assistance from GRI colleagues within our own Department of Contemporary Art and Architecture. We want to express our sincere thanks to our co-curator, Rani Singh, for her many critical contributions to the exhibition, especially her oral histories with architects and her selection of contemporary works of art. Curatorial assistant Lyra Kilston was the backbone of our project. She managed all of the endless details of the exhibition and was always able to maintain her clarity of vision and enthusiasm. Our exceptional intern and assistant, Johnny Tran, skillfully sustained the project's momentum during a critical phase of its development. We are also grateful to Glenn Phillips, Beverly Faison, and Jacob Semler for their important efforts and insights. We thank Joshua Machat for his digital-image and rights research as well as his exciting archival discoveries.

During the writing and production of this catalog, we profited from the expertise and hard work of Gail Feigenbaum, associate director of Research and Publications at the GRI; Michele Ciaccio; and especially Lauren Edson, the extraordinary editor of this book. And we are grateful to John Hicks, Melanie Lazar, and Ashley Newton for their image-rights detective work and careful attention to detail. The talents of Catherine Lorenz and Amita Molloy resulted in the beautiful design and production of the catalog.

As the exhibition is a collaboration between the GRI and the Museum, we have had the opportunity to work closely with numerous colleagues across the Getty. We thank Timothy Potts, director of the Museum; Quincy Houghton, Amber Keller, and their staff for coordinating all aspects of the exhibition; and Betsy Severance, who as registrar tracked all loans. We are also grateful to Cherie Chen, Leigh Grissom, Irene Lotspeich-Phillips, and Lora Chin Derrien, who handled rights for many of the images used in the exhibition and the book. We thank Sahar Tchaitchian for her skillful eye in ensuring that the written information about each exhibition object was clear, compelling, and accurate.

The Design Department at the Museum has harnessed all of its creativity to produce an installation that is as compelling as the objects on display. We are extremely grateful to Merritt Price, head of the department, Nicole Trudeau, Christina Webb, and all the others who participated in this dynamic process. We also want to thank the Art Center College of Design's faculty, students, and staff, who during a special collaborative studio course in the summer of 2012 took on the comprehensive design of our exhibition as an assignment and provided the Getty's design team with extraordinary visions for the installation, interpretation, and dissemination of the narratives on view.

We are very grateful to the conservators, in both the GRI and the Getty Museum, who worked meticulously to prepare all exhibition objects for their presentation in the gallery. We thank Mary Reinsch-Sackett, Jane Bassett, Brian Considine, Marc Harnly, Albrecht Gumlich, Lynne Kaneshiro, Theresa Mesquit, Juliane Wattig, Stephan Welch, and Nancy Yocco.

One of the engaging aspects of the exhibition is its extensive use of digital media; this rich content for all the exhibition's screens would not have been possible without the hard work of the Department of Collections Information and Access. We express our sincere thanks to Erik Bertellotti, Heather MacMillan, Jason Patt, Douglas Blush, and Karen Voss. The exhibition's informative website, implemented by the Web and New Media Development Department, informs diverse audiences far beyond the Getty Center campus. We offer our thanks to Jack Ludden, Molly Callender, Paula Carlson, and Susan Edwards for their creativity and expertise.

The intricate evolution of Los Angeles's urban landscape was elegantly visualized thanks to our excellent collaboration with the following digital-content contributors: University of Southern California professor Philip J. Ethington; Mia Lehrer, Astrid Diehl, and Michelle Frier of Mia Lehrer + Associates Landscape Architecture; and Bill Jepson, Zachary Rynew, David P. Sartoris, and Lisa M. Snyder of the Urban Simulation Team at the University of California, Los Angeles.

New dimensions of the exhibition's themes came to life as a result of the outstanding efforts of those in the Getty's Education and Programs Departments, including Tuyet Bach, Cathy Carpenter, Rebecca Edwards, Laurel Kishi, Rebecca Peabody, Sandy Rodriguez, Theresa Sotto, Catherine Taft, and Peter Tokofsky.

Inspired by the success of the Pacific Standard Time initiative of 2011–12, the Getty Trust decided to serve as the catalyst for an institutional collaboration dedicated to the region's built environment, titled Pacific Standard Time Presents: Modern Architecture in L.A. The Getty has funded concurrent exhibitions at eight other venues (the A+D Museum; Cal Poly Pomona; the Hammer Museum; the Los Angeles County Museum of Art;

the MAK Center; the Museum of Contemporary Art, Los Angeles; SCI-Arc; and the Art, Design and Architecture Museum at the University of California, Santa Barbara) and a series of events and programs at numerous other locations throughout Los Angeles. We are extremely grateful to Deborah Marrow, director of the Getty Foundation, Joan Weinstein, Anne Helmreich, and Kathleen Johnson for their vision and generosity.

During the preparation of the exhibition, we were assisted by many scholars and curators outside the Getty. We are grateful to Eric Avila, Emily Bills, Eve Blau, Beatriz Colomina, Sandy Isenstadt, and Stephen Phillips, who, during a workshop in June 2010, helped us shape the exhibition's concept. And we would like to recognize our advisory committee—Ken Breisch, Margaret Crawford, Thomas S. Hines, Greg Hise, D. J. Waldie, and Gwendolyn Wright and architects Lorcan O'Herlihy, John Friedman, and Alice Kimm—who reviewed all our plans for the exhibition and catalog and gave us very helpful feedback. During the academic year 2011–12, we were able to bring in four guest scholars who specialize in the history of Los Angeles architecture—Catherine Gudis, Hillary Jencks, Linda C. Samuels, and Martino Stierli—to review the object selections with us and give us many suggestions about the archival collections that might be of use. Their insight was invaluable.

Finally, we extend our deepest appreciation to our family and friends for their advice and encouragement during this complex and rewarding project.

—Wim de Wit and Christopher James Alexander

LENDERS AND CONTRIBUTORS TO THE EXHIBITION

We are very grateful to the following individuals and institutions for assisting us with exhibition research, facilitating loans, and lending objects to the exhibition.

AC Martin Partners, Inc.
Raj Ahuja and James Frankel, Philip Johnson Archives
Akademie der Künste, Berlin
Peter Alexander
Alexander Architectural Archive, Architecture and Planning Library, University of Texas at Austin
Katie Anderson, Unitarian Universalist Church
Architecture and Design Collection, Art, Design & Architecture Museum, University of California, Santa Barbara
Arkansas Architectural Archives, Special Collections, University of Arkansas, Fayetteville
Antonio Beecroft
The Benjamin and Gladys Thomas Air Photo Archives, Department of Geography, University of California, Los Angeles
Gregg E. Brandow
Edward Cella, Edward Cella Art + Architecture
L. J. Cella
Center for Architecture, Design and Engineering, Prints and Photographs Division, Library of Congress
Charles E. Young Research Library Department of Special Collections, University of California, Los Angeles
Randall J. Corcoran, Wallspace Gallery, Santa Barbara
Craig Krull Gallery
George Credle
Doheny Memorial Library, University of Southern California
Steven Ehrlich, Steven Ehrlich Architects
Julie Eizenberg and Hank Koning, Koning Eizenberg Architecture
ENV Archives Special Collections, California State Polytechnic University, Pomona
Environmental Design Archives, University of California, Berkeley
Carol Espinoza and Ian Espinoza, Carlos Diniz Archives
Frank Gehry and Meaghan Lloyd, Gehry Partners, LLP
Thomas S. Gibson and JuanCarlos Chan, City of Los Angeles Department of Recreation and Parks
Alan Eliot Goldberg
Lawrence B. Gotlieb and Linda M. Bourbeau, KB Home
Helen Topping Architecture & Fine Arts Library, University of Southern California
Amy Heller, Milestone Films
Craig Hodgetts and HsinMing Fung, Hodgetts + Fung Design and Architecture
Harvey M. Holt, Jim Hergenrather, and David Lumbar, CBS Television City
Karen E. Hudson, Paul R. Williams Archives
The Huntington Library
Internet Archive
David Iscove, Capitol Music Group/EMI Music NA Archives
Jeffrey Daniels Architects
Jon A. Jerde, Janice A. Jerde, and Matthew Heller, The Jerde Partnership
Yvonne Johnson, KCET
David Kellen, David Kellen + Associates, Inc.
Steven Keylon, Baldwin Hills Village and Village Green
Adam King
Craig Krull, Vicki Rand, Peter Rand, and Marvin Rand Estate
Brian Lane
Langdon Wilson International
Mark Langill, Los Angeles Dodgers
Jack Laxer
LAX Flight Path Learning Center Museum
David Lebrun
Alan Leib
Los Angeles County Metropolitan Transportation Authority Library and Archive
Anne Lumsden
MAK Vienna: Austrian Museum of Applied Arts/Contemporary Art
Maureen Murphy Fine Arts
Michael McGee and Bob Clauser, Pardee Homes

Morphosis Architects, Inc.
Eric Owen Moss and Eric McNevin, Eric Owen Moss Architects
Layne Murphy, Budget Films
Victor Newlove, Armet Davis Newlove Architects
Don Normark
Thomas Ochoa, Gruen Associates
Office of Historic Resources, Los Angeles Department of City Planning
Peter O'Malley, Brent Shyer, and Robert N. Schweppe, Walteromalley.com
Thomas Prelinger, Prelinger Archives
Andrew Rakos
Miranda Rectenwald, University Archives, Washington University in St. Louis
Matthew W. Roth and Morgan P. Yates, Automobile Club of Southern California
Michael Salmon, LA 84 Foundation
San Diego Gas & Electric
San Francisco Museum of Modern Art
Diane Scoglio and David Stern, Slide Library, Walt Disney Imagineering
Abby Sher, Edgemar Archives
Jim Simmons, Annette Del Zoppo Archive
John Spohrer, Archisystems International
William Stout, William Stout Publishers, Richmond, CA
Deborah Sussman, Paul Prejza, and Gene Treadwell, Sussman/Prejza & Company, Inc.
Hoodie Troutman, Hoodie Troutman Productions, Inc.
University of Southern California Libraries, Special Collections
D. J. Waldie
Walt Disney Imagineering, Archives
Katharina Weingartner, Pooldoks
Stephen White, Stephen White Associates
The Wolfsonian–Florida International University
Buzz Yudell and Rebecca Bubenas, Moore Ruble Yudell Architects & Planners

INDEX

The Getty Research Institute Publications Program

Thomas W. Gaehtgens, *Director, Getty Research Institute*
Gail Feigenbaum, *Associate Director*

© 2013 J. Paul Getty Trust
Published by the Getty Research Institute, Los Angeles
Getty Publications
1200 Getty Center Drive, Suite 500
Los Angeles, California 90049-1682
www.getty.edu/publications

Lauren Edson, *Manuscript Editor*
Leigh Grissom, John Hicks, Ashley Newton, *Photo Researchers*
Catherine Lorenz, *Designer*
Amita Molloy, *Production Coordinator*
Diane Franco, *Typesetter*
Printed by Graphicom, Verona, Italy
Type composed in Forza and Gotham Narrow

17 16 15 14 13   5 4 3 2 1

Library of Congress Cataloging-in-Publication Data

Overdrive : L.A. constructs the future, 1940-1990 / edited by
Wim de Wit and Christopher James Alexander.
    p. cm.
  Includes index.
  "This volume accompanies the exhibition Overdrive: L.A.
Constructs the Future, 1940–1990, held at the J. Paul Getty
Museum, 9 April to 21 July 2013. Organized by the Getty
Research Institute and the J. Paul Getty Museum, this exhibition
is part of the initiative Pacific Standard Time Presents: Modern
Architecture in L.A."—CIP t.p. verso.
ISBN 978-1-60606-128-2
  1. Modern movement (Architecture)—California—Los Angeles—
History—20th century. 2. Architecture—California—Los
Angeles—History—20th century. 3. City planning—California—
Los Angeles—History—20th century. I. Wit, Wim de. II.
Alexander, Christopher James. III. Getty Research Institute. IV. J.
Paul Getty Museum. V. Pacific Standard Time (Project)
  NA735.L55O94 2013
  720.9794'940904—dc23
              2012036941

This volume accompanies the exhibition
Overdrive: L.A. Constructs the Future, 1940–1990,
held at the J. Paul Getty Museum, 9 April to 21 July 2013.
Organized by the Getty Research Institute and the J. Paul Getty
Museum, this exhibition is part of the initiative Pacific Standard
Time Presents: Modern Architecture in L.A.

The Getty gratefully acknowledges our sponsors for the
Overdrive exhibition, including Bank of America, which was
the lead sponsor of the 2011–12 initiative Pacific Standard Time:
Art in L.A. 1945–1980, and Hathaway Dinwiddie Construction
Company, which, during its fifty-year partnership with first
J. Paul Getty and subsequently the J. Paul Getty Trust, built
two of Los Angeles's most iconic public arts institutions: the
Getty Villa and the Getty Center.

Other books published by the Getty Research Institute:

Las Vegas in the Rearview Mirror:
The City in Theory, Photography, and Film
Martino Stierli
ISBN 978-1-60606-137-4 (paper)

Farewell to Surrealism: The Dyn *Circle in Mexico*
Annette Leddy and Donna Conwell
ISBN 978-1-60606-118-3 (paper)

Surrealism in Latin America: Vivísimo Muerto
Edited by Dawn Ades, Rita Eder, and Graciela Speranza
ISBN 978-1-60606-117-6 (paper)

Pacific Standard Time: Los Angeles Art, 1945–1980
Edited by Rebecca Peabody, Andrew Perchuk,
Glenn Phillips, and Rani Singh, with Lucy Bradnock
ISBN 978-1-60606-072-8 (hardcover)

Brush and Shutter: Early Photography in China
Edited by Jeffrey Cody and Frances Terpak
ISBN 978-1-60606-054-4 (hardcover)

G: An Avant-Garde Journal of Art, Architecture, Design,
and Film, 1923–1926
Edited by Detlef Mertins and Michael W. Jennings
Translation by Steven Lindberg with Margareta Ingrid Christian
ISBN 978-1-60606-039-1 (hardcover)

Visual Planning and the Picturesque
Nikolaus Pevsner
Edited by Mathew Aitchison
Introduction by John Macarthur and Mathew Aitchison
ISBN 978-1-60606-001-8 (hardcover)

California Video: Artists and Histories
Edited by Glenn Phillips
ISBN 978-0-89236-922-5 (hardcover)

Art, Anti-Art, Non-Art: Experimentations in the
Public Sphere in Postwar Japan, 1950–1970
Edited by Charles Merewether with Rika Iezumi Hiro
ISBN 978-0-89236-866-2 (hardcover)